American Missionaries and the Middle East

D1570473

AMERICAN MISSIONARIES AND THE MIDDLE EAST

Foundational Encounters

EDITED BY

MEHMET ALI DOĞAN AND HEATHER J. SHARKEY

THE UNIVERSITY OF UTAH PRESS
Salt Lake City

The Defiance House Man colophon is a registered trademark
of the University of Utah Press. It is based upon a four-foot-tall,
Ancient Puebloan pictograph (late PIII) near Glen Canyon, Utah.

15 14 13 12 11   1 2 3 4 5

LIBRARY OF CONGRESS CATALOGING-IN-PUBLICATION DATA
Middle East Studies Association of North America. Meeting (2005 :
Washington, D.C.)
 American missionaries and the Middle East : foundational encounters /
edited by Mehmet Ali Dogan and Heather J. Sharkey.
    p. cm.
 Proceedings of the 2005 and 2006 annual meetings of the Middle East
Studies Association of North America.
 Includes bibliographical references (p.   ).
 ISBN 978-1-60781-038-4 (pbk. : alk. paper)
    1. Missions, American—Middle East—History—19th century—Congresses.
2. Middle East—Church history—19th century—Congresses. 3. Missions,
American—Middle East—History—20th century—Congresses. 4. Middle
East—Church history—20th century—Congresses. I. Dogan, Mehmet Ali,
1976- II. Sharkey, Heather J. (Heather Jane), 1967- III. Middle East
Studies Association of North America. Meeting (2006 : Boston, Mass.) IV.
Title.
 BV3160.M53 2010
 266ʹ.0237305609034—dc22

                                                        2010035084

Printed and bound by Sheridan Books, Inc., Ann Arbor, Michigan.

To our families

NOTE ON TRANSLITERATION

Arabic terms are italicized, except for those that recur often. The symbol (')
is used for the Arabic letter ayn and the reverse symbol (') is used for hamza.

CONTENTS

Illustrations follow page 164

INTRODUCTION

AMERICAN MISSIONARIES AND THE MIDDLE EAST

A History Enmeshed

HEATHER J. SHARKEY

IN AN INTERVIEW CONDUCTED SHORTLY BEFORE THE EVENTS OF SEPtember 11, 2001, Edward Said (1935–2003) reflected on the subject that his own research had defined. This was Orientalism, the product of Western discourses that asserted the corruption and weakness of the "Orient," or Islamic "East," in order to justify intervention in its affairs. During this interview, Said remarked that the United States, unlike Britain and France, had had no direct experience of military intervention in the Middle East, with the result that American Orientalism had been qualitatively different—perhaps less overtly "imperialist"—than its European counterparts. Said spoke too soon. A few years later, writing in the post-9/11 milieu, he expressed his bafflement and concern over "the sheer belligerency of the verbal assaults on the average citizen" as the U.S. government mobilized to invade Iraq and sought to rally public support.[1]

American engagement in Iraq, following the U.S. invasion of 2003, forced historians to confront questions about the deeper and wider context of American engagement with the modern Middle East. When did American involvement begin? What did it entail? How did U.S.-Middle Eastern relations evolve from early encounters? Have American overtures been altruistic or imperialistic?[2] And how did encounters transform the parties involved? Amid these interrogations of history, Christian missionaries stand out for their participation in so many of America's "foundational encounters"[3] with the Middle East and its peoples beginning in the early nineteenth century.

Edward Said, the theoretician of Orientalism, could have attested to the importance of these encounters, since his own family was shaped by—and helped to shape—American missionary engagements in what is now Lebanon, Israel/Palestine, and Egypt.[4]

During the nineteenth and early twentieth centuries, American missionaries mediated U.S.-Middle Eastern relations and helped to determine U.S. foreign policy toward the region.[5] They presented examples of American culture to Middle Eastern peoples, just as they interpreted the Middle East for Americans back home.[6] They established schools, publishing houses, hospitals, and other institutions whose legacies persist today. American missionaries were so influential in this period because they represented the largest and most educated group of Americans living abroad.[7] Their engagements in the Middle East prompt us to ask larger questions about the consequences of American Christian cultural projections into the wider world.[8]

This volume, which grew out of a series of discussions that occurred at the 2005 and 2006 meetings of the Middle East Studies Association (MESA) in Washington, D.C., and Boston, surveys the nature and impact of American missionary encounters in the region. Its essays focus on places that were once part of the Ottoman Empire. Together they consider the ramifications of American missionary activities not only for religious life and international relations, but also for such cultural phenomena as education and literacy, gender relations, and even popular understandings of science. By bridging the histories of the United States, the Middle East, and their respective peoples, its essays contribute to the kind of transnational history that recognizes that nations and peoples "lie enmeshed in each others' history."[9]

The following pages set out to introduce the essays in this volume while providing a larger, synoptic view of nineteenth-century American missions in the Middle East. Four sections follow. The first sketches out the distinctly American dimension in the Middle East missions. It addresses an obvious question, namely, given the diversity of American missions and missionary experiences, why does it make sense to study American missions together? The second section considers the political context against which American missions developed in the nineteenth- and early twentieth-century Middle East, and assesses broad assumptions that guided missionary policies. The third section surveys the essays in this volume and identifies their primary arguments and achievements. The concluding section sets out what remains to be done and suggests avenues for future research.

A note on terminology is necessary before proceeding. For Americans, the "Middle East" has been more of an idea than a fixed place, so that the region associated with the term has shifted. Alfred Thayer Mahan (1840–1914), the American military naval historian, reportedly coined the term "Middle East" in 1902 to suggest the area stretching from the Arabian Peninsula and the Persian Gulf eastward to the fringes of Pakistan. Mahan intended the "Middle East" to complement rather than replace the extant term "Near East," which connoted the region from the Balkans and Asia Minor to the eastern Mediterranean. In this volume, a study about the American missionary encounter with a Bulgarian nationalist—with whom the Americans worked, significantly, in Istanbul, not in "Bulgaria"—acknowledges the continuing relevance of both the "Near East" and an Ottoman cultural orbit during the late nineteenth century. After World War I, however, the term "Middle East" gained momentum, until by World War II it was displacing "Near East" for current affairs.[10]

Reflecting larger geopolitical trends, some places that Americans had once deemed "Near Eastern" did not make the transition to "Middle Eastern." Thus during the Cold War era of the early 1950s, the U.S. government's Central Intelligence Agency (CIA) reclassified Greece and Turkey as "European" rather than "Near Eastern" countries for purposes of its analysis.[11] At the same time, other regions—notably the Arabic-speaking countries of North Africa as far west as Morocco—became more closely associated with the "Middle East."[12] Bearing this history in mind, readers should understand that use of the term "Middle East" in this volume is simply shorthand for evolving American conceptions of the region across decades of political flux.

THE AMERICAN DIMENSION IN THE MIDDLE EAST MISSIONS

What was distinctly American about the missionaries who went to work in the nineteenth- and early twentieth-century Middle East? And how did their American culture influence the missions that they pursued?

For a start, the Americans who went to the Middle East were integral parts of an American foreign missionary movement that reflected a culture of pluralistic, evangelical Protestantism. This movement was the product of two episodes of Christian revivalism, the First Great Awakening in the 1730s and 1740s, and the Second Great Awakening in the first half of the nineteenth century. It was evangelical in the sense that its supporters emphasized the Christian's inner, heartfelt religion over doctrines, creeds, and church rituals; it also valued common language, that is, the vernacular, as a vehicle for religious devotion.[13] In the American context, the movement developed along with the westward-moving frontier and grew out of missions to Native Americans. The latter provided experiences in cultural imperialism that Americans subsequently brought to the Middle East.[14] The movement was distinctly American, furthermore, in its particular brand of populism and egalitarianism, in its "refus[al] to defer to learned theologians and traditional orthodoxies," and in its "overt rejection of the past as a repository of wisdom."[15] This is not to say, however, that the American missions that emerged from this milieu were themselves egalitarian. On the contrary, often the most durable missions in the Middle East developed bureaucracies and institutions that had clear leadership hierarchies and structures, as well as gendered divisions of labor.

Contrasting nineteenth- and early twentieth-century American missions with their British counterparts, a leading missiologist elaborated on the distinctly American dimensions of the American Protestant missionary movement. American missions flourished, he noted, within networks of voluntary societies; these societies involved women as often as men and functioned as auxiliaries to churches. They flourished, too, within an American social system that allowed for "plurality of choice." This system valued individualism, and did not expect people to follow their neighbors or even their relatives.[16]

There were also *economic* aspects to the American culture of missions. Not only did American churchgoers have the "cash surpluses" that enabled them to donate to missions, but they had no embarrassment about fund-raising— and even about "conspicuous financing"—when Christian causes were at stake.[17] The United States, in other words, had a culture in which pious widows were as likely to donate to missions as merchants and magnates; it was a place where families like the Rockefellers bankrolled mission projects even as women and children raised pennies from bake sales.[18] These economic attitudes, another scholar argued, were central to the "liberal" evangelical culture of nineteenth-century American churches, where not only individualism and democratization were valued, but also "market-making."[19]

These features of American evangelical culture were discernible in the work of nineteenth- and early twentieth-century missionaries in the Middle East, as essays in this volume attest. American missionaries showed preferences for vernaculars in worship, along with disregard for tradition and orthodoxy, for example, by promoting Arabic over Coptic as a language of the Bible. At the same time they often promoted what they regarded as "national" vernaculars, for example, by favoring Greek Bibles among "Greeks," and Bulgarian Bibles among "Bulgarians." In this way American evangelicals sharpened the contours of emerging nationalisms in the region.

The American evangelical esteem for "market-making" also found its expression in missions to the region. Thus when American missionaries found themselves short of money, they started businesses or sought donors, sometimes going on fund-raising tours in the United States for such purposes. Consider Cyrus Hamlin, the principal of Bebek Seminary, which trained Armenians for the Protestant clergy in mid-nineteenth-century Istanbul: when funds ran short, he organized a student-run bakery and laundry service. A century later, Lillian Trasher, the Pentecostal founder of an orphanage in Egypt, starred in a promotional film in which she pleaded for funds from American donors unknown.[20] In that regard, Trasher evinced another feature of American evangelical culture: a ready embrace of mass media and communication technologies for the sake of transmitting messages.[21]

The inherent diversity of American missions in the Middle East also reflected the larger picture of American Christian culture. In this volume, the work of American Presbyterians and Congregationalists looms largest. There is a reason for this: Presbyterians, together with Congregationalists, led the earliest American missions to the region, as members of the American Board of Commissioners for Foreign Missions (ABCFM). After 1870, the ABCFM decided to focus its work in Anatolia, leaving mission work in the Arabic-speaking regions of the Fertile Crescent to the foreign missions board of the Presbyterian Church in the U.S.A. (PCUSA). (The Presbyterians were also active in what is now Iran, which was not part of the Ottoman Empire, and which is therefore not included in this volume.) By this time, a second American Presbyterian denomination, the United Presbyterian Church of North America (UPCNA), was also active in Egypt.[22] In 1925, Presbyterians were still the largest contingent of American missionaries in the Middle East, and they were running many schools, hospitals, and other institutions that endure in some form today.[23] More than any other group of missionaries, Presbyterians set foundations for subsequent American cultural initiatives in the region.

Nevertheless, as the nineteenth century ended, increasingly diverse groups of American evangelicals were arriving in western Asia and North Africa. Members of the Reformed Church of America started work in southern Iraq and the Gulf as far south as Oman, where they developed medical missions especially.[24] Mormon missionaries visited Turkey and Palestine and started their first mission which lasted from 1884 to 1909. (They later resumed work, in Syria and Palestine, in 1921.) Pentecostals and Plymouth Brethrenites undertook work in Egypt and organized churches among local Copts.[25] As the twentieth century dawned, an American Methodist Episcopal Mission began work in Algeria, where Augustine of Hippo had written his *Confessions* fifteen centuries before. After the emergence of Israel in 1948, the Society of Friends (Quakers) began work among Palestinian refugees in Gaza and in neighboring Arab states. Their efforts built upon the earlier work of British and American Quakers, who had established networks of schools near Beirut and in Ramallah beginning in the 1860s.[26] Likewise, in the post-World War II period, American Lutherans became more actively involved in the Middle East, building upon the earlier missionary efforts of German-speaking Lutherans, including Pietists.[27]

Given the American evangelical fascination for the lands where Jesus once lived, it is remarkable that, during the nineteenth century, there emerged no organized American mission in what is now Israel (especially in Jerusalem or Nazareth) or in the West Bank (which contains Bethlehem). Of course, many Americans visited the Holy Land as tourists or pilgrims, and together they produced a body of travel accounts that attests to the impact of the region on American popular literature.[28] Still others—and particularly those who expected Christ's imminent return—even settled down. Examples of the latter include Horatio and Anna Spafford, who in 1881 left Chicago and arrived with a group of their followers in Jerusalem. The Spaffords organized their (mostly American and Swedish) followers into an "American Colony," which supported itself by operating a hotel and associated businesses for tourists.[29] (Note that the American Colony was more of a sect and commune than a mission, since it made no effort to proselytize or attract members from the local community.) During the mid-nineteenth century, several other Americans settled near Jerusalem and started farms, making them, in the words of one Israeli historian, "the pioneers of modern agricultural settlement in the Holy Land."[30]

An important reason for the lack of Holy Land missions among the ABCFM, the Presbyterians, and other large American mission-sponsoring organizations may have related to issues of turf. Rather than setting up operations in the vicinity of Jerusalem, which was already crowded with churches and sects, the large American missions looked for open spaces—or what they sometimes called "unoccupied fields"—where few other Protestants were active.[31] Note that British, German, and later Swedish Protestant organizations operated in Jerusalem and its environs, not to mention Catholic or Orthodox Christians, and this probably induced Americans to venture elsewhere.[32] Moreover, and notwithstanding the Protestant rhetoric of Christian "fellowship," competition between missionary organizations could be intense. An awareness of such rivalries later contributed, in Sudan after 1900, to the British colonial policy of awarding missionary societies distinct territorial "spheres" so that they would not overlap.[33]

Of course, not all large American missions represented a single denomination. In some cases, Americans in the Middle East represented non- or interdenominational organizations like the World Sunday School Association or WSSA (which had its international headquarters in Philadelphia), and the Young Men's and Young Women's Christian Associations (YMCA and YWCA); they also represented the New York City-based American Bible Society, which was a publishing mission.[34] Some missions were small and focused: the Kansas City-based Gospel Missionary Union, for example, funded work in Morocco during the interwar period. In other cases, some missions operated as independent or solo enterprises, like the "Gospel Center" that operated in 1930s Cairo under the direction of an American woman and her Egyptian husband. Still other organizations, which did not appear to be American, drew upon substantial American funding. In Egypt, for example, a British publishing mission in Cairo known as the Nile Mission Press depended on funds from the interdenominational American Christian Literature Society for Moslems, which was based in New York City, while the Swedish Salaam Mission of Port Said, in the Suez Canal Zone, drew upon contributions from Scandinavian immigrants in Michigan.[35] Again, the diversity of these missions and their support bases was in keeping with the culture of American Protestantism, where individual choice fostered Christian pluralism, and where men and women across the social spectrum were ready to donate to missionary causes.

Members of all these American missions shared a culture of English, too. Their use of the language facilitated contact with British missionaries, and led to collaborations that buoyed an emergent Protestant ecumenical movement. This ecumenical movement, and Anglo-American cooperation in particular, gained momentum at the World Missionary Conference held in Edinburgh in 1910.[36] Anglophone culture also facilitated cooperation between missions and the region's Protestant publishing houses—above all, the American Bible Society, the British & Foreign Bible Society, the Nile Mission Press, and the American Mission Press in Beirut—and joined English-speaking missions into a network through which the circulation of Bible portions, tracts, and other literature occurred. At the same time, the Americans' use of English confirmed the rift that divided them from Catholic missionaries—a rift spanning a tradition of "Protestant anti-Romanism [that] was a staple of the American theological world" and that traced its roots to the sixteenth-century Reformation.[37] Language differences compounded Protestant-Catholic alienation on the ground, even when American missionaries were working in the same big cities (like Beirut and Istanbul) or small towns (like Tahta, in Upper Egypt) where Catholic missionaries were active. That is because Catholic missionaries tended to use French first, and Italian second, as lingua francas. At the same time, American missionaries and other Protestant groups were more likely than Catholic missionaries to support education and publishing in local languages.[38]

Finally, it is worth noting that American missionaries, regardless of their diversity in denominational or other terms, shared common pools of information and misinformation about the Middle East.[39] Above all, they shared popular resources for biblical knowledge, which led them to map their own scheme of the "Bible Lands" onto the nineteenth-century Ottoman territories. Appealing to this popular interest was a thriving American genre of illustrated Bibles or Bible geographies that included, for example, William Thomson's *The Land and the Book* (1859), Henry J. Van-Lennep's *Bible Lands: Their Modern Customs and Manners Illustrative of Scripture* (1875), and Philip Schaff's *A*

Dictionary of the Bible (1881).[40] New nineteenth-century technologies—above all, the steamship and photography—also enabled Americans to envision the Holy Land more vividly by making it possible for American tourists (or journalists like Mark Twain) to go there for themselves and take or buy pictures of biblical sites.[41]

For the American Presbyterians and Congregationalists who founded the ABCFM in 1810 and who sent missionaries toward Jerusalem a decade later, many of their impressions of the Middle East would have also come from "a flood of books on the Muslim world" which had appeared in the 1790s. This was a decade during which the popular American press was reporting attacks by the "Barbary Pirates" of North Africa on American ships in the Mediterranean. The "War with Tripoli," which the United States fought from 1801 to 1804 in an effort to quell these raids, "carried great ideological importance" for the young American republic and for its president, Thomas Jefferson.[42] The war over the Barbary Pirates, which sharpened an American myth of U.S. exceptionalism, was a critical event in early U.S. relations with the Arabic-speaking world and provided some of the political context against which American missionary activity to the region began.

American evangelicals gained a footing in Ottoman domains during the 1820s and one thing was clear from the start. Religion, politics, and culture were—and would continue to be—inextricably bound together within the history of American missions to the Middle East.

AMERICANS IN THE MIDDLE EAST: POLITICAL CONTEXT AND CULTURAL ASSUMPTIONS

American missionaries appeared in the Middle East during a period of staggering political and social changes.[43] Secession movements were threatening the integrity of the Ottoman Empire, most visibly in Greece, where in the 1820s Greek nationalists drew upon French, British, and Russian support to revolt and claim independence. More importantly, in a swathe of territory stretching from Algeria (conquered by France in 1830) eastward to the Balkans and the Arabian coast, the European imperial powers were chipping away at Ottoman domains. At the same time, in the years from 1839 to 1876, Ottoman authorities were initiating far-reaching internal reforms known as the "Tanzimat."[44]

For missionaries, the most consequential reform of the Tanzimat era was the imperial edict of 1856. Known as the Hatt-i Humayun, this edict declared all Ottoman subjects, including Muslims, Christians, and "other non-Muslims" (notably Jews), to be equals, with equal rights and responsibilities vis-à-vis the Ottoman state and freedom in building places of worship.[45] Many American missionaries interpreted the Humayun decree, at the time and years later, to indicate support for freedom in both the pursuit and choice of religion. Missionaries also hoped that the edict would somehow empower local Christians while reversing centuries of Christian attrition in the lands of Islam.[46] In theory, the Hatt-i Humayun overturned Islamic social conventions that had defined Christians (and Jews) as *dhimmi*s, meaning people who were tolerated but subordinate to Muslims. In practice, however, the extent, nature, and impact of the edict's implementation proved to be ambiguous.[47]

In 1882, Britain invaded and occupied Egypt, which was still officially part of the Ottoman Empire. This event accelerated the European "Scramble for Africa," and with it the expansion of Christian (including American) missionary activity in the continent.[48] Among both American and British missionaries, the British Occupation also deepened the sense of a modern contest between Islam and Christianity, which some missionaries plainly called a new "crusade."[49] The post-1882 period witnessed, too, the intensification of British and American missionary overtures to Muslims.[50] Thus by 1900, the American missionary statesman John Mott argued that the "evangelization of the world"—including the Muslim world—would be possible in one generation in part because "the influence and protection of Christian governments" would "make possible the free preaching of the Gospel."[51]

World War I was the turning point of modern Middle Eastern history. Disgusted by decades of French and British imperial intrusion, the Ottoman government chose to side with Germany and the Central Powers. But the Central Powers lost the war. Afterward, the victorious Allies dismantled the Ottoman Empire. In the predominantly Arabic-speaking, formerly Ottoman territories of the Fertile Crescent, they established French- and British-administered "mandates" over countries which, in the words of the League of Nations covenant that approved them, were "inhabited by peoples not yet able to stand by themselves under the strenuous conditions of the modern world."[52] Britain and France thereby gained a set of de facto colonies and at the same time invented new countries, namely, Palestine (including what eventually became Israel, Jordan, and the Palestinian territories of the West Bank and Gaza), Iraq, Syria, and Lebanon. Following the terms of the Balfour Declaration, which the British government had issued in 1917, the mandate for Palestine made special provisions for Jewish immigration and the establishment of a "Jewish homeland." This support for the Zionist movement and Jewish settlement fostered conditions that led, in 1948, to the emergence of Israel and with it the Arab-Israeli conflict and Palestinian refugee crisis.[53]

In the core of what had been the Ottoman Empire, some Turkish-speaking nationalists managed to unravel the postwar settlements outlined in the 1920 Treaty of Sèvres. The result was the emergence of a new republic of Turkey, whose leader, an Ottoman World War I veteran named Mustafa Kemal (later known as Ataturk), tried to renounce the Ottoman past and to make a fresh start in nation-building.

War, imperial contraction and expansion, and nationalist ferment: against this complicated context, American missions in the Middle East developed. Bearing this history in mind, one can identify several tendencies regarding the nature of American missionary encounters in the region. Six points stand out.

First, within reports, memoirs, and other writings, nineteenth- and early twentieth-century missionaries argued that the Orient was spiritually and culturally impoverished and in need of the enlightenment that Americans could bring. Even the indigenous Christians of the Orient, missionaries declared, were merely "nominal Christians" who had become weak under the pressure of "Muslim fanaticism" and whose churches were in need of reform.[54] These assumptions explain, in part, why so much American missionary effort in the region was directed at people who were already Christian, such as Armenians, Maronites, and Copts. More broadly, American missionaries portrayed the Middle East as the site of ancient, but decrepit, civilizations and contrasted this with America's own newness and vigor. In this way, the Middle East provided a foil for the construction of American modernity.[55] Meanwhile, the missionaries' modes of imagining, speaking about, portraying, and behaving toward the Islamic Middle East shaped American Orientalism and justified American involvement in Middle Eastern life and affairs.[56] Herein lies the tragedy, and paradox, of the American missionary enterprise in the

Middle East. For indeed, like Cotton Mather, who "wanted to save Indians [though] he detested them," many American missionaries wanted to save Ottoman peoples while holding them in private contempt.[57]

Second, although the Middle East formed only one part of the American Protestant "errand to the world"[58] as it evolved over the nineteenth century, and although it ultimately yielded few converts and church members relative to other mission "fields" (such as Korea), the region was essential to popular American Christian imaginations. The Middle East held the Holy Land, the lands of the Bible; it was the cradle of Christianity; and it fascinated some Christians as a likely site for an anticipated return, or second coming, of Christ (thereby feeding into channels of American millenarian thought). "Millennialism," one scholar has argued in a study of American missionaries in Asia Minor and the Levant, "was part of an American identity that constituted itself religiously in the interaction with and the representation of the Near East, the 'cradle of Zion'"; thus "going Near East" [sic] was in significant ways more important than colonizing the American West, at least to American evangelicals.[59] This millennialism alone helps to explain why the Middle East was so important as a stage for the construction and production of American Christian identities, and why American churchgoers were so eager to fund missionary ventures in the wider region.[60]

Third, if "conversion" is understood relative to church memberships, or relative to formal declarations of changed religious allegiance, then American missionaries in the Middle East had meager records of effecting conversions.[61] Yet if conversion is understood in the broad sense to refer to significant turns or changes in character or outlook, then American missionary influences were substantial. For example, American missionaries encouraged the use of vernacular Bibles in Orthodox churches, thereby changing the way that local Christians worshipped. They transformed cultures of modern schooling by introducing new ideas about what and how children and adults should be taught. They influenced the history of everyday life (including such things as how schoolgirls dressed and how "modern" families arranged their households) in ways that historians have only begun to assess.[62] They even introduced Muslim reformists to debates over Darwinist thought and evolutionary biology, thereby stimulating discussions among Muslims about Islam and science.

Fourth, the impact was reciprocal. Missionaries may have assumed that they were delivering a message in a one-way stream of transmission, but close study of their history shows that missionaries and missions came out transformed by their encounters. Missionaries often revised their activities and goals in light of what Middle Eastern peoples sought or demanded. In many cases, for example, mission schools became increasingly "secular" insofar as they minimized their explicitly Christian or evangelical dimensions in order to appease or reassure governments, religious authorities, and families, and thereby to bolster enrollments.[63] Missionary encounters also had consequences for American mission-sponsoring communities at large, as a study of the "reflex story" of the foreign missionary enterprise can show.[64] For example, they galvanized American women within churches, producing foreign mission-supporting societies whose members also promoted social causes such as temperance reform and suffrage in the United States.[65] Certainly in the Middle East, American women often came out of the mission experience possessing greater influence within the organizations that sponsored them. Moreover, by focusing on the provision of schools and services for females, American women missionaries broadened opportunities for their Middle Eastern counterparts, suggesting that the history of changing gender relations bound American and Middle Eastern women together.[66]

Fifth, missionaries in the Middle East operated against the complex and ambiguous context of Western imperialism, while their evangelical overtures ran counter to Islamic laws and expectations regarding Muslim-Christian relations and religious conversions. Islamic law held that anyone could convert into Islam but that no one could leave it. Even in a period like the mid-nineteenth century, when Tanzimat reforms were dismantling the *"millet* system" (according to which Ottoman society was organized or envisioned as a cluster of religious communities, or *millet*s) and proclaiming ideals of religious equality, Muslim authorities recognized the ban on Christian evangelization among Muslims.[67] At the same time, Muslim communities at the grass roots stood ready to apply legal and social sanctions against apostates from Islam.[68] This (and not only missionary beliefs about eastern Christian backwardness) helps to explain why American missionaries in the Middle East concentrated so much attention on local Christians, whose ecclesiastical leaders resented Protestant overtures but were largely powerless to stop them. It also explains why evangelical overtures to Muslims remained so controversial and sensitive.

In the long run, American missionary evangelization among Muslims became more possible—and more common—as the grip of British and French imperialism tightened in the region and therefore as local Muslim authorities lost the power to restrict Christian missionary activities. The links between imperialism and evangelization were particularly pronounced in North Africa. In Egypt, for example, Christian missions to Muslims accelerated only after Britain invaded and occupied the country in 1882.[69] The same applied to Algeria, once the westernmost outpost of the Ottoman Empire, where a firmly entrenched French settler colony was flourishing by the nineteenth century's end.[70]

The complicity of missionaries in imperialism has remained a source of enduring controversy.[71] In the twentieth century, some Muslim critics have portrayed missionaries as the "shock troops of imperialism,"[72] even as some supporters of Christian missions have emphasized missionaries' roles as cultural ambassadors and humanitarian workers.[73] Historians remain divided. Some have concluded that missionaries sowed ethnic and sectarian discord (however inadvertently), while others have suggested mixed motives in their philanthropy. Still others have acknowledged the ways in which missionaries faced ethical dilemmas and coped with their own uncertainties.[74] Without a doubt, missionaries were complicated creatures. It makes things even harder for historians to generalize about them given that they could be so fractious, disagreeing among themselves over matters of policy and practice.

OVERVIEW OF THE ESSAYS

The essays in this volume elaborate on many of the issues set out above. They are divided into two sections. The essays in Part 1, "Shifting Foundations of American Missions," highlight the evolution of American missions in the Middle East from the arrival of the first ABCFM missionaries in 1820 until the Young Turk revolution of 1908. This first section focuses on American missionaries and on the origin and evolution of their practice, and includes articles by Mehmet Ali Doğan, Christine Lindner, Cemal Yetkiner, Karen Kern, and Carolyn Goffman. Part 2, entitled, "Ripples of Change: The Consequences of Missionary Encounters," examines the local implications of missionary encounters from the late nineteenth century through the mid-twentieth and includes articles by Marwa Elshakry, Barbara Reeves-Ellington, Heather J. Sharkey, and Beth Baron.

In "From New England into New Lands: The Beginning of a Long Story," Mehmet Ali Doğan examines the ABCFM and its early forays in the Middle East during the 1820s. He introduces Rufus Anderson (1796–1880), who outlined the organization's early goals in converting the "heathen" and shaped missionary policies from New England. Doğan considers how the first AB-CFM missionaries to the region, starting with the "pioneers" Levi Parsons and Pliny Fisk, approached their task of "spiritual conquest" among local Muslims, Christians, and Jews, while distributing tracts and Bibles and starting schools. These first ABCFM missionaries antagonized Maronite and Greek Orthodox leaders almost immediately by threatening to draw their followers away. Local clergy soon appealed to Ottoman Muslim authorities for help. Responding to this plea in 1824, the Sublime Porte declared a ban on missionaries' distribution of tracts, yet the ban was not enforced. Doğan concludes that, by 1830, the pattern was firmly established whereby AB-CFM missionaries were concentrating their evangelical efforts on converting "nominal Christians."

In "The Flexibility of Home," Christine Lindner examines the history of everyday life by considering how ABCFM missionaries structured their households in early to mid-nineteenth-century Ottoman Syria. Only able to rent houses on the fringes of Beirut, and depending on the goodwill of local Christian landlords, the American missionaries organized their interior space while asserting or revising their own understandings of family and social hierarchy. The missionary house, Lindner argues, was therefore a site for self-definition within the small American missionary colony. Lindner's article offers a Christian missionary analogue to historical research on the "architecture of memory." Buildings are treated in such research as frameworks for social encounters.[75]

Cemal Yetkiner shows how rifts within the ABCFM, rooted in policy disagreements, were emerging by the mid-nineteenth century. His article, "At the Center of the Debate," considers Bebek Seminary in Istanbul, which Cyrus Hamlin founded in 1840. In keeping with ideals set out by Rufus Anderson and others, Hamlin envisaged this seminary as a place for training "native assistants and preachers of the gospel," particularly Armenians, and thereby helping to establish "self-supporting," "self-governing," and "self-propagating" churches among them. But problems arose and changed Hamlin's plans. In 1846, the Armenian Apostolic Church began to excommunicate Armenians who turned toward Protestantism; those who persisted were ostracized, so that the Armenian students remaining in the seminary were shunned and impoverished. Hamlin tried to ameliorate the students' financial situation and to raise funds for the seminary by starting a steam-operated flour mill, bakery, and laundry business on the seminary grounds; these enterprises flourished by supplying British troops in the Crimean war. Their very success, in turn, displeased Hamlin's missionary colleagues; some suggested that he was becoming too secular and money-minded, and that he was doing more to Americanize than to Christianize students. Disgusted, Hamlin resigned from the ABCFM. He went on in 1863 to found Robert College in Istanbul as an independent, American-run, but only loosely Christian institution. Soon becoming one of the most prestigious institutions in the region, Robert College set institutional foundations for what is now the Turkish-government-run Boğaziçi University.[76]

In "From Religious to American Proselytism," Carolyn Goffman studies the career of the ABCFM missionary Mary Mills Patrick, who was first assigned, in 1875, to teach Armenian girls in the Constantinople Home School while cultivating a form of "heart Christianity" among them. When circumstances placed Patrick in the role of principal of the American College for Girls in Istanbul, her vision and personal mission changed. She abandoned evangelization (Goffman suggests, with much relief), bolstered the academic content of the school's curriculum, and set a "non-sectarian" tone that made Muslim and Orthodox Christian students comfortable. Eventually, Patrick oversaw the separation of the college from the ABCFM and made the American College for Girls in Istanbul self-supporting. Like Cyrus Hamlin at Robert College, Patrick developed the American College for Girls as a kind of secular, postevangelical institution that pursued an American cultural mission. Moreover, her growing respect for the religious and social identities of her students, and her support for incipient Turkish nationalism, guaranteed the survival and success of the college into the twentieth century. Goffman concludes that Patrick developed "a new style of proselytism...in which feminist and nationalist goals supplanted Protestant conversion."

Drawing upon government reports in the Ottoman archives as well as American church records, Karen Kern considers how and why the Church of Jesus Christ of Latter-day Saints (commonly known as the Mormon Church) faced particularly acute challenges when it sent its first missionary—a German-speaking convert of Swiss origin—to Istanbul in 1884. In her article, entitled, "'They Are Not Known to Us,'" Kern explains that Sultan Abdülhamid II was eager to clamp down on Christian missionaries and foreign activities in general. He was especially distrustful of foreign Christians—Mormons included—who were working with Armenians, among whom nationalism was starting to simmer. At the same time, the Ottoman authorities refused to recognize the Mormons as a distinct and official sect, which would have afforded them important legal privileges vis-à-vis publishing, protection of converts, and more. To make matters worse, American missionaries from other churches (who since 1850 had enjoyed Ottoman government recognition as part of a "Protestant sect") treated the Mormons with contempt and circulated rumors about them. Kern shows that Ottoman authorities were aware of Mormon history in the United States—and regarded the Mormon history of polygamy with equanimity—although this did not help to ameliorate the Mormons' situation in Ottoman territories.

Incorporating Arabic and English sources, Marwa Elshakry's article on "The Gospel of Science and American Evangelism in Late Ottoman Beirut" shows how the dissemination of contemporary sciences proved crucial to the missionary enterprise in the Middle East (as it did elsewhere). Yet, missionary efforts to teach science at the Syrian Protestant College (later known as the American University in Beirut) backfired, led to bitter disputes among the American faculty, and in the long run "convert[ed] them to a different sense of themselves and their own mission."[77] The dispute arose in 1882, when an American professor of geology and chemistry delivered a graduation lecture that paid tribute to Charles Darwin and the ideas set out in his influential book, *On the Origin of Species*. By this time, the college had established a reputation among local Muslims and Christians as a center for scientific study in engineering, medicine, and other fields, and as a pace-setting publisher of Arabic science textbooks. But the college's Board of Trustees in New York decided that praise for Darwinist thought went too far in challenging biblical "truth." Thus the board decided that faculty would have to sign a "Declaration of Principles" affirming "sound and reverent views on the relation of God to the natural universe." Several faculty refused to sign and gave up their positions, among them Cornelius Van Dyck, the distinguished translator of the Arabic Bible. Some of the college's best students were also suspended, such as Jurji Zaydan, who went on to become one of the most prolific Arabic writers of the late nineteenth century. Occurring forty-three years before the Scopes Trial (the Tennessee court case that pitted biblical creationism against evolutionary theory in American public school teaching), this dispute at the Syrian Protestant College showed how American missionaries could become bitterly divided over religion and science even as Arab intellectuals (like the Muslim reformer, Muhammad 'Abduh) were eagerly embracing the two.

Barbara Reeves-Ellington relies on English and Bulgarian sources to tell a similar story of the unexpected in missionary encounters. By studying the American-Bulgarian encounter relative to developments in Istanbul, she implicitly reminds us that the Ottoman Empire was a European empire, and that "Europe" and "the Middle East" are blurry as ideas and as regions.[78] Entitled "Petko Slaveykov, the Protestant Press, and the Gendered Language of Moral Reform in Bulgarian Nationalism," her article tells the story of Petko Slaveykov, who in 1864 accepted a job in Istanbul with missionaries of the ABCFM and the Methodist Episcopal Church, who were translating the Bible into Bulgarian on behalf of the British and Foreign Bible Society. Interactions with Protestant missionaries and their publishing programs led Slaveykov to revise his attitudes about roles for women in Bulgarian nation-building, and sharpened his belief in the Bulgarian Orthodox Church as the supreme vehicle of Bulgarian nationalism. His work with translation and publishing also deepened his commitment to the Bulgarian vernacular, which was supplanting Greek as the language of Bulgarian religious and academic high culture. Slaveykov came out of his encounters with American missionaries transformed, but more ideologically committed to Bulgarian Orthodox Christianity than before.

Heather J. Sharkey examines the cultural consequences of missionary publishing with regard to the Arabic Bible. In "American Missionaries, the Arabic Bible, and Coptic Reform in Late Nineteenth-Century Egypt," she considers how American Presbyterians, cooperating with both the American and British Bible societies, promoted a culture of Bible-reading among

Egyptians and coordinated a system of Bible distribution throughout Egypt and extending into northern Sudan. This system, in turn, involved Egyptians in grass-roots missionary enterprises, particularly as colporteurs (male Bible distributors) and Bible Women, and helped to establish an Egyptian evangelical culture that was only partly tied to the Egyptian Evangelical (Presbyterian) Church. In the long run, Sharkey argues, efforts to propagate the Bible among Egyptians accompanied and fostered the expansion of literacy and helped to cultivate a Christian print culture, and perhaps, too, a culture of trans-sectarian "Copticity" among Orthodox, Protestant, and Catholic Egyptians. Her article also shows that while American missionaries may have planted a system of Bible distribution, Egyptians grew and sustained it.

In "Comparing Missions: Pentecostal and Presbyterian Orphanages on the Nile," Beth Baron takes the story beyond Presbyterians and shows how American attitudes, policies, and cultures could differ dramatically from one mission to the next. She contrasts the Fowler Orphanage, a Presbyterian institution in Cairo, with the orphanage of the Pentecostal missionary Lillian Trasher in Assiut. Both were ostensibly faith-based. However, Fowler Orphanage was tied into a larger Presbyterian network of schools and hospitals, and into formal budgetary structures that sometimes drew upon donations from other Protestants (and notably, in the case of Fowler Orphanage, from Quakers). By contrast, Trasher's orphanage in Assiut (which later became associated with the Assemblies of God Church in the United States) operated more informally, by relying for support on "answers to prayers" in the form of occasional gifts in cash or kind. Lillian Trasher herself encouraged speaking in tongues, initially advocated faith healing over hospital treatment, and disapproved of advanced education for girls; in this last respect, her attitudes were at odds with those of the flourishing Egyptian nationalist and feminist movements.[79] Baron shows that visions of modernity and cultures of evangelism could differ markedly from one American group to the next, and reminds us that missionaries "reflected a broad spectrum of Christian thought and practice."

In spite of all the human and financial resources that American missions poured into the region during the nineteenth and early twentieth centuries, they gained limited numbers of official converts in the Middle East, so that local Protestant communities remained small. In 1906–1907, for example, the Ottoman census reported a mere 520 Protestants in the province of Jerusalem; by 1908, the city of Aleppo in Syria had only 191 Protestants.[80] Even in Egypt, where the Egyptian Evangelical (Presbyterian) Church alone claimed nearly 22,000 official members by 1939, an American missionary acknowledged that the Protestant population was still proportionally tiny: "There are fifteen Muslims for each Copt," he wrote, "and nineteen Copts for every Protestant." Protestants, he concluded, were a minority of a minority.[81] One scholar estimates that by 1914 there were "about 65,000 Protestants in the Ottoman Empire out of a total of 10 million people," with a majority of these being Armenians who had left the Armenian Apostolic Church.[82]

Given the small scale of Protestant missionary conversions, then, what do the articles in this volume show? Together they make four related points. First, historians cannot gauge missionary impact in terms of numbers of official converts. Second, American missionaries built important institutions that changed—in often unexpected ways—the lives and the thinking of Middle Eastern peoples, including non-Protestants (such as Armenian, Bulgarian, and Coptic Orthodox Christians) and non-Christians (above all Muslims and Jews). Third, the transformations initiated through missionary encounters extended to the missionaries themselves, suggesting possible "conversions" of personal faith or identity. And fourth, through the interactions of American missionaries with Middle Eastern peoples, U.S.-Middle Eastern history unfolded on common ground.

THE WAY FORWARD

Scholars still need to explore two broad avenues that lead through the history of American missionary encounters in the Middle East. The first avenue goes beyond the ABCFM and later Presbyterian missionaries by examining the activities of either the many other American organizations that sent missions to the Middle East, or of individuals who set out alone. The second avenue considers the local consequences of, and responses to, missionary encounters by using Arabic, Turkish, and other non-English sources more fully. (Two contributors to this volume already take both approaches. Beth Baron studies an independent faith mission that later affiliated with the Assemblies of God, and does so while using some Arabic sources. Karen Kern examines the Latter-day Saints, while drawing upon Ottoman Turkish sources.)

From reading these articles one may see why the ABCFM and the Presbyterians loom so large relative to other American missionaries in the Middle East and why their roles as educators and publishers were significant. Yet their hegemonic place in the historical literature on Middle Eastern missions is also the result of their own history-mindedness. That is, the ABCFM and Presbyterian missionaries and educators tended to keep and preserve detailed records. Many were prolific letter-writers or diarists, some even wrote memoirs, and many either bequeathed their papers to archives or had historically minded heirs who did so for them. Harvard University holds extensive ABCFM records, while many other documents and books related to American Board history are housed in the private library and archive of the Amerikan Bord Heyeti in Istanbul. The Presbyterian Historical Society in Philadelphia has copious records as well. The American University of Beirut and the American University in Cairo, both founded by Presbyterians, have troves of records, too. As Beth Baron noted in her article here, "The sheer volume and diversity of [the Presbyterian] material can be overwhelming."

Other archives are still waiting to be explored. Drew University holds the United Methodist Archives Center; the University of Minnesota maintains the Kautz Family YMCA Archives; New Brunswick Theological Seminary (in New Jersey) contains the archives of the Reformed Church in America; and the American Bible Society keeps records in New York City. Columbia University has recently acquired the archives of Istanbul's Robert College and the American College for Girls. Additional resources are deposited in the Day Missions Library at Yale Divinity School. Admittedly, all of these collections represent either mainline Protestant churches or (in the case of the YMCA and American Bible Society) organizations that drew upon mainline Protestant directors. The term "mainline," as a dictionary of Christianity in America explains, "seems to take its meaning from the traditional aristocratic community ('The Main Line') just outside Philadelphia, Pennsylvania, once served by the main line of the former Pennsylvania Railroad."[83] Mainline implies historically established, mainstream Protestantism, with clearly organized and geographically broad church networks. Mainline missions, as products of an establishment, tend to be relatively easy for historians to study.

A challenge for historians of American missions in the Middle East and elsewhere is to find records from non-mainline groups. In the 1920s, non-mainline evangelicals were becoming increasingly important in American Protestant overseas missions; by 1950, mainline and non-mainline missionaries had reached numerical parity; and by 1990, non-mainline evangelicals accounted for some 90 percent of American missionaries abroad. Yet by the late twentieth century, the scholarship available on non-mainline missions was minimal. Non-mainline groups tended not to keep and organize detailed records regarding their missions, while non-mainline missionaries, who were less likely to have attained the same academic credentials as mainline missionaries, tended not to write or publish as much as Presbyterians.[84] These record-keeping conventions were arguably related to fundraising strategies, too, since Presbyterians, as a matter of policy, tried to use their foreign missions literature to generate interest and raise funds.

The second avenue of research that calls for greater exploration pertains to the local reception, response, and mutual impact of missionary encounters, and demands that historians seek out printed or manuscript sources in local languages. Major American research libraries are likely to hold relevant books in languages like Arabic, Turkish, and Bulgarian, while some hold print runs of relevant periodicals as well.[85] (In the United States, for example, one can find print runs of Egyptian Arabic periodicals like *Majallat al-Azhar*—the magazine of the Sunni Muslim al-Azhar University—and in the 1930s these occasionally discussed American missionaries.) However, what one is unlikely to find in even the best American research libraries are local church journals: for that, one needs to go to the Middle East to visit churches or seminaries that maintain their own archives. In Egypt, for example, during a long stretch within the twentieth century, the Evangelical Church published an Arabic journal that was first called *al-Murshid* and later called *al-Huda*. Journals like these, which offer windows into the life of the church community, are waiting for historians to read them. Occasionally, even manuscript sources, such as personal letters, have found their way into missionary archives. Finally, historians should note that many documents related to American missionary activities in the Middle East are preserved in the Prime Ministerial Ottoman Archive (Başbakanlık Osmanlı Arşivi), located in Istanbul.[86]

With regard to twentieth-century developments, historians may also seek out the Middle Eastern dimensions of missionary encounters by utilizing oral history. Researchers can visit institutions in the Middle East and speak to local pastors or administrators, some of whom may be able to share information on family histories regarding missionary encounters. (For example, the Fowler Orphanage discussed in Baron's paper is still operational, albeit now under the supervision of the Egyptian Evangelical Church.) Another promising line of research may be in finding and speaking to the Muslim, Christian, and Jewish graduates of missionary-founded institutions.[87] Time is running out, however, and those who recall first-hand encounters with American missionaries are often elderly, especially given that active and formal American missions to the Middle East rarely persisted beyond the decolonization movements of the mid-twentieth century. Those wishing to do research on the late twentieth century may need to shift their attention from American Christian missions to what one may arguably call secular development missions. These include American nongovernmental organizations (NGOs), U.S. government organizations like the U.S. Information Agency, and philanthropies like the Ford Foundation, which have professed goals of fostering economic and social advancement.

The resourceful historian may also find sources in photographs, including school pictures, which may suggest how missionary encounters affected social conventions like girls' clothing and physical deportment. Picture postcards, which functioned as both tourist souvenirs and popular art during the late nineteenth and early twentieth centuries, may be helpful as well.[88] With luck, historians may be able to find other "artifacts" of missionary cultures, too, such as embroidery samples produced by girls in mission schools.[89] Finally, researchers may examine more closely some of the most durable and tangible products of American missions—such as churches, book depots, and school buildings—and thereby use architecture as a prism for history and social geography.[90]

Research on American missionary encounters in the Middle East is still in its infancy. Exciting work awaits students and scholars.

NOTES

1. *Edward Said on Orientalism*, produced by Sanjay Talreja, directed by Sut Jhally (Northampton, MA: Media Education Foundation, 2002) VHS; Edward W. Said, *Orientalism* (New York: Pantheon Books, 1978); Edward Said, "Misinformation about Iraq," *CounterPunch*, December 3, 2002, http://www.

counterpunch.org/said1203.html (Accessed July 29, 2008). For an analysis of his works and their impact on Middle Eastern studies, see Daniel Martin Varisco, *Reading Orientalism: Said and the Unsaid* (Seattle: University of Washington Press, 2007).

2. Eleanor H. Tejirian and Reeva Spector Simon, eds., *Altruism and Imperialism: Western Cultural and Religious Missions in the Middle East* (New York: Middle East Institute, Columbia University, 2002); Abbas Amanat and Magnus T. Bernhardsson, eds., *U.S.-Middle Eastern Historical Encounters: A Critical Survey* (Gainesville: University Press of Florida, 2007).

3. Ussama Makdisi, *Artillery of Heaven: American Missionaries and the Failed Conversion of the Middle East* (Ithaca: Cornell University Press, 2008), 1.

4. Edward W. Said, *Out of Place: A Memoir* (New York: Knopf, 1999). Said's family converted to Protestantism after encountering American missionaries in the Levant. His aunt, Emilia Badr, also served for more than forty years as a supervisor at a Presbyterian institution, the American College for Girls in Cairo, which survives today as Ramses College.

5. Joseph L. Grabill, *Protestant Diplomacy and the Near East: Missionary Influence on American Policy, 1810–1927* (Minneapolis: University of Minnesota Press, 1971).

6. David H. Finnie, *Pioneers East: The Early American Experience in the Middle East* (Cambridge: Harvard University Press, 1967).

7. William R. Hutchison, *Errand to the World: American Protestant Thought and Foreign Missions* (Chicago: The University of Chicago Press, 1987), 1.

8. Robert Wuthnow, *Boundless Faith: The Global Outreach of American Churches* (Berkeley: University of California Press, 2009).

9. Daniel T. Rodgers, *Atlantic Crossings: Social Politics in a Progressive Age* (Cambridge: Harvard University Press, 1998), 1–2.

10. Zachary Lockman, *Contending Visions of the Middle East: The History and Politics of Orientalism* (Cambridge: Cambridge University Press, 2004), 96–97.

11. Roby Carroll Barrett, *The Greater Middle East and the Cold War: U.S. Foreign Policy under Eisenhower and Kennedy* (London: I. B. Tauris, 2007), 331n3. Greece was still occupying a position on the borders of "Europe" and the "Near East" or "Middle East," when George Lenczowski first published his political survey of the region in 1952. Thus Lenczowski wrote about the formation of the North Atlantic Treaty Organization (NATO): "largely to assuage Turkish fears, Dean Acheson, the American secretary of state, declared on March 23, 1949, that the United States' continuous interest in the security of the nations of the Middle East [*sic*], particularly Greece, Turkey, and Iran, had in no way been lessened by the [NATO] negotiations." George Lenczowski, *The Middle East in World Affairs* (Ithaca: Cornell University Press, 1952), 149. This line remained unchanged in the fourth edition (1980) of Lenczowski's study (pages 137–138). In all editions of his book, however, Lenczowski explained in the introduction

that Greece was part of the "Near East" but not really of the "Middle East" (see 1952 edition, xvii; 1980 edition, 21). By contrast, the regional status of Turkey remained more ambiguous.

12. Inclusion of North Africa within the "Middle East" is becoming increasingly common, while many scholars and organizations (such as the World Bank) recognize "the Middle East and North Africa" (rendered by its acronym, MENA) as a distinct region. See, for example, The World Bank, "Countries and Regions," http://www.worldbank.org/ (Accessed May 27, 2009).

13. Sydney E. Ahlstrom, *A Religious History of the American People* (New Haven: Yale University Press, 1972); Hutchison, *Errand to the World*; Mark A. Noll, *The Old Religion in a New World: The History of North American Christianity* (Grand Rapids: William B. Eerdmans Publishing Company, 2002); and Mark A. Noll, *American Evangelical Christianity: An Introduction* (Oxford: Blackwell Publishers, 2001).

14. Makdisi, *Artillery of Heaven*. Regarding the early context of missions to Native Americans, see Hutchison, *Errand to the World*.

15. Nathan O. Hatch, *The Democratization of American Christianity* (New Haven: Yale University Press, 1989), 5, 9–10.

16. Andrew F. Walls, "The American Dimension in the History of the Missionary Movement," in *Earthen Vessels: American Evangelicals and Foreign Missions, 1880–1980*, ed. Joel A. Carpenter and Wilbert R. Shenk (Grand Rapids: William B. Eerdmans Publishing Company, 1990), 1–25.

17. Walls, "The American Dimension in the History of the Missionary Movement," 5–6, 12–13. Contrast this with his overview of British missions, which emphasizes a British missionary aversion to traders: Andrew F. Walls, "British Missions," in *Missionary Ideologies in the Imperialist Era: 1880–1920*, ed. Torben Christensen and William R. Hutchison (Århus, Denmark: Aros, 1982), 159–165.

18. On John D. Rockefeller and John D. Rockfeller, Jr., see Heather J. Sharkey, *American Evangelicals in Egypt: Missionary Encounters in an Age of Empire* (Princeton: Princeton University Press, 2008), 12, 138–139, 157, 165–166, 235n57. On women and fund-raising in missions, see Shirley S. Garrett, "Sisters All: Feminism and the American Women's Missionary Movement," in *Missionary Ideologies in the Imperialist Era*, ed. Torben Christensen and William R. Hutchison (Århus, Denmark: Aros, 1982), 221–230.

19. Noll, *The Old Religion in a New World*, 24.

20. Beth Baron, "Talking in Tongues: Lillian Trasher, the Asyut Orphanage, and Pentecostals on the Nile" (paper presented at the Conference on "Christian Missionaries in the Middle East: Re-Thinking Colonial Encounters," North Carolina State University, Raleigh, North Carolina, May 4, 2007).

21. Noll, *American Evangelical Christianity*.

22. Both were antecedents of today's Presbyterian Church (U.S.A.), which is often known by its acronym PC(USA). For an explanation of these distinctions, see James H. Smylie, *A Brief History of the Presbyterians* (Louisville: Geneva Press, 1996).

23. See Harlan P. Beach and Charles H. Fahs, *World Missionary Atlas* (New York: Institute of Social and Religious Research, 1925). On American schools in what is now Turkey, see Frank Andrews Stone, *Academies for Anatolia: A Study of the Rationale, Program and Impact of the Educational Institutions Sponsored by the American Board in Turkey, 1830–2005* (San Francisco: Caddo Gap Press, 2006). On Protestant and Catholic mission schools more broadly, see Mehmet Ali Doğan, "Missionary Schools," in *Encyclopedia of the Ottoman Empire*, ed. Gábor Ágoston and Bruce Masters (New York: Facts on File, 2009), 385–388.

24. Eleanor Abdella Doumato, *Getting God's Ear: Women, Islam, and Healing in Saudi Arabia and the Gulf* (New York: Columbia University Press, 2000); Fatma Hassan Al-Sayegh, "American Women Missionaries in the Gulf: Agents for Cultural Change," *Islam and Christian-Muslim Relations* 9:3 (1998): 339–356.

25. John Thomas Nichol, *Pentecostalism* (New York: Harper & Row Publishers, 1966), 167–168. By 1966, Nichol wrote, there were 170 Pentecostal congregations in Egypt. Published material on Plymouth Brethrenites in Egypt is scanty, though American Presbyterian sources date their entry to 1874, when a former Presbyterian, the Rev. B. F. Pinkerton, started to establish churches in Egypt. See, for example, J. R. Alexander, *A Sketch of the Story of the Evangelical Church of Egypt* (Alexandria: Whitehead Morris Limited, 1930), 23–28.

26. Nancy Gallagher, *Quakers in the Israeli-Palestinian Conflict: The Dilemmas of NGO Humanitarian Activism* (Cairo: American University in Cairo Press, 2007). See page 22 regarding the nineteenth-century Anglo-American antecedents of Quaker outreach in Palestine.

27. David D. Grafton, *Piety, Politics, and Power: Lutherans Encountering Islam in the Middle East* (Eugene, OR: Wipf and Stock Publishers, 2009).

28. Brian Yothers, *The Romance of the Holy Land in American Travel Writing, 1790–1876* (Aldershot, UK: Ashgate, 2007).

29. Ruth Kark, "Sweden and the Holy Land: Pietistic and Communal Settlement," *Journal of Historical Geography* 22:1 (1996): 46–67; and Jane Fletcher Geniesse, *American Priestess: The Extraordinary Story of Anna Spafford and the American Colony in Jerusalem* (New York: Nan A. Talese, 2008).

30. Ruth Kark, "Millenarism and Agricultural Settlement in the Holy Land in the Nineteenth Century," *Journal of Historical Geography* 9:1 (1983): 47–62.

31. In the 1850s, this search for space prompted the (American) Associate Reformed Presbyterian Church (a precursor of the United Presbyterian Church of North America) to relinquish its work in Damascus to British missionaries

and instead "to occupy Cairo"—and all of Egypt—"at their earliest convenience." Sharkey, *American Evangelicals in Egypt*, 18.

32. On British missions in Israel/Palestine, see, for example, Nancy L. Stockdale, *Colonial Encounters among English and Palestinian Women, 1800–1948* (Gainesville: University Press of Florida, 2007); Michael Marten, *Attempting to Bring the Gospel Home: Scottish Missions to Palestine, 1839–1917* (London: I. B. Tauris, 2006); Inger Marie Okkenhaug, *The Quality of Heroic Living, of High Endeavour, and Adventure: Anglican Mission, Women, and Education in Palestine, 1888–1948* (Leiden: Brill, 2002); Laura Robson, "Archaeology and Mission: The British Presence in Nineteenth-Century Palestine" (paper presented at the conference on "Great Powers in the Holy Land: From Napoleon to the Balfour Declaration," European Institute, Columbia University, April 4, 2009); and Philippe Bourmand, "Public Space and Private Spheres: The Foundation of St. Luke's Hospital of Nablus by the CMS (1891–1901)," in *New Faiths in Ancient Lands*, ed. Heleen Murre-van den Berg, 133–150. On German missions see, for example, Nicholas Railton, *No North Sea: The Anglo-German Evangelical Network in the Middle of the Nineteenth Century* (Leiden: Brill, 2000); Roland Löffler, "The Metamorphosis of a Pietistic Missionary and Educational Institution into a Social Services Enterprise: The Case of the Syrian Orphanage (1860–1945)," in *New Faiths in Ancient Lands*, ed. Heleen Murre-van den Berg, 151–174; Uwe Kaminsky, "German 'Home Mission' Abroad: The *Orientarbeit* of the Deaconess Institution Kaiserswerth in the Ottoman Empire," in *New Faiths in Ancient Lands*, ed. Heleen Murre-van den Berg, 191–209; and the classic work by Julius Richter, *A History of Protestant Missions in the Near East* (Edinburgh: Oliphant, Anderson & Ferrier, 1910). On Swedish missions to the Holy Land, see Kark, "Sweden and the Holy Land"; and Inger Marie Okkenhaug, "Signe Ekblad and the Swedish School in Jerusalem, 1922–1948," *Svensk Missionstidskrift* 94:2 (2006): 147–161. A collection of essays that includes materials on British, German, and Russian missions in Palestine, as well as on Jesuit and Dominican Catholic, American, and Scottish missions in the wider region, is Martin Tamcke and Michael Marten, eds., *Christian Witness between Continuity and New Beginnings: Modern Historical Missions in the Middle East* (Berlin: LIT Verlag, 2006).

33. Hence historians of Sudan speak about a missionary "spheres system." See, for example, Roland Werner, William Anderson, and Andrew Wheeler, *Day of Devastation, Day of Contentment: The History of the Sudanese Church across 2000 Years* (Nairobi: Paulines Publications Africa, 2000), 373. Lilian Sanderson wrote extensively about this "spheres system" in southern Sudan. See, for example, Lilian Passmore Sanderson and Neville Sanderson, *Education, Religion, and Politics in Southern Sudan, 1899–1964* (London: Ithaca Press, 1981). British authorities had another reason for spreading the missionaries out: in southern Sudan, their geographic diffusion helped to establish colonial rule by proxy.

34. Historians have not written much about the YMCA, YWCA, or WSSA in the Middle East, though the Sunday Schools Movement as a whole exerted critical influences on the twentieth-century Coptic Orthodox Church. Some coverage of the YMCA is in Sharkey, *American Evangelicals in Egypt*. Regarding the Sunday Schools Movement, see S. S. Hasan, *Christians versus Muslims in Modern Egypt: The Century-Long Struggle for Coptic Equality* (Oxford: Oxford University Press, 2003). On the American Bible Society in the Ottoman Empire, see Marcellus Bowen, *The Bible in Bible Lands: History of the Levant Agency* (New York: American Bible Society, 1917).

35. On these examples from Egypt, see Sharkey, *American Evangelicals in Egypt*.

36. William Richey Hogg, *Ecumenical Foundations: A History of the International Missionary Council and Its Nineteenth-Century Background* (New York: Harper & Brothers, 1952); and Brian Stanley, *The World Missionary Conference, Edinburgh 1910* (Grand Rapids, MI: William B. Eerdmans Publishing Company, 2009).

37. Noll, *American Evangelical Christianity*, 116.

38. On the connections between Catholic mission schools and French education, see, for example, Jérôme Bocquet, "Francophonie et langue arabe dans le Syrie sous mandat: l'exemple de l'enseignement missionnaire à Damas," in *The British and French Mandates in Comparative Perspectives,* ed. Nadine Méouchy and Peter Sluglett (Leiden: Brill, 2004), 303–319. Regarding the heavy French-language emphasis in the Catholic missions of Egypt, see, for example, Victor Guérin, *La France Catholique en Égypte* (Tours: Alfred Mame et Fils, 1894); and Jack Sislian, "Missionary Work in Egypt during the Nineteenth Century," in *Educational Policy and the Mission Schools: Case Studies from the British Empire,* ed. Brian Holmes (London: Routledge & Kegan Paul, 1967), 175–240; see especially 178, 218. In general, there is a dearth of scholarship in English on the history of Catholic missions in the Middle East. Exceptions include Alastair Hamilton, *The Copts and the West, 1439–1822: The European Discovery of the Egyptian Church* (Oxford: Oxford University Press, 2006); Bernard Heyberger, "Individualism and Political Modernity: Devout Catholic Women in Aleppo and Lebanon between the Seventeenth and Nineteenth Centuries," in *Beyond the Exotic: Women's Histories in Islamic Societies*, ed. Amira El Azhary Sonbol (Syracuse: Syracuse University Press, 2005), 71–85, 407–412; Haim Goren, "The German Catholic Holy Sepulchre Society: Activities in Palestine," in *Jerusalem in the Mind of the Western World, 1800–1948*, ed. Yehoshua Ben Arieh and Moshe Davis (Westport, CT: Praeger, 1997), 155–172; Bruce Masters, "Competing for Aleppo's Souls: The Roman Catholic and Protestant Missions in the Ottoman Period," *Archaeology & History in Lebanon* 22 (2005): 34–50; and Akram Khater's forthcoming book on religious women in eighteenth-century Aleppo.

39. On the relevance of sharing information and misinformation, see Hamilton, *The Copts and the West.*

40. Daniel Martin Varisco, "Framing the Holy Land as an Art: Illustrations of Arabs in 19th Century Bible Custom Accounts" (paper prepared for the conference of the Middle East Studies Association (MESA), Boston 2009); and Daniel Martin Varisco, "Lithographica Arabica," *Tabsir: Insight on Islam and the Middle East,* http://tabsir.net/?p=746 (Accessed May 12, 2009).

41. Issam Nassar, "Biblification in the Service of Colonialism: Jerusalem in Nineteenth-Century Photography," *Third Text* 20:3–4 (2006): 317–326; and Edward L. Queen II, "Great Powers, Holy Powers, and Good Powers: American Protestants Tour the Holy Land, 1867–1914" (paper presented at the conference on "Great Powers in the Holy Land: From Napoleon to the Balfour Declaration," European Institute, Columbia University, April 4, 2009).

42. Robert J. Allison, *The Crescent Obscured: The United States and the Muslim World, 1776–1815* (Chicago: The University of Chicago Press, 1995), xvi–xvii.

43. Lively synthetic histories of the nineteenth and early twentieth centuries include James L. Gelvin, *The Modern Middle East: A History,* Second edition (New York: Oxford University Press, 2008); and William L. Cleveland and Martin Bunton, *A History of the Modern Middle East,* Fourth edition (Boulder: Westview Press, 2009).

44. A valuable study of this period is M. Şükrü Hanioğlu, *A Brief History of the Late Ottoman Empire* (Princeton: Princeton University Press, 2008). On demographic trends, see Justin McCarthy, *Muslims and Minorities: The Population of Ottoman Anatolia and the End of Empire* (New York: New York University Press, 1983). A pithy overview of Ottoman attitudes toward missionaries appears in Bruce Masters, "Missionaries," in *Encyclopedia of the Ottoman Empire,* ed. Gábor Ágoston and Bruce Masters (New York: Facts on File, 2009), 384–385.

45. J. C. Hurewitz, *Diplomacy in the Near and Middle East: A Documentary Record, 1535–1914* (Princeton: D. Van Nostrand Company, 1956), 149–153.

46. On the diminishing of Christian populations, see Youssef Courbage and Philippe Fargues, *Christians and Jews under Islam,* Trans. Judy Mabro (London: I. B. Tauris, 1997); and Heather J. Sharkey, "Middle Eastern and North African Christianity," in *Introducing World Christianity,* ed. Charles Farhadian (Oxford: Blackwell, forthcoming).

47. Sharkey, *American Evangelicals in Egypt,* 55–63; Bruce Masters, *Christians and Jews in the Ottoman Arab World: The Roots of Sectarianism* (Cambridge: Cambridge University Press, 2001), 137–139.

48. Valuable general studies, with some information on North Africa, include Bengt Sundkler and Christopher Steed, *A History of the Church in Africa* (Cambridge: Cambridge University Press, 2000); Adrian Hastings, *The Church in Africa, 1450–1950* (Oxford: Clarendon Press, 1994); and Brian Stanley, *The*

Bible and the Flag: Protestant Missions and British Imperialism in the Nine-teenth and Twentieth Centuries (Leicester: Apollos, 1990).

49. Heather J. Sharkey, "A New Crusade or an Old One?" *ISIM Newsletter* 12 (June 2003): 48–49.

50. Andrew Porter, *Religion versus Empire? British Protestant Missionaries and Overseas Expansion, 1700–1914* (New York: Manchester University Press, 2004), 211–224.

51. John R. Mott, *The Evangelization of the World in This Generation* (New York: Student Volunteer Movement for Foreign Missions, 1900), 115.

52. On the mandates, see Méouchy and Sluglett, eds., *The British and French Mandates in Comparative Perspectives.*

53. A useful collection of materials on this history appears in Walter Laqueur and Barry Rubin, eds., *The Israel-Arab Reader*, Seventh revised edition (New York: Penguin Books, 2008).

54. A classic exposition of this view appears in Richter, *A History of Protestant Missions in the Near East*. Richter was German but his works were widely read by Americans.

55. Allison, *The Crescent Obscured.*

56. Douglas Little, *American Orientalism: The United States and the Middle East since 1945* (Chapel Hill: The University of North Carolina Press, 2002). A more focused study of this phenomenon, relative to late twentieth-century Morocco, is Brian T. Edwards, *Morocco Bound: Disorienting America's Maghreb* (Durham, NC: Duke University Press, 2005).

57. Makdisi, *Artillery of Heaven*, 29.

58. Hutchison, *Errand to the World.*

59. Hans-Lukas Kieser, *Nearest East: American Millennialism and Mission to the Middle East* (Philadelphia: Temple University Press, 2010).

60. Melani McAlister, *Epic Encounters: Culture, Media, and U.S. Interests in the Middle East, 1945–2000* (Berkeley: University of California Press, 2001), 3; Michael B. Oren, *Power, Faith, and Fantasy: America in the Middle East, 1776 to the Present* (New York: W. W. Norton & Co., 2007); Thomas S. Kidd, *American Christians and Islam: Evangelical Culture and Muslims from the Colonial Period to the Age of Terrorism* (Princeton: Princeton University Press, 2008); Timothy Marr, *The Cultural Roots of American Islamicism* (Cambridge: Cambridge University Press, 2006).

61. Consider, for example, the case of the American Presbyterians, who after 1854 developed the largest Protestant mission in Egypt. By 1957, they counted 26,662 communicants, almost all of whom came from Coptic Orthodox families that were already Christian. Wallace N. Jamison, *The United Presbyterian Story: A Centennial Study, 1858–1958* (Pittsburgh: The Geneva Press, 1958), 198; and Sharkey, *American Evangelicals in Egypt*. The total population of Egypt in 1957 was approximately twenty-five million.

62. This school of history is particularly developed among German scholars. See Alf Lüdtke, ed., *The History of Everyday Life* (Princeton: Princeton University Press, 1995). Recent works that acknowledge the impact of American missions on women and households are: Mona L. Russell, *Creating the New Egyptian Woman: Consumerism, Education, and National Identity, 1863–1922* (New York: Palgrave Macmillan, 2004); and Lisa Pollard, *Nurturing the Nation: The Family Politics of Modernizing, Colonizing, and Liberating Egypt, 1805–1923* (Berkeley: University of California Press, 2005). Examples specific to the impact of missionaries include Barbara Reeves-Ellington, "Gender, Conversion, and Social Transformation: The American Discourse of Domesticity and the Origins of the Bulgarian Women's Movement, 1864–1876," in *Converting Cultures: Religion, Ideology, and Transformations of Modernity*, ed. Dennis Washburn and A. Kevin Reinhart (Leiden: Brill, 2007), 115–140; Barbara Reeves-Ellington, "Women, Gender, and Missionary Education: Ottoman Empire," in *The Encyclopedia of Women and Islamic Cultures*, Vol. 4, gen. ed. Suad Joseph (Leiden: Brill, 2007), 285–287; and Heather J. Sharkey, "Women, Gender, and Missionary Education: Sudan," *The Encyclopedia of Women and Islamic Cultures*, Vol. 4, gen. ed. Suad Joseph (Leiden: Brill, 2007), 287–288.

63. Betty S. Anderson, "Liberal Education at the American University of Beirut," in *Liberal Thought in the Eastern Mediterranean*, ed. Christoph Schumann (Leiden: Brill, 2008), 99–120; Michael P. Zirinsky, "A Panacea for the Ills of the Country: American Presbyterian Education in Interwar Iran," *American Presbyterians* 72:3 (1994): 187–201; Jasamin Rostam-Kolayi, "From Evangelizing to Modernizing Iranians: The American Presbyterian Mission and Its Iranian Students," *Iranian Studies* (April 2008): 213–240; and Kieser, *Nearest East*.

64. Daniel H. Bays and Grant Wacker, eds., *The Foreign Missionary Enterprise at Home: Explorations in North American Cultural History* (Tuscaloosa: The University of Alabama Press, 2003).

65. Dana L. Robert, *American Women in Mission: A Social History of Their Thought and Practice* (Macon, GA: Mercer University Press, 1996); R. Pierce Beaver, *American Protestant Women in World Mission: A History of the First Feminist Movement in North America* (Grand Rapids, MI: Eerdmans, 1980); Patricia R. Hill, *The World Their Household: The American Women's Foreign Mission Movement and Cultural Transformation, 1870–1920* (Ann Arbor: University of Michigan Press, 1984); Frederick J. Heuser, Jr., "Culture, Feminism, and the Gospel: American Presbyterian Women and Foreign Missions, 1870–1923" (PhD diss., Temple University, 1991). The last study includes some discussion of Iran.

66. Marilyn Booth, "'She Herself Was the Ultimate Rule': Arabic Biographies of Missionary Teachers and Their Pupils," *Islam and Christian-Muslim Relations* 13:4 (2002): 427–448; Heleen Murre-van den Berg, "Nineteenth-Century Protestant Missions and Middle Eastern Women: An Overview," in *Gender,*

Religion and Change in the Middle East: Two Hundred Years of History, ed. Inger Marie Okkenhaug & Ingvild Flaskerud (Oxford: Berg, 2005), 103–122; Barbara Reeves-Ellington, "A Vision of Mount Holyoke in the Ottoman Balkans: American Cultural Transfer, Bulgarian Nation-Building, and Women's Educational Reform, 1858–1870," *Gender & History* 16:1 (2004): 146–71; and Ellen Fleischmann, "Evangelization or Education: American Protestant Missionaries, the American Board, and the Girls and Women of Syria (1830–1910)," in *New Faiths in Ancient Lands,* ed. Heleen Murre-van den Berg, 263–280. On the American side, see, too, Lisa Joy Pruitt, *"A Looking-Glass for the Ladies": American Protestant Women and the Orient in the Nineteenth Century* (Macon: Mercer University Press, 2005); and these two articles by Ellen Fleischmann: "The Impact of American Protestant Missions in Lebanon on the Construction of Female Identity, c. 1860–1950," *Islam and Christian-Muslim Relations* 13:4 (2002): 411–426; and "'Our Moslem Sisters': Women of Greater Syria in the Eyes of American Protestant Missionary Women," *Islam and Christian-Muslim Relations* 9:3 (1998), 307–323.

67. Benjamin Braude, "Foundation Myths of the *Millet* System," in *Christians and Jews in the Ottoman Empire*, Vol. 1, ed. Benjamin Braude and Bernard Lewis (New York: Holmes and Meier, 1982), 69–88; Masters, *Christians and Jews in the Ottoman Arab World*; and Courbage and Fargues, *Christians and Jews under Islam.*

68. Heather J. Sharkey, "Muslim Apostasy, Christian Conversion, and Religious Freedom in Egypt: A Study of American Missionaries, Western Imperialism, and Human Rights Agendas," in *Proselytization Revisited: Rights, Free Markets, and Culture Wars*, ed. Rosalind I. J. Hackett (London: Equinox, 2008), 139–166.

69. Sharkey, *American Evangelicals in Egypt.*

70. Whereas in Egypt only Protestants focused on missions to Muslims, in Algeria Catholics did so as well. Consider the work of Cardinal Lavigerie, founder of the White Fathers, and of Charles de Foucauld. Aylward Shorter, *Cross and Flag in Africa: The "White Fathers" during the Colonial Scramble, 1892–1914* (Maryknoll, NY: Orbis Books, 2006); and Jean-Jacques Antier, *Charles de Foucauld*, Trans. Julia Shirek Smith (San Francisco: Ignatius Press, 1999).

71. Regarding the impact of imperialism and postcolonial nationalism on American missions and mission studies, see Dana L. Robert, "From Missions to Beyond Missions: The Historiography of American Protestant Foreign Missions since World War II," in *New Directions in American Religious History*, ed. Harry S. Stout and D. G. Hart (New York: Oxford University Press, 1997), 362–393. This article also provides a superb bibliography on American Protestant missions and missionary thought.

72. This phrase comes from Marwa Elshakry's essay in this volume. See Heather J. Sharkey, "Arabic Antimissionary Treatises," *International Bulletin of Missionary Research* 28:3 (2004): 112–118.

73. The Layman's Inquiry on Foreign Missions, a project supported by John D. Rockefeller Jr., emphasized that foreign missionaries either were or should be purveyors of humanitarian and development aid. The team's report was highly controversial upon its debut, but its arguments did reflect, influence, or predict changes in missionary policies. The summary report was William Ernest Hocking, ed., *Re-Thinking Missions: A Laymen's Inquiry after One Hundred Years* (New York: Harper & Brothers Publishers, 1932). An excellent assessment of the report and its long-term impact appears in John R. Fitzmier and Randall Balmer, "A Poultice for the Bite of the Cobra: The Hocking Report and Presbyterian Missions in the Middle Decades of the Twentieth Century," in *The Diversity of Discipleship: The Presbyterians and Twentieth-Century Christian Witness,* ed. Milton J. Coalter et al. (Louisville, KY: Westminster/John Knox Press, 1991), 105–125.

74. On missionaries as sowers of discord: Ussama Makdisi, *The Culture of Sectarianism: Community, History, and Violence in Nineteenth-Century Ottoman Lebanon* (Berkeley: University of California Press, 2000); and Eleanor Abdella Doumato, "Joyful Death: The Romance of Americans in Mission to the Nestorians" (paper presented at the Conference on "Christian Missionaries in the Middle East: Re-Thinking Colonial Encounters," North Carolina State University, Raleigh, North Carolina, May 5, 2007). On missionaries, philanthropy, and NGOs, see Gallagher, *Quakers in the Israeli-Palestinian Conflict*; and Eleanor H. Tejirian, "Faith of Our Fathers: Near East Relief and the Near East Foundation—From Mission to NGO," in *Altruism and Imperialism*, ed. Tejirian and Simon, 295–315.

75. In the Middle Eastern context, this idea has otherwise been more fully developed among French scholars with regard to Jewish-Muslim relations. Joëlle Bahloul, *The Architecture of Memory: A Jewish-Muslim Household in Colonial Algeria, 1937–1962*, Trans. Catherine Du Peloux Ménagé (Cambridge: Cambridge University Press, 1992). Another study of a mixed Jewish-Muslim household in Turkey appears in the film *Camondo Han* directed by Peter Clasen (2005), which is based in part on works by Nora Seni including *Les Camondo* (Arles: Actes Sud, 1997) and her article "The Camondos and Their Imprint on 19th-Century Istanbul," *International Journal of Middle East Studies* 26:4 (1994): 663–675.

76. John Freely, *A History of Robert College, the American College for Girls, and Boğaziçi University* (Istanbul: YKY, 2000).

77. An earlier version of this article appeared as Marwa Elshakry, "The Gospel of Science and American Evangelism in Late Ottoman Beirut," *Past & Present* 196:1 (2007): 173–214.

78. On these issues of European-ness, see Donald Quataert, *The Ottoman Empire, 1700–1922* (Cambridge: Cambridge University Press, 2000); and Talal Asad, "Muslims and European Identity: Can Europe Represent Islam?" in Anthony Pagden, ed., *The Idea of Europe: From Antiquity to the European Union* (Cambridge: Cambridge University Press, 2002), 209–227.

79. See Beth Baron, *Egypt as a Woman: Nationalism, Gender, and Politics* (Berkeley: University of California Press, 2005).

80. Bruce Masters, *Christians and Jews in the Ottoman Arab World*, 151.

81. H. E. Philips, *The Question Box: A Catechism on Missions in Egypt*, ([Pittsburgh?] The Publicity Committee of the Egyptian Mission of the United Presbyterian Church of North America, 1939).

82. Masters, "Missionaries," in *Encyclopedia of the Ottoman Empire*, ed. Gábor Ágoston and Bruce Masters (New York: Facts on File, 2009), 385.

83. Daniel G. Reid, ed., *Dictionary of Christianity in America* (Downers Grove, IL: InterVarsity Press, 1990), 700–701.

84. Joel A. Carpenter and Wilbert R. Shenk, eds., *Earthen Vessels: American Evangelicals and Foreign Missions, 1880–1980* (Grand Rapids, MI: William B. Eerdmans Publishing Company, 1990), preface and xii–xviii.

85. See Ami Ayalon, *The Press in the Arab Middle East: A History* (New York: Oxford University Press, 1995).

86. A searchable database of this Ottoman government archive is available at: http://www.devletarsivleri.gov.tr/katalog/ (Accessed June 15, 2009).

87. Ellen Fleischmann, "'I Only Wish I Had a Home on This Globe': Transnational Biography and Dr. Mary Eddy," *Journal of Women's History* 21:3 (2009): 108–130.

88. Christraud M. Geary and Virginia-Lee Webb, eds., *Delivering Views: Distant Cultures in Early Postcards* (Washington, DC: Smithsonian Institution Press, 1998); and Christraud M. Geary, "Photographs as Materials for African History: Some Methodological Considerations," *History in Africa* 13 (1986): 89–116. Neither of these works includes a discussion of the Middle East but they are both useful methodologically nonetheless. On the Middle East, see, for example, Sarah Graham-Brown, *Images of Women: the Portrayal of Women in Photography of the Middle East, 1860–1950* (New York: Columbia University Press, 1988); and Annelies Moors, "Presenting Palestine's Population: Premonitions of the Nakba," *The MIT Electronic Journal of Middle East Studies* 1 (2001). The last article includes a discussion of postcards.

89. Several years ago, while doing research at Birmingham University on British CMS missionaries in northern Sudan, I found some small but intricate specimens of mission-school embroidery that were included among the papers from

a CMS school. Perhaps an American missionary archive preserves similar items. See Heather J. Sharkey, "Christians among Muslims: The Church Missionary Society in the Northern Sudan," *Journal of African History* 43 (2002): 51–75.

90. A description of Robert College in Istanbul appears in the following memoir: Godfrey Goodwin, *Life's Episodes: Discovering Ottoman Architecture* (Istanbul: Boğaziçi University Press, 2002). A noteworthy study—albeit one that studies British mission buildings in the Middle East—is Mark Crinson, *Empire Building: Orientalism and Victorian Architecture* (London: Routledge, 1996).

PART 1

SHIFTING FOUNDATIONS OF AMERICAN MISSIONS

1

From New England into New Lands

The Beginning of a Long Story

Mehmet Ali Doğan

For Jerusalem's sake let us give ourselves no rest.[1]

In every direction to which we can turn our eyes, we may discover regions which claim the compassionate regard of Christians. From the North and the South, from the East and the West, we may hear the same call that was heard, by Paul in vision, from a man of Macedonia: "Come over and help us." In Europe, in Asia, in Africa, how many millions of our apostate race are perishing for want of the Bread of Life! What darkness covers, what idolatry debases. Heathen nations! On the borders of our own country, how many Indian tribes to civilize and christianize! Within the limits of our own territory, how many populous settlements seldom hear a sermon from a minister of Jesus![2]

So said the chairman of managers of the Philadelphia Missionary Society in an address to his colleagues in 1813. His words captured the spirit of a nineteenth century that was marked by the rapid, global pursuit of foreign missions among North American and European churches. In the United States, many evangelical Protestants believed that the Middle East, as the heart of the "Bible Lands," was a particulary promising field for missionary activities. They therefore set out to establish missions in the region.

This article examines the historical roots of American missions in the Middle East. These missions began amid the early nineteenth-century movement that historians call the Second Great Awakening. Critical to this missionary engagement was the establishment of the American Board of Commissioners for Foreign Missions (ABCFM), which in the 1820s sent American missionary "pioneers" to the Levant. These early ABCFM initiatives in the Middle East were of an experimental nature. Nevertheless, they set the foundations for subsequent American Protestant missionary encounters in the region.

The Second Great Awakening

The earliest American missions to the Middle East developed against the context of a series of Christian evangelical revivals, which occurred during the early nineteenth century and became collectively known as the Second Great Awakening. The term Second Great Awakening suggested succession from an earlier revival movement, namely, the First Great Awakening, which had emerged during the 1730s and 1740s. Both movements profoundly affected the characteristics of American Christianity and extended the influence of Christianity over the nation. The First Great Awakening influenced political and social thought, and transformed the religious and social life of the colonies before the American Revolution. The Second Great Awakening was a series of revivals, in which American society experienced an outpouring of religious concern, a flowering of spiritual sentiment, a vast mobilization of people, and an unparalleled growth in church membership.[3] Alexis de Tocqueville, the French aristocrat who visited the United States in the early nineteenth century, observed that "there is no country in the whole world in which the Christian religion retains a greater influence over the souls of men than in America."[4]

This "awakening" emerged in various regions mainly as a reaction to the deism of the Enlightenment and the general decline in religious interest in America. Many local congregations had been disrupted during the American War of Independence, while some were dissatisfied with Christianity as previously practiced. The Second Great Awakening was a galvanizing event that boosted attendance in churches throughout the country. All denominations such as Congregationalists in New England, Presbyterians in the mid-Atlantic region, and Methodists and Baptists in the Southeast participated in these revivals; so did Christians who were moving westward with the frontier.[5] Moreover, the Awakening provided the impetus for the foundation of several new American denominations such as the Disciples of Christ, the Church of Jesus Christ of Latter-day Saints (the Mormons), and the Transcendentalists.[6] Its revivals, which fortified the Protestant culture of the early American republic, had a wider social and political impact. Namely, the revivals enhanced American Christian discourses about creating a godly republic. They also stimulated a wave of social activism that led to the foundation of several benevolent societies and missionary organizations. Among these were the American Board of Commissioners for Foreign Missions (1810), the Home and Foreign Mission Society (1812), the General Missionary Convention of the Baptist Denomination in the United States for Foreign Missions (1814), the American Education Society (1815), the American Bible Society (1816), the American Colonization Society (1817), the Missionary and Bible Society of the Methodist Episcopal Church (1819), the American Sunday School Union (1824), the American Tract Society (1825), the American Home Missionary Society (1826), and the American Temperance Society (1826).[7] Between 1810 and 1870, American evangelicals established approximately twenty-four American societies dedicated to evangelism and Bible and tract distribution.[8] "Earlier deistic elements," says Robert Linder, "now combined with a virile evangelical faith to produce for the fledgling republic a civil religion which emphasized America's godly connections, unique history and millennial mission to convert the world to Christianity and democracy."[9]

Donald Mathews argues that the Second Great Awakening was "an organizing process that helped to give meaning and direction to people suffering in various degrees from the social strains of a nation on the move into political, economic and geographical areas."[10] Indeed, the United States was rapidly changing. The country was not a narrow band along the eastern seacoast anymore and already extended many hundreds of miles inland.[11] The Louisiana Purchase had doubled the size of the country in 1803. The population had increased rapidly, from slightly fewer than four million to almost thirteen million between 1790 and 1830.[12] Additionally, the country was receiving new waves of immigrants daily.[13] Along with the nation's population growth, there were also two demographic shifts: a strong westward movement of people from the seaboard states and migration from rural areas to towns and cities.[14] "The incredible dimensions of national expansion were a daunting challenge," Mark Noll observes, "and the ecclesiastical response was the voluntary society."[15]

New England

The Second Great Awakening brought about a major revitalization of the New England social order[16] and signaled the inception of missionary work in New England, where Congregational and Presbyterian churches dominated the revivals of the Awakening. In 1798, Connecticut pastors established the Missionary Society of Connecticut[17] to carry out home missionary work in order to evangelize both European settlers and Native Americans.[18] After the formation of the Massachusetts Missionary Society in Boston in May 1799, a missionary endeavor developed among the Congregational churches in New England.[19] Similar societies were organized in the other New England states. The members of the Massachusetts Missionary Society declared their aim as "to diffuse the knowledge of the Gospel among the heathens, as well as other people in the remote parts of our country, where Christ is seldom or never preached."[20]

Missionary literature was also expanding in the region. Missionary biographies, sermons, narratives, and tracts were circulating. Missionary publications in New England such as *Connecticut Evangelical Magazine, the Massachusetts Missionary Magazine,* and *Panoplist*[21] were reporting on the foreign missionary work of the European missionaries regardless of denominational affiliation in order to promote missionary activities at home and abroad.[22] These overseas examples certainly convinced many people in New England of the need for foreign missions as the revivals of the Second Great Awakening spread across New England during two or three generations.[23] Ultimately, too, these examples of missionary cooperation or mutual awareness also planted the seeds of Protestant ecumenism.

The Second Great Awakening was also a turning point in the history of theological education in New England. Andover Theological Seminary, whose faculty were associated with the Congregational and Presbyterian churches, opened its doors in September 1808 and became an important center of missionary spirit for foreign missions.[24] In a sermon preached at the opening, Timothy Dwight, president of Yale, stated that "it is the design of this Institution to furnish students with a sufficient opportunity to prepare themselves for the Ministry of the Gospel."[25] According to its constitution, the seminary "shall be equally open to Protestants of every denomination."[26] In addition to being America's first postgraduate theological school and offering a new style of American theological education, the seminary was the training center for the missionaries of the ABCFM from the beginning.[27] According to Leonard Woods, author of *History of the Andover Theological Seminary*, all but one of its missionaries studied at the seminary during the first decade of the American Board.[28] Andover Theological Seminary retained considerable influence, so that over the next fifty years, 40 percent of the board's missionaries attended it. No other institution claimed anything close to that proportion.[29] Andover Theological Seminary became the premier missionary school, Glenn Miller states, "in part because its students desperately needed the inspiration of a new spiritual vision."[30]

THE ESTABLISHMENT OF THE ABCFM

In the midst of the Second Great Awakening, inspired by a student missionary movement, the American Board of Commissioners for Foreign Missions (ABCFM) was born.[31] With support from several Andover faculty members and other interested people, four students from Andover Theological Seminary—Adoniram Judson Jr., Samuel Nott Jr., Samuel J. Mills, and Samuel Newell,[32]—presented a petition of carefully formulated questions to the annual meeting of the General Association of Massachusetts Proper[33] on June 27, 1810, in Bradford, Massachusetts.[34] They stated that "their minds have been long impressed with the duty and importance of personally attempting a mission to the heathen" and asked for advice "whether they may expect patronage and support from a Missionary Society in this country, or must commit themselves to the direction of a European society."[35] The petition was turned over to a committee on the subject of foreign missions. The following day, the committee recommended the organization of a foreign missionary board and the recommendation was unanimously accepted by the association, which forthwith organized the American Board of Commissioners for Foreign Missions "for the purpose of devising ways and means, and adopting and prosecuting measures, for promoting the spread of the gospel in heathen lands."[36]

The ABCFM was the first foreign mission board founded in the United States, as well as being the largest in the nineteenth century. It served as an interdenominational foreign mission society for Congregationalists, Presbyterians, and for some Reformed churches. Initially an organization of Massachusetts and Connecticut Congregationalists, the ABCFM shunned the term *Congregationalist* in its title and recruited Presbyterian and Dutch Reformed members until they established their own foreign mission boards.[37]

The ABCFM held its first meeting in Farmington, Connecticut, in September 1810 and elected Samuel Worcester, pastor of the Tabernacle Congregational Church in Salem, Massachusetts, corresponding secretary. The Prudential Committee, a smaller executive committee under the direction of the board, was appointed. In January 1811, in search of financial support, the ABCFM sent Adoniram Judson to Britain in order to seek the possibilities of cooperation with the London Missionary Society (LMS)[38] in the foreign missions.[39] The LMS found the offer impracticable mainly because of administrative difficulties.[40]

Soon after Judson's return from Britain, the Prudential Committee announced to the Christian public in the Second Annual Meeting in Worcester, Massachusetts, that "prophecy, history, and the present state of the world, seem to unite in declaring, that the great pillars of the Papal and Mahommedan impostures are now tottering to their fall." "Now is the time" the committee added, "for the followers of Christ to come forward, boldly, and engage earnestly in the great work of enlightening and reforming mankind." According to the board, people in New England were in a very important position in the missionary enterprise: "*a great and effectual door* for the promulgation of the Gospel among the heathen is now opened to all Christian nations; but to no nation is it more inviting, than to the people of New England" and "no nation ever experienced the blessings of the Christian religion more evidently, and uniformly, than the inhabitants of New England."[41]

While trying to raise the necessary funds, the Prudential Committee decided to send the first missionaries to the Indian subcontinent. At a widely publicized ordination ceremony, Leonard Woods, professor of theology at Andover Theological Seminary, encouraged the first group of ABCFM missionaries to adopt the following objectives: "I would excite you by motives which no follower of Christ can resist, to make the spread of the Gospel, and the conversion of the world, the object of your earnest and incessant pursuit."[42] Five young men commissioned by the American Board—Adoniram Judson, Samuel Newell, Samuel Nott, Gordon Hall, and Luther Rice (the first three with wives)—departed for India in two separate ships in February 1812.[43]

The First Missionaries

The target of the ABCFM's first foreign mission was Burma,[44] but it proved to be a complete disaster. By the time the first missionaries of the ABCFM arrived in Calcutta, the United States had declared war on Britain (the War of 1812) which isolated the board from its missionaries. The British East India Company, which controlled the region, was not friendly toward these new American missionaries. Samuel Newell and his wife went to Mauritius where Harriett Newell died during childbirth.[45] Adoniram Judson, his wife, and Luther Rice became Baptists. They resigned from the service of the American Board and connected themselves with the Baptist Church.[46] Rice returned to the United States and the Judson family obtained passage to Burma. Gordon Hall and Samuel Nott went to Bombay and tried to avoid deportation to Britain by petitioning the British governor for permission to stay in India.[47] Afterward, the Nott family left India because of Samuel Nott's health problems.[48] Charles Maxfield properly describes the situation: "Each pocket of letters received from the missionaries was a new chronicle of disaster."[49] According to the ABCFM, "disappointments in the great work of evangelizing the world are to be expected"[50] and "the immediate consequences may be such as to disappoint the hopes and try the faith of Christians. But that ultimate consequences of *all* attempts to diffuse the Gospel among mankind will be glorious."[51] The ABCFM also invited Americans to engage in a cause "which aims directly and supremely at the glory of God, and the salvation of the whole human race."[52] John Andrew III, however, appropriately states that "even the most passionate supporters of the enterprise clearly recognized that their dream of millions of new Christian converts was far from realization."[53]

At home, Mary Norris, widow of a wealthy Salem merchant, bequeathed thirty thousand dollars to the ABCFM.[54] The litigation over the bequest demonstrated the need for legal recognition and the ABCFM procured an act of incorporation for securing its funds in June 1812.[55] Therefore, by acquiring legal existence, it obtained the right to receive bequests and estates, and the opportunity to arrange widespread fund-raising projects and develop its group of auxiliary societies. During its first years, the ABCFM employed agents whose main responsibility was to encourage the missionary spirit and raise funds from local congregations to support its missionaries. The ABCFM also received donations from several local benevolent and missionary societies although many of the donations were small sums. Although the ABCFM received no more than one thousand dollars during its first year, in 1816, for example, the donations to the ABCFM exceeded twenty-seven thousand dollars.[56]

"The object of the Board," the ABCFM announced, "is *one*—the promulgation of Christianity among the heathen. The means, by which this object is designed to be effected, are two kinds;—the publication and distribution of the Scriptures in the different languages of the nations; and the support of faithful missionaries to explain, exemplify, and impress on the mind, the great truths which the Scriptures contain."[57] Trying to increase the support for foreign missions, the American Board claimed that, "*the readiest and most efficacious method of promoting religion at home, is for Christians to exert themselves to send it abroad.*"[58] It was the same argument that the ABCFM had used during the debates on the act of incorporation in the Massachusetts legislature.

The expenses of the board were increasing as well. Immediately after the War of 1812 ended, the ABCFM decided to send reinforcements to India. Five more missionaries arrived in Ceylon in March 1816.[59] In the same year at home, the Prudential Committee declared its intention to send missionaries to the Indian tribes and to establish schools among them "under the missionary direction and superintendence" in order to "make the whole tribe English in their language, civilized in their habits, and Christian in their religion."[60] By 1819, the ABCFM had twenty-three missionaries and many assistants under its direction in Bombay, Ceylon, the Sandwich Islands (Hawaii), and among American Indian tribes (Cherokees and Choctaws).[61]

To the Holy Land: From New England to Jerusalem

In the autumn of 1818, the Prudential Committee of the ABCFM determined to send missionaries to "Western Asia" in order to establish a mission ultimately in Jerusalem and assigned two missionaries, Levi Parsons and Pliny Fisk, to that service.[62] When the decision was announced by the AB-CFM, the idea of initiating the first American mission to Jerusalem and conveying the Gospel to the Jews and Muslims excited the religious public in the United States.[63] "After ages of darkness, the light of the gospel is soon to re-illumine the shores of Palestine," a Boston newspaper wrote.[64] In a letter received by a newspaper in Ohio, a missionary said: "The glory of the Lord will return. The Jews are to be gathered in from their dispersions, and acknowledge that Jesus, whom their fathers crucified, to be their Saviour and their God. I consider this mission a grand link in the chain of events, which are preparatory to the second coming of our blessed Lord."[65]

Indeed, it was widely believed that the missionaries must prepare the world for the approaching millennium by the restoration of the Jews which was "endemic to American culture."[66] Millennialist anticipation was very popular among American Christians, and religious societies used millennial motifs extensively in their activities.[67] Many sermons called people to take action in order to hasten the advent of Christ's millennial reign. "The world is forming anew," the *Panoplist and Missionary Herald* claimed; "the men of this generation will be the patriarchs of the millennial age."[68] Moreover, Jerusalem was an exceptionally attractive city for missionary activities. New Englanders in general considered New England as a "New Jerusalem." Indeed, in order to benefit from such interest for Jerusalem and raise funds for missionary enterprise, the American Board was very quick to take action and launch a Palestine mission.[69]

American missionaries' interest in the Ottoman Empire was not new. Even one of the first missionaries to India had tried to encourage the Prudential Committee to open a mission in western Asia when the first American missionaries had troubles with the local authorities in British India. "A mission to western Asia would be our own," Samuel Newell wrote from Ceylon to the Corresponding Secretary of the Prudential Committee, "and it would be free from the objections which I stated to establishing our mission in British India. We should be in the neighborhood of Mesopotamia, Syria, Palestine, and Egypt, those interesting theatres, on which the most wonderful and important events, recorded in sacred history, took place." After mentioning his desire of bringing *"a great light"* to "the regions of thick darkness," he added that "when I think of these things, I long to be on my way towards Jerusalem."[70]

In their book entitled *The Conversion of the World*, which was published in Andover in 1818, Gordon Hall and Samuel Newell pointed to the imminence of the millennium and mentioned the western part of Asia as an interesting and worthy field for "missionary exertions." According to them, the people in the region were "destitute of the gospel, immersed in gross ignorance, and led away by the delusions of Mahomet."[71] Besides the encouragement of American missionaries in India, Samir Khalaf argues, "the early volumes of the *Missionary Herald* were replete with appeals from travelers and merchants returning from exploratory visits to the region."[72]

In 1819, the report of the Prudential Committee wrote the following:

> In Palestine, Syria, the Provinces of Asia Minor, Armenia, Georgia and Persia, though Mohammedan countries, there are many thousands of Jews, and many thousands of Christians, at least in name. But the whole mingled population is in a state of deplorable ignorance and degradation,—destitute of the means of divine knowledge, and bewildered with vain imaginations and strong delusions.[73]

The missionaries of the ABCFM regarded the Christians of the Ottoman Empire as "nominal" Christians. They believed that Ottoman Christianity lacked Christian virtue and represented a deteriorated form of the religion. Thus, they reasoned, Ottoman Christians were Christians in name only and needed guidance toward a better form of Christianity. This denigration of Ottoman Christianity was typical of all foreign missionaries in this period—American as well as European, Protestant and Catholic.

MISSIONARY PIONEERS: LEVI PARSONS AND PLINY FISK

Levi Parsons and Pliny Fisk, the missionary pioneers to the Holy Land, were both graduates of Andover Theological Seminary. After having been appointed by the ABCFM, while preparing for their journey to Jerusalem, they were sent on preaching tours in the United States as agents for the board in order to enlist enthusiasm and raise funds to support the new mission. Before their departure, both of them preached in Boston and presented their hopes and dreams for the mission to Jerusalem. In his farewell sermon, Fisk presented a survey of Eastern lands and focused mainly on the Christians in the region. According to Fisk, "though they call themselves Christians, [they] are still destitute almost entirely of the Scriptures, and deplorably ignorant of real Christianity."[74] He anticipated spreading "true Christianity" among the Eastern Christians as well as making "spiritual conquests" among the Muslims.[75] Levi Parsons believed that "many of the Jews are willing to receive the New Testament." "The millions of Jews," Parsons noted in his sermon entitled *The Dereliction and Restoration of the Jews*, "must be furnished with the *word of God*, and with the instruction of *Missionaries*. But this cannot be done without *charity*; without the *liberal*, and *persevering* efforts of the Christian world."[76]

After the sermons, the instructions of the Prudential Committee were delivered in public by Samuel Worcester, the secretary of the Prudential Committee. "Your mission," he said, "is to be regarded as a part of an extended and continually extending system of benevolent action, for the recovery of the world to God, to virtue and to happiness."[77] The ABCFM wanted Parsons and Fisk to stop at Malta and Izmir (Smyrna), study the languages of the region (especially Arabic), visit the historic Seven Churches of Asia,[78] gather information about the region, not offend laws and customs, survey the new field in the Ottoman Empire, and keep communication with Boston. The main aim was to establish a mission in Jerusalem, if possible, or otherwise in Bethlehem, and investigate what could be done for the Jews, pagans, Muslims, and Christians. Worcester also added his millennialist view that "the Jews have been for ages an awful sign to the world. But the period of their tremendous dereliction, and of the severity of God, is drawing to a close. You are to lift up an ensign to them, that they may *return and seek the Lord their God and David their king*. They will return."[79] Since use of the printed word and distribution of Bibles were very important for the missionaries in order to reach potential converts in the region, Parsons and Fisk also received detailed instructions regarding the Bible and other publications:

> Whether copies of it exist and are read,—of what kind, and to what extent? Whether the circulation of it might be increased?—In what versions, by what means, and in what amplitude? It will be an object also to ascertain what other books are in use, or are held in esteem; and what useful books or tracts might be circulated, and in what languages."[80]

Motivated by the desire to spread Christianity in the Mediterranean region, Parsons and Fisk left Boston in November 1819 and entered the harbor of Malta the next month. After receiving hints and information for their prospective missionary activities in the region from William Jowett, missionary of the Church Missionary Society, and other westerners, they arrived at Izmir in January 1820.[81] They were welcomed by Charles Williamson, chaplain to the British consulate, and by an international trading community.[82] In a letter written to Boston in February 1820, they claimed that "in all the populous Catholic and Mahomedan countries on the north and south sides of the Mediterranean, there is not a single Protestant missionary." They mentioned three missionaries in the Aegean Islands: William Jowett in Malta, Isaac Lowndes from the London Missionary Society in Zante, and Samuel Sheridan Wilson in Malta. They added that "in all the Turkish empire, containing perhaps 20,000,000 of souls, not one missionary station permanently occupied, and but a single [Protestant] missionary besides ourselves [James Connor]."[83] Although Parsons and Fisk found the situation in the region more encouraging than expected, they reported that "the prevalence of the plague" and "the nature of the Turkish government" which might be considered unfavorable to Christian missions were the two main obstacles to their activities.[84]

As expected, in order to evangelize people, first they needed to learn the languages of the region. After spending the summer in Chios (Sakız), an island in the Aegean Sea, in order to study modern Greek, they visited the sites of the seven biblical churches of Asia in Western Anatolia. At the end of 1820, Parsons went to Jerusalem to look into the conditions in order to establish a mission station and Fisk remained in Izmir.[85] Parsons arrived at Jerusalem in February 1821 and it was regarded as a significant event by the ABCFM and the religious public in the USA. He became one of the first missionaries to enter the city, and, according to the ABCFM, he was the first Protestant missionary who "entered that field, with a view of making it the centre of his own evangelical exertions."[86] He distributed Bibles and tracts and continued the missionary explorations and excursions to the interesting localities in the vicinity.[87] His memoir contains the record of his thoughts with respect to a missionary station in Jerusalem:

The reading of the scriptures is perhaps the most effectual method of doing good at Jerusalem. In this respect, the time from Christmas to the Passover is invaluable. Multitudes, and among them men of influence and literature, from almost every part of the world, are literally assembled in one place; and the information they receive will be communicated to thousands of souls. This station I view as one of the most important that can be selected, and one which cannot be relinquished, without great criminality on the part of the Christian community.[88]

Parsons quickly realized it would be impossible to reside in Jerusalem. He came to the conclusion that it was best for him to return to Izmir in order to join Fisk in the preparation of tracts to be distributed in different languages among the pilgrims.[89] While returning to Izmir, Parsons became sick. Both Parsons and Fisk went from Izmir to Alexandria where Parsons's health continued to fail. Parsons died of dysentery in Alexandria in February 1822.[90] Three years later, in 1825, the pioneer Fisk died in Beirut while preparing an Arabic-English dictionary for use by missionaries.[91]

The Construction Years
of the American Missionary Establishment

After the Second Great Awakening, as Bruce Masters argues, the Protestant missionary enterprise "was marked by an almost innocent enthusiasm to bear witness for the 'light of Christ,' as well as a casual arrogance that Anglo-Saxon culture was indeed superior to any the missionaries would encounter in the 'field.'"[92] According to the American missionaries, there was misery and ignorance in the Mediterranean, and people were waiting to be given spiritual truth. "By enlightening and reforming nominal Christians in Turkey," Pliny Fisk and Jonas King wrote from Egypt, "we are preparing the way, and raising up agents to bear a part when they shall be prepared, in convincing the followers of the false prophet of their errors, and teaching them the truth."[93]

Many others followed the two American missionary pioneers. Jonas King replaced Levi Parsons. Since Parsons and Fisk had tried to convince Boston of the need for printed materials, the ABCFM sent Daniel Temple with a printing press to Malta in 1822 and a mission press was established.[94] More-over, the next year, the ABCFM reinforced its mission field by sending two other missionaries to Malta: William Goodell and Isaac Bird, as well as their wives (who in this period the ABCFM did not officially count as missiona-ries). All three, Temple, Goodell, and Bird, were graduates of Andover Theo-logical Seminary.[95]

AMERICAN MISSION PRESS IN MALTA

Malta, under British rule, was an ideal location for a mission station and a fa-vorable place for the American missionaries to print their materials. How-ever, even in Malta, there were constraints. So as not to alarm the Catholics of the island, British authorities allowed the ABCFM missionaries to print only for export.[96] While in Malta, they were mostly occupied with the prepa-ration, publication, and distribution of books and tracts in the region in addi-tion to making exploratory journeys and corresponding with other Western missionaries. The mission press was printing copies of the Bible, other religi-ous tracts, and, later, school books in the vernacular in order to reach those whom they referred to as the "nominal Christians" of the Eastern churches. As it was said during the arguments related to a printing establishment in the Mediterranean in early 1821, "a missionary, by means of the press, increases his power to do good, in an incalculable ratio. They, who can hear his voice, may be, comparatively, few. But tracts and books reach thousands."[97]

The American missionaries regarded the island "only as the fulcrum for the lever, which is to move all the Levant at a future day."[98] By 1832, the printing presses of the ABCFM in the world had produced sixty-one million pages in eleven different languages from their inception.[99] The next year, the ABCFM decided to transfer the mission press from Malta to Beirut and Izmir as two separate presses. According to the ABCFM reports, the mission press in Malta printed some 350,000 copies of books and tracts in total.[100]

THE ABCFM'S FIRST SCHOOL IN BEIRUT

After establishing a mission press in Malta, the missionaries of the ABCFM, Jonas King, Pliny Fisk, Isaac Bird, and William Goodell, the last two with their wives, came to the eastern Mediterranean and established a mission station in Beirut. In 1824, the ABCFM founded its first school in the city. By the middle of 1825, the school had between eighty and ninety students, all of whom were Arabs.[101] Although the schools were suspended by the Greek attacks on Beirut and subsequent incidents in 1826, the American missionaries had thirteen schools with about six hundred students by the next year.

According to the missionaries, the spread of the Bible required the establishment of "civilized Christian institutions" and literacy was a paramount requirement in order to gain personal knowledge of the Bible and its teachings. They considered schools as an important means of multiplying their opportunities to make contact with the children and their friends and families. However, in 1828, since their safety was under threat because of the conditions in the eastern Mediterranean caused by the Greek revolt and Ottoman-Russian war, the missionaries in Beirut together with a few Armenian converts moved to Malta.[102] After two years, they returned and reopened the station.

The American missionaries in Beirut repeatedly requested that Boston send a physician to their mission station in order to help the missionary labor in the region and preserve the health of the missionaries and their families. They claimed that a well-educated physician could reach people very easily, acquire information about the customs and opinions of the people, and gain access to many individuals and families in ways which others could not. In addition, the influence of a physician over local governors and officials might be the most effective protection for the missionaries.[103] In another letter, Goodell claimed that a physician could reside wherever he pleased without a *ferman* and could "go into any town or city, and Turks, Jews, and Christians would all beseech him to take up his residence among them." The ABCFM eventually sent a medical missionary, Asa Dodge, and regarded his medical skill and all his future practice "only as a means of furthering the spiritual objects of the mission."[104]

Obstacles to the American Missionaries

In the early nineteenth century, the ABCFM missionaries failed to convert Muslims. In addition, they found little interest among Ottoman Jews, particularly in Jerusalem, toward the American missionary activities. Christian communities in the Ottoman Empire were very conservative and the ecclesiastical

authorities of both the Maronite and Greek Orthodox churches strongly opposed the American missionaries during the 1820s when they tried to distribute Bibles and tracts among their followers. According to the board, however,
"difficulties great and many do, indeed, lie in the way. The errors of a thousand
years are not to be easily and at once eradicated.... Opposition, however, will
be the signal and the proof of success."[105]

At the urging of the Maronite and Greek Orthodox leaders, the Sublime
Porte issued a decree in 1824 forbidding the distribution of tracts and Bibles
printed in Europe. According to the Ottoman authorities, their circulation
agitated relations between the various religious communities in the empire.
Abu-Ghazaleh appropriately argues that "although Protestant missionaries
ascribed the decree to Catholic pressure, the Ottoman decision was primarily administrative, designed to protect the operation of the millet system in
the empire and in this way it was similar to the decree of 1723 which tried to
check the activity of the Catholic missions among Orthodox Christians."[106]
At first, the decree vastly panicked the American missionaries. However, in
the long run, it did not have an effect on the missionaries of the ABCFM and
they continued selling and distributing their printed materials.[107]

As expected, the relations between American and Catholic missionaries
were not very cordial. According to the missionaries of the ABCFM, the
Jesuits were giving a false impression to the people of Lebanon that the Protestants "have no religion, no priesthood, no churches, and so on." After ten
years the ABCFM opened their first school in Beirut, the American missionaries claimed that "the bigotry, intolerance, unreasonableness, and worldly-
mindedness of the priests have been brought to light by their opposition to
the Scriptures and the schools" and according to them the wrong impression
seemed to be widely removed.[108]

As far as controversy with the local churches was concerned, William
Goodell thought that the American missionaries must avoid agitation. In
1829 he wrote:

> I do not think that this is the time for controversy in these countries.
> There is, so to speak, no foundation. There is not knowledge enough.
> There is not conscience enough. There is not religion enough. We
> must labor to give the people knowledge, an enlightened conscience,
> and pure and undefiled religion, and controversy will then commence

among themselves, and be carried on between themselves, and not between them and us who are strangers and foreigners, and of course regarded with more or less jealousy, and who, from the strength of our
convictions respecting the whole system of truth, would be in danger
of attempting too much at once.

After mentioning a quotation from Jesus, "I have yet many things to say
unto you, but ye cannot bear them now," he put his position in plain words:
"Missionaries in this part of the world must, I think, often remember this
text, and act in some measure accordingly."[109] The American missionaries believed, moreover, that their object was "not to pull down or build up a sect, but
to make known and inculcate the great fundamental truths of the Gospel."[110]
By the beginning of the 1830s, the ABCFM was trying to redefine its objectives and shift its focus to different sects in the region, including Greeks in
Izmir and Greece, as well as Armenians in Istanbul and Anatolia.

This redefinition of the objectives had its roots in the previous decade, of
course. In the early years of mission, the American missionaries in the region
informed headquarters in Boston about the necessity of activities among the
Armenians. In a joint letter written from Beirut in May 1824, Fisk, King,
Bird, and Goodell recommended the extension of the printing activities particularly for the Armenians and added: "We are anxious to see something
done, as soon as possible, for the Armenians. The readiness with which they
purchase the Scriptures, encourages us."[111] By the end of 1826, two Armenians, Dionysius Carabet and Gregory Wortabet, were admitted to the mission church in Beirut.

After Greece asserted its independence from the Ottoman Empire, the
ABCFM attention was also drawn to that country.[112] Pliny Fisk, however,
had already come to regard Greece and the Greek population of the Mediterranean region as a great field of opportunity for American missionary
activities:

The Greeks need missionaries; for though nominal Christians, they
pay an idolatrous regard to pictures, holy places and saints. Their clergy
are ignorant in the extreme. Out of hundreds, you will scarcely find
one who is capable of preaching a sermon. Of course, there is little
preaching; and that little is oftener an eulogium on some saint, than

an exhibition of Christ's Gospel. The people are consequently ignorant and vicious. Before the Bible society began its work, the Scriptures
were rare, and in most of the schools that exist, the children merely
learn to read ancient Greek, without understanding it. Greece offers to
view an extensive missionary field.[113]

Moreover, twelve Greek youth were sent to be educated in the United States at the expense of the ABCFM between 1823 and 1831.[114] In 1828, Rufus
Anderson, the assistant secretary of the ABCFM, was appointed by the Prudential Committee to visit the eastern Mediterranean mainly to confer with
the missionaries there and to investigate the situation for future missionary
operations particularly in Greece.[115] The ABCFM was very cautious about
missionary work in Greece: "[T]he first evangelical operations in Greece
should be conducted with judgment and caution. The people are ignorant
and superstitious, and their prejudices are easily excited. Books and schools
seem likely to exert more beneficial influence, with less liability to opposition
or suspicion, than any other means that can be freely used at present."[116] Boston appointed Jonas King to work in Greece in 1830.[117]

Conclusion

It was apparent that the early years of ABCFM activities in the Ottoman
Empire were of an experimental nature. It was obviously necessary for the
incoming American missionaries to learn the languages of the people in the
region before trying to evangelize them. Several exploratory journeys were
undertaken during the 1820s mainly to investigate conditions in the region,
and to find suitable locations for mission stations and congregations to be
evangelized. In addition to compiling reports on the conditions of the mission, the ABCFM missionaries recorded their observations about things that
they saw in the region, including the political dynamics of religious "denominations"[118] and their arguments with the local churches.[119] They did so in
letters, detailed journals, memoirs, and more.[120] They used every opportunity
to make contact with the local people, for example Bird's Italian class[121] and
Goodell's religious instruction to the beggars in Beirut.[122]

From the beginning, the missionaries in the field demanded that the Prudential Committee should send more missionaries to the region. "It is our

united opinion," the missionaries in Malta wrote to Boston, "that an addition of laborers is extremely desirable in the extensive regions that border on the Mediterranean; and the unsettled state of affairs here should not be taken into account in deciding on the practicability of such a measure."[123] The Prudential Committee of the ABCFM was aware of the opportunities that the Mediterranean region presented: "It must be obvious to every intelligent and reflecting man, that the countries around the Mediterranean furnish one of the largest, most interesting, and most inviting fields of missionary labor, which the world now presents."[124] Apparently, preparations were being made for more extensive activities in this new missionary field over the following decades.

There were forty-seven missionary stations under the direction of the ABCFM in the world by 1830, thirty-three of them among the Indians in North America.[125] In the Mediterranean field, the ABCFM was active in Malta, Beirut, Jerusalem, and Izmir in the 1820s. For the American missionaries at that time the main obstacles were political turmoil, wars, clerical opposition, local disturbances, epidemics, plagues, and so on. With the help of the American missionaries' exploratory journeys in the 1820s, the Prudential Committee in Boston was reasonably well informed about the religious, moral, intellectual, and social situation in the region. "We know what needs to be done; what are the best methods of operating; what are the hindrances and delays to be expected; and what effects may reasonably be anticipated,"[126] said the committee while instructing the missionaries who were on the way to the Middle East in the 1830s. Obenzinger correctly states that Parsons and Fisk "approached their expedition with a deep sense that they were charting a newly-acquired territory for many others soon to follow."[127] Indeed, many others followed them and the American missionaries established an extensive network of mission stations in the Middle East throughout the nineteenth and early twentieth centuries in order to reach mainly those to whom they referred as the "nominal Christians" of the Eastern churches.

NOTES

1. Timothy Dwight, *A Sermon Preached at the Opening of the Theological Institu-
    tion in Andover, and at the Ordination of Rev. Eliphalet Pearson, LL.D. Septem-
    ber 28th, 1808* (Boston: Farrand, Mallory, 1808), 26.

2. "An Address of the Managers of the Philadelphia Missionary Society," *Religious
    Remembrancer* (September 11, 1813): 7.

3. See Barry Hankins, *The Second Great Awakening and the Transcendental-
    ists* (Westport: Greenwood Press, 2004); Frank Lambert, *Inventing the
    "Great Awakening"* (Princeton: Princeton University Press, 1999); Donald G.
    Mathews, "The Second Great Awakening as an Organizing Process, 1780–1830:
    An Hypothesis," *American Quarterly* 21:1 (Spring 1969): 23–43; William G.
    McLoughlin, *Revivals, Awakenings, and Reform: An Essay on Religion and So-
    cial Change in America, 1607–1977* (Chicago: The University of Chicago Press,
    1978); Nancy F. Cott, "Young Women in the Second Great Awakening in New
    England," *Feminist Studies* 3:1/2 (Autumn 1975): 15–29; Richard Carwardine,
    "The Second Great Awakening in Comparative Perspective: Revivals and Cul-
    ture in the United States and Britain," in *Modern Christian Revivals*, ed. Edith
    L. Blumhofer and Randall Balmer (Urbana: University of Illinois Press, 1993),
    84–100; Mark A. Noll, *A History of Christianity in the United States and Can-
    ada* (Grand Rapids, MI: William B. Eerdmans, 2003); and Sydney E. Ahl-
    strom, *A Religious History of the American People* (New Haven: Yale University
    Press, 2004).

4. Alexis de Tocqueville, *Democracy in America* (Washington, DC: Regnery,
    2002), 241.

5. J. R. Fitzmier, "Second Great Awakening," in *Dictionary of Christianity in
    America*, ed. Daniel G. Reid (Downers Grove: InterVarsity Press, 1990), 1067.

6. See Matt McCook, "Aliens in the World: Sectarians, Secularism and the Sec-
    ond Great Awakening" (PhD diss., Florida State University, 2005).

7. Wilbert R. Shenk, ed., *North American Foreign Missions, 1810–1914: Theology,
    Theory, and Policy* (Grand Rapids, MI: William B. Eerdmans Publishing Com-
    pany, 2004), 4; Mark A. Noll, *The Old Religion in a New World: The History of
    North American Christianity* (Grand Rapids, MI: William B. Eerdmans Pub-
    lishing, 2002), 68; McLoughlin, 112; and Hankins, 16. The reader can also find
    a list of American societies which were established during the first half of the
    nineteenth century, with their date of founding in Charles I. Foster, *An Errand
    of Mercy: The Evangelical United Front 1790–1837* (Chapel Hill: The University
    of North Carolina Press, 1960), 275–279. Foster admits that his list is not ex-
    haustive and the dates are not definite.

8. William R. Hutchison, *Errand to the World: American Protestant Thought and
    Foreign Missions* (Chicago: The University of Chicago Press, 1993), 45.

9. Robert D. Linder, "Division and Unity: The Paradox of Christianity in America," in *Dictionary of Christianity in America*, ed. Daniel G. Reid (Downers Grove: InterVarsity Press, 1990), 9.

10. Donald G. Mathews, "The Second Great Awakening," 27.

11. Keith J. Hardman, *Issues in American Christianity: Primary Sources with Introductions* (Grand Rapids, MI: Bakery Books, 1993), 111.

12. Mark A. Noll, *The Old Religion in a New World*, 68.

13. Edwin Scott Gaustad, *A Religious History of America* (New York: Harper & Row, 1990), 129.

14. Randall B. Woods and Willard B. Gatewood, *The American Experience: A Concise History* (Forth Worth: Harcourt College, 2000), 199.

15. Mark A. Noll, *The Old Religion in a New World*, 68.

16. Richard D. Birdsall, "The Second Great Awakening and the New England Social Order," *Church History* 39:3 (September 1970): 345.

17. "Missionary Society of Connecticut," *Connecticut Evangelical Magazine* 1:1 (July 1800): 13–14; James R. Rohrer, "The Connecticut Missionary Society and Book Distribution in the Early Republic," *Libraries and Culture* 34:1 (Winter 1999): 18.

18. *The Constitution of the Missionary Society of Connecticut: with an address from the Board of Trustees to the people of the state, and a narrative on the subject of missions: to which is subjoined, a statement of the funds of the Society* (Hartford: Hudson and Goodwin, 1800), 8.

19. "A Brief Abstract of the Proceedings and Fund of the Massachusetts Missionary Society," *The New-York Missionary Magazine, and Repository of Religious Intelligence* 1:6, 434–435; "An Address of the Massachusetts Missionary Society to the Public," *The New-York Missionary Magazine, and Repository of Religious Intelligence* 1:6, 436–440.

20. S. M. Worcester, "Origin of American Foreign Missions," in *American Missionary Memorial, Including Biographical and Historical Sketches*, ed. Hamilton W. Pierson (New York: Harper & Brothers, 1853), 10.

21. The *Panoplist* started in 1805 and became *Panoplist and Missionary Magazine United* after the absorption of the *Massachusetts Missionary Magazine* in 1808. It was published as *Panoplist and Missionary Magazine* (1812–1817) and *Panoplist and Missionary Herald* (1818–1820). In January 1821, it simply became *Missionary Herald* which was the official monthly publication of the ABCFM for more than a century. See Gaylord P. Albaugh, *History and Annotated Bibliography of American Religious Periodicals and Newspapers Established from 1730 through 1830*, 2 vols. (Worcester: American Antiquarian Society, 1994), 1: 618–626 and 2: 721–723. For the early years of *Panoplist*, see Peter Kawerau, *Amerika und die Orientalischen Kirchen: Ursprung und Anfang Der Amerikanischen Mission unter den Nationalkirchen Westasiens* (Berlin: Walter De Gruyter, 1958), 128–139.

22. For example, "London Missionary Society," *Connecticut Evangelical Magazine* 1:1 (July 1800); "A Dialogue between Africanus, Americanus, and Benevolus, on Sending Missionaries to Carry the Gospel to the Heathen in Africa. Dedicated to the Missionary Societies in the states of New-York, Connecticut, and Massachusetts," *The New-York Missionary Magazine, and Repository of Religious Intelligence* 2:1 (1801): 25–34; "Religious Intelligence: Abstract of the Account of the Protestant Missions in the East Indies for the Year 1803," *Christian Observer* 3:12 (December 1804): 781–784; "Religious Intelligence: Missions in India," *The Massachusetts Missionary Magazine* 4:5 (October 1806): 195–198; and "Religious Intelligence: Foreign. Missions in South Africa. East Indies. Otaheite. Great Britain. Methodist Conference," *Panoplist* 1:1 (June 1805): 29–33.

23. Sydney E. Ahlstrom, *A Religious History of the American People*, 416.

24. Henry K. Rowe, *History of Andover Theological Seminary* (Newton: Thomas Todd, 1933), 23; John A. Andrew III, *Rebuilding the Christian Commonwealth: New England Congregationalists & Foreign Missions, 1800–1830* (Lexington: University Press of Kentucky, 1976), 17 and 20; "Theological Institution," *The Panoplist and Missionary Magazine* 1:4 (September 1808): 191.

25. Timothy Dwight, *A Sermon Preached at the Opening of the Theological Institution in Andover*, 10.

26. *The Constitution and Associate Statutes of the Theological Seminary in Andover; with a Sketch of its Rise and Progress* (Boston: Farrand, Mallory, 1808), 13.

27. David W. Kling, "The New Divinity and the Origins of the American Board of Commissioners for Foreign Missions," in *North American Foreign Missions, 1810–1914*, ed. Wilbert R. Shenk, 30.

28. Leonard Woods, *History of the Andover Theological Seminary* (Boston: James R. Osgood, 1885), 200.

29. Glenn T. Miller, *Piety and Intellect: The Aims and Purposes of Ante-Bellum Theological Education* (Atlanta: Scholars Press, 1990), 78.

30. Ibid., 78.

31. For the general history of the ABCFM, see William E. Strong, *The Story of the American Board: An Account of the First Hundred Years of the American Board of Commissioners for Foreign Missions* (Boston: Pilgrim Press, 1910); Clifton Jackson Phillips, *Protestant America and the Pagan World: The First Half Century of the American Board of Commissioners for Foreign Missions, 1810–1860* (Cambridge: Harvard University, 1969); Rufus Anderson, *History of the Missions of the American Board of Commissioners for Foreign Missions to the Oriental Churches*, 2 vols. (Boston: Congregational Publishing Society, 1872); Rufus Anderson, *Memorial Volume of the First Fifty Years of the American Board of Commissioners for Foreign Missions* (Boston: The Board, 1861); and Joseph Tracy, *History of the American Board of Commissioners for Foreign Missions* (New York: M. W. Dodd, 1842).

32. Although two other students were also involved, Luther Rice and James Richards, their names did not appear in the petition because of the fear that a larger number would alarm the association. See Rufus Anderson, *Memorial Volume*, 42–43.

33. It was the General Association of the Congregational Churches of Massachusetts and came into being in 1802 in order to assist the closer coordination of the several local organizations of Congregational clergymen. *Proper* was erased from its name in 1820. It had a lot of influence over the Congregational churches in Massachusetts and ultimately became the Massachusetts Congregational Conference.

34. "Minutes of the First Annual Meeting," in *First Ten Annual Reports of the American Board of Commissioners for Foreign Missions, with Other Documents of the Board* (Boston: Crocker and Brewster, 1834), 9–10; and Joseph Tracy, *History of the American Board*, 24–26; M. Cutler and S. Worcester, "Religious Intelligence: Minutes of the General Association of Massachusetts Proper," *The Panoplist and Missionary Magazine* 3:2 (July 1810): 86–90.

35. "Minutes of the First Annual Meeting," 9–10.

36. William E. Strong, *The Story of the American Board*, 6; "Minutes of the First Annual Meeting," 10.

37. Peter G. Gowing, "American Board of Commissioners for Foreign Missions," in *Concise Dictionary of the Christian Mission*, ed. Stephen Neill, Gerald H. Anderson, and John Goodwin (Nashville: Abingdon Press, 1971), 18.

38. London Missionary Society formally founded in 1795. For a detailed account of the society, see Susan Elizabeth Thorne, "Protestant Ethics and the Spirit of Imperialism: British Congregationalists and the London Missionary Society, 1795–1925" (PhD diss., University of Michigan, 1990); and Richard Lovett, *The History of the London Missionary Society, 1795–1895*, 2 vols. (London: H. Frowde, 1899).

39. "Missionary Exertions," *The Panoplist and Missionary Magazine* 4:3 (August 1811): 144; "Minutes of the Second Annual Meeting," in *First Ten Annual Reports of the American Board of Commissioners for Foreign Missions, with Other Documents of the Board* (Boston: Crocker and Brewster, 1834), 16–24; Rufus Anderson, *Memorial Volume*, 45; John O. Choules and Thomas Smith, *The Origin and History of Missions: A Record of the Voyages, Travels, Labors, and Successes of the Various Missionaries, who have been sent forth by Protestant Societies and Churches to Evangelize the Heathen*... (Boston: Gould, Kendall and Lincoln, 1837), 2: 238.

40. *The Panoplist and Missionary Magazine* 4:4 (September 1811): 183.

41. "Minutes of the Second Annual Meeting / Address to the Christian Public," in *First Ten Annual Reports of the American Board of Commissioners for Foreign Missions*, 28; "An Address to the Christian Public, Prepared and Published by

a Committee of the American Board of Commissioners for Foreign Missions," *The Panoplist and Missionary Magazine* 4:6 (November 1811): 244–245.

42. Leonard Woods, *A Sermon Delivered at the Tabernacle in Salem, Feb. 6, 1812 on Occasion of the Ordination of the Rev. Messrs. Samuel Newell, A.M., Adoniram Judson, A.M., Samuel Nott, A.M., Gordon Hall, A.M., and Luther Rice, A.B., Missionaries to the Heathen in Asia, under the Direction of the Board of Commissioners for Foreign Missions* (Boston: Samuel T. Armstrong, 1812), 11.

43. William E. Strong, *The Story of the American Board*, 7–16; "Ordination," *The Panoplist and Missionary Magazine* 4:9 (February 1812): 425–426.

44. "Instructions: Given by the Prudential Committee of the American Board of Commissioners for Foreign Missions, to the Missionaries to the East, February 7, 1812," in *First Ten Annual Reports of the American Board of Commissioners for Foreign Missions*, 40.

45. "Letter from Mr. Newell," *The Panoplist and Missionary Magazine* (August 1813): 131–135.

46. See "Religious Intelligence," *The Panoplist and Missionary Magazine* (January 1813): 372–377; "Religious Intelligence," *The Panoplist and Missionary Magazine* (March 1813): 467–474; *The Massachusetts Baptist Missionary Magazine* 3:10 (May 1813): 291–293; and Edward Judson, *Adoniram Judson: A Biography* (Philadelphia: American Baptist Publication Society, 1894).

47. See "Minutes of the Fifth Annual Meeting," in *First Ten Annual Reports of the American Board of Commissioners for Foreign Missions*, 81–114; "Religious Intelligence," *The Panoplist and Missionary Magazine* (May 1814): 232–233; "Report of the Prudential Committee," *The Panoplist and Missionary Magazine* (October 1814): 458–470 and 471–477.

48. "American Missionaries," *The Panoplist and Missionary Magazine* 12:5 (May 1816): 243.

49. Charles A. Maxfield III, "The 'Reflex Influence' of Missions: The Domestic Operations of the American Board of Commissioners for Foreign Missions, 1810–1850" (PhD diss., Union Theological Seminary, 1995), 77.

50. *First Ten Annual Reports of the American Board of Commissioners for Foreign Missions*, 70.

51. Ibid., 47.

52. Ibid., 52.

53. John A. Andrew III, *Rebuilding the Christian Commonwealth*, 97.

54. *The Panoplist and Missionary Magazine* (March 1811): 480.

55. Rufus Anderson, *Memorial Volume*, 77–78 and 405–407.

56. "Minutes of the Eighth Annual Meeting," in *First Ten Annual Reports of the American Board of Commissioners for Foreign Missions*, 161.

57. *First Ten Annual Reports of the American Board of Commissioners for Foreign Missions*, 67.

58. Ibid., 76.

59. James Richards, Edward Warren, Daniel Poor, Benjamin C. Meigs, and Hora-tio Bardwell were ordained at the Presbyterian church in Newburyport in June 1815 and sailed in October of that year. See John O. Choules and Thomas Smith, *The Origin and History of Missions*, 2: 258.

60. "Minutes of the Seventh Annual Meeting," in *First Ten Annual Reports of the American Board of Commissioners for Foreign Missions*, 135.

61. "Report of the Prudential Committee," *The Panoplist and Missionary Herald* 15:11 (November 1819): 505–518, and 15:12 (December 1819): 545–562.

62. "Mission to Jerusalem," *The Panoplist and Missionary Herald* 15:2 (February 1819): 92; and "Mission to Jerusalem," *Boston Recorder* 3:43 (October 17, 1818), 179.

63. Several publications informed their readers of the new mission and usually used the news from *The Panoplist and Missionary Herald* and *Boston Recorder*. For example, "Mission to Jerusalem," *The Christian Monitor* (Hallowell) 6:5 (September 1818): 80; "Mission to Jerusalem," *The Latter Day Luminary* (Phil-adelphia) 1:9 (August 1819): 431–432; "Mission to Jerusalem," *The Religious Inteligencer* (New Haven) 3:41 (March 13, 1819): 665–666; "Mission to Jerusa-lem," *Religious Remembrancer* (Philadelphia) 6:10 (October 31, 1818): 40; "Mis-sion to Jerusalem," *Christian Chronicle* (Bennington) 1:20 (November 7, 1818): 318–319; "Mission to Jerusalem," *Christian Herald* (New York) 5:15 (Novem-ber 7, 1818): 460; and "Mission to Jerusalem," *Virginia Evangelical and Literary Magazine* (Richmond) 2:11 (November 1819): 531–532.

64. "Poetry: Mission to Jerusalem," *The Boston Recorder* 3:46 (November 10, 1818): 192. For another exmple of poetry, see "Lines on the Recent Designation of Messrs. Parsons and Fisk, as Missionaries to Jerusalem," *Christian Herald* 5:17 (December 5, 1818): 543–544.

65. "Mission to Jerusalem," *The Weekly Recorder: A Newspaper Conveying Important Intelligence and Other Useful Matter Under the Three General Heads of Theology, Literature, and National Affairs* 5:47 (July 2, 1819): 371.

66. Carl F. Ehle, *Prolegomena to Christian Zionism in America* (New York: New York University, 1977), 331. For the attitudes of various types of American Prot-estants toward the Holy Land, see Robert T. Handy, ed., *The Holy Land in American Protestant Life 1800–1948* (New York: Arno Press, 1981).

67. See James A. De Jong, *As the Waters Cover the Sea: Millennial Expectations in the Rise of Anglo-American Missions 1640–1810* (Laurel, MS: Audubon Press, 2006).

68. "Motives for Christian Exertion," *The Panoplist and Missionary Herald* 14:4 (April 1818): 153.

69. Rao H. Lindsay, *Nineteenth Century American Schools in the Levant: a Study of Purposes* (Ann Arbor: University of Michigan, 1965), 65–67.

70. *The Panoplist and Missionary Magazine* (November 1814): 518–519.

71. Gordon Hall and Samuel Newell, *The Conversion of the World, or, the Claims of Six Hundred Millions and the Ability and Duty of the Churches Respecting Them* (Andover: Flagg & Gould, 1818), 33–34.

72. Samir Khalaf, *Cultural Resistance: Global and Local Encounters in the Middle East* (London: Saqi Books, 2001), 130. For the nineteenth-century Holy Land writing in the USA, see Brian Yothers, *The Romance of the Holy Land in American Travel Writing, 1790–1876* (Aldershot, UK: Ashgate, 2007).

73. "Minutes of the Tenth Annual Meeting," in *First Ten Annual Reports of the American Board of Commissioners for Foreign Missions, with Other Documents of the Board* (Boston: Crocker and Brewster, 1834), 230.

74. Pliny Fisk, "The Holy Land an Interesting Field of Missionary Enterprise: A Sermon, Preached in the Old South Church Boston, Sabbath Evening, Oct. 31, 1819," in *Sermons of Rev. Messrs. Fisk & Parsons, just before their Departure on the Palestine Mission* (Boston: Samuel T. Armstrong, 1819), 28.

75. A. L. Tibawi, *American Interests in Syria 1800–1901: A Study of Educational, Literary and Religious Work* (Oxford: Clarendon Press, 1966), 16.

76. Levi Parsons, "The Dereliction and Restoration of the Jews: A Sermon Preached in Park-Street Church Boston, Sabbath, Oct. 31, 1819," in *Sermons of Rev. Messrs. Fisk & Parsons*, 19.

77. Samuel Worcester, "Instructions from the Prudential Committee of the American Board of Commissioners for Foreign Missions to the Rev. Levi Parsons and the Rev. Pliny Fisk, Missionaries designated for Palestine. Delivered in the Old South Church Boston, Sabbath Evening, Oct. 31. 1819," in *Sermons of Rev. Messrs. Fisk & Parsons*, 44.

78. The seven churches of Asia are the seven major churches of early Christianity in the Western Anatolia: Ephesus, Pergamos, Sardis, Laodicea, Smyrna, Thyatira, and Philadelphia.

79. Samuel Worcester, "Instructions from the Prudential Committee," 51.

80. Ibid, 47.

81. *Eleventh Annual Report of the American Board of Commissioners for Foreign Missions* (Boston: Crocker & Brewster, 1820), 30–31.

82. James A. Field, *America and the Mediterranean World 1776–1882* (Princeton: Princeton University Press, 1969), 93.

83. "Palestine Mission: Extract of a letter of the Rev. Mess'rs Fisk and Parsons, to the Cor. Sec. of the A.B.C.F.M., Smyrna, Feb. 8, 1820," *Religious Remembrancer* (June 24, 1820): 174.

84. "Religious Intelligence: Palestine Mission: Letter of the Rev. Messrs. Fisk and Parsons to the Corresponding Secretary of the A.B.C.F.M., Smyrna, Feb. 8, 1820," *The Panoplist and Missionary Herald* 16:6 (June 1820): 265–267.

85. For more information about the socioeconomic context of Izmir, see Daniel Goffman, "Izmir: From Village to Colonial Port City," in *The Ottoman City*

between East and West: Aleppo, Izmir, and Istanbul, ed. Edhem Eldem, Daniel Goffman, and Bruce Masters (Cambridge: Cambridge University Press, 1999), 79–134; and Christine May Philliou, "The Community of Smyrna/Izmir in 1821: Social Reality and National Ideologies" (master's thesis, Princeton University, 1998).

86. *Twelfth Annual Report of the American Board of Commissioners for Foreign Missions* (Boston: Crocker & Brewster, 1821), 93. The ABCFM also described Parsons as "the first Protestant missionary to Jerusalem went from a land of which the Apostles had no knowledge." See *The Missionary Herald* (January 1824): 4. Tibawi stated that at least three Protestant contemporaries visited Jerusalem before Parsons: Christian [Christoph] Burckhardt (1818), an agent of the British and Foreign Bible Society; James Connor (1820) on behalf of the Church Missionary Society; and Melchior Tschoudy (1820), a Swiss pastor and an agent of the London Society for Promoting Christianity amongst the Jews. See A. L. Tibawi, *American Interests in Syria,* 20.

87. Miles P. Squier, "Rev. Levi Parsons," in *American Missionary Memorial, Including Biographical and Historical Sketches,* ed. Hamilton W. Pierson (New York: Harper & Brothers, 1853), 270.

88. Daniel Oliver Morton, *Memoir of Rev. Levi Parsons, First Missionary to Palestine from the United States* (Burlington: Chauncey Goodrich, 1830), 389.

89. Ibid., 385.

90. *Thirteenth Annual Report of the American Board of Commissioners for Foreign Missions* (Boston: Crocker & Brewster, 1822), 72–76.

91. See "Death of Mr. Fisk," *The Missionary Herald* 22:4 (April 1826): 128–133. For a detailed account of their missionary activities, see Alvan Bond, *Memoir of the Rev. Pliny Fisk, A.M., Late Missionary to Palestine* (Boston: Crocker and Brewster, 1828); Morton, *Memoir of Rev. Levi Parsons*; and Richard Clogg, "Ὁ Parsons καὶ ὁ Fisk στὸ Γυμνάσιο τῆς Χίου τὸ 1820," Ἐρανιστής *(Eranistes)* 5:30 (1967): 177–193.

92. Bruce Masters, *Christians and Jews in the Ottoman Arab World: The Roots of Sectarianism* (New York: Cambridge University Press, 2001), 147.

93. "American Board of Missions: Proceedings and Intelligence: Palestine Mission: Journal of Messrs. Fisk and King, in Upper Egypt" *The Missionary Herald* 19:12 (December 1823): 376.

94. Before Malta, the only mission press of the ABCFM was in Bombay. See "Seventy Years in the Maratha Mission," *The Missionary Herald* 80:8 (August 1884): 301–302.

95. *Fourteenth Annual Report of the American Board of Commissioners for Foreign Missions* (Boston: Crocker & Brewster, 1823), 117–129; and ABCFM Microfilm, Unit 5: Near East, *Papers of the American Board of Commissioners for Foreign Missions,*) Reel 502.

96. E. D. G. Prime, *Forty Years in the Turkish Empire; or, Memoirs of Rev. William Goodell* (New York: Robert Carter, 1876), 75.

97. *Twelfth Annual Report of the American Board of Commissioners for Foreign Missions*, 201.

98. "Importance of the Printing Establishment at Malta," *The Missionary Herald* 22:4 (April 1826): 133.

99. *Twenty-Third Annual Report of the American Board of Commissioners for Foreign Missions* (Boston: Crocker & Brewster, 1832), 125. The press printed 4.8 million pages in 1831 alone.

100. *Twenty-Fifth Annual Report of the American Board of Commissioners for Foreign Missions* (Boston: Crocker & Brewster, 1834), 52. For printing activities in Malta, see Evra Layton, "The Greek Press at Malta of the American Board of Commissioners for Foreign Missions (1822–1833)," Ἐρανιστής *(Eranistes)* No. 53 (1971): 169–193; Geoffrey Roper, "Arabic Printing in Malta 1825–1845: Its History and Its Place in the Development of Print Culture in the Arab Middle East" (PhD diss., University of Durham, 1988); Geoffrey Roper, "The Beginning of Arabic Printing by the ABCFM, 1822–1841," *Harvard Library Bulletin* 9:1 (Spring 1998): 50–68; Geoffrey Roper, "Turkish Printing and Publishing in Malta in the 1830s," *Turcica*, No. 29 (1997): 413–421; W. J. Burke, "The American Mission Press at Malta," *Bulletin of the New York Public Library* 41:7 (July 1937): 526–529; Uygur Kocabaşoğlu, "Osmanlı İmparatorluğunda 19. Yüzyılda Amerikan Matbaaları ve Yayımcılığı," in *Murat Sarıca Armağanı* (İstanbul, Aybay Yayınları, 1988), 267–285; and Dagmar Glass, *Malta, Beirut, Leipzig and Beirut Again: Eli Smith, the American Syria Mission and the Spread of Arabic Typography in 19th Century Lebanon* (Beirut: Orient-Institut der Deutschen Morgenländischen Gesellschaft, 1998). For printing activities of the ABCFM in the world, see J. F. Coakley, "Printing Offices of the American Board of Commissioners for Foreign Missions, 1817–1900: A Synopsis," *Harvard Library Bulletin* 9:1 (Spring 1998): 5–34.

101. All except two of the students were boys. See *Seventeenth Annual Report of the American Board of Commissioners for Foreign Missions* (Boston: Crocker & Brewster, 1826), 93.

102. "Departure of the Missionaries from Beyroot," *The Missionary Herald* 24:11 (November 1828): 348–352.

103. "Joint Letter of the Missionaries," *The Missionary Herald* 21:1 (January 1825): 13–15.

104. *Twenty-Third Annual Report of the American Board of Commissioners for Foreign Missions* (Boston: Crocker & Brewster, 1832), 156. See also *The Missionary Herald* 28:12 (December 1832): 411; and 31:7 (July 1835): 281. Asa Dodge was the second medical missionary sent by the ABCFM to a foreign mission. The first one was John Scudder who went to Ceylon in 1819. See "Medical

Missionary Work under the American Board," *The Missionary Herald* 93:7 (July 1897): 268–270.

105. *Fifteenth Annual Report of the American Board of Commissioners for Foreign Missions* (Boston: Crocker & Brewster, 1824), 126.

106. Adnan Abu-Ghazaleh, *American Missions in Syria: A Study of American Missionary Contribution to Arab Nationalism in 19th Century Syria* (Brattleboro, VT: Amana Books, 1990), 20.

107. See "Opposition of the Catholics," *The Missionary Herald* 21:4 (April 1825): 108–109; "American Board of Missions: Palestine Mission," *The Missionary Herald* 21:3 (March 1825): 92. For Jonas King's conversation with "an Arab of the Roman Church" and another conversation relating to the Maronite Patriarch's Order, see "Palestine Mission: Journal of Mr. King," *The Missionary Herald* 21:10 (October 1825): 313–318.

108. "Syria: Extracts from a Communication of Messrs. Bird, Smith, and Thomson," *The Missionary Herald* 30:11 (November 1834): 414. Several years earlier, after John Keeling, a Methodist minister in Malta, was attacked in consequence of remarks made by a priest, the ABCFM stated in its annual report that "[t]he Pope is making great exertions to prevent the admission of light into countries which have been under the control of the Romish church." See *Sixteenth Annual Report of the American Board of Commissioners for Foreign Missions* (Boston: Crocker & Brewster, 1825), 83; and "Malta: Excitement among the Catholics," *The Missionary Herald* 21:9 (September 1825): 273.

109. "Malta: Extracts from Letters of Mr. Goodell," *The Missionary Herald* 26:1 (January 1830): 17–18.

110. *The Missionary Herald* 26:6 (June 1830): 177.

111. "Joint Letter of the Missionaries," *The Missionary Herald* 21:1 (January 1825): 13–15.

112. See Marcellus Bowen, *Historical Sketch of Mission Work in the Smyrna Field, 1820–1884* (manuscript), ABCFM archives at the Houghton Library, ABC 88.

113. Alvan Bond, *Memoir of the Rev. Pliny Fisk*, 411.

114. *Twenty-Second Annual Report of the American Board of Commissioners for Foreign Missions* (Boston: Crocker & Brewster, 1831), 43.

115. "American Board of Missions: Special Agency to the Mediterranean," *The Missionary Herald* 24:12 (December 1828): 394–396; "American Board of Foreign Missions: Special Agency to the Mediterranean," *The Missionary Herald* 25:5 (May 1829): 166–167; and Rufus Anderson, *Observations upon the Peloponnesus and Greek Islands made in 1829 by Rufus Anderson one of the Secretaries of the American Board of Commissioners for Foreign Missions* (Boston: Crocker & Brewster, 1830).

116. *Twenty-first Annual Report of the American Board of Commissioners for Foreign Missions* (Boston: Crocker & Brewster, 1830), 51.

117. William E. Strong, *The Story of the American Board*, 87.

118. For example, "Religious Denominations in Syria and Holy Land," *The Missionary Herald* 22:3 (March 1826): 92–93; 22:4 (April 1826): 126; and 22:5 (May 1826): 164–165.

119. For example, "American Board of Foreign Missions: Palestine Mission: Controversy of the Missionaries with the Maronite Patriarch," *The Missionary Herald* 23:10 (October 1827): 297–302.

120. For example, Goodell kept a meteorological journal and wrote from Beirut to Boston about the climate mainly to help future missionaries. In addition to advising future missionaries about matters of dress, his letters included many details: thermometrical observations (both at 9 am and 3 pm), the general range of the temperature, the course of wind, and the general state of the weather throughout 1825. "Climate of Syria," *The Missionary Herald* 21:11 (November 1825): 345–348; "Syria: Mr. Goodell's Observations on the Climate of Syria," *The Missionary Herald* 22:6 (June 1826): 183–185; and "Mr. Goodell's Observations on the Climate of Syria," *The Missionary Herald* 23:4 (April 1827): 102–103.

121. About thirty students attended, aged between eight and twenty. The missionaries proclaimed, "This school has greatly the advantage of the other in producing a greater degree of intimacy and friendship between us and the scholars, and thus affording a more ready access to the bosom of families." See *Literary and Evangelical Magazine* 8:12 (December 1825): 679.

122. Goodell and Bird wrote from Beirut in July 1825: "Four times a week through a part of the winter, and twice a week through the whole, we addressed a congregation of beggars, consisting frequently of an hundred and fifty persons." See *Literary and Evangelical Magazine* 8:12 (December 1825): 680; and *Christian Spectator* 7:10 (October 1, 1825): 551.

123. *Fourteenth Annual Report of the American Board of Commissioners for Foreign Missions* (Boston: Crocker & Brewster, 1823), 125.

124. Ibid.

125. *Twenty-first Annual Report of the American Board of Commissioners for Foreign Missions* (Boston: Crocker & Brewster, 1830), 104.

126. *Twenty-Third Annual Report of the American Board of Commissioners for Foreign Missions* (Boston: Crocker & Brewster, 1832), 152–157.

127. Hilton Obenzinger, "Holy Land Narrative and American Covenant: Levi Parsons, Pliny Fisk and the Palestine Mission," *Religion & Literature* 35:2–3 (Summer-Autumn 2003): 242.

The Flexibility of Home

Exploring the Spaces and Definitions of the Home
and Family Employed by the ABCFM Missionaries
in Ottoman Syria from 1823 to 1860[1]

Christine Lindner

Shortly after arriving in Beirut, Henrietta (Hetty) Smith described her "new mode of life."[2] In a letter to her mother, Hetty wrote that she and her husband, Eli,

> are very pleasantly accommodated in Mr. Thomson's family until we can procure a home of our own which we have not yet been able to do.... [We are residents in the] mission house [which] is sort of a central point. The family consists of Mr. and Mrs. Thomson, Miss Eliza Abbot, daughter of Mrs. Thomson, and three little children, Mr. Van Lennep, Mr. Smith and myself as their guests.[3]

Hetty's letter hints at the importance of the home within the work of the missionaries from the American Board of Commissioners for Foreign Missions (ABCFM) in Ottoman Syria; for it was within the home that the Protestants negotiated and performed their new identity on a daily basis.[4] Although the Thomson home was similar to others occupied by the AB-CFM missionaries,[5] their definition of the "home" and "family" was neither singular nor stable. Rather, these were highly malleable concepts, which were influenced by the realities faced by the ABCFM missionaries during their new life in Ottoman Syria.[6]

The aim of this chapter is to identify and analyze the way that the home and family were defined within this specific missionary encounter. The first section of this chapter investigates the locations of the ABCFM missionaries' homes in Ottoman Syria during the period 1823 to 1860. I argue that the choice of Beirut for the ABCFM's central station, the selection of specific buildings within Beirut and at out-stations on Mount Lebanon, as well as the division of space within their homes, were shaped by both the missionaries' ideologies and the complexities they faced while living in Ottoman Syria. The second section explores the definition of family employed by the ABCFM missionaries. The missionary family within this encounter was a flexible concept, for it was constructed from the ever-changing arrangements of different groups or units, in a manner that resembles a mosaic. While these "mosaic families" brought together different individuals, they nevertheless affirmed a racialized hierarchy that permeated the new Protestant community.

The material presented within this chapter reflects the expanding field of research on American and European missionary encounters in the Middle East. The number of scholars exploring this relationship has increased significantly over the past twenty-five years. Much of this work retells the "lost" histories of missionaries,[7] with a particular focus on the development of institutions such as schools.[8] Other researchers examine the complexities surrounding missionary encounters through narrowed case studies that employ anthropological and social historical tools.[9] Through exploring the differences in missionary organizations,[10] the channels of encounter,[11] and the historical contexts for the exchange,[12] these scholars demonstrate the complexities of how a specific form of Christianity was presented, received, negotiated, and subverted through such interactions.[13] Some of the more recent publications focus on the daily and mundane sites of the encounter, including the emotional connections created between missionaries and converts.[14] Stemming from this work, this chapter can thus be considered as adding another element to this diverse mission history.[15]

The writings of Pierre Bourdieu and Michel de Certeau support the investigation of daily exchanges. Both these scholars highlight that ideologies, which are defined as the ways of seeing, interpreting, and engaging with the world, are enacted through everyday activities. Specific ideologies are determined by the person's position within his/her society.[16] According to this theoretical model, the space for the home and the terms for the family reflect both the historical contexts in which these terms emerged, as well as the struggles amongst individuals to control the normative definitions of these concepts.[17] Employing this theoretical lens allows one to recognize that the ABCFM missionaries' definitions of home and family emerged from their historical background within American society, but were modified by their encounters with Syrians, negotiated within the nascent Protestant community (which included Americans, Europeans, and Syrians), and located in the dynamic space of Beirut and Mount Lebanon during the early to mid-nineteenth century. In other words, the missionary home and family were performances of the ABCFM missionaries' ideologies, which reflected their hybrid position within these various, but linked, contexts.

The letters and publications of the ABCFM missionaries serve as the primary sources for this research. These works include the *Missionary Herald* and other ABCFM publications, as well as the books written by the missionaries of the Syrian Station.[18] Also reviewed were the private correspondences between missionaries and their friends and family members. As noted by various historians, the unfortunate dearth of available accounts written by Syrian Protestants during this period results in an overemphasis of the missionary narrative.[19] Although these gaps render it difficult to delineate how Syrian Protestants perceived the missionaries' definitions of home and family, the sources point to the Syrians' inherent involvement within this definition process. Jean Said Makdisi recognizes that "[indeed] it was often the 'natives' who suggested the next bend in the road, the next step to be taken. Without them, the missionaries could have accomplished nothing."[20] Thus, cautiously reading missionary sources allows one to perceive that "this was a *dialectic* encounter in that it altered everyone and everything involved."[21] Taking this into consideration, the goal of this chapter is to delineate the terms for the home and family employed by the ABCFM missionaries during their encounters in Ottoman Syria. This approach intends not to render the Syrian voice silent, but rather to illuminate how this encounter affected the ideologies and lives of the ABCFM missionaries, while producing complex relationships with those living in the region.[22]

Locating the Missionary Home

Although the ABCFM missionaries arrived in Ottoman Syria with pre-conceived notions of both the region and their mission, these were quickly modified by the realities that they faced. Reflecting an increased biblical imaginary within American Protestantism, the ABCFM's original intent was to form a station in Palestine and specifically Jerusalem.[23] Unlike other missionary groups to the region, however, the ABCFM missionaries did not promote a premillennial eschatology, which demanded the conversion of the Jews to bring forth the Second Coming of Christ.[24] Rather, their goal was to share the gospel with all living in the region, including Jews, Muslims, and "nominal" Christians.[25]

Various challenges prevented the ABCFM missionaries' long-term residency at Jerusalem, both during the pioneering missions and on subsequent trials. As a result, and upon the advice of British colleagues, Beirut replaced Jerusalem as the site for the ABCFM's central station in the region.[26] Beirut was regarded as favorably located within regional trade routes, it had a comfortable and healthy climate, and was the location of the British consulate general, who was the diplomatic representative of American residents at that time.[27] Thus, the selection of Beirut for the central station resulted from the malleability of the ABCFM missionaries' ideologies, for which certain criteria, like climate and safety, took precedence over other, eschatological criteria.[28]

Beirut in the 1820s was on the eve of its transformation into a prominent port city. Space within the city was distributed among the different religious and economic communities that composed its small population. Although these groups were not divided into distinct quarters, different religious and economic clusters developed at certain localities within the city walls.[29] It appears that there was no available space for the ABCFM missionaries and their new religious identity within this distribution. When compared to other "new communities," like the Greek Catholic Church which emerged from the Greek Orthodox Church during the previous century, two ABCFM missionaries, George Whiting and William Thomson, argued that their colleagues "came into the country as *strangers and foreigners*. They had *no friends* here. They had *no character*. They had *no influence*."[30] These "Bible-men"[31] were regarded as being "neither Mussulman [*sic*], Jewish nor Christian."[32] As a result, the missionaries were "scattered" around this port city, for it was only in the scarcely populated suburbs, outside of the city walls, that the ABCFM missionaries found residencies available to them.[33]

This suburban residency nevertheless affirmed aspects of the ABCFM's ideology. For example, the missionaries described Beirut's city center as "disagreeable as any thing can be. Streets narrow… [and after a rain] as dirty as it could be."[34] In contrast, the suburbs were full of green gardens and situated as to allow for fresh wind and sea breezes to flow through the missionary homes. Access to fresh and breezy air was deemed necessary for it counteracted the feared "Sirocco winds" that struck Beirut during the summer months.[35] Even if their suburban residences did not neutralize the hot winds, the ABCFM missionaries could easily "remove" to Mount Lebanon, which became an annual occurrence for many.[36]

Another unforeseen challenge demanded flexibility from the ABCFM missionaries in regard to residency. Due to Ottoman legal policies, land within the Empire could not be purchased by "Franks." Rather, both land and property for homes had to be rented through Ottoman agents.[37] Being a new group within the region, the ABCFM missionaries needed to forge alliances with persons who owned land and with those who could serve as brokers to acquire property. Although neither the original broker nor the background for this agreement are clear, land was "purchased" or rented for an extended period of time to the southwest of Beirut's city walls, outside Bab Ya'qoub.[38] This home was initially occupied by the Goodell missionary family, but was later associated with their ABCFM colleagues, Isaac and Martha Bird. As a result, it was called "Burj Bird" or "the tower of Bird."[39] Burj Bird evolved into the "Mission House" and was the central point for the ABCFM's Syrian Station.[40] In subsequent years, the lease for this property was renewed by Tannous el-Haddad and witnessed by Butrus al-Bustani and Elias el-Fuaz, three prominent members of the Protestant community in Syria.[41]

Another home rented by the ABCFM missionaries was a house owned by "Old Susa." Located between the city center and Ras Beirut, the "Old Susa house" was about a mile from the Mission House, but within walking distance of the American Consulate at "Feteipah's house."[42] This illuminates another, political facet of the ABCFM missionaries' alliances in Ottoman Syria.[43] Like the Mission House, the details surrounding the original rental agreement are unclear, but it appears to have lasted until the death of "Old Susa" in 1855, when the missionaries were asked to pay their debts.[44]

Nevertheless, the relationship between the ABCFM missionaries and the Susa family continued, for other properties owned by the Susa family were rented to ABCFM missionaries and the American consuls, particularly those located in the Zoqaq el-Blat area, throughout the nineteenth century.[45] The history of both the Mission House and the Old Susa House demonstrates that the ABCFM missionaries were inherently dependent upon Syrians to acquire dwellings for them, even if the original details of these alliances are lost.[46]

The ABCFM missionaries' descriptions of their homes suggest that these buildings were architecturally similar to the homes of their Syrian neighbors. Henry Harris Jessup recalled that "[the] houses occupied by the missionaries in those days were the old-fashioned native houses in the cities and mountain villages."[47] Sarah Smith described her home at the "Old Susa house" as

> situated in the midst of gardens of mulberry trees, retired from the road, yet very accessible. It is built of stone, with a flat roof; and beside the rooms of the press, has upon the lower floor, a kitchen, store-room, lumber-room, servants' room and bath; all of which surround a large covered court, opening upon a pretty little flower garden, between which the court is an awning of grape vines, whose luxuriant fruit is beginning to enrich our social board. Upon the second story, which we occupy, are a large dining-room, a bed-room, study, room for Raheel, my little girl, and two rooms beside are now being built. These occupy the sides of a beautiful open court, where we can sit and gaze upon the illimitable sea.[48]

Twelve years later, Hetty Smith affirmed this description of the "Old Susa House" in a house plan she drew and enclosed in a letter to her sister.[49]

The missionaries' descriptions resemble the architectural plans for the modified "liwan" design identified by May Davie as the common housing structure for the local population.[50] Modifications made by the ABCFM missionaries to their homes enlarged these houses, but in a manner that maintained the original liwan format.[51] While scholars have recognized that the open spaces of Beirut's suburbs fostered architectural experimentation, specifically the development of the Triple-Arched or Central Hall House during the mid- to late nineteenth century, the ABCFM missionaries did not instigate this innovation.[52] Rather, their homes during this earlier period upheld the liwan model, while later structures, such as the buildings of the Syrian Protestant College (later American University of Beirut), followed Syrian innovation and adapted features of emerging architectural designs.[53]

The missionaries' homes on Mount Lebanon affirm that the ABCFM missionaries resided in houses constructed according to conventional Syrian design.[54] In 1843, the missionaries commenced an out-station at Abeih for the Whiting, Thomson, and Van Dyck families. By June 1844, however, the *Missionary Herald* printed that only the Thomson family had procured a home at this location.[55] In a letter dated 20 August 1844, the missionaries explained to the Prudential Committee in Boston the embarrassing crisis regarding the construction of a home for the Whiting family. Although the miscalculations of expenditures are interesting, what is most relevant for this analysis is the style of the proposed home. A floor plan was drawn in the letter that depicted a liwan design, with an external kitchen. This demonstrates that when given the opportunity to construct an entirely new structure, the ABCFM missionaries chose an architectural pattern that resembled their non-Protestant, non-American neighbors' homes. They did not (or could not) import a completely new, American design to the Syrian landscape.[56]

The choice to reside in Syrian-designed homes is significant for three reasons. Firstly, the motivation of the ABCFM missionaries, particularly after 1830, was to promote a revival of the Christian faith, but in a manner that did not excite "jealousy" or elicit negative reactions against Protestant activities.[57] The missionaries' choice of homes externally similar to their neighbors affirmed their hope for discretion, which they contrasted to the (perceived) ostentatious activities of Roman Catholic missionaries, whose churches occasionally included bell towers.[58] Slightly problematic for this stance, however, was the fact that the ABCFM missionaries occupied larger residences owned by the wealthier members of Syrian society, thus enacting a different form of social distinction.[59]

Second, the ABCFM argued that their mission was to instigate a religious revival among the Syrian populace, not to promote cultural or technological "modernity."[60] Superfluous acts to modify existing practices that were unrelated to religious reform were deemed unnecessary and possibly counter to the ABCFM's goal.[61] For example, the hybrid "Levantine" culture, which emphasized economic wealth and the knowledge of different languages, was criticized as a negative example of cultural modernity, which lacked proper moral and religious grounding.[62] As a result, any act that distanced the AB-CFM missionaries from their Syrian neighbors that was not grounded on religious objectives ran counter to their missiology.[63]

Third, Syrian homes were regarded as acceptable spaces for missionary residences despite being visually different from contemporary American homes, especially when viewed from the outside.[64] This suggests that the ABCFM missionaries' perceptions of home were not strictly linked to a specific housing type, but to ideological stances that allowed for Syrian architecture to be regarded as acceptable spaces for missionary domesticity.

Nevertheless, the missionaries' acceptance of Syrian domestic architecture was contingent upon their ability to modify the internal spaces of these homes. Most of the missionary homes in the suburbs of Beirut had two floors. On the ground floor were located storerooms, servants' quarters, a kitchen, bathroom, and study or work room for the male missionary, all of which led onto or surrounded a courtyard. The male missionary's study was occasionally employed as a room for the Mission Press or for the distribution of magazines and books. On the second floor were found the parlor, study, bedrooms for the missionaries, rooms for boarding students, and a dining room.[65]

This division initially suggests a gendered binary of space, with the male/public space on the ground floor separated from the female/domestic space of the upper levels. However, the missionaries' use of these spaces reveals fluidity in how the home was divided.[66] For example, the ground floor courtyard was a communal space used for a variety of activities, including schools, marriage and funeral ceremonies, social gatherings, and school examinations. Although the gendering of missionary work resulted in male missionaries overseeing the majority of these activities, female missionaries also organized schools and engaged in social activities within this communal space.[67] These activities were conducted for the benefit of the entire Protestant community, regardless of the participants' gender.

In a similar manner, the "domestic space" on the upper floor was neither a segregated female space nor the isolated domain of the missionary family. Although "she devoted herself to missionary work,"[68] Sarah Smith lamented that she missed being able to lock her door and hide within the privacy of her own chamber, as to not be distracted by "business, and absorbing, distracting care."⁶⁹ These "distractions" included visits from fellow missionaries, Syrian Protestants, and various non-Protestant visitors, who were mostly female but occasionally included male guests. These visitations occurred primarily within the parlor, although Smith's comment suggests that they might have taken place within her private chamber.⁷⁰ The parlor also served as the communal space for "family worship," when all family members, visitors, and occasionally servants assembled for prayers, readings from the Bible, or to hear a sermon given by a male missionary.⁷¹ Rooms for female boarding students were also set aside on the upper floor, if such arrangements occurred within the family. These students were educated by both the male and female missionaries, although they were under the primary care of the female missionary, and were considered part of the missionary family.⁷²

It can be concluded that the use of space within the missionary home differed from the gendered divisions commonly attributed to American Victorian, "traditional" Arab and "modern" Lebanese homes.⁷³ The spaces for men and women within the ABCFM missionary homes often overlapped, and were determined by the needs of the nascent Protestant community. This blurring of gendered space reveals the complexities of the Protestant identity, while complicating previous analyses of nineteenth-century American and Syrian domestic architecture.⁷⁴

Space within the missionary home was divided, but in a manner that ensured the appropriate channel of social interaction, as judged by the ABCFM missionaries.⁷⁵ This resulted in the fluid and at times inconsistent separation of the "family" from "non-family" members. One division was the segregation of missionary children and boarding students from "Arab servants" and other non-family "Arabs." In 1834, the biologically childless Sarah Smith commenced the practice of "adopting" Syrian girls to be educated by the missionaries and form part of their new, fictive kin. The first boarding student-daughter was Rahil Ata, who was from a Greek Orthodox family, but eventually became a model Protestant and married Butrus al-Bustani in 1844.⁷⁶ Describing Sarah's education of Rahil, Eli Smith wrote:

> Yet with the servants, [Rahil] was never allowed to associate. Mrs. Smith's hope of special benefit to the child from residing in her family, was based very much upon the principle of segregation and she had the

opinion most firmly fixed, that unless every avenue by which contamination might be contracted were strictly guarded, all her labour would
probably be lost. She was watched, therefore, with a care that parental
anxiety rarely gives rise to; and had no access to the kitchen, except on
an errand for a moment; nor was she even left alone in the house, with
the servants.[77]

In the Smith's residency at the "Old Susa house," the servants' quarters
and kitchen were located on the ground floor, while Rahil's room was on the
upper floor, alongside Eli and Sarah's room and the parlor. Some years later,
Hetty Smith complained how this arrangement affected her ankles, for she
constantly ran up and down the stairs, from the family space to the servants'
space, in order to monitor the practices of a new cook.[78]

This segregation gave way once servants demonstrated suitable, "non-
contaminating" behaviour and became part of the missionary family. Mary,
the daughter of Eli and Hetty Smith, was particularly fond of their cook and
"man of all works," Ichoeel. Other servants who were "accepted" into missionary families included Mennie and Khosma, two of the "Arab girls" who
served as nurses for various missionary families.[79] It appears that very few
servants were regarded as part of the missionary family and allowed into family spaces. This may have created a hierarchy among those employed by the
ABCFM missionaries.[80] Despite their elevated status, however, the above-
mentioned individuals continued to be regarded as servants, which emphasized a race- (and class-) based hierarchy within the Protestant community.

The perceived need for privacy also affected the ABCFM missionaries'
use of space within their homes. Missionary households in Ottoman Syria
were what I have called "mosaic" families. Like a piece of mosaic artwork,
these were combinations of different identifiable units, such as married couples, couples with children, adopted boarding students, and single persons.
Within two-story houses, each unit was given a separate bedroom on the upper floor.

The need for privacy was most clearly displayed with the ABCFM mission-
aries' modifications of the one or two-roomed houses on Mount Lebanon.
Within such homes, communal space was divided by curtains (sometimes
American flags) from the areas for sleeping, which were then subdivided to

maintain each unit's privacy. In 1856, Henry Harris Jessup described his home in Duma. He wrote:

> Mr. and Mrs. Lyon curtained off half of their large room with an American flag for a bedroom. The other half served as parlour, dining room and servant girl's room. My big room with a window was divided into my bedroom and the storeroom and cook's room.[81]

The privacy of the married couple was given the highest priority within this shared household. This stance was not concretely performed, however, for their room was separated by a flag, not a wall. It is also unclear how Jessup's room was subdivided so as to render it distinct from the cook's room. Moreover, this arrangement suggests that maintaining privacy was an important criterion for the missionaries, but not necessarily for their Syrian cohabitants. The privacy of both the servant girl and cook was compromised in this home, as their rooms were used for both private sleeping areas and communal spaces.

In other words, the selection of homes and the division of space within missionary households reflected the specific views of gender, familial affiliation, and privacy that were articulated by the ABCFM missionaries. Their criteria for choosing a home and living arrangements were not predetermined, but rather, flexible and open to the perceived needs of the ABCFM missionaries and their experiences in Syria.

THE FLEXIBILITY OF THE FAMILY

Similar to the ABCFM missionaries' homes, their definition of "family" was malleable and reflected the realities of their encounter in Ottoman Syria from 1823 to 1860. This produced the family arrangement that I have labelled the "mosaic" family. The following section will show that the mosaic family structure was employed by the ABCFM missionaries in an effort to construct new alliances and kinship patterns, while addressing the challenges faced by the nascent Protestant community. However, the manner in which mosaic families were created reinforced an underlying hierarchy based on race, which plagued this community.

As introduced above, the mosaic families of the ABCFM missionaries were composed of different units within a shared household. One unit consisted of a married missionary couple and their children. Marriages between missionaries (or more correctly between a male "missionary" and a female "assistant missionary") frequently took place immediately before sailing to Syria,[82] or at the station if both partners were originally sent as single missionaries.[83] Regardless of where the parents were married, missionary children were most often born at the mission station.[84] This basic family unit occupied one bedroom within the missionary household, although an 1844 floor plan for the Beadle's house in Aleppo noted a separate "children's room."[85]

Another unit was the single missionary, either male or female. The privacy of this unit was affirmed by single missionaries, especially women, being given separate rooms within missionary homes.[86] A childless married missionary couple functioned as a third unit and was treated in a similar manner.[87]

Although neither the ABCFM missionaries nor Syrian Protestants employed the terms "mosaic family" or "unit," these concepts were implied in the missionaries' discussions of their living arrangements. For example, Hetty Smith's 1847 description of "Mr. Thomson's family" reflected this mosaic combination of units, for it included the married Thomson couple; Eliza Abbot, a daughter from Maria Thomson's first marriage; three of William and Maria's own children; the single missionary Henry Van Lennep, and the then childless Smith couple.[88]

The mosaic structure of missionary families resulted from the limited availability of space for missionary homes described in the above section. Hetty Smith noted that her residency with the Thomson family at the Mission House was to last "until [Eli and she could] procure a home of our own which we have not yet been able to do."[89] Two months later, Hetty wrote that she was "a housekeeper now," meaning that the Smiths had secured their own home. Noticeably, seven additional persons, composing two units, joined the Smiths to form their new household.[90]

Modifications to the missionaries' homes were constructed to accommodate for the additions of units to mosaic arrangements. As stated above, each unit was given a separate bedroom within shared households. Sarah Smith explained in 1835 that an extension to the "Old Susa house" was for Rebecca Williams, a new single missionary at the station.[91] Although each unit was given a private bedroom, important social activities like meals and evening worship were communal events and occurred within the shared space of the parlor or dining room. This resulted in the overlapping of family activities. As a result, the definition of the missionary home and family were essentially linked. The specific conglomeration of units that defined a particular missionary household was determined by the availability of distinct rooms in order to accommodate for both the private spaces of each unit and the shared spaces for communal activities.

The duration of mosaic combinations was often short, for family arrangements were affected by the various needs of the station and individual missionaries. One situation that modified mosaic families was the removal of Protestants to Mount Lebanon during the summer. Conditions at these locations affected how mosaic families were reconfigured. They included the operation of schools, cost of living, need to return to Beirut, villagers' positive or negative reception of the missionaries, availability of buildings for occupancy, and illness. As a result, the arrangements of mosaic families during one summer differed from the previous summer's arrangements and the "normal" configurations at Beirut.

Other circumstances resulted in the break-up of mosaic families as well as basic units themselves. During the illness of a missionary, other missionaries stayed with the invalid. This role was most frequently performed by the missionary doctor and/or his wife. For example, pregnant missionary women were treated as being ill and were nursed by the wives of missionary doctors in their homes.[92] Catherine DeForest was specifically praised for her care of bedridden, pregnant missionary women. Catherine's role supplemented the nursing provided by biological sisters in the United States, during both the preparations of pregnancy and care of the post-partum mother. Such provisions tightened the "sisterly" bonds that formed among missionary women, but in a manner that broke up units, such as the married DeForest couple.

The death of a missionary, either male or female, produced another circumstance when a unit was broken apart and the mosaic family reconfigured. The most noticeable example of this was the Smith family. Eli Smith's second wife, Maria, died shortly after giving birth to a son, Charles Henry, in 1842.[93] Care of the then motherless Charlie was designated to Catherine DeForest.[94] In 1845, Eli went on furlough to the United States and returned two years later with a new wife, Hetty. Despite anticipating her new role as a wife and mother, Hetty waited almost five months before taking charge of her new stepson,

Charlie.[95] Although the primary care of Charlie was transferred to Hetty, his relationship with the DeForests remained strong, for Charlie resided with Catherine and Henry DeForest at different periods in subsequent years. Upon the death of Eli in 1857, the entire Smith family returned to the United States. At this point, Charlie was placed with his maternal grandfather (Maria's father), Moses Chapin.[96] Charlie nevertheless maintained correspondences with and visited both Hetty Smith and Catherine DeForest, both of whom had returned to the United States by this point.[97] Following the history of the Smith family, specifically the guardianship of Charlie, illuminates that even the basic unit of a biological family was malleable to the different challenges faced by the missionaries.

The mosaic missionary family was not limited to those employed by the ABCFM, but was open to include others. The ABCFM missionaries frequently housed travelers from the United States and Europe as guests within their homes. An American family named Martin resided with Hetty Smith in 1856 and functioned as a distinct unit within the Smith household. Although given a separate room, the additional burden of provisions for the Martins eventually grew to annoy Hetty.[98] In a more pleasant arrangement, Mr. and Mrs. Sergent, the parents of Catherine DeForest, lived with the DeForest family for a number of years. This couple assisted in running the DeForests' Female Boarding School after Catherine suffered a head injury from being kicked by a horse.[99]

Marriage was another channel through which nonmissionaries became members of mosaic families. While some missionary marriages occurred in the United States, others took place in Syria. For example, the single missionaries Story Hebard and Rebecca Williams were married in 1836, while Edward Aiken and Sarah Cheney were united in 1857. In other circumstances, single missionaries married non-ABCFM missionaries or other Protestant residents of the region. This was the case when William Thomson married Maria Abbott, the widow of Peter Abbott, a former British consul. The daughters of Peter and Maria Abbott were subsequently raised as missionary children within the "Thomson family." One daughter, Julia, married the ABCFM missionary Cornelius Van Dyck, while another, Eliza, married an English merchant, James Black, who was a resident of Beirut and member of the Free Church of Scotland's "Lebanon School Committee."[100] Martha Dodge, the widow of missionary Asa Dodge, remarried Rev. J. D. Paxton, an

American minister who visited Syria in the 1830s. As a result, Martha Dodge and her two daughters returned to the United States and she was released from her somewhat unconventional missionary commitment.[101]

Moreover, the missionary family was not restricted to the space of Ottoman Syria. Due to the unpredictable nature of missionary life, the ABCFM missionaries maintained connections to relatives and close friends back in the United States. These bonds were preserved primarily through letter writing. Upholding links to family in the United States was important for they were channels through which the missionaries obtained "necessary" items, such as American butter and clothing.[102] They were also essential in allowing missionaries to continue their role within biological families. For example, upon the death of her mother, Hetty Smith inquired about the distribution of the inheritance and claimed desired items.[103]

The maintenance of bonds with family back in the United States was especially important for the children of missionaries. Both the missionaries and the Prudential Committee felt that it was best to send missionary children back to the United States for schooling once the child reached the age of adolescence.[104] "Returned missionary children" lived with family members or close friends, if their parents remained in the field.[105] Monetary support for returned children was provided through grants from the ABCFM, the missionaries' private accounts, and/or family and friends living in the United States.[106] Tensions arose when the missionaries could not find adequate guardians for their children in the United States.[107] This was the case of Isaac and Anne Bird who had to leave Syria and return to the United States with their five children, for lack of a "good, pious schoolmaster" in Syria and "family friends with whom we could leave our children" in the United States.[108] Unlike other missionaries, whose endeavors were affirmed through continued links with family in the United States, the Birds' work was jeopardized by their failure to maintain (or forge) bonds with persons in the United States.[109]

As the above examples illuminate, the missionary family was a relatively open structure. It included, even if temporarily, a mosaic of persons and family units: missionaries, travelers, Americans, Europeans, those living in Syria, and those living in the United States. However, the criteria for acceptance within the missionary family were influenced by the ABCFM missionaries' perceptions on racial differentiation. People were included in the missionary family if they upheld certain ideologies and performed behaviors appropriate for a Protestant. This marked many, although not all, Syrians as unacceptable for the missionary family.

Justification for this separation/inequality was grounded on the ABCFM missionaries' views of the "Syrian" race along a scale of civility and piety.[110] This scale was found in American geography textbooks and "Moral and Political" maps of the world, which were employed at common schools and by families for evening convocation during the early nineteenth century.[111] Although the exact position of Syrians along this scale was indeterminate,[112] Syrians were generally regarded as "half-civilized."[113] This was attributed to the cultural and religious achievements of people from the Levant during antiquity (the remains of which were visited by the ABCFM missionaries) and the potential for reform granted to contemporary Syrians. The missionaries were told to remember "that however unlike our own the manners and customs of the oriental Christians may be, they are not barbarians; nor are they heathens."[114] As the rest of this section will show, the Syrians who were allowed entrance into the missionary family did so by being perceived as similar to the ABCFM missionaries, both culturally and (more importantly for the ABCFM) religiously. That is, these Syrians overcame their "half-civilized" status and became "almost a Frank."[115]

One channel through which Syrians were included into missionary families was through being "adopted." As introduced above, Sarah Smith initiated the practice of raising Syrian girls as boarding students within missionary families. Eli Smith recalled that Rahil "took a rank in the family, midway between a daughter and a servant" within the Smith household.[116] Even after Sarah's death, Eli maintained that Rahil was his "adopted daughter,"[117] while Rahil asserted that "his [Eli's] house is my home."[118]

Adoptions occurred within other missionary families and became part of the ABCFM's policy for the Syria Station.[119] In 1847, Henry and Catherine DeForest organized a formal Female Boarding School or seminary within their home. In addition to a rigorous study program, the students in this "family school" participated in morning and evening family worship, which blurred the line between school and family.[120] Unlike previous adoption arrangements, however, many of the girls at the DeForest school came from families already associated with the missionaries and maintained ties with their biological family members.[121]

A more formal boarding school was also created within the home of Martha Whiting. She wrote:

> My work in the *family school* began in October 1835, when Salome Carabet and Hannie Wortabet were placed by their parents in our family school. We afterwards added to the number Melita Carabet, and the two orphan girls Sada and Rufka Gregory.[122]

Although Martha asserted that "the parents of three of the girls in our family, being Protestants, always gave their sanction to our mode of instructing and training them,"[123] private correspondences reveal that tensions arose between Martha and Susan Wortabet over the care of Susan's daughter Hannie, while the grandmother of Sada and Rufka Gregory contested the ABCFM's claim of guardianship for these adopted students.[124]

Despite the high esteem granted to adopted boarding students by other members of the Protestant community, their position within missionary families illuminates the unequal distributions of power within this community. First, missionary women were promoted as being better mothers than the students' biological, Syrian mothers. This justified the missionaries' original removal of the girls from their biological families, which affirmed their use of the term "adoption" to describe this arrangement.[125] Second, although nurtured within missionary families, boarding students had to repeatedly prove their Protestant commitment. In contrast, the biological children of missionaries verbalized their pious commitment only once to be accepted as true Protestants.[126] This reveals an ever-present fear held by the ABCFM missionaries that the adopted students would revert to their original, "half-civilized" nature, despite the longevity of close association with the missionaries.[127]

Some "Arab girl" servants also formed close bonds with the missionary families that they worked for as nurses. As mentioned above, Khozma Ata (no relation to Rahil Ata) and "Mennie" were two Arab servants who lived with the DeForest and Smith families, respectively (although also interchangeably). Khozma was originally from a Druze family, but was "taken by [the missionary] Dr. Beadle" when she was a child.[128] By 1848, Khozma was referred to as Catherine DeForest's "Arab daughter."[129] Mennie served as a nurse for Hetty Smith and lived with the Smith family. It appears that Mennie traveled with Hetty and her children to the United States upon the death of Eli in 1856, but returned to Syria the following year.[130] Letters written by Charlie, who was then living with his maternal uncle, asked Hetty about Mennie and sent her his "salaams."[131] Charlie had "his likeness taken for Mennie,"[132] which meant that he had a daguerreotype taken of himself, as a gift for his Syrian nanny. Daguerreotypes were early experiments in photography, popular in the 1840s and 1850s, for which images were printed on small silver plates. The use of daguerreotype-exchange was first mentioned by Hetty Smith, as a method to maintain bonds with her family in the United States.[133] Charlie not only sent his image, but asked for Mennie's daguerreotype to be taken and sent to him in return. Charlie also asked for a lock of Mennie's hair, another exchange-symbol of familial bonds.[134] It is important to recognize that although strong bonds of affection allowed for both Khozma and Mennie to be considered part of missionary families, these relationships were forged on unequal exchanges: Khozma was "taken" from her family, while Mennie was a hired servant-nurse.[135]

Some Syrian Protestants were included as part of a mosaic missionary family due to their service and elevated position within the nascent Protestant community. This was the case of Tannous al-Haddad and his wife "Im Beshera." This couple developed close bonds with many ABCFM missionaries. During the early years of the mission, some of the missionaries, especially the single male missionaries, resided with the Haddad family. Eli Smith lived with the Haddads before his first marriage, with the hopes that he would

> be obliged to speak Arabic more, to be less interrupted in [his] studies, to become acquainted with the people of the mountain and their customs, to be less troubled by rumours of war and find opportunities of giving religious instructions to the people.[136]

In return, the Haddads asserted their affection for Eli and his first wife, Sarah, by naming one of their daughters after her.[137] Another daughter, Rufka, studied as a boarding student at the DeForests' Female Seminary and was an important member of this family-school. Although the Haddads were never regarded as equals by the ABCFM missionaries, they were perceived to be elevated above the "half-civilized" racialized positioning of their Syrian neighbors and welcomed parts of different missionary families.

The family of Rahil (née Ata) and Butrus al-Bustani forged the deepest bonds with the missionaries and was intertwined with some mosaic mission-ary families, particularly the Smith family. As noted above, Rahil was the first "adopted" boarding student at the Syrian Station. In that regard, Butrus al-Bustani was not only a colleague of Eli Smith, but his "adopted" son-in-law. When Hetty Smith commenced housekeeping in 1847, Rahil, Butrus, and their daughter Sarah Huntington (named after the first Mrs. Smith) resided in Hetty's home. Even when they moved to different, separate residences, the Bustani children remained playmates of the Smith children.[138] This was significant since Hetty prevented her children from interacting with other Syrian children "lest [they] should hear bad language."[139] Letters written by Rahil to Eli were similar to those he exchanged with Hetty and his biological children, for they were written in an informal journal format and included information concerning the mundane aspects of life.[140] Although the letters written by Butrus tended to focus on matters of business, they also included news of his family.[141] In other words, the Bustani family held a unique po-sition within the Protestant community, for they were perceived to be "al-most" overcoming a racial divide and integrated into the Smith family.[142]

It is important to note that the mosaic family of the ABCFM missionar-ies fulfills neither the definition of the "modern" nuclear family that emerged within Victorian America[143] nor that found in late nineteenth-century Ot-toman Syria.[144] It also confounds the template that some historians argue was promoted by Anglo-American missionaries as an ideal for the "Chris-tian home."[145] Nevertheless, these mosaic arrangements were comparable to the family structures found in the United States and in the Ottoman Empire during the late eighteenth and early nineteenth centuries. Within the United States, death, the pursuit of education, and the demands of economic develop-ment often fragmented families into smaller "mosaic" pieces.[146] For example, the future missionary Sarah Smith was raised by her father and a stepmother before being sent to a boarding school in Boston, where she spent the week-ends at her uncle's house.[147] In a similar manner, Zilfi argues that death, ap-prenticeships, the employment of servants, and the practice of slavery created similar family arrangements within wealthy families in Istanbul.[148] Meriwether describes a "continuum of household types" found within Ottoman Aleppo during this period, which ranged from "simple households to larger multiple-family households that remained undivided over several generations."[149] The "joint households" of Aleppo, for example, were "augmented through marriage, clientage, slavery, and possibly adoption," although "kin formed the core of the household."[150] While the mosaic arrangements were unique responses to the ABCFM missionaries' encounter in Ottoman Syria, this familial system appears to have resonated with household patterns already practiced in both the United States and the Ottoman Empire, and was thus part of a larger process of kinship reconfiguration during the early modern period.

CONCLUSION

As Fredrick Cooper illuminates, the definition of "colonialism" is multifaceted.[151] Recent debates over the role of European and American missionaries within the "colonizing endeavour" has (correctly) positioned missionaries along a spectrum of involvement.[152] While these studies offer new insights into missionary encounters, gaps remain regarding how such interactions affected the daily life of both the missionaries and those "targeted" by mission, and how the articulation of kinship and home life occurred. It is tempting to say that the ABCFM missionaries lived in homes and arranged their families according to concrete criteria imported from their home culture, such as a sharply gendered home that separated the public from the private, and which housed the American-European family, exclusive from all Arabs. It is just as appealing to say that Syrians resisted American household configurations, for it violated their own views of gender and kinship. However, by looking at how the home and family was actually manifested during this missionary encounter, even within the narrow context of the homes occupied (primarily) by the ABCFM missionaries, it becomes clear that this "colonial" encounter was very complex. The home and family were malleable terms, affected as much by the realities unfolding in Syria as by the ideological constraints imposed by the ABCFM missionaries themselves. As a result, by perceiving the home and family as important sites of ideological performance and cultural negotiation, one can better understand the development of the Protestant community and the true nature of the American mission in Ottoman Syria.

NOTES

1. An earlier version of this chapter was presented at the workshop: *Christian Missionaries in the Middle East: Re-Thinking Colonial Encounters*, North Carolina State University, North Carolina, USA, 4–5 May 2007. I am grateful for the positive feedback, suggestions, and stimulating conversations that took place over these two days. I would also like to thank Anthony Gorman and Frauke Matthes for their helpful comments on this chapter. The material presented in this chapter draws upon the research I conducted for my Doctoral thesis "Negotiating the Field: American Protestant Missionaries in Ottoman Syria, 1823 to 1860" (University of Edinburgh, 2009).

2. Henrietta Smith, "Letter," YDS: ES Box 1: Folder 16 (Beirut 18 January 1847).

3. Ibid.

4. Ellen Fleischmann notes the lack of analysis regarding the ABCFM missionaries' building projects in Ottoman Syria. Ellen Fleischmann, "Evangelization or Education: American Protestant Missionaries; the American Board, and the Girls and Women of Syria (1830–1910)," in Murre-van den Berg, *New Faith in Ancient Lands*, 266n10.

5. The term "Syria" within the Ottoman context describes the geographic region of Bilad al-Sham, which includes modern-day Lebanon, Syria, Jordan, Israel, and Palestine. Due to the nature of the ABCFM missionaries' work and their use of the term "Syria," this paper will focus upon the areas within present-day Lebanon.

6. Samir Khalaf, "On Doing Much with Little Noise: Early Encounters of Protestant Missionaries in Lebanon," in Tejirian and Simon, *Altruism and Imperialism*, 16. A similar description of the Jesuits has also been made. Bernard Heyberger and Chantal Verdeil, "Spirituality and Scholarship: The Holy Land in Jesuit Eyes (Seventeenth to Nineteenth Centuries)," in Murre-van den Berg, *New Faith in Ancient Lands*, 19–20; Habib Badr, "American Protestant Missionary Beginnings in Beirut and Istanbul: Policy, Politics, Practice and Response," in Murre-van den Berg, *New Faith in Ancient Lands*, 211–239.

7. Mehmet Ali Doğan in this volume; Adnan Abu-Ghazaleh, *American Missions in Syria: A Study of American Missionary Contribution to Arab Nationalism in 19th Century Syria* (Brattleboro, VT: Amana Books, 1990); Habib Badr, "Missions to 'Nominal Christians': The Policy and Practice of the American Board of Commissioners for Foreign Missions and Its Missionaries Concerning Eastern Churches Which Led to the Organization of a Protestant Church in Beirut (1819–1848)" (PhD diss., Princeton Theological Seminary, 1992); Ussama Makdisi, "Reclaiming the Land of the Bible: Missionaries, Secularism, and Evangelical Modernity," *The American Historical Review* 102:3 (1997): 680–713.

8. Cemal Yetkiner in this volume; J. Robertson Buchanan, "The Story of the Lebanon Schools and the Free Church of Scotland," (n.s.: n.s., 1957); Ellen

Fleischmann (2006); Aleksandra Majstorac Kobiljski, "Learning to Be Modern: Missionary Universities and the Formation of Secular Modernity in Lebanon and Japan, 1860s–1880s" (paper presented at Christian Missionaries in the Middle East: Re-Thinking Colonial Encounters Conference, Raleigh, North Carolina, 4–5 May 2007).

9. This is a trend found within the larger genre of research on missionaries. T. O. Beidelman, "The Organization and Maintenance of Caravans by the Church Missionary Society in Tanzania in the Nineteenth Century," *The International Journal of African Historical Studies* 15: 4 (1982): 601–623; Fiona Bowie, Deborah Kirkwood, and Shirley Ardner, eds., *Women and Missions: Past and Present: Anthropological and Historical Perceptions* (Oxford: Berg, 1993); John L. Comaroff and Jean Comaroff, *Of Revelation and Revolution: Volume One: Christianity, Colonialism and Consciousness in South Africa* (Chicago: University of Chicago Press, 1991); John L. Comaroff and Jean Comaroff, *Of Revelation and Revolution: Volume Two: The Dialectics of Modernity on a South African Frontier* (Chicago: University of Chicago Press, 1997); Mary Taylor Huber and Nancy C. Lutkenhaus, eds., *Gendered Missions: Women and Men in Missionary Discourse and Practice* (Ann Arbor: University of Michigan Press, 1999).

10. This diversity is reflected in the different edited volumes published within recent years focusing on mission work in the Middle East. Eleanor H. Tejirian and Reeva Spector Simon, eds., *Altruism and Imperialism: Western Cultural and Religious Missions in the Middle East* (New York: Middle East Institute, Columbia University, Occasional Papers IV, 2002); Martin Tamcke and Michael Marten, eds., *Christian Witness Between Continuity and New Beginnings: Modern Historical Missions in the Middle East* (Berlin: LIT-Verlag, 2006); Heleen Murre-van den Berg, ed., *New Faith in Ancient Lands: Western Missions in the Middle East in the Nineteenth and Early Twentieth Centuries* (Leiden: Brill, 2006).

11. Beth Baron in this volume; Nancy Stockdale, *Colonial Encounters among English and Palestinian Women, 1800–1948* (Gainesville: University of Florida Press, 2007).

12. See Fatma Hassan al-Sayegh, "American Women Missionaries in the Gulf: Agents for Cultural Change," *Islam and Christian-Muslim Relations* 9:3 (1998): 339–356; Bernard Heyberger and Chantal Verdeil, 19–42.

13. Willy Jansen, "Visions of Mary in the Middle East: Gender and the Power of a Symbol," in *Gender, Religion and Change in the Middle East: Two Hundred Years of History*, ed. Inger Marie Okkenhaug and Ingvild Flaskerud (Oxford: Berg, 2005), 137–154; T. O. Beidelman, 601–623.

14. Heleen Murre-van den Berg, "'Dear Mother of My Soul': Fidelia Fiske and the Role of Women Missionaries in Mid-Nineteenth Century Iran," *Exchange* 30:1 (2001): 33–48; Ellen Fleischmann, "The Impact of American Protestant Missions in Lebanon on the Construction of Female Identity, c. 1860–1950,"

Islam and Christian-Muslim Relations 13:4 (2002): 411–426; Marilyn Booth, "'She Herself Was the Ultimate Rule': Arabic Biographies of Missionary Teachers and Their Pupils," *Islam and Christian-Muslim Relations* 13:4 (2002): 427–448.

15. Also see Dana L. Robert, "The 'Christian Home' as a Cornerstone of Anglo-American Missionary Thought and Practice," in *Converting Colonialism: Visions and Realities in Mission History, 1706–1914,* ed. D. L. Robert (Grand Rapids, MI: William B. Eerdmans, 2008), 134–165.

16. Pierre Bourdieu, *Distinction: A Social Critique of the Judgement of Taste,* trans. Richard Nice (New York: Routledge, 1984); Michel de Certeau, *The Practice of Everyday Life,* trans. Steven Rendall (Berkeley: University of California Press, 1984), 43.

17. Pierre Bourdieu, *Outline of a Theory of Practice,* trans. Richard Nice (Cambridge: Cambridge University Press, 1977), 90–91; Michel de Certeau, 21.

18. For example Edward W. Hooker, *Memoir of Mrs. Sarah Lanman Smith, Late of the Mission in Syria* (London: The Religious Tract Society, 1839); Henry Harris Jessup, *Fifty-Three Years in Syria: Volume I and II,* originally published 1910 (London: Garnet Publishing Ltd., 2002); William M. Thomson, *The Land and the Book, or Biblical Illustrations Drawn from the Manners and Customs, the Scenes and Scenery of the Holy Land* (London: T. Nelson and Sons, Paternoster Row, 1860).

19. Eleanor Abdella Doumato, "Missionary Transformations: Gender, Culture and Identity in the Middle East," *Islam and Christian-Muslim Relations* 13:4 (2002): 373; Habib Badr (1992), 18. A small number of letters written by Syrian Protestants are kept at the Harvard University Houghton Library and the Yale University Divinity Library. Also considered were the published works of Syrian Protestants Butrus al-Bustani, Selim al-Bustani, John Wortabet, Gregory Wortabet, and Mikhayil Mishaqa.

20. Jean Said Makdisi, *Teta, Mother and Me: An Arab Woman's Memoir* (London: Saqi, 2005), 152.

21. John L. Comaroff and Jean Comaroff *(*1997), 5.

22. For other work, see Helena Michie and Ronald R. Thomas, eds., *Nineteenth-Century Geographies: The Transformation of Space from the Victorian Age to the American Century* (New Brunswick, NJ: Rutgers University Press, 2003).

23. *Missionary Herald* (1819), 271. From henceforth, *MH.*

24. Habib Badr (1992), 43–51. Compare this with the London Society for Promoting Christianity Amongst the Jews, also known as the the London Jews Society (LJS), whose primary focus was the conversion of the Jews and who advocated a premillenial theology. Reeva Spector Simon, "The Case of the Curse: The London Society for Promoting Christianity Amongst the Jews and the Jews of Baghdad," in Tejirian and Simon, *Altruism and Imperialism,* 45–65.

25. Habib Badr, 76–77.

26. Isaac Bird, *Bible Work in Bible Lands; Or, Events in the History of the Syria Mission* (Philadelphia: Presbyterian Board of Publication, 1872), 88.

27. Rufus Anderson, *History of the Missions of the American Board of Commissioners for Foreign Missions to the Oriental Churches: In Two Volumes* (Boston: Congregational Publishing Society, 1872), 40–41.

28. A similar argument is presented in Heleen Murre-van den Berg, "The Middle East: Western Missions and the Eastern Churches, Islam and Judaism," in *World Christianities c. 1815–1914: The Cambridge History of Christianity Volume 8*, ed. Sheridan Gilley and Brian Stanley (Cambridge: Cambridge University Press, 2006).

29. May Davie, *Atlas Historique Des Orthodoxes de Beyrouth et du Mont Liban: 1800–1940* (Balamand: Universite de Balamand, 1999), 24–26; Leila Tarazi Fawaz, *Merchants and Migrants in Nineteenth-Century Beirut* (Cambridge, MA: Harvard University Press, 1993), 10–12, 32.

30. Emphasis in original. George Whiting and William M. Thomson, "On the Results of Past Labours in the Mission," ABCFM microfilm Unit 5: Near East: Reel 538: 53B–56B (Beirut: 10 April 1844).

31. Gregory M. Wortabet, *Syria, and the Syrians; or, Turkey in the Dependencies, Volume I* (London: James Madden, 1856), 44.

32. William Goodell cited in Jeremy Salt, "Trouble Wherever They Went: American Missionaries in Anatolia and Ottoman Syria in the Nineteenth Century," in Tejirian and Simon, *Altruism and Imperialism*, 151.

33. Jens Hanssen, *Fin de Siècle Beirut: The Making of an Ottoman Provincial Capital* (Oxford: Clarendon Press, 2005), 151.

34. Hetty Smith (18 January 1847). For a similar description of Cairo see Eli Smith, "Letter to Brother," YDS: ES Box 1: Folder 2 (Beirut: 16 March 1827).

35. Edward W. Hooker, 181; Henrietta Smith, "Letter to Sister," YDS: ES Box 1: Folder 17 (Beirut: 11 May 1847).

36. Eli Smith, "Letter to Brother," YDS: ES Box 1: Folder 3 (Bhamdoun, 14 August 1834).

37. For an examination of the relationship between "renting" and "owning" land by "foreigners" in Ottoman Cyprus see Marc Aymes, "The Port-City in the Fields: Investigating an Improper Urbanity in Mid-19th Century Cyprus" (paper presented at Eighth Mediterranean Social and Political Research Meeting, Florence & Montecatini Terme, 21–25 March 2007, organized by the Mediterranean Programme of the Robert Schuman Centre for Advanced Studies at the European University Institute, 2007).

38. *MH* (1826): 354–356.

39. Ibid., 354–358; *MH* (1831): 148; Henry Harris Jessup (2002), 45; Henrietta Smith (18 January 1847).

40. Various terms for this house were employed including "Burj Bird," "Mission

House," and "Female Seminary." This site is the current location of the National Evangelical Church in Beirut.

41. Gabriel Chasseaud, "Registration of deed and transfer of deed for Beit Mikdash," PRO (Public Records Office): FO (Foreign Office); Box 616, Folder 1 (Beirut: 2 February 1831); n.s., "Deed of Tannous el-Haddad for Mission House and Garden," HHL: ABC 8.2.17, box 4: folder 26 (n.s.: 19 April 1844).

42. The exact location of this house is unclear, but I disagree with those who suggest that it was the Abdallah Soussa house, which was occupied by Henry Harris Jessup during the late nineteenth century and is currently located near the Patriarchal School. Ralph Bodenstein et al., "Walking through Zokak el-Blat: A Rhythmanalysis of the Quarter," in *History, Space and Social Conflict in Beirut: The Quarter of Zokak el-Blat*, ed. Hans Gebhardt (Beirut: Ergon Verlag Würzburg in Kommission, 2005), 29.

43. Eli Smith, "Letter to Brother Bird," YDS: ES Box 6: Folder 10 (Beirut: 27 November 1850).

44. William M. Thomson, "Letter to Eli Smith," HHL: ABC 60 (111) (Beirut: 28 December [1838]).

45. Ralph Bodenstein et al., 29.

46. Jean Said Makdisi, 201–202.

47. Henry Harris Jessup (2002), 115.

48. Edward W. Hooker, 182.

49. Henrietta Smith, "Letter to Sister," YDS: ES Box 1: Folder 17 (Beirut: 16 April 1847).

50. May Davie (1999), 21–22.

51. Friedrich Ragette, *Architecture in Lebanon: The Lebanese House during the 18th and 19th Centuries* (Beirut, Lebanon: American University of Beirut, 1974), 72.

52. May Davie, "Genèse D'une Demeur Patrimoniale: La Maison Aux Trois Arcs de Beyrouth," in *La Maison Beyrouthine Aux Trois Arcs: Une Architecture Bourgeoise du Levant,* ed. M. Davie (Beirut: ALBA, 2003), 73–77.

53. The red-tiled roof of Syrian Protestant College, now American University of Beirut, is a striking feature, which draws upon later developments of the Center Hall/Triple Arched House. Friedrich Ragette, 112.

54. Also see Charles Benton, "The Benton Home: B'hamdoun, Mount Lebanon, Syria," in *A Diary and Some Reminiscences of Loanza Goulding Benton (Mrs. William Auston Benton): Missionary to Syria*, Loanza Benton (Sophia Smith Collection, Smith College Religion Collection: Box 5: Folder 56), n.d.

55. *MH* (1844): 205.

56. Noticeably, this letter does not tackle the question of how the missionaries, as foreigners, were granted permission to construct a new building.

57. George Whiting and William M. Thomson (10 April 1844); Habib Badr (1992), 119.

58. Eli Smith noted that the Jesuits were ordered by the Turkish authorities to stop the "extensive improvements" they commenced on a convent in Beirut, which included a bell tower. Eli Smith, "The Papal Sects of Syria are the Maronites, Greek Catholics, Armenian Catholics, Syrian Catholics and Latins," ABCFM microfilm Unit 5: Near East: Reel 540: 49B-69, (n.s.: n.d.). For more on Protestant anti-Catholic rhetoric see Heleen Murre-van den Berg, "Simply by Giving to Them Maccaroni...': Anti-Roman Catholic Polemics in Early Protestant Missions in the Middle East, 1820–1860," in Tamcke and Marten, *Christian Witness Between Continuity and New Beginnings*, 63–80.

59. Edward W. Hooker, 182.

60. n.s., *Minutes of the Special Meeting of the Syrian Mission, Held in September and October, 1855, on Occasion of the Visit of One of the Secretaries of the American Board of Commissioners for Foreign Missions* (Boston: T. R. Marvin, 1856), 9–12.

61. Ibid., *MH* (1851): 136; Henrietta Smith (11 May 1847).

62. Similar stances were asserted by various social reform groups during the Antebellum period, such as the Home Missionary Society and the American Tract Society. Robert T. Handy, *Religion in the American Experience: The Pluralistic Style* (New York: Harper & Row Pub., 1972), 85–89.

63. Despite the presentation of a unified missiology, the ABCFM missionaries often differed on how to balance religious refinement with "modernity" and conflicted with the Prudential Committee's views on the matter. This led to tensions and a tightening of ABCFM regulation of the station. n.s., *Minutes of the Special Meeting of the Syrian Mission.*

64. Henrietta Smith (18 January 1847).

65. Edward W. Hooker, 182.

66. Zilfi argues that this gendered divide of domestic workspace was itself fluid within Ottoman households during this period. Madeline C. Zilfi, "Servants, Slaves, and the Domestic Order in the Ottoman Middle East," *Hawwa* 2:1 (2004): 10–22.

67. Henrietta Smith, "Letter to Sister," YDS: ES Box 1: Folder 18 (n.s.: 9 May 1848).

68. Edward W. Hooker, 266.

69. Ibid., 198–199.

70. Karin Calvert, *Children in the House: The Material Culture of Early Childhood, 1600–1900* (Boston: Northeastern University Press, 1992), 130.

71. Henrietta Smith (18 January 1847).

72. Gregory Wortabet, 70.

73. Patricia R. Hill, *The World Their Household: The American Woman's Foreign Mission Movement and Cultural Transformation, 1870–1920* (Ann Arbor: University of Michigan Press, 1985), 25–26; Pierre Bourdieu, *Algeria 1960*, trans. Richard Nice (Cambridge: Cambridge University Press, 1979), 133–153; Mirna

Lattouf, *Women, Education, and Socialization in Modern Lebanon* (Lanham, MD: University Press of America, Inc., 2004), 116–127.

74. Notable exceptions within the Ottoman contexts are Margaret L. Meriwether, *The Kin Who Count: Family and Society in Ottoman Aleppo, 1770–1840* (Austin: University of Texas Press, 1999); and Madeline C. Zilfi.

75. The fear of contamination from servants was common within the United States during this period. Karin Calvert, 74 and 122–123.

76. Edward W. Hooker, 278–280; Henry Harris Jessup, *The Women of the Arabs: With a Chapter for Children*, ed. C. S. Robinson and Isaac Riley (New York: Dodd & Mead, Publishers, 1873), 120–139.

77. Edward W. Hooker, 280.

78. Henrietta Smith, "Letter to Sister," YDS: ES Box 1: Folder 23, (Beirut: 1 May 1854).

79. Ibid.

80. Madeline C. Zilfi, 17–18.

81. Henry Harris Jessup (2002), 120.

82. Barbara Reeves-Ellington hypothesizes that justification for this practice was to prevent giving birth while en route to the missionary station. Conversation with Reeves-Ellington, November 2007.

83. This was the case with Story Hebard and Rebecca Williams in 1836 and Edward Aiken and Sarah Cheney in 1857.

84. This frequently caused tension for the children's identity, both in regards to their claim to American citizenship and identification of "home." Eli Smith (8 May 1840). See also n.s., "Missionaries' Children Returned to the United States ca. 1831–1881: Records of Grants, Etc.," HHL: ABC 77.8.3, (1866) and n.s., "Missionaries' Children Returned to the United States; Questionnaire Circulated by Rufus Anderson," HHL: ABC 11.8.2, (1881).

85. Elias R. Beadle, "Letter to Rev. and Sir," ABCFM microfilm Unit 5: Near East: Reel 539: 153, (Aleppo: 10 June 1844).

86. Sarah Smith, "Letter to Rebecca Williams," HHL: ABC 60 (110) (Beirut: 5 August 1835).

87. Henrietta Smith (18 January 1847).

88. Ibid.

89. Ibid.

90. Henrietta Smith, "Letter to Sister," YDS: ES Box 1: Folder 17 (Beirut: 15 March 1847).

91. Sarah Smith (5 August 1835).

92. Catherine DeForest, "Letter to Mrs. Butler," YDS: ES Box 1: Folder 17 (Bhamdoun: 11 August 1847).

93. Eli Smith, "Letter to Parents," YDS: ES Box 1: Folder 6. 30 May 1842 (Beirut: 30 May 1842). Eli's first wife, Sarah, passed away in 1836.

94. Ibid.

95. Henrietta Smith (11 May 1847).

96. Charles H. Smith, "Letter to Mother," YDS: ES Box 2: Folder 2 (n.s.: 16 September 1857).

97. Ibid.

98. Henrietta Smith, "Letter to Husband" YDS: ES Box 2: Folder 1, (Bhamdoun: 19 July 1856); Henrietta Smith, "Letter to Husband," YDS: ES Box 2: Folder 1 (Bhamdoun: 31 July 1856).

99. George Whiting and Henry DeForest, "Letter to Dr. Anderson" (n.s.: 5 August 1850), in Jamil M. Yazigy, "American Presbyterian Mission Schools in Lebanon" (master's thesis, American University Beirut, 1964), 138–142; ABCFM, "Annual Report 1850" (Beirut).

100. Rev. J. Robertson Buchanan, 9.

101. Martha Dodge, "Letter to Mr. Anderson," ABCFM: Reel 539: 600–601B (Beirut, 17 June 1837). Unlike other widows, Martha remained in Syria with her daughters after her husband's death and continued her missionary work until she remarried.

102. Henrietta Smith, "Letter to Sister," YDS: ES Box 1: Folder 16 (Beirut: 20 February 1847); Henrietta Smith, "Letter to Sister: attached to Eli Smith's letter to Brother," YDS: ES Box 1: Folder 7 (Bhamdoun: 29 June 1849); Henrietta Smith, "Letter to Sisters," YDS: ES Box 1: Folder 20 (Beirut: 8 May 1850).

103. Henrietta Smith, "Letter to Sisters," YDS: ES Box 1: Folder 19 (Beirut: 15 December 1849).

104. *MH* (1846): 333–337.

105. Catherine M. Scholten, *Childbearing in American Society: 1650–1850* (New York: New York University Press, 1985), 5.

106. See n.s., "Missionaries' Children Returned to the United States: Questionnaire"; n.s., "Missionaries' Children Returned to the United States. Ca. 1832–1881."

107. *MH* (1846): 333–337.

108. Isaac Bird, "Letter to Sir-Private," ABCFM microfilm: Reel 537 (Smyrna: 4 December 1835); Isaac Bird, "Letter to Dear Brother," ABCFM microfilm: Reel 538: 3224 (Gilmanton [USA]: 26 August 1841).

109. Two of the Birds' children, William and Emily, returned to the Ottoman Empire and served as ABCFM missionaries as adults.

110. Sylvester Bliss, *Analysis of Geography; For the use of Schools, Academics, &c.* (Boston: John P. Jewett & Co., 1850), 33; Rev. J. L. Blake, *American Universal Geography, for Schools and Academics. On the Principles of Analysis and Comparison* (Boston: Lilly, Wait &c., 1833), 140–141.

111. Rev. William D. D. Jenks, "Missionary Map," in *The Explanatory Bible Atlas and Scripture Gazetteer; Geographical, Topographical and Historical...* (Boston: Charles Hickling, 1849).

112. Christine Lindner, "Historical Perceptions of Muslim Women by American Women" (paper presented at MESA Annual Conference, Boston, MA, 20

November 2006).

113. Ussama Makdisi, "Mapping the Orient: Non-Western Modernization, Imperialism, and the End of the Romanticism," in *Nineteenth-Century Geographies: The Transformation of Space from the Victorian Age to the American Century*, ed. Helena Michie and Ronald Thomas (New Brunswick, NJ: Rutgers University Press, 2003), 49.

114. *MH* (1839): 41–42.

115. Henrietta Smith (15 March 1847); Henrietta Smith (11 May 1847).

116. Edward W. Hooker, 279–280.

117. Eli Smith, "Letter to Brother," YDS: ES Box 1: Folder 4, (Beirut: 6 February 1843).

118. This is the printed response during the dispute between Rahil and her birth family. *MH* (1843): 283. In another version, Rahil proclaimed "I wish to go home to Mrs. DeForest." Henry Harris Jessup, (1873), 135.

119. George Whiting, "Report: Native Girls Under Instruction in the Mission Families," ABCFM microfilm: Reel 538: 80B-82A (Beirut: 20 March 1844).

120. Henry DeForest, "Letter to R. Anderson," (Abeih: 15 August 1850), in Jamil M. Yazigy, "American Presbyterian Mission Schools in Lebanon" (master's thesis, American University Beirut, 1964), 138–142.

121. A list of the students educated at the DeForests' Female Seminary are listed in Christine B. Lindner (2009), Appendix II:C.

122. George Whiting quoted in Henry Harris Jessup (1873), 60. Emphasis added.

123. Ibid., 62.

124. Sarah Smith, "Letter to Matilda Whiting," HHL: ABC 60 (110) (Beirut: 4 June 1835), *MH* (1841): 203; Henry Harris Jessup (1873), 60–62; Colonel Rose, "Dispatch to Foreign Office" (Beirut, 9 January 1845): PRO: FO Box 615, Folder 5.

125. See the story of "Sitt Abla" in Henry Harris Jessup (1873): 30–33.

126. George Whiting et al., ABCFM, "Annual Report," ABCFM microfilm: Reel 540: 26. 31 (Abeih: 1844).

127. Rahil al-Bustani, "Letter to Eli Smith," HHL: ABC 60 (12) (n.s., n.d.).

128. Henry Harris Jessup (1873), 33.

129. Henrietta Smith (9 May 1848).

130. Henry Harris Jessup, "Letter to Mother," YDS: HHJ Box 1: Folder 4 (Beirut: 3 April 1857).

131. Charles Henry Smith (16 September 1857).

132. Ibid.

133. Henrietta Smith (15 December 1849).

134. Charles Henry Smith, "Letter to Mother," YDS: ES Box 2: Folder 2 (Rochester [NY, USA]: 7 October 1857).

135. An overview of this class-based division of missions, with regard to women's education in domestic economy, is presented in Robert (2008): 155–157.

136. Eli Smith, "Journal as Resident on Mount Lebanon," YDS: ES Box 6: Folder 35 (n.s.: 27 December 1827).

137. *MH* (1838): 475.

138. Henrietta Smith, "Letter to Mother," HHL: ABC 60 (107) (n.s.: 30 September 1852).

139. Henrietta Smith, "Letter to Mother," YDS: ES Box 1: Folder 18 (Beirut: 11 March 1848); Henrietta Smith, "Letter to Mother," YDS: ES Box 1: Folder 18 (Beirut: 10 April 1848).

140. Rahil al-Bustani (n.d.).

141. Butrus al-Bustani, "Letter to Sir [Eli Smith]," HHL: ABC 60 (12) (Beirut: 30 May 1853); Butrus al-Bustani, "Letter to Sir [Eli Smith]," HHL: ABC 60 (12) (Abeih: 27 June 1853).

142. Eli explained that Raheel was "almost" a daughter while Hetty explained that Raheel was "almost Frank." Eli Smith, "Letter to Sir [Mr. Lanman]," YDS: ES Box 6: Folder 2 (Beirut: 2 November 1842); Henrietta Smith (15 March 1847).

143. Catherine M. Scholten, 99.

144. The triple-arch house, the symbol of the late nineteenth-century "modern family" in Beirut and Syria, was concentrated on the nuclear family. Michael F. Davie, ed., *La Maison Beyrouthine Aux Trois Arcs: Une Architecture Bourgeoise du Levant* (Beyruth: ALBA, 2003), 20.

145. Though not overtly stated, Robert's analysis associates the nuclear family with the "Christian home" template promoted by American and British missionaries during the nineteenth and twentieth centuries. See Robert (2008).

146. Karin Calvert, 21–43 and 60–65; John Modell and Tamara K. Hareven, "Urbanization and the Malleable Household: An Examination of Boarding and Lodging in American Families," in *The American Family in Social-Historical Perspective* (Second Edition), ed. Michael Gordon (New York: St. Martin's Press, 1978), 51–68.

147. Edward W. Hooker, 2–4.

148. Madeline C. Zilfi, 1–22.

149. Margaret L. Meriwether, 84.

150. Ibid., 87.

151. Frederick Cooper, *Colonialism in Question: Theory, Knowledge, History* (Berkeley: University of California Press, 2005), 1–31.

152. This has been highlighted by collected volumes, such as Eleanor H. Tejirian and Reeva Spector Simon (eds.); Martin Tamcke and Michael Marten (eds.); Heleen Murre-van den Berg (ed.), and this volume.

At the Center of the Debate

Bebek Seminary and the Educational Policy of the American Board
of Commissioners for Foreign Missions (1840–1860)

Cemal Yetkiner

Introduction

Incorporated in Boston in 1810, the American Board of Commissioners for Foreign Missions (ABCFM) expounded a clear educational policy. Under the dominating leadership of Rufus Anderson (1796–1880), who served as the board's corresponding secretary from 1832 to 1866, the ABCFM insisted that mission education should serve the cause of "Christianization." By the mid-nineteenth century, however, this policy was leading to strains in institutions like Bebek Seminary, which the American Board missionary Cyrus Hamlin founded in 1840. In 1860, Hamlin split with the ABCFM, disagreeing with the Board's single-minded, inflexible, and perhaps, too, unrealistic focus on Christian conversion as the centerpiece of education.

The ABCFM and its missionaries recognized education as a principal component of evangelizing and "civilizing" the "heathen." Moreover, its Prudential Committee, which was the decision- and policy-making body of the organization, considered primary, secondary, and higher educational institutions as valuable recruiting centers for native preachers and assistants who might ultimately facilitate the development of Protestant Christian churches. These preachers and assistants would also enable what Rufus Anderson called the

"Three-Self" program, which entailed developing native Protestant churches that would be "self-supporting," "self-governing," and "self-propagating." Anderson and his colleagues believed, in turn, that this institutional self-reliance would foster the development of indigenous Christianity.

Missionaries eventually questioned the educational policies and priorities of the American Board. In the Ottoman Empire, Bebek Seminary and its founder, Cyrus Hamlin, were at the center of this debate. Cyrus Hamlin (1811–1900) designed Bebek Seminary in 1840 to train native assistants and preachers of the gospel, and within a few years it became a popular institution. However, tension grew in time between Hamlin and Rufus Anderson, as the latter began to question Hamlin for ostensibly "secularizing" the seminary. This study therefore is an attempt to analyze the educational policy of the American Board in general and to explore how Cyrus Hamlin gradually came to disagree with the center's instructions and developed and implemented his own educational method at Bebek Seminary in years to come.

THE AMERICAN BOARD MISSION

The American Board of Commissioners for Foreign Missions (ABCFM), incorporated in 1810, was organized to evangelize the nations of the world.[1] It was born in a time and place when liberal and conservative strains of Protestantism were competing for the hearts and minds of college students and educated men and women in and around the New England region of the United States. During the nineteenth century, the American Board transformed itself and became the biggest and most famous missionary institution representing American Protestant doctrine abroad. The board had its origin in the desire of several students at the Andover Theological Seminary, which was founded in 1808 by an "orthodox coalition" led by Jedidiah Morse against the "Boston Harvard liberals," to "preach the pure gospel" in the "heathen world."[2] The purpose of the American Board was, according to its constitution, "to devise, adopt, and persecute, ways and means for propagating the gospel in heathen lands and among those who are destitute of the knowledge of Christianity by supporting missionaries and diffusing knowledge of the Holy Scriptures."[3] As Paul William Harris, biographer of Rufus Anderson, states, it was with the success of evangelical revivals during the Second Great Awakening (1800–1850) that mid-nineteenth-century

Protestants proclaimed their confidence in the ability of the "Holy Spirit" to "convert" sinners without elaborate preparatory measures.[4]

Enlisting in the missions of the American Board was voluntary and so was contributing to them. Building on the religious revivalism of the Second Great Awakening in the northeastern United States, the board quickly enlisted many students from Andover and beyond as "missionaries" and "missionary wives" for foreign lands. According to the laws of the board,[5] a missionary was described as "one who has been ordained a minister of gospel and has actually come under its direction."[6] Rufus Anderson, one of the strongest figures in the Prudential Committee and policy-making body of the American Board for years, suggested that missionaries should go to the heathen lands as "the forerunners of the Spirit, as pioneers, as healers. Their whole prescribed duty is to make proclamation of the truth."[7] The ABCFM rejected other religious truths, including those of Eastern Orthodox churches. Their view of "truth" therefore was an imperial one by definition.

At first, the American Board committee members and missionaries genuinely believed that they would be able to convert "sinners" and "heathens" without much resistance. However, they experienced difficulties soon after their explorations beyond the Atlantic Ocean. Missionaries went out into the world to bring people to the "true religion," and did succeed in converting some. Yet they faced tremendous disappointment when many others in the Sandwich Islands, Ceylon, East India, China, the Ottoman Empire, and elsewhere heard but rejected their message, preferring to maintain their own truths and religions. Accordingly, the American Board developed new policies and strategies to face the challenges of rejection.

THE ROLE OF EDUCATION
IN THE AMERICAN BOARD'S FOREIGN MISSION

The American Board had almost no specific educational policy at its foundation. Nonetheless, as early as 1816, the board decided to set up a school fund, stating that "it must be the ardent desire of Christian benevolence to extend the benefits of education to as many as possible, and for that purpose, to enlarge and multiply schools to the utmost extent of the means which can be obtained for supporting them."[8] Like the printing press and translation work of the missions, in time, education was seen by the board as one of the most powerful elements of missions for a principal component of evangelizing. By 1831, the board started to consider the schoolroom as one of the best places for preaching the gospel and disseminating literature.[9] The board stated in its annual report of 1833 that "schools ought everywhere to form an integral part of missionary operations; they ought to be established by missionaries, and to exist under their immediate superintendence and directions."[10]

The American Board began its educational campaign as a means of "propagating the gospel," especially in the first half of the nineteenth century. According to Rufus Anderson, schools should be more prominent at the outset than in the later stages of progress. The missionary schools, Anderson stated, formed a part of the machinery most "readily" put in motion and most "appreciated" by the heathen. He believed that if in these schools native teachers were employed, it would be possible to start schools at once and with "little danger of opposition."[11]

There was no question whether or not to have schools as part of the board's mission in the "heathen" lands since its members considered education as one of the principal elements of their evangelizing. However, the board's Prudential Committee and missionaries debated the form education should take in mission schools and the means of its delivery. According to Harris, at that time, the question was what form of mission education would be most effective in controlling indigenous clients and what form could be "bent most effectively to indigenous purposes."[12] Obviously, primary schools (usually called "common schools") were not enough for the American Board mission. Higher education was needed for the production of "native preachers, teachers, assistants, and even good wives for native helpers." As a result, the educational policy of the board preoccupied the policy-making committee, and schools became the key element in the development of native ministry in an effort to establish self-propagating and self-supporting indigenous churches in foreign lands. In short, schools for the American Board mission in various parts of the world were considered necessary for the development of Protestant Christian churches and Christians, but indispensable only for that purpose.

According to Rufus Anderson, there was a great need for native agents who would act as missionaries within their native communities in order to make the "Three-Self" programs possible. However, he was very clear about the role of education in the missionary establishments and its connection with the evangelical program. Education apart from evangelization, Anderson strongly pointed out in 1869, had "no place in the program of the Board at this or any other period in the history of the Board."[13] If native agents became too much like American missionaries through education, two of their chief attractions would be endangered, according to Anderson. First of all, their education would weaken their cultural bonds with their society, which would no longer enable them to communicate easily with their own people. Second, if they became as capable as the missionaries from the United States, they might expect similar salaries and standards of living, which ultimately would make them very expensive for either the board or the native church to support.[14] If this was the case, then they would become "vain" and "denationalized."

According to Anderson, the graduates or "unsatisfactory scholars" of these missionary schools "longed for more cultivated hearers than they found in the village, and for larger salaries than they could receive, or ought to receive, and shrank from pastorates in obscure places, among low-caste, ignorant people; and sometimes they were impatient of advice and wholesome restraint from their missionary fathers." Anderson continued, "[I]n some quarters the graduates of the missionary schools were tempted to contract business relations with the world, and thus the labor and money bestowed on their education were in great measure lost to the course."[15] Consequently, he strongly stressed his point of view that the proper test of success in mission would be not the "progress of civilization," but the "evidence of a religious life."[16]

As a result of this viewpoint, for Anderson, educational policy was the key to the native ministry and should lead to self-propagating and self-supporting native churches. Any other educational mission had no place in the board's policies and should not be practiced. This point of view was important because, as Harris points out, when students took advantage of mission schools to gain broader access to the Western world, those schools no longer served the goals established by the American Board.[17] If that happened, then the education implemented in the missionary schools would not serve the cause of the mission but would help prepare the natives intellectually and materially for the challenges of the nineteenth century. This then was opposite to the policy of the American Board. It would subvert the purpose of the mission and role of education in the "heathen world" and would financially drain the American Board and its sources of income, American donors in hundreds of churches in the States.

Anderson insisted that mission education should have a Christian core. However, as the case of Bebek Seminary shows, other members of the board opposed this idea and believed that education for its own sake had merit. As will be shown, according to many members of the board mission, schools were important because "they are to have intelligent hearers of the preached gospel, and intelligent readers of the Bible and of religious tracts."[18]

INITIAL EDUCATIONAL WORKS
OF THE AMERICAN BOARD IN THE OTTOMAN EMPIRE

The first overseas movement of "God's people," as missionaries often called themselves, of the American Board mission for the "spiritual renovation" of different societies, was to India in 1812. Later, the Ottoman Empire was chosen as a new destination for the work of the mission. Clearly, the Prudential Committee wanted the missionaries to go to the Islamic Ottoman Empire "to acquire particular information respecting the state of religion and to ascertain the most promising place for the establishment of Christian missions."[19] The prime objects of the board's mission at the very beginning were Jews in the Holy Land. However, they were also curious about Muslim Turks and Arabs and other nationalities and religious communities in the Levant, including Greeks, Copts, Armenians, and others of the "Oriental Churches" for possible future missions.[20]

In November 1819, the first two missionaries of the American Board, Pliny Fisk and Levi Parsons, were sent to explore the unknown lands of the Ottoman Empire and were instructed to establish a missionary station in Jerusalem to work primarily for the conversion of the Jews. However, the very first missionaries for the American Board appointed to the Ottoman Empire died in the field after a short tenure. Parsons began to work among the pilgrims at the Church of the Holy Sepulcher. But, later, he died on his way to Jerusalem in Alexandria, Egypt, in February 1822.[21] Eventually, Fisk, who had been busy with preparation of an Arabic and English dictionary, died while evangelizing among the Jews of Palestine in 1825.[22]

After the death of Levi Parsons, the American Board attempted to establish a missionary station in the same region but in a relatively more secure place, Beirut, Lebanon. They sent two new missionaries, William Goodell and Isaac Bird, along with their wives, Abigail Goodell and Ann Bird, in 1823.

For a time, Goodell, Bird, and their native helpers worked in Beirut without opposition from either civil or ecclesiastical authorities. They met Turks, Arabs, Maronites, Jews, and Greeks and distributed the Bible and read it to them. The study of languages spoken in the region was their prime occupation but not their only employment right after they settled in Beirut. In July 1824 the American missionaries opened their first home school in the Ottoman Empire with the instruction of Abigail Goodell and Ann Bird under the supervision of a Christian Arab teacher, Tannus Al Haddad.[23] Although it did not continue to operate after the missionaries left Beirut in the late 1820s for security reasons, the establishment of the first home school was important because it was for girls. This signaled the beginning of home or regular schools for girls in the region operated by missionaries.

In time, however, the unstable situation in the Levant, the opposition of the local church leaders to missionaries in general, and the inexperience of the missionaries made it impossible for them to stay permanently in Beirut. The missionaries recognized the Greco-Turkish warfare of 1827, which made the situation worse and threatened their safety. Once British and French consuls had left the region, Goodell, Bird, their wives, along with two native Armenian helpers, Dionysius Carabet and Gregory Wortabet, left Beirut too, and headed for Malta. There Goodell worked on a translation of the New Testament into Armeno-Turkish and completed it just before his departure to Istanbul in 1831.[24]

AT ISTANBUL

The first continuous mission of the American Board of Commissioners for Foreign Missions in the Ottoman Empire was only established in Istanbul when Reverend William Goodell arrived in the city in 1831.[25] Goodell would become famous as the founder of the Constantinople Mission, working actively in establishing numerous schools for various sects of the Ottoman millets, translating evangelical literature and the Bible into the main language used by the constituents of the Armenian Church.

Rufus Anderson, corresponding secretary for the ABCFM, visited the Ottoman Empire in 1829, and this visit indeed helped to direct attention once again to the East and the unfinished business there. After Anderson's visit to the region, two of the American Board missionaries were instructed to go to the Ottoman Empire to make an extended tour of Eastern Anatolia and Western Iran to map Armenians living there for possible future missions. In 1830, Harrison Gray Otis Dwight and Eli Smith began their famous exploratory trip, spending a year and a quarter on the road. Their observations were important for the future missions to the Armenians and were later published in a volume.[26] In 1832, Harrison G. O. Dwight joined Goodell in Istanbul together with William G. Schauffler as new missionaries appointed by the board to the region. The former targeted Armenians, the latter Jews.[27]

The missionaries would have liked to evangelize among Muslims, but this was almost impossible during their first years in the field. The Ottoman Porte allowed missionaries in, but forbade them from proselytizing among Muslims. Thus, they focused instead on those whom the American Board called the "nominally Christian populations."[28] That is why, like almost all the board's Middle Eastern missionary efforts, the Constantinople Mission was outwardly concerned not with the Muslim community but with the members of the Eastern churches, which they sought to "reform."[29] William Goodell was selected to open the station at the Ottoman capital and went to Istanbul with a special mandate to work among the Armenian people in June 1831.[30] Istanbul thus became the center of the American mission in the Ottoman Empire.

Goodell had as his first objective the social welfare of the Armenians and a plan to begin a Lancastrian school. Lancastrian schooling was a movement then led by Joseph Lancaster (1778–1838) to establish schools that would use the Monitorial System in which more-advanced students would teach less-advanced ones, enabling a small number of adult teachers to educate large numbers of students at low cost in basic and often advanced skills.[31] Yet, soon after his arrival to Pera, one of the suburbs of Istanbul where nearly all the European ambassadors resided, Goodell lost his house, furniture, library, papers, and other items in a big fire.[32] Due to the fire, Goodell moved from Pera to Buyuk Dere, from the Armenian community into the middle of the Greeks, residing together with three other American representatives in the city. Thereafter, he started to work with the Greeks of Istanbul and in November he was able to establish four Greek Lancastrian schools in and around Istanbul with 155 male students.[33]

According to the policy of the American Board outlined in the Annual Report of 1833, the program for a common school under the mission should have included "not only reading and writing, and the doctrines and duties of Christianity, but also, as far as possible, the elementary principles of arithmetic, geography, astronomy, and other sciences; endeavoring to make them subservient to the better understanding and appreciation of gospel."[34] Since schools were considered part of the evangelical mission and were church schools, religious instruction took a significant place in the curriculum. According to the instructions of the American Board to its outgoing missionaries, they were to teach "not the commandments, or the dogmas of men; but the pure doctrines of the gospel, drawn directly from the Scriptures of truth."[35] The "truth" of the Bible was to be implemented in such schools, and the Bible became the main textbook of the schools established not only in the Ottoman Empire, but in other missionary centers in the rest of the world.

Like the American schools of the same period, classes of the very first Lancastrian schools in Istanbul remained ungraded and had a relatively simple curriculum focused mainly on reading, writing, basic arithmetic, and the Bible as a text. Instructions were in local languages, either Greek or Armenian. As Robert L. Daniel states, the classrooms were very simple with little furniture, a floor covered with mats, benches for students to be seated, and if possible, desks in the American style.[36] These initial projects of Goodell also received significant aid from the charge d'affaires of the United States to Istanbul, Commodore David Porter.[37] Porter himself believed in missionaries and reported to the State Department that they were "generally men of liberal education and well-cultivated minds," and foresaw that by their Gospel work, their establishment of free schools, and their "historical and scientific researches, these countries, and mankind in general, will be much enlightened, and the United States in particular will derive…both honor and benefit."[38] In addition to these initial Lancastrian-type common schools, missionaries opened a high school at Pera in the fall of 1834 to educate and train Armenian boys and young men for their possible future missions. This high school became the first school among the Armenians of Istanbul established directly by the missionaries.[39] It ended in 1837, however. The Armenian Patriarchate regarded the school as a Protestant mission center and thus a challenge to the ecclesiastical order and hierarchy in the city. Its prohibition movement broke up the school by forbidding Armenians to go under threat of excommunication.

As mentioned earlier, one of the primary objectives of the American Board Mission in the Ottoman Empire in general, and Istanbul in particular, was to establish indigenous stations and churches that would eventually become self-propagating, self-governing, and self-supporting establishments aimed at preparing native preachers and helpers for the American Board Mission in the region. Because the board would not be able to supply enough missionary preachers, teachers, and/or helpers from the United States to meet the increasing needs of missionary activities abroad, it was deemed necessary to educate natives to take part in missionary activities in their own societies. Thus, in the mid-1830s, the American Board began to consider the establishment of higher educational institutions, such as seminaries that would work toward that particular mission. The result was the formation of establishments in foreign lands that would train a select group of native students to become preachers and teachers or at least native helpers to their own people for the American Board mission.[40] The added benefit to training native students for the mission as preachers and teachers was that it would be less costly and more efficient for the American Board. Having finished the course work in the seminaries, these native students would be ready to assist the American Board mission among their own people. Moreover, the graduates of these schools would not need to spend time learning the language or the manners and customs of their own communities as foreign missionaries had to do.

It is imperative to note that while the American Board was elaborating the idea of the establishment of seminaries in foreign lands, it clearly did not approve of a policy of educating natives in the fields of law or medicine, or training them for civil office or trade, "except so far as this will directly promote the legitimate object of the mission."[41] Once again, the board envisioned seminaries in years to come as only being "training schools" for missionary workers. The program that Cyrus Hamlin developed at Bebek Seminary in Istanbul ran counter to this policy, even though the institution did include a seminary component.

Bebek Seminary was the first of several higher educational institutions that the ABCFM established in Asia Minor. In time, the founding of schools became the main enterprise of American missionaries in the region, as they created first home, then elementary and secondary schools, and finally seminaries for the purpose of educating girls and boys in Istanbul and the wider region. Although the affirmed purpose of these schools was to develop native preachers and teachers, in time—and contrary to the original goal of Christianization—they helped also to spread American culture and an American lifestyle among the native students. As early as 1832, Commodore David Porter commented that the founding of schools among the Turks is "astonishing, perhaps among the greatest benefits which the Empire has derived from its alliance with the United States."[42]

CYRUS HAMLIN AND BEBEK SEMINARY

It was in 1839 that Cyrus Hamlin (1811–1900) from Maine joined William Goodell and the other missionaries in Istanbul as a new missionary of the American Board after having graduated from Bowdoin College and Bangor Seminary. Born into a relatively poor family in Waterford, Maine, Hamlin lost his father when he was seven months old. He, his older brother, and his two sisters grew up on a farm in Waterford helping their mother. At the age of sixteen, he started to work for a firm owned by his brother-in-law as an apprentice silversmith in Portland. In Portland, Hamlin started participating in activities at a Congregational church. Later, it was the members of this church who convinced him to continue his education, a decision that ultimately led him to the ministry.

Having finished Bowdoin College in Brunswick, Hamlin entered Bangor Theological Seminary in 1834.[43] During his third year in the seminary, Hamlin decided to apply to the American Board for missionary service in foreign lands, naming China as his first choice and Africa his second.[44] The board, however, appointed him to Istanbul for mission work in education. Shortly before he moved to Istanbul for missionary work, he married Henrietta Jackson from Dorset, Vermont. Two months later they sailed for the Ottoman Empire and arrived in Istanbul in January 1839. By the time of his arrival in the city, the number of missionaries of the American Board in Istanbul had reached four: Goodell, Dwight, Schauffler, and Hamlin, along with their wives, who also served the mission in various capacities. Although not formally labeled "missionaries," missionary wives were expected to assist their husbands by running model homes, teaching at home schools, and carrying the Bible to homes; thus they were often called "Bible women." There were also five native male helpers. In Istanbul, Hamlin became the leader of Bebek Seminary, where young men were trained for the Christian ministry.

Cyrus Hamlin designed the Bebek Seminary to train native assistants and preachers of the gospel, and it was opened in November 1840.[45] All the missionaries agreed that educating Armenians for such work was of the highest importance. The 1844 annual report of the ABCFM stated that the Bebek Seminary would be a "liberal institution." Students would also receive education in other fields than the natural sciences, like ancient and modern history, especially ecclesiastical, intellectual, and moral philosophy, and theology, which was to be gained by the constant study of the Bible, sermons, lectures, and textbooks. Moreover, according to the missionaries, students would be taught "not only what the facts and truths of the Bible are," but "how to use them in the statement and enforcement of truth and in opposition to error."[46] This meant that the students educated in Bebek Seminary would receive, more or less, the same education as that taught in theological seminaries in the United States. They would not, however, be given a religious education only. Students were also taught mathematics, physics, and chemistry. Instruction was mainly in the Armenian language. Although the American Board began to question the policy of "English study" in seminaries and high schools as early as the mid-1830s, upon finding that intense English language study was making the natives "foreign in their habits, sympathies, and manners," the policy at Bebek Seminary in the early 1840s was to teach in the English language, as it was the "instrument" for acquiring knowledge, whereas Armenian would be the language for passing it on.[47]

After visiting the Ottoman Empire a second time, in 1844, Anderson gave his account of Bebek Seminary as well as his opinion concerning the work that the board mission was doing in this institution in his report to the Prudential Committee at Boston. In this report, Anderson stated that "the object of the institution (Bebek Seminary)—and the only object that will justify the expense—is to raise up native pastors and evangelists." He noted that "it will still come to pass, owing to the imperfection of human beings and plans that but a part of our beneficiaries will in fact enter it; yet many who do not make preachers will make school-teachers, and we shall be more likely to create such school-teachers, on this plan, as it will be worth while to employ, than if our seminary had an inferior and less exclusive aim."[48]

For those educated in such an institution, Anderson outlined his point of view and stated that "none are to be received on the charity foundation, except with reference to the ministry, and none but those who give good evidence of piety and talents." He also stressed the need of a boarding system for students and signified that day-scholars, extraordinary cases excepted, were not to be received, as they would tend to weaken the religious influence exerted on the boarding pupils. In addition to these remarks, Anderson also noted in his report that in view of the present exigencies of the mission, it was not necessary for all the "theological students to be required to go through the entire course of study." He assured that many of the evangelists now needed, and some who were actually employed, would be greatly benefited by spending six months or a year in the seminary, in theological or other studies. He also did not advocate the policy of English language study in the seminary and advised that students should not have any immediate connection with English.[49] As mentioned earlier, Anderson, and many others in the American Board Mission, considered the goal behind the policy of opening seminaries and institutions of higher education in foreign lands to be to serve the evangelical movement by producing native preachers, teachers, and obviously assistants to a larger mission of the American Board.

That is why Anderson and others strongly suggested that "education apart from evangelization had no place in the program of the Board at any time in the history of the Board."[50] He ended his remarks on Bebek Seminary by advising, "[S]till the chief danger to which this young and promising institution is exposed (in common with all other institutions) is that of losing its spirituality in the eager pursuit of literature and science; and it will be well if the friends of missions can be induced to remember it in their prayers."[51] All this can be interpreted as an important message to Hamlin and his contradictory practices at the seminary which were already underway.

Most of the students at Bebek Seminary were very poor, according to Hamlin. This was because their families had adopted openly "evangelical principles" to the "great injury" of their worldly affairs and declared themselves as Armenian Protestants. After the official separation in 1846, many excommunications were issued against Protestant Armenian families by the Apostolic Armenian Church of Istanbul, and local merchants and trade guilds excluded them from business or trade. All of these factors ultimately increased the poverty of Armenian Protestants in the city. While Hamlin was busy with the seminary, he was also involved with measures that focused on improving the economic situation of the students and, if possible, their families, through philanthropic works.

Some of the seminary students were young men of eighteen to twenty years old. According to Hamlin, students were "polite" and "deferential" since these qualities were "natural" to the "Oriental." In Hamlin's narrative, many of them needed training, discipline, instruction, and the development of a good conscience before "God" and "man." Hamlin believed that very few of them had "personal religion" and they had not "put on Christ." Most of them were also married.[52] In addition to financial difficulties of the students, the early years of the seminary were characterized by struggles with the Armenian patriarchal anathemas and boycotts against the seminary. The *Missionary Herald*, a monthly magazine of the American Board in the United States, published numerous letters sent by Hamlin during the 1840s on the conflict with the patriarch.

While busy fighting the opposition against him and the seminary, Hamlin worked to solve the financial problems of the students enrolled in the seminary. Rather than asking for money from the American Board, Hamlin, with help from some Englishmen, found his own solution. He added a small industrial workshop in the basement of the seminary which manufactured stoves, stovepipes, and other metal implements. This way, students were able to earn money through the workshop to buy clothes and to better support themselves.[53] Thus, with Hamlin's help, shortly after its establishment, the seminary became a self-supporting institution. According to Paul William Harris, the students learned to be more industrious and self-denying.[54] In addition to the small workshop in the basement of the seminary, Hamlin later established a steam-powered flour mill. The mill sent shiploads of wheat and baked hundreds of thousands of loaves of bread for the English troops in the channels of the Crimea during the Crimean War (1853–1856) and to the hospital at Uskudar where the wounded soldiers were treated and nursed by Florence Nightingale and others.[55] Baking bread was not the only service Hamlin provided to the British army in Istanbul. As the war went on, he came up with the idea of starting a laundry business for the British army, designing and building washing machines using old beer barrels. Like the bakery business in Istanbul, the laundry business also made him a great deal of money in a short period of time, which he used for the mission for years to come.[56]

Even though part of the profits from the bakery supported Bebek Seminary and its students, and a surplus of twenty-five thousand dollars was used to build thirteen churches for the American Board in many parts of the Ottoman Empire, the board did not approve of Hamlin's works in the secular world.[57] Hamlin's secular activities conflicted with the mission of the seminary, which was to produce native preachers for the purpose of evangelizing to the "heathen." In time, his business dealings raised the question of what type of education the missionaries ought to provide in these institutions, such as Bebek Seminary.[58] According to many members of the American Board, their organization had been established primarily for the purpose of "propagating the Gospel in the heathen lands." Thus Hamlin's activities forced them to ask the question, "was it necessary and proper to engage in secular philanthropic ventures as well?"[59] In particular, Henry Van Lennep, the American Board's missionary who was posted in Istanbul to teach biblical literature at the seminary, criticized his colleague's involvement with the secular world. According to Van Lennep, Hamlin was "Americanizing" the students. Through his philanthropic works in and for the seminary, Hamlin had already incorporated manual labor into seminary life. If things continued like this, the seminary would become an industrial enterprise, Van Lennep stated. According to him, these developments at the seminary diverted students from their religious studies and worsened the "money making" and "complaining spirit" of the students by forcing them to become obsessed with their financial situation.[60] More conservative members of the board, also disapproving of Hamlin's activities, turned to the Bible and observed: "We do not find…that Christ or his Apostles made any inventions or discoveries in the arts and sciences, or sought directly to promote literature." They stated that the "American Board could not be a society for promoting civilization, or literature, or the arts."[61]

Although Rufus Anderson and many of the missionaries became concerned that Hamlin was secularizing the seminary, Hamlin defended his policies at Bebek Seminary by stating that the "ability to engage in some secular pursuit, the conscious power to live by one's own exertions, is a necessary safeguard to the purity of the native ministry. He who enters the ministry because there is nothing else for him to do will hardly be a very spiritually minded worker."[62] In a paper he delivered in a conference in Istanbul in 1855, Hamlin outlined his perspective on the education of a native ministry and the role of the Seminary at Bebek. According to Hamlin, for the American Board's missionary work to be carried out, a second group of preachers would be required, and training them would be the work of the seminary at Bebek. He indicated that the culture of these students should be of a "different and higher nature."[63] He strongly supported the study of the English language at the seminary since it would allow opening all its stores of biblical literature to the minds of students. Others joined Hamlin and stated that "whatever conduces to human happiness and welfare, or is adapted to elevate men, intellectually or socially as well as morally, is Christian in its character, and deserving the attention of a Christian missionary." Reverend David Greene, secretary of the American Board from 1832 to 1848, had already been leading the so-called liberal ideas with what he had previously stated on the mission and the role of education. According to Greene, "Christianity did not of itself teach the native to make an alphabet, invent a press or establish a system of schools. It did not teach him to construct a plough, make an axe or weave a garment. Nor could one depend upon intercourse with more cultivated nations to furnish the 'unenlightened communities' of the earth with all the means which they need for improving their intellectual and social condition." He declared that without cultural and economic growth in native societies, Christianity could accomplish little. According to him, the task of the missionary was to help natives learn to use agricultural utensils, to construct comfortable dwellings, to make decent clothes, to teach literature and science, and to promote "all the useful arts and invention."[64]

Even though this was indeed what Hamlin was trying to achieve at the seminary, the American Board was increasingly dissatisfied with Bebek Seminary. In reality, the board's concerns about secularization were well founded. After graduation from the seminary, many students chose to pursue employment opportunities outside mission service making many of the missionaries unhappy that the seminary was failing to meet the need for native agents. Moreover, enrollment began to decline. For instance, in 1848, the number of students in the seminary at Bebek dropped from forty-seven to twenty-eight. Though the reasons for that dramatic decrease were varied (some of the students had been dismissed for incompetence and others could not bear the financial burden of education anymore), the main reason was that many students had been forced to withdraw in order to seek employment in different fields in order to support themselves.[65]

In time, tension grew between Hamlin and Rufus Anderson and other missionaries over the seminary at Bebek and its role in the American Board.

Because of differences on this issue, Hamlin left Istanbul for some time and traveled throughout Europe and America. Finally, in 1860, he left the American Board permanently, feeling that he could not agree with its educational methods. Instead, he dedicated himself to the establishment of a college on the American pattern, which he hoped would serve as "a channel through which to irrigate the parched fields of the ancient Churches, and perhaps even the corrupt Turkish society, with the life giving streams of English Christian culture."[66] The school he founded was Robert College, the forerunner of today's Boğaziçi University. The establishment of Robert College became Hamlin's most important endeavor. Christopher Robert, a wealthy merchant and philanthropist in New York City, who shared the same views as Hamlin on religion and education, wanted to fund an educational institution. Hamlin's collaborations with Robert led to the foundation of a higher educational center. When Robert College opened in 1863 there were five teachers and four students.[67] Hamlin served seventeen years as president of the college.

CONCLUSION

In 1860, the seminary at Bebek was closed in Istanbul and moved to inner Asia Minor, in Merzifon, where it was transformed into a theological seminary.[68] As indicated earlier, the Bebek Seminary was originally designed with the purpose and the anticipation of training native (initially and, mostly, Armenian) assistants and preachers of the gospel for the greater mission. However, as a result of Hamlin's engagement with philanthropic endeavors and the so-called secular world on the one hand and Anderson's persistent emphasis on the role of Christianization in education on the other, the institution quickly found itself at the heart of a critical debate between the American Board's ideological center in Boston and its mission periphery in Istanbul.

The center, represented primarily by Rufus Anderson and others, insisted on the point of view that the proper test of success in mission was not the progress of civilization, but the evidence of a religious life. Hamlin, on the other hand, understood the conscious employment of some degree of secular pursuit as a necessary safeguard to the purity and success of native ministry in the periphery. That is why he split with the American Board after a short tenure in order to establish a college in Istanbul on that particular pattern.

After debates over its role, the seminary at Bebek had to be moved into Asia Minor to better serve the Protestant Mission of the American Board, due to the center's emphasis on Christianization in education.[69] The Bebek Seminary experience became a lesson to the American Board, which decided after 1860 to refrain from opening seminaries in cities like Istanbul where the attractions of cosmopolitan urban life could distract students from religious instruction. Henceforth, the board preferred instead to open seminaries in small towns within Asia Minor, such as Merzifon, Harput, Mardin, and Maras.

Notes

1. James L. Barton, "Our Evangelistic Policy," *Envelope Series* 9:3 (October 1906): 3.
2. Sydney E. Ahlstrom, *A Religious History of the American People*, 2d ed. (New Haven: Yale University Press, 2004), 415.
3. Henry Otis Dwight, Allen Tupper, and Edwin Munsell Bliss, *The Encyclopedia of Missions: Descriptive, Historical, Biographical, Statistical*, 2d ed. (New York: Funk and Wagnalls Company, 1910), 26.
4. Paul William Harris, *Nothing but Christ: Rufus Anderson and the Ideology of Protestant Foreign Missions* (Oxford: Oxford University Press, 1999), 3.
5. For the American Board's constitution, laws, and regulations, see *Constitution, Laws and Regulations of the American Board of Commissioners for Foreign Missions* (Boston: Crocker & Brewster, 1835).
6. For more information on American Board missionary candidates and their appointment, see *Manual for Missionary Candidates and for Appointed Missionaries before Entering Their Fields* (Boston: The Board, 1853; revised edition, Boston: Beacon Press, 1887).
7. Rufus Anderson, *Missionary Paper: Promised Advent of the Spirit for the World's Conversion* (Boston: Crocker & Brewster, 1841), 13.
8. *Annual Report of the American Board of Commissioners for Foreign Missions* (1821), 133.
9. Marion A. Nosser, "The Educational Policies of the American Board of Commissioners for Foreign Missions in Turkey; 1823–1923" (master's thesis, University of Chicago, 1924), 20.
10. *Annual Report of the ABCFM* (1833), 137.
11. Rufus Anderson, *Memorial Volume of the First Fifty Years of the American Board of Commissioners for Foreign Missions* (Boston: Missionary House, 1861), 304.
12. Harris, *Nothing but Christ*, 39.

13. Rufus Anderson, *Foreign Missions: Their Relations and Claims* (New York: Charles Scribner and Company, 1869), 328.

14. Harris, *Nothing but Christ*, 39.

15. David H. Finnie, *Pioneers East: The Early American Experience in the Middle East* (Cambridge, MA: Harvard University Press, 1967), 122.

16. Anderson, *Foreign Missions*, 118.

17. Harris, *Nothing but Christ*, 40.

18. *Annual Report of the ABCFM* (1833), 23, quoted in Nosser, "The Educational Policies of the American Board," 24.

19. Ussama Makdisi, "Refusing Comparison: How Middle Eastern Violence is Narrated by the American Missionary" (paper presented at a conference in honor of Professor Robert L. Tignor, "The Empire and Its Discontents," Department of History, Princeton University, September 16–17, 2005), 20. For more about Andover Theological Seminary, see Leonard Woods, *History of the Andover Theological Seminary* (Boston: James R. Osgood and Company, 1885).

20. Clifton Jackson Phillips, *Protestant America and the Pagan World: The First Half Century of the American Board of Commissioners for Foreign Missions, 1810–1860* (Cambridge, MA: Harvard University Press, 1969), 136.

21. "Palestine Mission: Letter from Mr. Fisk to the Corresponding Secretary, Respecting the Sickness and Death of Mr. Parson," *The Missionary Herald* 18:7 (July 1822): 214.

22. Joseph Tracy, *History of the American Board of Commissioners for Foreign Missions: Compiled Chiefly from the Published and Unpublished Documents of the Board*, 2nd ed. (New York: M. W. Dodd, 1842), 164.

23. Uygur Kocabaşoğlu, *Kendi Belgeleriyle Anadolu'daki Amerika: 19. Yüzyılda Osmanlı İmparatorluğu'ndaki Amerikan Misyoner Okulları* (İstanbul: Arba Yayınları, 1989), 35.

24. For more on Goodell's memoirs in Beirut and Malta, see E. D. G. Prime, *Forty Years in the Turkish Empire; or Memoirs of Rev. William Goodell, D.D., Late Missionary of the A. B. C. F. M. at Constantinople* (New York: Robert Carter and Brothers, 1876), 71–111.

25. Sydney Nettleton Fisher, "Two Centuries of American Interest in Turkey," in *A Festschrift for Frederick B. Artz*, ed. David H. Pinkney and Theodore Ropp (Durham, NC: Duke University Press, 1964), 117.

26. For their trip and observation, see Eli Smith, *Researches (of the Rev. E. Smith and Rev. H. G. O. Dwight) In Armenia* (Boston: Crocker and Brewster, 1833).

27. "Mission to Constantinople," *New York Observer* 11, no. 40, whole no. 543, 05 October 1833.

28. *Historical Sketch of the Missions of the American Board of Commissioners for Foreign Missions, in European Turkey, Asia Minor, and Armenia* (New York: John A. Gray, Printer Stereotyper, and Binder, 1861), 12.

29. James A. Field Jr., *America and the Mediterranean World 1776–1882* (New Jersey: Princeton University Press, 1969), 177.

30. Heleen Murre-van den Berg, "Why Protestant Churches? The American Board and the Eastern Churches: Mission Among 'Nominal' Christians (1820–70)," in *Missions and Missionaries*, ed. Pieter N. Holtrop and Hugh McLeod (Rochester, NY: Boydell Press, 2000), 98–111.

31. For more on Lancastrian schools, see Carl F. Kaestle, ed., *Joseph Lancaster and the Monitorial School Movement: A Documentary History* (New York: Teachers College Press, 1973). Paul D. Sedra, "John Lieder and His Mission in Egypt: The Evangelical Ethos at Work among Nineteenth-Century Copts," *The Journal of Religious History*, 28:3 (2004): 219–239.

32. "Constantinople: Missions to Greeks and Armenians," *Annual Report of the ABCFM* (1832), 64–69. *RABCFM, Read at the 23rd Annual Meeting*, which was held in the City of New York, October 3, 4, and 5, 1832 (Boston: Crocker and Brewster, 1832).

33. *Annual report of ABCFM* (1832), 65.

34. *Annual Report of the ABCFM* (1833), 23, quoted in Nosser, "The Educational Policies of the American Board," 28.

35. Ibid., 29.

36. Robert L. Daniel, "American Influences in the Near East before 1861," *American Quarterly* 16:1 (Spring 1964): 79.

37. Tracy, *History of the American Board*, 248.

38. Dispatches, Turkey: Porter to Sec. of State, 6 August 1835, quoted in Field, *America and the Mediterranean World*, 184.

39. Leon Arpee, *The Armenian Awakening: A History of the Armenian Church, 1820–1860* (Chicago: University of Chicago Press, 1909), 97.

40. *Annual report of ABCFM* (1835), 25.

41. *Annual Report of the ABCFM* (1837), 23, quoted in Nosser, "The Educational Policies of the American Board," 31.

42. Daniel, "American Influences in the Near East before 1861," 80.

43. Malcolm P. Stevens and Marcia R. Stevens, "A College on the Bosporus," *Saudi Aramco World* 35:2 (March/April 1984): 16–21.

44. A. R. Thain, "Cyrus Hamlin D.D., LL.D. Missionary, Statesman, Inventor: A Life Sketch," *Envelope Series* 10:2 (July 1907): 9–10.

45. William E. Strong, *The Story of the American Board: An Account of the First Hundred Years of the American Board of Commissioners for Foreign Missions* (Boston: Pilgrim Press, 1910), 199.

46. "Western Asia: Mission to the Armenians," *Annual Report of ABCFM* (1844), 98–117. *RABCFM, Presented at the 35th Annual Meeting*, which was held in Worcester, Massachusetts, September 10–13, 1844 (Boston: T. R. Marvin, 1844).

47. Nosser, "The Educational Policies of the American Board," 34–35.

48. Rufus Anderson, *Report to the Prudential Committee of a Visit to the Missions in the Levant* (Boston: T. R. Marvin, 1844), 20.

49. Ibid.

50. Rufus Anderson, *Foreign Missions*, 328.

51. Anderson, *Report to the Prudential Committee*, 20.

52. Cyrus Hamlin, *My Life and Times*, 5th ed. (Boston: The Pilgrim Press Chicago, 1893), 250.

53. Thain, "Cyrus Hamlin D.D., LL.D. Missionary, Statesman, Inventor: A Life Sketch," 13.

54. Harris, *Nothing but Christ*, 129.

55. David Brewer Eddy, *What Next in Turkey: Glimpses of the American Board's Work in the Near East* (Boston: The American Board, 1913), 66–67.

56. Stevens and Stevens, "A College on the Bosporus."

57. Thain, "Cyrus Hamlin D.D., LL.D. Missionary, Statesman, Inventor: A Life Sketch," 20.

58. Field, *America and the Mediterranean World*, 353–354.

59. Daniel, "American Influences in the Near East before 1861," 82.

60. Henry J. Van Lennep to Anderson (Tokat, 9/2/1857), ABC: 16.7.1, V. 15, quoted in Harris, *Nothing but Christ*, 130.

61. *Annual Report of the ABCFM* (1856), 64, quoted in Daniel, "American Influences in the Near East before 1861," 82–83.

62. Cyrus Hamlin, *Among the Turks* (New York: Robert Carter and Brothers, 1881), 214.

63. Cyrus Hamlin, "Education of a Native Ministry," in *Minutes of a Conference of Missionaries held at Constantinople, in November, 1855, on Occasion of the Visit of one of the Secretaries of the American Board of Commissioners for Foreign Missions* (Boston: T. R. Marvin, 1856), 12–13.

64. Rev. David Greene, "The Promotion of Intellectual Cultivation and the Arts of Civilized Life in Connection with Christian Missions," *Annual Report of the ABCFM* (1842), 69–75, quoted in Daniel, "American Influences in the Near East before 1861," 83.

65. "Western Asia: Mission to the Armenians," *Annual Report of the ABCFM* (1849), 108–116. *RABCFM, Presented at the 40th Annual Meeting*, which was held in Pittsfield, Massachusetts, Sept. 11–14, 1849 (Boston: T. R. Marvin, 1849).

66. Julius Richter, *A History of Protestant Mission in the Near East* (New York: Fleming H. Revell Comp., 1910), 128–129.

67. Kocabaşoğlu, *Kendi Belgeleriyle Anadolu'daki Amerika*, 179.

68. Field, *America and the Mediterranean World*, 355.

69. Kocabaşoğlu, *Kendi Belgeleriyle Anadolu'daki Amerika*, 84–85.

From Religious to American Proselytism

Mary Mills Patrick and the "Sanctification of the Intellect"

Carolyn Goffman

Introduction: An American Woman Missionary and the New Secularist Project

In the summer of 1871, Mary Mills Patrick said a tearful goodbye to her family in Iowa and set out for Eastern Anatolia to serve as a missionary to the Armenians. She was a twenty-one-year-old American Board of Commissioners for Foreign Missions (ABCFM) recruit whose task it would be to proselytize in the homes of Armenian women and to assist in establishing schools for girls. The posting was arduous, and in her early years, Patrick was disappointed to witness little improvement in Armenian women's lives. She confessed to feeling a great sense of relief when, four years later, she was transferred to the Constantinople Home School. Patrick would remain in Istanbul for almost forty years, leading her school through a separation from the ABCFM and transforming it into the influential American College for Girls. In the process she forged a new style of proselytism, one in which feminist and nationalist goals supplanted Protestant conversion.

Patrick's strong leadership and her progressive educational initiatives at the Constantinople Home School anticipated the missionary movement's own loosening of evangelical purpose and its heightened sensitivity to the needs of its target communities. At the same time, her personal development as a career academic mirrored changes in women's education in both the United States and the Ottoman Empire. During her long residence in the Ottoman capital, Patrick reconstructed her identity as an American woman missionary educator. Her self-definition as Christian, teacher, and scholar evolved from a young and earnest evangelist into a politically astute academic administrator. She changed the Constantinople Home School, which provided a high school education, into the American College for Girls, a degree-granting institution with academic standards comparable to those of American colleges. In 1908 Patrick increased her school's autonomy when she severed the college's ties with the American Board and in the process finally rejected the unavailing task of recruiting Ottoman souls for Christ. In its place, she substituted the far more gratifying campaign of winning the minds, and she hoped the hearts, of young Ottoman women. Patrick saw the American College for Girls as an educational initiative that would be integral to Ottoman progressive social and political movements, effectively shifting the college's center of gravity from Boston to Istanbul.

Patrick's restructuring of the college was a conscious incursion into nationalist rhetoric reverberating in Ottoman realms during the late nineteenth and early twentieth centuries. Taking advantage of the desire of progressive Ottomans to advance the role of women, Patrick maintained that her college was a crucial component of the nation-building project. But even though she seemed to be moving away from missionary goals, in fact Patrick's ideas were also in step with changes in American missionary practice in the Ottoman Empire. Some female missionary educators were finding it expedient to abandon aggressive Protestant evangelism, and instead were redirecting their unabated missionary fervor to the cause of women's education. While Boston did not always welcome such changes, Patrick forged ahead with her new vision for the college. More confident in her leadership, she no longer felt compelled to make the Gospel the school's pedagogical center. She promoted instead a new educational approach that was, in her words, "non-sectarian."

This term, *non-sectarian*, served two highly useful purposes for Protestant educators. First, it asserted the hegemony of American Protestant practice, in the form of American schools, without openly tying itself to the project of conversion. Second, it allowed non-Protestants to enter the school with less fear of proselytism. Parents could send their daughters to the school without relinquishing control over their faith; indeed, Patrick's stance was to celebrate religious diversity among her students. Though Patrick's new educational project resembled the old in much of its practice and rhetoric, and it remained firmly grounded in the American Protestant worldview, its professed purpose was starkly different. In place of religious conversion, Patrick's aim was secular education in the universal causes of feminism and nationalism.

This paper will trace Patrick's evolution in Istanbul from her early years as an earnest evangelist to her final role as powerful president of the American College for Girls in the new Republic of Turkey. Several important convictions underlay Patrick's evolution. First was her belief in women's education as a vital precondition for a healthy nation. Second was the belief that the American model of secular nationalism was the ideal one for Turkey's own emerging nationalism. And last, but hardly least, was her practical concern for the continued existence of her college during the end of the empire and the emergence of the new Turkish Republic. Indeed, the necessity of adapting to outward social and political circumstances to ensure the preservation of the school was an important reason behind Patrick's decision to move away from religious proselytism. She sought to open the door to friendlier relations with the empire's elite Ottoman Muslim population, which was naturally suspicious of aggressive attempts at conversion. By the early twentieth century, Patrick's success and the popularity of the college encouraged her to move even further from missionary practice, and she launched a successful campaign to garner independent financial support for the American College for Girls.

As college president, Patrick labored diligently, even at the risk of her health, to create an educational environment that emphasized its American identity but did not threaten students' religious faiths. Patrick was fortunate in her timing: Progressive Ottomans were actively seeking education for their daughters and the college was ideally positioned to meet their needs.[1] While Patrick saw the college's "non-sectarian" philosophy as instrumental in attracting the Ottoman elite to her school, at the same time she exploited the political mood of the moment, wholeheartedly supporting first the Young Turks (1908–1909) and later the new Turkish Republic (1923). She also weathered less hospitable regimes, and at times quietly waited for more promising opportunities to promote her school.[2] In her untiring advocacy of the college in reports, letters, books, and college documents, Patrick demonstrated an awareness of political realities tempered with a stubborn allegiance to a worldview still suffused with her American Protestant missionary origins. Thus Patrick, like other American missionary educators, both promoted the Protestant worldview and accommodated the nationalist and feminist agendas of progressive Ottoman thought. She turned the proselytizing mission into one that sought, to use the word of fellow ABCFM missionary Robert Chambers, a "sanctification" of the intellect that would subsume, but not deny, the spirit.[3]

Patrick's late nineteenth-century move to secularism had its origins in the antebellum evangelistic and millenarian fervor that emerged in reaction to early nineteenth-century liberal Protestant practices. Any idea of "secularism" was decidedly absent from this early view, and the opportunities for women in missionary work were in most cases strictly limited to the role of the wife of a male missionary. After the American Civil War, however, the role of women in foreign missions expanded rapidly.[4] Women's missionary activity paralleled other changes in the United States: Protestant congregations were becoming more socially conscious, Americans' sense of manifest destiny was seeking frontiers beyond North America, and women had developed a new sense of agency during the Civil War.[5] When Rufus Anderson, longtime foreign secretary of the American Board of Commissioners for Foreign Missions (ABCFM), resigned in 1866, the new secretary, N. G. Clark, invited Congregationalist women in Boston to form a female auxiliary, the Woman's Board of Missions. At the same time, the ABCFM began at last to recruit single women to missionary posts in the field. These two events, the founding of a women's missionary organization at home and the opening of new opportunities for unmarried women to participate in worldwide missionary work, marked the beginning of a period of enormous growth in women's missionary activity and set the stage for Mary Mills Patrick's entry to the field. The Woman's Board of Missions (WBM), which would make the Constantinople Home one of its first projects, assembled for the first time in 1868, three years before Patrick set off for Anatolia.

The WBM conceived the Constantinople Home as a three-fold project intended to change the role of local Armenian women in the family and the community through Protestant evangelism, literacy training, improved domestic skills, and medical instruction and service, all directed toward women by women. The hoped-for result was the eventual conversion not only of Ottoman Armenians to Protestant Christianity, but also, through the influence of missionary good works and newly converted women, of all the peoples of the Ottoman territories. The succeeding two decades, however, saw a definitive shift in the Home's agenda. The medical component, originally intended to include at least one female physician, never got off the ground, and the mission center likewise never came into being. Instead, the educational part of the venture quickly became the centerpiece of the Home.

This lopsided growth was a source of continued distress to the WBM in Boston, and it reflected an important difference in missionary goals between the women in Constantinople and their supporters in the United States. The Constantinople Home was in the process of changing its character, diverging from its founders' idealistic hope of mass Ottoman conversions. From dedicated yet amateur religious proselytizers, these women missionary teachers increasingly saw themselves as, above all, professional educators. During the 1870s and 1880s, these women teachers came to view the educating, or "civilizing," nature of their mission to women in the Ottoman Empire as their foremost concern, even if it meant diminishing their own efforts at Protestant proselytism. Mary Mills Patrick was instrumental in this newly charged vision, which extended not only to an expanded idea of what an educator of women could accomplish in the Ottoman Empire, but also to a greater sense of professional possibilities for American women.

Three rhetorical "moments" serve to illustrate Patrick's evolution from evangelist to secularist and the increasing distance she put between the Missionary Board and her job as professional educator. The first "moment" occurred in 1883, during her early stint at the Constantinople Home School, where the young Patrick threw herself into the mission of Protestant Christian conversion with an intensity that affected her physically and emotionally, and resulted in severe migraines. Although Patrick herself wrote little about this time, she made a strikingly evangelistic appearance in one Bulgarian student's diary. The student's narrative depicted a terrifyingly earnest young teacher who implored her young charges both to embrace Jesus and to lead a life of "purity." In time, however, Patrick evidently found that admonishing innocent young girls to eschew sin was an unsatisfactory pedagogy, and her teacher's persona soon changed dramatically. When after 1889 the Home School's increasing emphasis on academics allowed her to focus on scholarship rather than to compel students to seek Christ, she quickly bloomed in the role of teacher and principal.

Later, in her first year as president of the newly chartered and still intimately small American College for Girls, Patrick immediately cultivated a more secular stance, one reflected in a second rhetorical "moment" that appeared in her 1890 Annual Report to the Woman's Board of Missions in Boston. As did other missionary reports on the Ottoman Empire, Patrick's documented the religious diversity among the students; however, to the dismay of some board members in Boston, she barely acknowledged the evangelical project of conversion. While Patrick had once believed in imminent mass conversions throughout the Near East, she now seemed suddenly aware of the social and political realities of the Ottoman Empire occurring outside the school walls. If her students were unlikely to become Protestant Christians, she reasoned, perhaps another kind of conversion was within her grasp. In a period when Ottoman intellectuals and activists were increasingly preoccupied with the question of how to build a nation, Patrick firmly believed that the American Protestant model, in which the concepts of "American" and "Protestant" were essentially interchangeable, was an attainable ideal in the Ottoman Empire. Patrick's 1890 Annual Report displayed her confident expectation that the college, in concert with other progressive movements, would propel the Ottoman Empire into democratic nationhood.

The Young Turk Revolution of 1908 further stirred Patrick's hopes for an Ottoman nation in which women would be full citizens. In a third rhetorical "moment" in which she rallied student rhetoric to the Young Turk cause, Patrick optimistically interpreted the 1908 Revolution as a harbinger of positive social, political, and educational changes not only for the Ottoman Empire but also for the college. Indeed, the familiar missionary trope of the Ottoman Empire's impressively diverse population reinforced the idea that the American concept of "nation" was an appropriate model for the nationalist movement in the Ottoman Empire. Unfortunately, the subsequent counterrevolution, Balkan War, and the First World War delayed those hopes, but by 1924 Patrick felt that the ascendant Turkish Republic at last augured a democratic state in which women would participate fully. A decade later, in retirement in California, Patrick wrote a final postscript to her career in which she enthusiastically described the emerging Turkish Republic and envisioned a permanent status for the college in the new nation.[6] Patrick believed that the Turkish nation was destined to follow the American model, and the American College for Girls would be an integral part of Turkey's educational system and a positive force in creating an enduring sense of Turkish nationalism.

THE FIRST RHETORICAL MOMENT:
THE ARDENT EVANGELIST AND THE CONSTANTINOPLE HOME SCHOOL

The Constantinople Home School opened in 1871 with three students and the goal of promoting "Christian culture" through a three-fold project of missionary work, academics, and a medical department. The Woman's Board of Missions (WBM) planned not only to operate a city mission and a school, but also to set up a "lady physician" who, as described by a board member a few years later, would find a "great opening" to the "houses of all women, particularly those of higher rank."[7] However, just as Cyrus Hamlin had reshaped his Bebek Seminary to meet certain needs of his Armenian proselytes and thus displeased the ABCFM,[8] so did the Constantinople Home find itself adjusting to its Ottoman students in ways that worried the Woman's Board of Missions. Problems began with the first principal, Julia A. Rappeleye, an 1855 graduate of Oberlin College who had taught at the Oakland Seminary in California for several years. Rappeleye was by all accounts devoted to her students, and even spent her holidays "visiting the parents of her pupils."[9] Her reportedly "high-spirited" and "impetuous" personality,[10] however, caused some friction between her and the ABCFM men in Istanbul; moreover, the ABCFM had appropriated funds that the women had expected to use in establishing a "physician's room and dispensary."[11] The WBM argued that the failure to establish the medical department was a "violation of good faith" to the American women's groups who had "come forward so generously with their gifts,"[12] and Rappeleye resigned in frustration from the Home School and was replaced by Catherine (Kate) Pond Williams in 1875.

Williams, a Mount Holyoke graduate and widow of an ABCFM missionary,[13] served as principal until 1883. Her goal was to expand "the course of study" until it embraced "nearly everything that is considered important in Young Ladies Seminaries in America."[14] When Mary Mills Patrick arrived in Istanbul in 1875, Armenian (which Patrick spoke well) was still the school's language of instruction. The board, however, wanted to encourage other linguistic groups to send their daughters to the Constantinople Home, and it determined that "the English language" would be "so thoroughly taught that it may be made the medium of instruction in advanced studies."[15] This policy had another practical benefit: It eliminated the need to provide a year or more of language instruction for new teachers from America.

In 1879 the first Bulgarian student arrived at the school; by 1881 twenty Bulgarians were in residence.[16] In this multi-ethno-linguistic environment, Williams insisted on "family arrangements" at the Home, with the principal as its "recognized head." Teachers lived with and closely supervised the boarding students and, like the students, were required to attend prayer, chapel, and Sunday services. The American teachers were trained missionaries who subjected their students to an unremitting and intimate barrage of proselytizing. In December 1882 a Bulgarian student, Penka Racheva, began a journal that demonstrates much about Patrick's teaching methods and the intensely personal relations between teachers and students.[17] Penka noted that she received the journal, "beautifully bound" in "red leather and gold," and inscribed "with the love of M. M. Patrick and C. H. Hamlin,"[18] as a Christmas present in 1882.[19] Over the next six months, Penka's documentation of her spiritual struggles reveals the concentrated pressure on the students to embrace evangelical Christian belief. Penka recorded daily reminders to "love Christ with my whole heart,"[20] words that echoed the missionary refrain of "heart Christianity," implying that this evangelical faith was to be as much emotionally experienced as intellectually understood.

Penka's vivid recollections constitute the earliest of what I call Mary Mills Patrick's rhetorical "moments." Penka shows that the earnest young Patrick did not simply encourage spiritual introspection, but pushed her students to agonize about their personal religious struggles. While committing "sin" seemed a remote danger in Penka's life, sermons and lessons nonetheless continually reminded her of the guilt and transgressions that even a well-intentioned girl like herself might indulge. In the absence of any clear transgression, Penka wrote,

> I wonder what my [lasting?] sin is, yet I think it is idolatry, but pride, jealousy, vanity my hatred are they not formed in me [sic]. Oh when will I be free of them. Today I feel a little better than yesterday. I feel God a little nearer, but what have I done today? Nothing. But it is comforting that God sees our weak trials.[21]

Writing in English, Penka echoed the words of her teachers. She despaired of the "vanity" and "earthly affection" that, as Patrick and other teachers reiterated, "tie her down," and she sought with anguish ways to "show that I am

Christ's" so that she could attain the beauties of the afterlife, as she heard them described. Other students, too, were overwhelmed by these matters, as Penka recorded:

> I forgot to write that on the 14 of March I think, Monday morning [T?] Kazakoba threw herself in the pond with the hope of drowning, but just as she was in that agony Hosanna of her father passed and took her out [sic]. The reason was remorse. She thought there is no salvation for her. Her brother came and she went home after several days.[22]

Penka seems to accept this suicide attempt as punishment for spiritual "remorse," a state with no hope of salvation. The remaining students were left, perhaps, clinging to their own "heart Christianity," trying to escape a similar dark hopelessness. As Penka neared her graduation date, Patrick and Hamlin, Penka's favorite teacher, exhorted her to "confess Jesus." But Penka was afraid she would "feel ashamed" to do so in her Orthodox community at home. Caught between the pressures of her home community and the fear of punishment with which the school had indoctrinated her, Penka agonized about what would happen to her spiritual future if she were to "please my friends and displease my father in Heaven."[23] In contemplating a return to home, Penka and other students felt increasingly anxious about their earthly and spiritual allegiances.

Penka wrote frequently of Patrick's advice, both spiritual and practical. For example, Patrick warned in frightening terms about the dangers of "balls and parties." As Penka wrote, "Miss Patrick said, if any one is in doubt for such a question, she has only to ask herself, will the spirit of God be there?...That decided the question." While "balls and parties" may not have been a difficult sacrifice for Bulgarian boarding school girls far from home in Istanbul, even these young women were, according to Patrick, susceptible to terrible temptations. As Penka recorded, Patrick admonished the girls that "it is not only ambitious people" who might succumb to sin, and "your temptation after you leave school will be pleasure. [Living] a life of pleasure and [having a bad] character" are "just the same." If one succumbs to "pleasure," one will eventually suffer guilt. As Patrick warned the girls, "The sinner after death will see the love that God had for him and his punishment will be remorse, which is terrible."[24]

On one occasion, "Miss Patrick" requested Penka's presence in the parlor to meet some American visitors, including a "tall gentleman with [a] white beard." Penka wrote, he "showed us a little book. He opened it. It was a black page representing our natural hearts full of sins. The next page was red which represented the blood of Christ then white—cleansing of our hearts and lastly gold color—glory."[25] Later, Penka recorded, Patrick explained the symbolism of the alarming book in a way that suggested her own proximity to an emotional breakdown:

> [Miss Patrick] looked pale and her voice sweet, her eyes once filled with tears and she tried to smile. She looked a perfect picture of beauty. But that is not all. She talked beautifully…[she said] those who are pure not only have the blessed promise of seeing God for eternity in the beautiful home above, but also they can see him in their hearts. Every girl she said who has given her heart to Christ is growing every day more pure, Jesus is helping her, he is preparing their heart. A pure heart is like a white dress, we have to be very careful not to soil it."[26]

Patrick's tearful sincerity, while genuine, seems to have placed her in a pedagogical dead end: There was no more she can do for these girls than to urge them to evangelical ecstasy. However, escape from this untenable situation lay ahead. This Mary Mills Patrick, the earnest spiritual advisor, constructor of metaphoric white dresses and a stern voice of warning about the dangers of balls and parties, was about to disappear forever. In 1883 Kate Pond Williams retired, leaving Patrick and Hamlin co-principals of the school.[27] In only a few years, Patrick would be the president of a new American college and she would begin, with evident relief, to replace the highly wrought language of evangelical Christianity with the civic-minded rhetoric of American secularism.

The Second Rhetorical Moment: The Christian Secularist and Early Years at the American College for Girls

In 1889 Patrick traveled to the United States to persuade the Woman's Board of Missions to establish a college in place of the Constantinople Home. She succeeded in acquiring a college charter in Massachusetts, and the Woman's

Board of Missions of the ABCFM appointed her president of the American College for Girls (also called the Constantinople College for Women).[28] With the new college charter in hand, Patrick began the delicate process of transforming a religious school into an academic college without jarring the evangelical sensibilities of conservative board members. The board insisted that the missionary goal of Christian conversion remain intact, but Patrick's own agenda was already changing. Intent on attracting an elite Ottoman clientele, she wished to minimize the school's former emphasis on the Gospel. In this second rhetorical "moment," Patrick used the 1890 Annual Report of the college to place one foot firmly in both camps. In a rhetorical turn remarkable for its appeal to two opposing agendas, she claimed allegiance both to the missionary credo and to Ottoman desire for women's education. In so doing, she effectively delineated the tensions that would shape the institution for the next thirty years.

Patrick was well aware that the Constantinople Home's new incarnation did not sit well with its missionary backers who still believed that mass religious conversion of the Near East was attainable if the American schools would only do their job. The 1890 *Annual Report* was Patrick's first, albeit cautious and at times deliberately opaque, sally in the ideological power struggle that would continue between her and the Woman's Board of Missions for the next eighteen years. She declared herself ready to tackle challenging administrative and pedagogical issues, including faculty hiring, curriculum development, physical infrastructure, library acquisitions, and relations with the Ottoman government. Notably absent from her agenda were resisting sin, giving one's heart to Christ, and finding admittance to the Kingdom of Heaven. Instead, the 1890 Report demonstrated a new vision of missionary education and a new sense of awareness of the Ottoman milieu; moreover, it blurred the already muddy distinction between religious and cultural proselytizing, thus propelling Patrick's faculty into new missionary terrain. The ABCFM had already expanded its opportunities for women by permitting them full missionary status[29]; building on this reform, Patrick set out to hire missionaries who were also excellent teachers.

In the 1890 Report, Patrick discovered her voice as a professional educator. Her rhetoric was still colored with American missionary phrase and tone, but her message was that something more than the project of proselytism was at stake. Indeed, she proclaimed the college essential to the betterment of the Ottoman people, if not to their ultimate spiritual salvation, then to their imminent social, moral, and intellectual redemption. In her vision of the powerful effects of education, Patrick was not alone. Cyrus Hamlin, founder of the non-missionary-affiliated Robert College of Istanbul, had written in 1877 that the Ottoman "governing class," as opposed to the "ignorant multitudes," had "wonderfully changed" toward Christianity due to the subtle influences of "The Scriptures, newspapers, books, education…and the religious freedom is coming in slowly, and in the only possible way, by *enlightenment*" (Hamlin's emphasis).[30] Patrick, too, believed that secular American educational practices would transform individuals who in turn would contribute to American-style nationalism in the Ottoman Empire.

In anticipation of criticism from the Woman's Board of Missions about the decline of evangelism at the college, Patrick's 1890 Report directly addressed one of the missionaries' most pressing problems, "the animosity of the native Christian nationalities to Protestant schools."[31] What the missionaries called "heart Christianity" could well have been viewed as insidious proselytizing by many locals and could only have increased the long history of mutual irritation between the missionaries and (in Patrick's term) the "native Christian" churches. Since Ottoman law prevented the missionaries from proselytizing Muslims, the Americans had long looked to the Christian communities, and with less optimism to the Jews, for new recruits. At least partly in response to the competition from the Protestant missionary schools, Ottoman Armenians, Greeks, Muslims, and Jews had during the nineteenth century expanded and improved their systems of education and had even introduced some schools for girls. Advances in Ottoman education at many levels had been initiated during the Tanzimat ("reorganization") Period (1839–1876) as a critical part of the modernization process, and even the missionaries had to admit that it was no longer accurate to set the American schools apart in their higher standards of education. Indeed, Patrick mentioned in the 1890 Report the "constant improvement" of the "native schools." Such local "improvement," however, was also a potential obstacle to American success. The Armenian, Greek, and Catholic schools, she noted with concern, "compete well with us in French and accomplishments, and offer a more extended, though less thorough, course in the native languages."[32] Thus, the final verdict was reassuring: These programs did not offer real competition to the American College, even in the "native" languages. In response to these local rivals,

Patrick had overseen a "greatly improved" French department and, bowing to the necessary, if crass, desire for "accomplishments," had added a German music teacher to "make our College attractive."[33]

But Patrick knew that such curricular additions would not satisfy the board members who still hoped for mass Christian conversions. In a rhetorical move aimed at both placating the evangelists and staking a claim to secularism, Patrick claimed that the school's Christianity was not explicit, but was so embedded in its teachings as to cause offense in unenlightened people. "Our teaching is not sectarian," she declared, "[but] the *heart Christianity* that our students learn, prejudices many parents against our institution that teaches the daughters to live more righteous lives than those of their parents."[34] Patrick implied here that "heart Christianity" went beyond mere theology; indeed, it was not even a threat to other beliefs, but was a means of elevating faith and morality in general. The college's "non-sectarian" education, she argued, did not demand that students profess the Protestant faith; rather, they should live a "righteous" life, a coded term that implied a specific system of behavior, one evidently not hitherto practiced by non-Protestants, yet nonetheless accessible to them. That the college might turn students away from the customs of their families was, as in Penka Racheva's time, still a laudable goal. Patrick used the term "non-sectarian" as a salve to Ottoman fears about proselytism, but at the same time she implied to the board that the college was still at heart the same Christian institution as always. Thus, this "heart Christianity" was both exclusive and universal; it transcended the kind of religious association that Patrick called "sectarian" without sacrificing the college's Protestant identity.

In finessing the proselytism issue, Patrick clearly wanted to have it both ways: She disavowed aggressive proselytism but claimed vague moral advantages for the college. Even without overt proselytism, she hinted, new religious feelings would inevitably emerge in the students. The paradoxical outcome, in which the college would inspire religiously motivated thought by *not* enforcing it, Patrick explained, was evidenced by the increased enrollment at the college.

The 1890 Report especially emphasized the conspicuous success of the non-sectarian approach among the college's non-Christian students, of whom there were, of course, only a few. The presence of Jewish students provided welcome evidence that the college was at once intellectually secular yet essentially Christian. The simple fact of Jewish student attendance proved that the college had transcended its missionary label, yet Patrick argued that the college exerted a profound moral influence over them. Of these girls, Patrick wrote, "we find them more interesting and teachable than we had supposed" and cited the hopeful case of "[o]ne of our Jewish boarders, Miss Elize Pilosophe, [who] asked for a library book one Sunday about Jesus, adding, 'We have no Jesus in our religion.'"[35] Such instances, Patrick suggested, were evidence of more than intellectual curiosity: They showed the subtle success of the college's moral influence. Other students also displayed effects of the school's embedded spiritual teachings:

> During the year we have had no marked religious interest at any one time, but the change of sentiment towards religious things was more wonderful than anything we have ever experienced. Until Christmas about thirty of the strongest characters in the College, many of them new students, were banded together in strong and avowed opposition to all religious influence. This spirit changed entirely long before the end of the year, and those who came to us with the most prejudice against our teaching became enthusiastic in Bible study, attentive in the prayer meetings, and very much softened in every way. It is our hope and prayer that another year may find them ready to give their hearts to the Savior.[36]

Thus, even the "strongest characters" found themselves "softened" by the experience of "heart Christianity," "new students" were gently converted from rebels to loyalists, and the board in Boston could rest assured that even the most obdurate girl would turn around before the end of her second year. Patrick noted that not only did "about thirty" girls attend the "voluntary prayer meeting on Saturday afternoon" but also that "the students have had a great many prayer meetings among themselves, even the little girls often asking permission to do so, and quite a number of day-scholars have attended the Sunday Bible classes."[37] Such statements must have been balm indeed to the anxious trustees in Boston.

In describing the college's pervasive religious influence, Patrick demonstrated an ambivalence of purpose that was resolutely, if unconsciously, paradoxical. The college permitted students the freedom of their own faiths with the understanding that such tolerance was a fundamental characteristic of American Protestantism. Patrick presented "secularism" and freedom of religion as essential to an American Protestant education; at the same time, it was only through such a "secular" education that one might experience the "heart Christianity" of American Protestantism. The "voluntary" and purportedly spontaneous religious gatherings of students served to underline in seeming contradiction *both* the Christian character of the college and its "secular" commitment to religious freedom. What is crucial here is that for Patrick there was no contradiction: The American ideal of religious freedom sprang from Protestant belief; religious freedom set the Americans apart from the Ottomans; and, once a person of any faith was thoroughly exposed to the American system, the superiority of the American faith inevitably would rise and assert itself.

In the absence of a significant Muslim presence at the college in the 1880s and 1890s, Patrick was quick to point to Jewish students as useful markers of the effectiveness of the college's indirect proselytism and its ability to attract all religions, as well as to remind the board members of the extraordinary heterogeneity of the Ottoman people. In the 1890 Report, Patrick related a story about a government inspector from the Ministry of Education "who gives us such constant trouble in regard to our textbooks" and who asked the school to "receive two Jewish protégés of his, at half price, hinting that our troubles with the Government might thereby be lessened." The school agreed, "but the girls did not appear." Finally, the inspector "sent us word that they had decided to send one girl for nothing, instead of two for half-price!"[38] (Clearly, Patrick implies, the machinations of the Oriental mind are absurd.) The girl, named Rose, appeared, but she was a "mere atom" of a child, not old enough to be a student. The teachers decided to send her home, but after the first night they changed their minds. The above-mentioned Elize Pilosophe took charge of the little girl,

> teaching her a little prayer without any suggestion from anyone. "What is it to make a prayer," said Rose, "I never made a prayer at home.'" Then she confided to Elize that she intended to work very hard in school in order to help her father soon to retrieve his fortunes. This was such a remarkable statement for a child of seven that we began to regard her with a new interest.[39]

In the end, the college "kept her as a nucleus for our kindergarten."[40] Patrick did not explain the relationship between Rose's family and the inspector; rather her concern was to present this child as a college success story, a girl who could be changed by exposure to the school, and was indeed transformed in only one night.

Rose's story also demonstrated to Boston the college's close relation to powerful people in the Ottoman Empire. Patrick did not have to entice students to attend; rather, elite families from all religious and linguistic groups sought out the college on their own initiative. Moreover, the college reflected the Ottoman Empire's diverse population. The 1890 Report included what would become a regular feature of all Patrick's annual reports, the obligatory breakdown of students by "nationalities." In 1890, Patrick listed all the graduates of the Home School, past and present, by "nation": "Armenian 52, Bulgarian 13, Greek 4, English 3, Jewish 1, Danish 1, American 1, Turkish 1."[41] Of these, Patrick adds, "34 have engaged in teaching—some of them many years—20 are married, and two have died."[42] Of the last, one student,

> Miss Manoushag Besharian…died in Mardin last winter, where she had been a most valuable teacher in the mission school for nearly four years. She was very much beloved in Mardin, and her sister writes that all the city mourned her death, and that she was considered a saint by both Papists and Protestants.[43]

Miss Besharian's brief career spanned the trajectory of female experience in mission work: She was the familiar figure of the martyred, indeed, saintly, female missionary, she was a "native" converted to Protestantism and trained to teach her own people, and, finally, she was the newly professionalized single woman teacher. Her death, like those of missionary wives of sixty years earlier, was appropriately elevated in the context of missionary lore, and Patrick, although undoubtedly genuinely saddened by the demise of this former student, effectively exploited that aspect while at the same time exhibiting Miss Besharian as an example of the professional success of the school.[44]

Patrick's descriptions of Protestant osmosis and missionary martyrdom certainly must have soothed Mission Board forebodings about her self-proclaimed "non-sectarian" proselytizing project. But for Patrick the high point of the year occurred during the 1890 commencement exercises. This last commencement exercise for students of the Constantinople Home was also the first graduation of a Muslim student, Gulistan Ismet Hanum. The event defined Patrick's vision of secularism by demonstrating, first, the college's remarkable popularity in Istanbul, and, second, its success in penetrating the most resistant Ottoman population, the Muslims, the "ruling nationality" of the empire.

The spectators alone provided visual evidence of the college's prominent position in Istanbul. This "brilliant occasion" was attended by "more than the usual number of representatives of the Government, and diplomatic circles."[45] Patrick wrote,

> The graduating class of this year is distinguished from all others in numbering among its members the first graduate from any Christian school belonging to the ruling nationality of the land, Gulistan Ismet Hanum, a young lady calculated by her character and attainments to bring honor to her alma Mater. The father of Gulistan, a colonel in the Turkish army, has shown great courage and independence of thought in continuing to send his daughter to us, notwithstanding the pressure brought to bear upon him in consequence of the bitter animosity of the Turkish government to Christian education.[46]

Patrick carefully described Gulistan's appearance, depicting her clothing, her female relatives, and even the location of her seat in the audience. This loving attention to detail revealed Patrick's new sense of values, in which she turns toward the Ottoman milieu and away from Boston. Rather than claiming Christian souls and seeking approval only from the Mission Board, she now sought and found acceptance in her Ottoman surroundings. She wrote that during the graduation ceremony Gulistan "did not sit with her class, as no Mohammedan girl could appear in public unveiled, but she sat, closely veiled, with her mother near the stage, partly concealed from curious eyes by the piano which stood in front of her seat." Likewise, Gulistan "did not rise with the others to receive her diploma, but when it was handed to her, the applause of the audience was almost beyond control, and the curiosity to see her was intense."[47]

In focusing on Gulistan's physical separation from the other students, marked especially by her veil, Patrick staked a claim to a new achievement for an American educator. Patrick not only attracted a Muslim student to a Christian school, but also, as evidenced by the presence of Ottoman officials and Gulistan's upper-class parents, she had integrated the college into Ottoman society. Moreover, her description suggested a special feminine closeness between this student and her teachers, a closeness only achieved by this college. Patrick's clear pleasure in the presence of these Ottoman Muslim women, Gulistan and her mother, also demonstrated her belief that she, as head of this women's college, could accomplish goals that would have been impossible for men. Gulistan had to be veiled in this public ceremony, but she did not have to be covered when she was in class. The female American teachers had a private view behind the veil, a privileged position that could only exist in a college tolerant of religious difference, since observant Muslim girls would not have found their way into a conventional missionary school. Patrick's description showed that the college's special role was now to welcome, to protect, and to enlighten, but not to convert, the Muslim girl.

Unlike Penka Racheva before her, Gulistan had not been asked to "give her heart to the Savior." Indeed, 1890, like previous years, had failed to entice any significant number of girls into the Protestant fold; however, it had significantly expanded the college's body of loyal alumni. Patrick's interest now lay in the growth of the college and its place in the Ottoman milieu, and her concern had shifted from "heart Christianity" to a mission, both personal and professional, to educate Ottoman women. Paralleling her turn from evangelistic to cultural proselytism was the high value she now placed on Ottoman response to the college.

In 1890, then, Patrick was forging a rhetorical path that both satisfied her new educational goals and suited her two important audiences. For the trustees in Boston, she implied that she would replace mass conversions by something better, an Ottoman enthusiasm for American influence. For the young Ottoman women and their families, she made room for religious diversity and sought to unite all students in loyalty to their alma mater. But Patrick's campaign to attract a more elite student body by advertising the college's secular stance did not alter the college's Protestant perspective in its structure, its curriculum, and its continued inclusion of religious lessons. Why did this double-voiced rhetorical strategy succeed? Perhaps both sides found the messages that they sought. The administrators in Boston were pleased because the lady missionaries were increasing the college's enrollment and expanding its influence. The students and, more importantly, their families, were watchful, but, in a society that offered few alternatives, they appeared satisfied with the level of education and the type of curriculum offered to their daughters.

Amid the success stories in this Annual Report, Patrick hinted at impending changes in the missionary stance of the college. She cited Dr. Washburn, president of Robert College, who, in his Commencement Day speech,

> emphasized the fact that the change in our institution, which was the subject of the day, was not merely a change in name, but a natural outgrowth of the inward progress of the institution to meet the ever increasing outward demand for better educational advantages for the youth of Turkey.[48]

The "inward" progress had dovetailed with the "outward demand" and Patrick added for the benefit of her Boston readers that the trustees must "enable us to meet the added responsibility that this change involves."[49] Patrick here prepared the way for future requests for funding, not for a missionary school, but for a college that was now integral to the Ottoman system of education. The trustees, Patrick suggested, needed to understand that the college was moving away from its evangelistic origins toward a project of cultural proselytism, one that would not only enhance the American Board's profile, but that would also have global implications for the future of the Ottoman Empire. Such an enterprise would indeed demand more resources, and the board needed to understand that Patrick's de-emphasis of religion would expand, not weaken, the college's influence.

This change in tone rankled with some Missionary Board members, both in Ottoman territories and in the United States. In April 1891, H. G. O. Dwight[50] of the American Board Mission in Turkey wrote to Judson Smith of the ABCFM in Boston asking "whether there has been a change in the missionary character of the college or in the relation of the ladies who teach in it to the Western Turkey Mission."[51] Smith took the letter to the members of the Woman's Board and with their collaboration drafted a reply to Dwight affirming that the "administration of the school…did not touch its missionary aim and relations" and that the teachers are all "assistant missionaries" of the American Board, "appointed in the same way as other female assistant missionaries." He continued, "It is a deep conviction of all at these rooms that the special glory and chief value of the college are found in its distinctive missionary character and aims."[52]

Dwight had been in the habit of frequently visiting the Home School and later the college, providing lectures, sermons, and Bible classes for the students. He wrote voluminously about the Ottoman territories and peoples for American readers, and usually mentioned the college in highly positive terms. His view of the Ottomans, however, was uniformly negative, and in his descriptions, the culture, institutions, and peoples of the Empire always fell short. The title of his book, *Constantinople and Its Problems: Its People, Customs, Religions and Progress* (1901), set the stage for the analysis that followed, in which "problems" predominate and "progress" comes only with the aid of American missionaries. Dwight expressed the familiar missionary view that the Ottomans had better look to the West to improve every aspect of their intellectual capacity, since they were clearly unable to match Western output of scholarly books with anything comparable in any of the languages of the Ottoman territories. Already, Dwight wrote, they had benefited by modeling lower schools on Western forms, namely, missionary schools.[53]

Patrick, while she welcomed Dwight's visits, had veered away from his uniformly pessimistic view of Ottoman prospects for improvement. Ultimately, she would use Judson Smith's abovementioned "distinctive" aims as justification for the college's departure from the board; in the meantime, she became more insistent in her requesting funds for academic improvements. In her 1891 Annual Report to the Board of Trustees, she wrote,

> We greatly need a permanent professor in [the "Scientific"] department, who has had the best advantages offered in America, and with a sufficient knowledge of German to avail herself of the opportunities offered in Europe to keep herself in touch with the progress of the day. Such a one would do much to build up the department satisfactorily."[54]

Patrick identified her faculty members with their academic areas rather than with missionary work, thus not only raising the intellectual level of the curricular offerings but also setting the stage for an overall more sophisticated academic environment. But even as the educational mission subsumed the proselytizing one, the Christianizing purpose did not disappear. Instead, the college's more tolerant approach to religion became a way of approaching the familiar "civilizing" objective by different means. As Patrick wrote,

> In regard to the religious life of the College, we can say that all who share in the teaching feel that an education, to be complete, must quicken and nurture the spiritual life, and desire most earnestly to inculcate the Christianity of the New Testament. Public worship has been conducted in the College every Sabbath morning in the English language, and the students also had opportunities to attend services conducted in their own languages.... The religious occasions at the College have been marked by a spirit of devotion that has helped greatly to promote the harmony that has distinguished the College life of the year.[55]

The above comments followed a discussion of the qualifications of newly hired teachers, the academic departments, the need for a "Science Hall" with "better facilities for experimental work," and the inevitable break-down of students by religion and language.[56] Patrick concluded with a plea for funding that was both admonishing and self-righteous:

> It is difficult to render our methods of teaching the best and most progressive, and to keep our College abreast with other institutions of its kind, so far away from educational centers, and can be accomplished only by expenditure of time and money, and only by devoted efforts on the part of all interested in it. The necessity for self-denial on the part of the teachers will always exist. To promote the best interests of each member of a family like ours, composed of so varied and susceptible elements, and of characters so young, will always demand from the teachers a high degree of moral personal power, which must be exercised with loving wisdom and patience.[57]

Patrick emphasized that personal interests did not motivate her or her faculty; indeed, the low salaries were a constant source of worry for the board as well as for those "on the ground" in the expensive city of Istanbul. Her phrases, "self-denial," "moral personal power," and "loving wisdom and patience," invoked the familiar ideals of the missionary who sought not personal gain but the greater good. But Patrick made it clear that moral strength was not sufficient to do the job: "time and money" as well as "devoted efforts" were required. She noted that "imperative needs" had been "presented to you in private letters" and added the hope that "you will use every means in your power to attract attention to our College," which promised to be "one of the most useful institutions of the coming century."[58] Patrick's new mission, it would seem, was to jolt the board into providing more support.

These tensions would continue to flare throughout the decade, and indeed, in 1894, just five years after the college gained its charter, the ABCFM was worried enough about the Christianity of the college to send someone to check up on it. The subsequent report of Reverend Robert Chambers of Bardezag (now Bahçecik, Izmit), however, was reassuring. Chambers, a member of the ABCFM Advisory Board, reported to Abbie Child, vice-president of the college's Board of Trustees and an officer of the Woman's Board of Missions, that he had "gained an impression that the trend in the College was rather toward intellectual advancement than toward spiritual power, but on closer acquaintance I have been surprised and deeply impressed by the depth of spiritual experience in the teachers."[59] Chambers noted approvingly the time devoted to "Biblical instruction and heart culture," an expression that, as in Patrick's use of the term in her 1890 *Report*, seemed to refer to a kind of spiritual infusion, a Christianity felt rather than learned. Evidently Chambers found the religious side of the curriculum more than sufficient, adding, "The W.B.M. may well thank God that it has been led to found and support this center of Gospel power in the East." He was, he wrote, "devoutly grateful" to these "educators of women," who indeed seemed to have entirely won him over. He assured Child that if "the members of the board of trustees could once in a while drop in to a meeting of prayer and spiritual communion with their devoted fellow workers here; how soon all misunderstandings would disappear, and heart sympathy be increased!" Evidently Patrick was successful in persuading Chambers that, as he wrote to the board, "the sanctification of the intellect is no less important than the conversion of the soul."

Thus, in her first years as president of the American College for Girls, Patrick created an environment in which Christian and secular education seemed to coexist as philosophical bases of the college. But if the "progressive" American college was at the forefront of Ottoman social change, where was the Protestantism in this image? Although the vocabulary had changed and overt expressions of faith were repressed, the missionary ideals were still very much in evidence. Indeed, for Patrick, the cultural proselytism implicit in the college's educational program subsumed but did not exclude the idea of religious conversion. Patrick continued optimistically to see signs of Protestant belief and behavior even among her Muslim students and those who steadfastly maintained their "native" religious allegiance. Patrick's abiding faith in the ideology of American Protestantism constituted a peculiarly American extension of the Orientalist worldview. She viewed the Ottomans as people in need of Western, that is, Protestant and American, enlightenment, and the Ottoman world as a retrogressive civilization now slowly turning toward the ways of the West. These views marked the first two decades of Patrick's leadership of the college, when her dual performances of ideological inflexibility and social liberalism most exemplified the ambivalence of projects of cultural colonization.

As Patrick redefined the missionary purpose of the American College in its shift from spiritual to cultural proselytism, she reinvented her rhetorical construction of the Ottoman people to accommodate the multiethnic and multireligious character of the declining Ottoman Empire. Even as she advocated social emancipation and religious freedom, however, her depictions of students remained doggedly stereotyped. Patrick's rhetorical production of Ottoman women performed two seemingly contradictory tasks at once: It racialized the female students by stereotyping them according to their particular religious, ethnic, or language group, but it also elevated them by virtue of their contact with American education.

These uneasy balances, between the evangelist and the scholar, and between the Orientalist and the liberal, would soon tip, and Patrick and the college would edge further from their missionary roots.

THE THIRD RHETORICAL MOMENT: THE PROGRESSIVE EDUCATOR
AND THE 1908 YOUNG TURK REVOLUTION

Between 1890 and 1908, Patrick recruited Muslim students, expanded enrollment overall, and hired faculty members with post-graduate degrees. Tensions over the missionary function of the college as well as governance issues (such as hiring nonmissionary teachers) finally prompted Patrick and her supporters to declare independence from the Woman's Board of Missions and the ABCFM. In 1908, Patrick again traveled to America, this time to acquire a new charter that would make the American College for Girls a private, nonmissionary institution with a new board of trustees. Thus she was absent from Istanbul during the 1908 Revolution, but she did not fail to note the opportunities the Revolution offered for expanding the college's sphere of influence. Patrick greeted the Young Turks as heralds of a new era of Western-style nationalism; moreover, she believed that a Westernizing Ottoman state promised widespread education and emancipation of women. Patrick's rhetorical "moment" of the post-1908 period, then, spreads across time, including the charter of the newly independent college, her post-missionary annual reports, and her later reflections on the era's significance.

The coincidence of revolutionary events, in which the Ottoman state seemed to advance toward a more Westernized system of government and the college cut itself loose from the hampering effects of the board, was not lost on college personnel. Indeed, Patrick viewed the college's existence as integral to the Ottoman Empire. She described the newly independent college as not merely benefiting from the new Ottoman politics, but also as deeply enmeshed in Ottoman affairs and even acting as inspiration to the reformers; moreover, she saw both the college and the political movement as not merely local, but as part of a worldwide network of positive revolutionary change.

Patrick later wrote, "The formation of our new college committee...and the enlarged status of our administration culminating in 1908 were symptoms of general transformations taking place in world affairs."[60] Certainly, the immediate effects were positive for the college, as the reforms increased enrollment; indeed, in Patrick's view, this brief era was a "temporary heaven on earth."[61] In her memoir, *A Bosporus Adventure* (1934), Patrick unabashedly placed the college at the forefront of the march to the social and political transformation of the Ottoman Empire:

> The change in our college life [after the revolution] was dramatic in the extreme. For thirty-two years we had been forbidden to admit Turkish [Muslim] students. The three distinguished Turkish women who had studied with us during that period had suffered many things from attending an institution under the ban of their government. Now overnight the bars were removed. Turkish officials called to congratulate us on our progressive college. A procession of new Turkish students

appeared at our gates, many of them paid for by the government itself, and frequent messages were received from prominent Turkish officials regarding them.[62]

Here, Patrick implied that the college occupied a position *within* the Ottoman system: that is, rather than obtaining strength from its American association, it derived power from its "progressive" stance in concert with the Young Turks. Even as she celebrated the swelling numbers of "Turkish" students, however, Patrick could not suppress her old evangelistic impulses, and she allowed the missionary's habitual depiction of the Christian as martyr to surface, albeit obliquely. The unenlightened women who had "suffered" were now redeemed, and the "bars were removed" as in a long-awaited Second Coming. This time, of course, the revelatory moment was not inspired by Christ, but by progressive intellectual enlightenment. The joy lay in the freedom to seek a secular education that would delight, rather than offend, the elite Muslim class. If further proof was needed of the college's secure position in the new Ottoman state, it lay in the government's eagerness to pay Muslim students' tuition. Thus, in those tumultuous times, Patrick adapted her educational policies to the dynamic change occurring both within the college's own organization and beyond its walls. The spirit and the state banded together to affirm the college's worth, and Patrick deployed inspirational rhetoric to extol not only the virtues of democracy and progress but also the college's role in promoting them.

Despite the college's severance from the Board of Missions, in 1908 Patrick was not yet willing to cut away entirely from missionary goals. The college charter of 1908 asserted that the American College for Girls would remain a "positive Christian institution" and "carry on [its] work in harmony and cooperation with the missionary operations" in Istanbul.[63] The president, other administrators, and the faculty would "decide questions relative to the personal life and conduct of the students, and the social and religious life of the college."[64] Students and faculty were "expected," but not, it seems, required, to attend chapel "or some other public religious service," thus further loosening the Christian mandate but still maintaining a vaguely spiritual stance.[65]

Patrick not only permitted the Christian affiliation, in rhetoric if not in actuality, to remain, but also she allowed the racializing depictions of the missionary mindset to remain in place. As the college scrambled to accommodate itself to the rapid social changes of the late Ottoman Empire, the rhetorical forms of Patrick's representations of the Ottomans remained undisturbed: Ottoman women still needed social, moral, and intellectual enlightenment, especially if they were to play a role in new political events. Moreover, Patrick continued to characterize the college itself as not merely a positive influence, but also as a major player in the cultural upheavals of this period.

Patrick's documentation of the nonsectarian nature of the newly independent college was well timed. When she returned from America, she found Muslim women, "veiled ladies of the ruling race," crowding the school grounds and begging for admittance to the college.[66] For the first time, "Turks" numbered among the largest enrollments: at thirty-two students they were second only to the Bulgarians, who numbered forty-three.[67] As Patrick wrote later, "It constantly thrilled us to welcome groups of these black-robed students, eager for a life of study. Once across the threshold, the black veils disappeared and modern seekers for knowledge came to view."[68] The idea of "modernity" seemed to have firmly displaced Christianity, even of the "heart" version, and the college's mission now had become one of creating moral and "righteous" female citizens for a new democracy. This "morality," however, was still tinged with Protestant rhetoric: The "moral" citizen would be one who upheld values intrinsic to Protestant ideals. Patrick addressed this issue in her 1909–1910 Annual Report:

> The East at the present time is in great need of strong centres not only of education but of religious and moral influence. The breaking up of the old customs and laws endangers the loss of the strong old faith in an over-ruling power for good in the universe. Many students enter our College with this belief greatly shaken if not lost. It is therefore a leading aim of the College to be a centre of strong faith and an inspiration to a high spiritual life.[69]

Here, Patrick has identified an opportunity for the college to integrate itself further into the Ottoman educational structure while still satisfying the American desire for cultural proselytism. The "breaking-up of old customs and laws" presented a strategic void for the American College to fill.

As political events of the decade continued to resonate within the college walls, Patrick stressed the exceptional preparation her students received. In her 1911–1912 Annual Report, Patrick wrote,

> Conditions are steadily improving in the Near East, with the result of constantly bringing the subject of higher education of women into greater prominence. In this respect Constantinople College occupies a unique place, in scope, organization, and aspirations. It seeks to share in the development of the nations of eastern Europe and western Asia, and desires to furnish each one with the intellectual, moral, and religious help that is most needed.[70]

The college, Patrick said, was positioned to offer the "help that is most needed"; however, she was not complacent about the inimitability of her product. She noted in this Annual Report the presence of women students in universities in Greece, Hungary, Romania, and Bulgaria. In fact, there was "no university in the Near East *except in Turkey* [my emphasis] where women were not found," and, glancing over her shoulder at the competition, she added, "If Constantinople College is to succeed in helping to shape the moral and religious ideals of the young nations in this part of the world, it must provide advantages that are superior in comparison with the growing excellence of those offered by [neighboring] schools and universities."[71] The spread of educational opportunities for women and men was, of course, laudable, and one that the college was happy to accept credit for, but it was already becoming clear that the unique "advantage" that the college could offer was in teaching Muslim students. With this in mind, Patrick could safely maintain that the American College still stood above the competition because it alone could lead in the education of "Turkish" women, the one group still underrepresented in Western schools. In attracting these students, Patrick argued, the college was a crucial component in the advances in women's education, where "conditions in the schools of the Turkish Empire are also rapidly improving." The young educated classes would be the new leaders, and the college had to maintain its high status even as other schools began to develop. The American College stood at the top of the educational pyramid, waiting for the arrival of the brightest students:

A number of Turkish schools for girls have recently been organized which aim to prepare students to enter college; and while the majority of the Mohammedan students are necessarily in the preparatory department...the number of Turkish women in our higher classes will increase each year.[72]

Always eager to note constructive growth, Patrick added, "[W]hen we remember how recent the time was when Turkish women were debarred from all education, the progress made by them is truly remarkable."[73] The college's role, Patrick implied, was correspondingly indispensable. But it was not simply in educating women that the college was so crucial. Rather, its power lay in its American philosophy of education in which the Protestant mission was still firmly inscribed. The college, she wrote, had "attracted the people of the East" because of the "freshness and power of American methods of education" and "the high place given to moral and religious ideals."[74] American education was inseparable from its unique moral stance, which, in turn, was enmeshed in its Protestant base. Patrick justified continued religious instruction as a means of "shaping the highest issues of life."[75] Students were required to attend "[d]aily chapel exercises and Sunday-morning services" where "the attempt is made...to bring personal knowledge of God into the lives of the students—and to show the relation of religion to high and pure moral ideals, to home and national life and to the laws of the state." Religious "addresses" sought to "promote thoughtful seeking on the part of the students for sincerity in religious worship, nearness to God, and uprightness in personal life."[76]

These were extraordinary claims for a purportedly secular school. The concept of "personal" acquaintance with God was one firmly rooted in Protestant missionary evangelism, in which individual Bible study, rather than following the dicta of a hierarchical religious order, was the correct path to faith. The association of this missionary-style approach with the concept of "national life" unambiguously pointed to the fusion of the "American" and the Protestant.

But Patrick went further: "the influence of the College" would affect not only personal conduct and belief, but also it would be "a force for international peace." The "large number of races" in the college was often, Patrick acknowledged, "a source of difficulty," but it also furnishes an unusual opportunity to unite and amalgamate members of antagonistic nations in the common aim of promoting larger and freer national life. The political problems of the Near East would be easily solved were a union of interests possible among the different nations. To this end there could be no stronger influence than that exerted by a cosmopolitan college where equality of the races and the common interests of all nationalities are the practical experience of daily life.[77]

Educating women, then, created a "union of interests" that served "nations," such as the Armenian, the Jewish, and the Greek, but it also served *the* nation, that is, the Ottoman state.

In crediting the college with being a major player in the shifting political patterns of the twentieth century, Patrick reiterated the refrain of "equality of races" and "nationalities" as a means to "international peace." If there were "no stronger influence" than the college, then it must continue to exist. Her proposal for preserving the college rested on the educational principle that the "academic and cultural advantages" offered in the English language must be "superior to those that could be obtained elsewhere in the best institutions."[78]

Moreover, students had to be allowed to study "their own vernacular language in its ancient and modern form and to acquaint themselves with the literature and history of their own land"; similarly, "theoretical, practical, and vocational training" in "domestic art and science, and in sanitation, hygiene, and physical education" must be available.[79] These 1912 goals were surprisingly reminiscent of those of the 1890s: The purpose was still "to find the kind of training for individuals that will show the largest results in the progress of the communities to which they belong."[80] The linguistic- and religious-based cultural differences among students had to be preserved and even strengthened, befitting the college's vision of future political entities to which each group, or "nation," might belong; at the same time, the overarching "morality" infused throughout the content and methods of the American teaching would draw these disparate groups together under the umbrella of "international peace."

Despite such idealism, the political and societal conflicts within the Ottoman Empire could not help but impinge on the college. In the 1912–1913 Annual Report, Patrick noted tensions brought on by the Balkan War. She wrote that "the larger portion of the student body belonged to the allied nations at war with Turkey"; that is, most of the students were Bulgarian.[81] The college at this time was in the midst of building a new facility in Arnavutkoy, on the European side of the Bosphorus. Patrick wrote that "during the panic" of the early part of the war in November 1911, the American Ambassador advised the college to suspend operations and send as many students home as possible. Those who lived too far away, mostly "Bulgarians and Greeks," were sent to Arnavutkoy. It was, Patrick wrote, "in one sense a relief to have all the Bulgarian students over on the European side of the Bosphorus where they could be easily taken off on a steamer if necessary."[82] But public opinion also weighed heavily on Patrick, and she noted that "the news of the breaking up of the College appeared in the press of Bulgaria and Greece and made it an extremely difficult matter to hold the student body together."[83]

Fortunately, after three weeks "it was found that the armies of the Allies would not enter the city of Constantinople, the panic subsided…and the College resumed its regular work in Scutari."[84] Patrick accentuated the college's calm stoicism through these hard times and its refusal to be diverted from academics. In the 1912–1913 *Report*, Patrick glossed over what must have been a tense environment:

> During the [Balkan] war the students of the various nationalities were for the most part harmonious. A condition of perfect harmony, however, was difficult to maintain as there was hardly a girl in the College who did not have a father or a brother or some relative in one or the other of the conflicting armies.[85]

According to Patrick, "the students agreed among themselves" to "control their feelings in regard to national events," and the Bulgarian legation in Istanbul reinforced this effort by sending a "strong letter" to students "bidding them remain quietly in the College and to live as far as possible at peace with students of other nationalities."[86]

Peace, however, did not mean the disappearance of "national" identity at the college; on the contrary, the "nation" of each student remained always at the forefront. Patrick explained that in the interests of school harmony, "the representatives of the different nationalities among the students and the [native] faculty were in general careful not to discuss what was going on in any way to cause irritation," and they went about "their daily work" with "outward calmness."[87] This public face of neutrality was an important expression of the college's ability to rise above local disturbances, but Patrick's point was also that the college contributed to peace, and, indeed, set an example that others would do well to follow. This microcosm of a peacefully diverse democratic state demonstrated the American ability to find harmony even among different peoples.

Patrick's assertion that the college played an important role in Ottoman society shows how far Patrick and this institution had come from the admonition of Rufus Anderson, the ABCFM's secretary from the 1830s to the 1860s, to "plant the seed and move on."[88] Patrick's writings following 1908 reveal her ambivalence about her mission: Even as she allowed her students to assert their own national identity, she assumed the superiority of the American model. In the process, she created a singular philosophy, her "sanctification of the intellect," to use Reverend Chambers's term, in which she persisted in using the language of proselytism and the stereotypes of Orientalism while at the same time adapting her rhetoric to the changing demands of her Ottoman clientele, her American supporters, and the college's own drive for survival. Although Patrick had severed the connection between herself and the American Board and heightened the emphasis on the college's role as educator of Ottoman women and especially on her own ardent desire to bring more Muslims to the college, she did so without relinquishing her essentially missionary point of view. In short, Patrick's leadership of the American College in the final years of the Ottoman Empire provides a revealing case of Orientalist ambivalence in action.

Before 1908, Patrick's depictions of multicultural amity and Ottoman gratitude for the college, as in the narrative of Gulistan's graduation, had garnered American financial and moral support. But Patrick always kept an anxious eye on her Ottoman clientele and she continued to concern herself with the college's future existence in a rapidly changing world. Following the First World War, she shifted her rhetorical appeal to focus on Ottoman as well as American support for the college. She intimated to Ottoman parents and government officials that the American College was not only tolerant, but also actively sympathetic to and supportive of nationalist ideals, both from the Young Turks and later in the new Turkish Republic. She appealed to the Ottoman and later to the Turkish government to recognize in her college a philosophy that accorded with new nationalist goals.

POSTSCRIPT: MARY MILLS PATRICK AS MISSIONARY OF AMERICA:
THE SECULAR COLLEGE AND THE TURKISH NATION

The wars and political upheavals after 1912 served to distance Patrick even further from her missionary roots. Muslim student enrollment continued to increase, and Patrick remained intent on integrating the college into the Ottoman system, even as she maintained its American persona. The events of these difficult years affected the college physically, in shortages of students and supplies, and emotionally, in tensions between ethnic student groups and between the college faculty and students. The British occupation of Istanbul at the end of World War I, for example, brought to the surface internecine stresses at the college that had hitherto remained in check, especially pitting Muslims against the college's Christians, who welcomed the British presence. Writing from the vantage point of 1924, at the beginning of the Turkish Republic and the end of her last year at the college, Patrick walked a fine rhetorical line between Muslim hatred of the British and their Allies and the birth of the new Turkish nation. She wrote that the people of Istanbul gave the Allied armies a "comparatively friendly welcome when they entered the city."[89] But she added: "It is, however, a most unnatural state of things for any city to be occupied by the armies of the forces of the enemy for a long period" and "the constant irritation of foreign occupation" and the "interference which necessarily followed in the normal life of the city, was too great to be borne."[90] In her usual dry manner, Patrick noted that after the British Army of Occupation pulled out on October 2, 1923, the "Turkish Republic then carried out its legal right of possession."[91] In the overthrow of unwelcome occupiers and the subsequent bloody conflict, Patrick represented the birth of the Turkish Republic as organic and natural. Most importantly, in claiming their "legal right of possession," she presented the Turks as behaving just as Americans would, indeed, modeling themselves, as she later wrote, on the "people of the United States in 1776" who also "desired freedom to develop in their own way."[92]

The selected "moments" described above—Patrick's evangelism in Penka Racheva's diary, her attempts to create a "secular" image in the early years of the college, and her optimism about the college's role following the Young Turk Revolution—illustrate Patrick's fluid vision of her educational mission and her ability to change and adapt to the demands of the historical moment. These "moments" also demonstrate her desire for the college to be more, not less, inclusive of diverse religious views, and more, not less, deeply entwined with the real population of the Ottoman Empire, rather than only with those individuals who had converted, or who might convert, to Protestant Christianity. Finally, these moments show that Patrick's construction of herself as educator also changed: From being merely a female "assistant missionary" and an appendage to the evangelistic American Board project, she created her own, unique plan for the intellectual, social, and political conversion of Ottoman women to an American-style matrix of intellectual and moral behavior. As she moved further away from the missionary organization, Patrick's effectiveness as an educator grew. At the same time, her sense of vocation, her personal calling to proselytize in the Ottoman Empire, also blossomed as she became more successful at recruiting students from the ranks of the Ottoman elite.

By 1924, Patrick's construction of her educational mission and her rhetorical presentation of her students, the Ottoman Empire, and the new Turkish Republic included a broad vision of the possibilities of nationhood and womanhood, but the role of Christian evangelism had shrunk practically to nonexistence. As she transformed the Constantinople Home School into the American College for Girls, and the college into an important Ottoman, then Turkish, institution, Patrick advanced from the suffocating perspective of her young missionary days to more enlightened leadership of a secular, but still determinedly Protestant American, educational project. As missionary, she had admonished her girls to eschew parties and balls, guard against sin, and embrace the spirit of Christ; in her early days as college president, she dipped into the well of missionary rhetoric to invoke "heart Christianity" as a way of gathering all her students—Christian, Jewish, and Muslim—in the embrace of the college's "secular" Protestantism. After 1908, far from boasting of the proselytes who accepted Christ into their hearts, she sought instead to advertise students' Western standards of behavior, dress, family life, and intellectual achievement: to make them appear to be, in effect, American Protestants in all but their adherence to Christian belief. Although the college's secular spirit reverberated with Protestant values, in her final retrospective Patrick stubbornly asserted her affinity with the new Turkey, celebrated the "new national thinking" of Kemal Ataturk, and declared the college's "absolutely neutral" position in this "startling period of Turkish history."[93] By dissociating herself from the missionaries and instead foregrounding the college's American identity, Patrick had defined her sphere of influence as an integral part of the educational project in the Ottoman and then the Turkish state.

Patrick's wholehearted support of the Turkish Republic showed how far she had traveled in the course of her career as missionary educator. Her devotion to the American Board's goal of mass conversion had shifted to a more idiosyncratic faith in post-imperial nation building. In the process, Patrick's essential Protestant worldview was transformed but not eliminated. Patrick consciously altered, in ways both opportunistic and heartfelt, her educational mission to the Ottomans. In the rapidly changing social and political environment of the late Ottoman Empire, she steered the college away from an evangelical devotion to Scripture and toward an ideology of secular nationalism. By so doing, she secured her most cherished goal, the continued existence of her college in the new Turkish Republic, and the conviction that the American College was an integral part of the birth of the Turkish nation itself.

NOTES

1. On Ottoman interactions with foreign educators, see Selim Deringil, *The Well-Protected Domains: Ideology and the Legitimation of Power in the Ottoman Empire 1876–1909* (London: Tauris, 1998); Aron Rodrigue, *French Jews, Turkish Jews: The Alliance Israélite Universelle and the Politics of Jewish Schooling in Turkey, 1860–1925* (Bloomington: Indiana University Press, 1990).
2. For example, as Patrick documents in her books about the college, she endured many visits from Hamidian spies. See Mary Mills Patrick, *A Bosporus Adventure: Istanbul (Constantinople) Woman's College, 1871–1924* (Stanford: Stanford University Press, 1934), and *Under Five Sultans* (New York: Century, 1929).
3. See below for Chambers's reactions to his visit to the college in 1894 in which he complimented Patrick's "sanctification of the intellect." Robert Chambers, Letter to Abbie Child. 22 February 1894. ACG Box 2. Robert College Archives, New York. I used sources from the Robert College Archives when it was housed independently in New York City, and now the archive is at the Columbia University's Rare Book and Manuscript Library.
4. For discussions of missionary women in the Middle East, see essays in *New Faith in Ancient Lands: Western Missions in the Middle East in the Nineteenth and Early Twentieth Centuries*, ed. Heleen Murre-van den Berg (Leiden: Brill, 2006); Lisa Joy Pruitt, *"A Looking Glass for the Ladies": American Protestant Women and the Orient in the Nineteenth Century* (Macon: Mercer University

Press, 2005); R. Pierce Beaver, *American Protestant Women in World Mission: History of the First Feminist Movement in North America* (Grand Rapids, MI: Eerdsman, 1980); Patricia R. Hill, *The World Their Household: The American Woman's Foreign Mission Movement and Cultural Transformation, 1870–1920* (Ann Arbor: University of Michigan Press, 1985); Amanda Porterfield, *Mary Lyon and the Mount Holyoke Missionaries* (New York: Oxford University Press, 1987); Dana L. Robert, *American Women in Mission: A Social History of Their Thought and Practice* (Macon, GA: Mercer University Press, 1996).

5. For a general discussion of these changes, see Michael B. Oren, *Power, Faith, and Fantasy: America in the Middle East 1776 to the Present* (New York: Norton, 2007); and Lester I. Vogel, *To See a Promised Land: Americans and the Holy Land in the Nineteenth Century* (University Park: Pennsylvania State University Press, 1993).

6. Patrick, *A Bosporus Adventure.*

7. Pauline Durant et al., Letter to Prudential Committee of the ABCFM, 10 May 1875, ABC 16.7.1, vol. 16, ACG Folder 2, Item 1. By permission of the Houghton Library, Harvard University.

8. See Cemal Yetkiner's essay in this volume.

9. Charles T. Riggs, "Julia Rappeleye," "Near East Missionary Biographies," ts. n.d.

10. Ibid.

11. Pauline Durant et al., Letter to Prudential Committee.

12. Ibid.

13. May N. Fincanci, *The Story of Robert College Old and New: 1863–1982* (1983; rev. ed., Istanbul: Redhouse, 2001).

14. Katherine Pond Williams, "Ten Years Review of the Constantinople Home," Typescript, File 1-C, Robert College Archives, Istanbul, 17 May 1881.

15. Caroline Borden, "Constantinople Home," two versions— published and typescript, ABC 16.7.1, vol. 16, ACG Folder 6, Item 2. By permission of the Houghton Library, Harvard University.

16. Patrick, *A Bosporus Adventure*, 46.

17. Penka Racheva, Diary. Robert College Archives, New York.

18. Clara Hamlin was the daughter of Cyrus Hamlin of Robert College.

19. Penka Racheva, Diary, 1 January 1883.

20. Ibid., 4 March 1883.

21. Ibid., 5 April 1883.

22. Ibid.

23. Ibid., 3 March 1883.

24. Ibid., 5 April 1883.

25. Ibid., 7 May 1883.

26. Ibid., 19 May 1883.

27. Patrick, *A Bosporus Adventure*, 89. Clara Hamlin's work at the Constantinople Home fulfilled her father, Cyrus Hamlin's, desire that his daughters find "work and home" in a female version of Robert College. For a discussion of Hamlin and his family, see Keith Greenwood, *Robert College: The American Founders* (İstanbul: Boğazici University Press, 2000).

28. Hester Donaldson Jenkins, *An Educational Ambassador to the Near East: The Story of Mary Mills Patrick and an American College in the Orient* (New York: Fleming H. Revell, 1925), 58–9.

29. For discussion of "assistant missionary status" for missionary wives, see Patricia Grimshaw, *Paths of Duty: American Missionary Wives in Nineteenth-Century Hawaii* (Honolulu: University of Hawaii Press, 1989); Hill, *The World Their Household*; and Robert, *American Women in Mission*.

30. Cyrus Hamlin, *Among the Turks* (New York: Robert Carter and Brothers, 1877), 90.

31. The American College for Girls at Constantinople. *Annual Report of the American College for Girls, 1889–1890*, Ms., Robert College Archives, New York, 3–4.

32. Ibid., 3–4.

33. Ibid., 4.

34. Ibid.

35. Ibid., 5.

36. Ibid., 7–8.

37. Ibid., 8.

38. Ibid., 5–6.

39. Ibid., 6.

40. Ibid.

41. Ibid., 3.

42. Ibid.

43. Ibid.

44. Examples of missionary wives eulogized in such terms appeared in missionary magazines and other publications, such as *Mother's Magazine* and *Missionary Friend*. Mary Van Lennep, who died in Istanbul in 1844, after only one year of marriage, was praised in a biography for her saintly forebearance and ethereal beauty. Mary Elizabeth Van Lennep, *Memoir*, published in "Stereotype," xii, [13]–382. Micropublished in "History of Women" (New Haven: Research Publications, Inc. 1975).

45. *Annual Report, 1889–1890*, 8.

46. Ibid.

47. Ibid., 9.

48. Ibid., 10.

49. Ibid.

50. Penka's diary also mentions a visit from Dwight: "In the night Mr. Dwight spoke to us. He read to us the description of heaven and began by saying:

When we read of heaven every one of us feels how much she wants to go to heaven, yet it is under certain conditions. No girl who tells lies or steals can go there. Then he went on talking of character and how it is the little acts every day that form the character." Penka Racheva Diary, 2 April 1883.

51. Judson Smith, Letter to Miss Abbie B. Child, Secretary. The letter appears in the Women's Board of Missions Minutes, 30 April 1891. ABC 16.7.1 Vol. 16. ACG Box, Folder 6. By permission of the Houghton Library, Harvard University.

52. Ibid.

53. Henry G. Otis Dwight, *Constantinople and Its Problems: Its People, Customs, Religions and Progress* (New York: Young People's Missionary Movement, 1901).

54. The American College for Girls at Constantinople, *The President's Report to the Board of Trustees for the Year 1890–91* (London: Sir Joseph Causton & Sons), 9.

55. *President's Report 1890–91*, 13.

56. Ibid., 9.

57. Ibid., 15.

58. Ibid.

59. Robert Chambers, Letter to Abbie Child, 22 February 1894, ACG Box 2, Robert College Archives, New York.

60. Patrick, *A Bosporus Adventure*, 133. Patrick significantly titles the chapter on the separation of the college from the Board of Missions, "The Struggle for Freedom."

61. Ibid., 135.

62. Ibid., 135–136.

63. *Charter of the Trustees of the American College for Girls at Constantinople in Turkey; also the By-Laws* (Boston: Fort Hill Press, 1908), 5.

64. Ibid., 13.

65. Ibid., 15.

66. The American College for Girls at Constantinople, *Report of the Year 1909–1910*, Robert College Archives, New York, 17.

67. Ibid., 18.

68. Patrick, *Under Five Sultans*, 210.

69. *Report of the Year 1909–1910*, 21.

70. The American College for Girls at Constantinople, *Reports for the Year 1911–1912* (Constantinople: H. Matteosian, 1912), 20.

71. Ibid.

72. Ibid., 21.

73. Ibid.

74. Ibid., 22.

75. Ibid., 23.

76. Ibid.

77. Ibid.

78. Ibid., 21.

79. Ibid.

80. Ibid.

81. Constantinople College: The American College for Girls at Constantinople. *Bulletin. President's Report, 1912–1913*, Robert College Archives, New York, 14–15.

82. Ibid., 15.

83. Ibid.

84. Ibid.

85. Ibid.

86. Ibid.

87. Ibid.

88. See William R. Hutchinson, *Errand to the World: American Protestant Thought and Foreign Missions* (Chicago: University of Chicago Press, 1987), and Paul William Harris, *Nothing but Christ: Rufus Anderson and the Ideology of Protestant Foreign Missions* (New York: Oxford University Press, 1999), for useful discussions of Rufus Anderson's philosophy.

89. *Bulletin: Constantinople Woman's College: President's Report, 1923–1924.* Robert College Archives, New York, 18.

90. Ibid.

91. Ibid.

92. Patrick, *Under Five Sultans*, 330.

93. Patrick, *A Bosporus Adventure*, 3.

"They Are Not Known to Us"

The Ottomans, the Mormons,
and the Protestants in the Late Ottoman Empire[1]

Karen M. Kern

The missionaries from the Church of Jesus Christ of Latter-day Saints (Mormons) were latecomers to the Ottoman Empire when they opened their first Turkish mission in Istanbul on December 31, 1884. This was not a particularly auspicious time to establish a new church. The reigning Sultan, Abdülhamid II (1876–1909), was attempting to reinforce Sunni orthodoxy throughout the empire, and his policy to expand Sunni missionary work among marginal and disparate tribes was in direct conflict with foreign missionary activity.[2]

The first phase of the Mormon Turkish mission lasted for twenty-five years from 1884 until 1909, with a brief interruption between 1895 and 1897. As the missionaries embarked on their labors, they encountered the same challenges experienced by their Protestant counterparts in seeking converts in a Muslim empire. The door was essentially closed to Muslim conversion out of Islam, which left proselytizing possible only among the Christian communities. At the end of the nineteenth century, however, the Ottoman government also placed many obstacles in the path of the Mormon missionaries that did not exist for the Protestants. Ottoman refusal to officially grant recognition to the Mormon sect, a certification already achieved by the Protestants, led to restrictions on publishing and distributing religious tracts, and a prohibition on preaching in public and establishing social service institutions. In addition to these difficulties, the Mormons also encountered complaints and slander from Protestant sects that fed into Ottoman suspicions of Mormon activities. The Mormon missionaries, like their Protestant counterparts, worked with the Armenian community at a moment of extraordinary political instability. Their involvement with the Armenians further spread the belief that they were supporters and facilitators of Armenian separatist activities. For all of these reasons, the Mormon sect was never able to achieve official Ottoman recognition and, therefore, labored under exceptionally difficult circumstances.

The current state of scholarship on the Mormon experience in the Middle East consists primarily of research generated by the Mormon academic community, which utilizes missionary diaries and local newspaper articles from the archive and library of the Church of Jesus Christ of Latter-day Saints. They examine the history of the missions, the activities of the missionaries, and the obstacles to their work from the perspective of the missionaries themselves.[3] Relatively little attention has been paid to the Mormon mission from the broader community of scholars who research Western missionary movements to the Middle East. Those few articles that have appeared also rely primarily on Church archives and, therefore, are again framed from the perspective of the missionaries.[4] This chapter takes a step beyond the current state of research by examining not only Church archives but also Ottoman archival documents. It places the Mormon missions within the larger context of the relationship of the Ottoman government to missionary activity, and also examines Mormon relations with native churches and other foreign missions. Current scholarship on Western missionary movements is engaged with the broader question of whether or not missionary activities had political dimensions that were a part of larger imperial projects. This study does not engage in this debate but instead examines the Mormon missions within the more "fragile process of staking out claims of cultural and historical belonging to the biblical land."[5]

This chapter begins with a brief discussion of the history of missionary activity in the Ottoman Empire in order to establish the commonalities between the Protestant and Mormon movements. The focus moves to reports from the Ottoman Embassy in Washington that show familiarity with Mormon history and an appreciation of Mormon problems with the U.S. government over their practice of polygamy, a fundamental principle of the faith. The next section then turns to the various attempts of the Ottomans under Sultan Abdülhamid II to control Mormon missionary activities. Rumors and slander generated by Protestant sects also influenced Ottoman government policy and created opposition to the Mormons that manifested in physical and verbal attacks. The chapter next examines the fundamental theological force behind most missionary activity to the Middle East in the nineteenth century. As with other missionaries, the Mormons saw themselves as participants in the process of prophetic fulfillment of the millennium and the ingathering of the Jews, which would lead eventually to judgment day. The final section of this chapter discusses the Mormons' intention to establish a colony that would witness and enable the fulfillment of biblical prophesy in Palestine. By placing the Mormon Turkish Mission within the larger context of Protestant missionary activity, and by examining Mormon missionary work from both the Mormon and Ottoman perspective, this study intends to bring this smaller, less wealthy missionary movement out of the provinces and into the mainstream of foreign missionaries who labored during the final decades of the Ottoman Empire.

A Short History of Missions to the Ottoman Empire

Missionaries had a presence in the Ottoman Empire that began as early as the sixteenth century with the arrival of Catholic missions. By the eighteenth century, British evangelicals, spurred on by tales from explorers of the horrible condition of native inhabitants, formed missionary societies and sent missions to the region.[6] The United States began to export American Christianity when the Boston-based American Board of Commissioners for Foreign Missions (ABCFM), a group of Congregational, Presbyterian, and Reformed congregations, sent their first missionaries to Jerusalem in 1820.[7] The missionaries of these various denominations shared some common tenets. They believed in spreading the gospel throughout the world, in the return of the Jews to Palestine and their eventual conversion to Christianity, in the destruction of the Papacy, and in the overthrow of the Ottoman Empire and the fall of Islam.[8] Their biblical prophesies conjoined the coming millennium in 1866 with the conversion of the world to Christianity, events that would lead to the Day of Judgment.[9]

American missionaries in the Ottoman Empire began working among Armenians and Nestorians in the late 1820s. Missionary activity increased in the next decade after the Treaty of Commerce and Navigation of 1830 came into force. Article IV of the treaty offered a measure of protection for missionaries by requiring the presence of an American consul in litigation between Ottoman subjects and citizens of the United States. The United States immediately established diplomatic missions throughout the Ottoman Empire and appointed David Porter as the first American ambassador to the empire in 1831.[10] Throughout the nineteenth century, the United States and the Ottomans disagreed about the extent of extraterritorial rights granted by Article IV, but in 1905, before final acceptance of the article's revision, the American ambassador John G. Leishman demanded fairer treatment for American missionaries as a prerequisite for ratification.[11]

American missionaries confronted obstacles from the Ottoman government because of lack of certification. An officially recognized church could publish religious literature, hold meetings, proselytize, collect taxes, and manage social services, including educational institutions. Without official recognition, however, converts lost their connection to their original churches, were without representation at the Sublime Porte, and were subject to extortion and abuse. In 1850, under strong British pressure, Sultan Abdülmecid issued an imperial decree that recognized the difficulties experienced by the Protestants. They received official recognition as a separate community and were subjected to, and received the benefits from, the same system allowed to other non-Muslim Ottoman subjects.[12]

Difficulties for American missionaries continued, however, due to resistance from native churches. The Armenian patriarch continually complained about Protestant missionaries who were poaching among the members of his community.[13] Irrespective of the resistance from native churches, Ottoman law allowed for proselytizing by foreign missionaries. Edicts and legislation enacted during the Tanzimat reform period provided for religious freedom and formed the legal basis for proselytizing in the empire. The "Reform Edict" (Hatt-ı Hümayun) of 1856 took an important step toward legalizing missionary activity by providing that no obstacles should hinder the right of Ottoman subjects to choose their religion.[14] The Criminal Code of 1858 reinforced the right of freedom of religion and dealt a punishment of between one week to three months for anyone who interfered with or threatened Ottoman subjects during worship and religious ceremonies.[15] The Sublime Porte also ensured religious freedom in Article Sixty-Two of the Treaty of Berlin (1878), which stated that no person was to be denied civil or political rights, opportunities, or honors because of their religion. The treaty guaranteed freedom of worship, freedom of travel for ecclesiastics, pilgrims, and monks of all nationalities, and freedom to establish religious and charitable institutions.[16]

The rights guaranteed under Ottoman law did not halt the "mutual suspicion and dislike" that marked the relationship between the Ottoman government and the missionary communities.[17] Selim Deringil has shown, for example, that Article Sixty-Two of the Treaty of Berlin was in actuality defensive and was meant to establish European acceptance of the Ottoman definition of religious liberty. The treaty defined a political principle that was "designed to maintain the strictly Mohammedan character of the Turkish Government, and to retain all political power in the hands of the Turks."[18] Sultan Abdülhamid II was instead intent on preventing Muslims from converting out of their faith. He recognized the wealth and influence of foreign missionaries and knew that Bible societies in England, Russia, and France had political leverage over their governments. If the Ottoman government moved against these societies, it risked intervention by the Powers on behalf of their subjects. In the Sultan's view, the only way to counter this influence was to reinforce Sunni Islam by spreading the faith and increasing the Muslim population.[19]

OTTOMAN VIEWS OF MORMONISM

The Mormons began their investigations in the Middle East during the 1840s, but for various reasons discussed below, the first Turkish mission in Istanbul was not opened until Elder Jacob Spori, a German-speaking convert from Switzerland, arrived on December 31, 1884.[20] The impetus for establishing the mission came from Hagop T. Vartooguian, an Armenian, who invited the Mormons to send missionaries to Turkey. They quickly established branches in the Anatolian towns of Zara (Sivas), Maraş (Marash), and Antep, and in Aleppo in northern Syria. Antep became the largest center for missionary activity and remained their headquarters until 1907 when they moved to Aleppo.[21]

When Jacob Spori arrived in Istanbul, he immediately reported back to Salt Lake City, "As Mr. V [Vartooguian] says, the Turkish authorities are rather indifferent about our doctrines."[22] Ottoman authorities may have appeared indifferent to Spori, but officials in the foreign ministry and in the Ottoman Embassy in Washington were well aware of the Mormon religion. The Ottomans, like other empires, monitored and reported on missionary activity throughout the world.[23] As early as November 1871, the Ottoman Embassy in Washington sent a detailed account of the Mormon community to Server Pasha, the Ottoman foreign minister. This sympathetic portrayal began with a description of early Mormon history in the 1830s as they tried to build a community in Missouri and Illinois and continued to 1847 when, under the leadership of Brigham Young, they went into unexplored wilderness between the Rocky Mountains and the Sierra Nevada and established their settlement in the Great Salt Lake Basin. In a short period of time the territory was an oasis for caravans of pioneers who were crossing the deserts of the West in search of California gold. The Latter-day Saints also rendered a great service to the expansion of the American Republic because of their material support to the builders of the great Pacific railroad. The railroad facilitated the colonization of the West as well as bringing the Mormon community into more frequent contact with the rest of the Union.[24]

The Ottoman Embassy took special interest in Mormon difficulties with U.S. authorities over the issue of polygamy. Showing sympathy and support, the embassy reported that U.S. authorities were influenced by the "fanaticism of the Puritans of Protestantism," which was against polygamy, a fundamental principle of Mormonism.[25] The embassy reported on a court case brought by Harriet Hawkins, the wife of a Mormon bishop, Thomas Hawkins, whom she accused of polygamy.[26] Officials noted that the court found Hawkins guilty and levied a punishment of five hundred dollars and three years in prison.[27] According to the embassy's analysis, this case was a prelude to more serious and energetic prosecution, since arrest warrants were also issued for Brigham Young and several of the main Mormon leaders.[28] The Ottoman Embassy believed that the U.S. administration intended to remove this sect from Union territory in order to benefit unscrupulous land speculators who were enemies of the Mormons. In clear sympathy with the Mormon settlers, embassy officials wondered how Mormon leaders and their adherents would respond to this persecution. Would the more fanatical members resist with arms, or would they come to a much wiser decision and relocate farther into the wilderness of the continent, or even leave the United States and emigrate to Tahiti? The report correctly predicted that Brigham Young would try to come to terms with U.S. authorities and eventually pronounce the end of polygamy among the Latter-day Saints.[29]

In December 1887, the Ottoman Embassy in Washington sent a report to Said Pasha, the Ottoman foreign minister, which discussed the intense fascination of the U.S. press with the subject of Mormon polygamy.[30] There was concern in the United States that polygamy would continue to flourish if Utah Territory was admitted to the Union. Congress did not want to see this occur and believed that if the Senate waited to confer statehood on the territory, then the non-Mormon population might increase enough to cease being dominated by the Mormons.[31] It is clear from these reports that by the time of the establishment of the Mormon Turkish mission in 1884 both the Ottoman Embassy in Washington and the Ottoman Ministry of Foreign Affairs were well aware of the existence of the Mormon sect and of their long, contentious history with U.S. authorities. This knowledge, however, did not appear to translate into a willingness to recognize and facilitate Mormon missionary activities in the empire.

POLYGAMY IN ISLAM AND MORMONISM

The institution of polygamy in both Islam and Mormonism was bound to become a major narrative component among the Mormons, Ottoman Muslims, and native Ottoman-Christian populations. Polygamy in Islam and Mormonism was based on different historical contexts. In the seventh century CE, Muhammad curtailed an existing polygamous tradition among the Arabs by limiting the number of wives to four. In contrast, in the nineteenth century Joseph Smith introduced the institution of polygamy into a monogamous society in Illinois. For both Muslims and Mormons, however, the institution of plural marriage was a divinely inspired law.[32]

Polygamous marriages among the Ottomans, historically, were never as numerous as imagined by Western travelers. Alan Duben and Cem Behar's seminal research on Istanbul households examined census data to determine its frequency. They found that between 1885 and 1907 only 2.29 percent of men and only about 5 percent of women in Istanbul were engaged in polygamous unions. The authors noted that this percentage was low when compared to the 10 to 12 percent of Mormon men in polygamous marriages. They emphasized further that, although Islamic law allowed for up to four wives, the main form was bigamy and not polygamy. Duben and Behar maintained that even though polygamy was accepted in the society, the institution met with increasing opposition in the late nineteenth and early twentieth century.[33]

By the mid- to late nineteenth century, in fact, many Ottoman writers and intellectuals were quite critical of this tradition in their society, and they made reference to Mormon polygamy as evidence of the decadence inherent in the institution. The journalist İbrahim Şinasi (1825–1871), for example, used his newspaper *Tasvir-i Efkar* (*Description of Ideas*) as a vehicle in support of liberal politics and social reforms. He translated articles from the foreign press and used poetry for his own commentary on the issue at hand. In 1863, the newspaper published a translation of a French article about the Mormon sect that made a connection between polygamy in Utah territory and the civil war between the northern and southern states. The president of the republic of the northern states was attempting to prevent polygamy among the Mormon sect. Şinasi added his critique in two poetic phrases, imagining how a Mormon man would react to the prohibition of this fundamental ordinance of his religion. This imaginary Mormon male thought "what an evil [it is] to be limited to one wife" and "to stop being able to lust after a young girl."[34] This poetic critique was an interesting turn of perspective since Şinasi was essentially "orientalizing the occident." He depicted a Christian sect as exotic and erotic in the same manner that Western writers long portrayed the "Orient."[35]

When reading the diaries and reports of Mormon missionaries, one is struck by Mormon interest in Ottoman polygamy and Ottoman curiosity about Mormon polygamy. Ottoman subjects who listened to Mormon missionaries were apparently as interested in polygamy as they were in the gospel. When Ferdinand Hintze arrived in Beirut in 1889, he preached the principles of the gospel and although people listened respectfully they appeared to be disappointed because "we did not tell them how they could obtain a plurality of wives."[36]

In 1890, Janne Sjodahl wrote that Mormon polygamy was superior to polygamy in Islam. In certain ways, Sjodahl's view was similar to Şinasi's position. Both noted that the other's form of polygamy was based on male lust and female repression and unhappiness. Sjodahl wrote,

> [I] have it from a reliable informant that the Moslem ladies are generally opposed to the system of polygamy as practiced here. They are sometimes crazy from jealousy, and the husbands are many a time afraid of eating food prepared by the wives, for fear of being poisoned. Thus the peace of families often vanishes with the introduction of a new wife. But the reasons for this are also obvious. The husbands act without consulting their wives, and transact the business "on the sly" as much as possible. Mohammedan polygamy is, therefore, essentially legalized prostitution, and that causes here, as in all the world, jealousy…it is an affair of no higher importance than the gratification of the flesh. There is no heaven in it; all is in earth…. One lamentable result…I have been told, is that many Moslems' wives seek other company than that of their husbands. This is mentioned as a public secret, and the fact illustrates how the transgression of God's laws always result in misery and degradation, while strict adherence to those laws ennobles mankind and fosters virtue, bringing with it peace and happiness.[37]

Brother Fred A. Huish seemed particularly interested in marriage customs and also noted differences between polygamy among the Mormons and the Ottoman Turks. In 1893, he remarked that Ottoman polygamy was the cause of crimes such as licentiousness and theft, and it is a wonder that "the nation has not been swept away by disease; no wonder that cholera has such an affinity for them."[38] On another occasion Huish received a visit from an Armenian man who had an invalid wife and wanted to remarry. He asked Huish if this would be a sin in Mormonism, because it was a sin in the Armenian Church. The man said that he had a lot of money and he would become a Mormon if he could have a new wife. Huish told him that it would be a great sin.[39] Huish also noted that polygamy was indeed rare in Islam because only the wealthy could afford more than one wife. He reported that a Muslim with multiple wives committed a sin if he did not have intercourse with each of them once a week. This was to prevent old or ugly wives from neglect.⁴⁰ Huish's distaste for polygamy, as he believed it was practiced in Islam, is indeed interesting since only three years earlier, in 1890, the Mormon leadership had outlawed polygamy as a step toward statehood. The outlawing of polygamy did not mean that polygamy suddenly ceased to exist in Utah Territory. It is reasonable to assume that Huish was not far removed chronologically or psychologically from the institution, and felt the need to draw distinctions between the Mormon and Muslim versions that elevated Mormon belief.

THE OTTOMAN GOVERNMENT'S CONTROL OVER MISSIONARY ACTIVITY

Early in the long reign of Sultan Abdülhamid II, the Ottomans sustained tremendous loss of territory and Muslim population to the Russians in the Russo-Ottoman War of 1877–1878. Fearing the disintegration of the empire, the sultan established a policy in the 1880s to restore Islamic unity by bringing heterodox Muslim groups into mainstream Sunni Islam. Protestantism became the "main ideological enemy in the eyes of the Sultan."⁴¹ By the early 1890s, the Ottomans also came to believe that Protestant missionaries were fostering subversion and sedition by facilitating Armenian revolts. Armenian separatists inside and outside of the empire hoped to create an Armenian republic in six eastern Anatolian provinces. During the three years from 1890 to 1893, attacks and counterattacks occurred in predominantly Armenian villages. The worse of the massacres took place during the winter of 1895–1896, and the army was not able to reestablish control until the spring months. The Ottoman government accused American missionaries of being the "spiritual fathers of the social unrest."⁴²

Sultan Abdülhamid II sought to closely control all forms of missionary activity from the publishing of pamphlets and books to the opening of schools and churches. Such control had, from time to time, been a part of Ottoman-missionary relations. In November 1862, the minister of foreign affairs, Ali Pasha, informed embassies and legations in Istanbul that the government was censoring all publications containing political or religious propaganda. Confiscations of Christian publications began immediately.⁴³ In 1864, the Ottomans took stricter measures by enacting the "Act of Publication," which required permission from the Sublime Porte before missionary materials could be imported, published, or distributed. The police closed an American mission bookstore and seized its contents because of accusations that the missionaries were spreading false information about Islam.[44] New regulations in 1875 required that the Ministry of Public Instruction approve the printing of religious materials. Missionaries continued, however, to publish and distribute books and pamphlets, despite these regulations.[45] In the 1880s, the Ottoman government attempted to increase their control and began to investigate the importation of missionary publications at the point of entry to the empire. Many publications were confiscated and destroyed and, when the missionaries tried to seek redress for the value of their books, the Ottoman government refused to compensate them for their financial losses. Regulations on the importation, printing, and distribution of missionary pamphlets and books continued until the constitutional revolution in 1908 when the Committee of Union and Progress finally lifted these restrictions.[46]

The Mormon experience in attempting to import, publish, and distribute their pamphlets and books offers a microcosm of the obstacles facing foreign missionaries. At the beginning of the Mormon mission, Elder Jacob Spori remarked on the difficulty in transporting published materials into the Ottoman Empire. After arriving in Istanbul, officials seized and examined his tracts and pamphlets. With the help of a few piasters, however, he was able to regain possession of his belongings.[47]

When Elder Ferdinand F. Hintze was appointed president of the Turkish Mission in 1887, he immediately set about seeking permission to publish in Turkish. Over the course of that year, he took petitions to the Grand Vizier, to the Publishing Council, and finally to the minister of education. The minister of education refused permission, however, until the government officially recognized the Mormon Church.[48] Hintze was not deterred and continued for another year to petition the Ottoman government for certification. The Ottoman cabinet maintained that since "they are not known to us, it is illegal to publish and distribute books in the empire."[49] The cabinet ordered the ministries of religion and education to investigate the sect in order to ensure that no harm would come to the fundamentals of the Muslim faith. Once that assurance was given, the Mormon sect could be granted permission to publish and distribute books.

Protestant opposition also influenced the government in its decision to prevent the Mormons from publishing and distributing their tracts. In

1891, Frederick Stauffer received permission to publish but the Protestants immediately created such an outcry that the government reversed its decision. Stauffer and other missionaries continued, nonetheless, to petition for the right to publish and distribute their doctrines throughout the remaining decade.[50]

Obstacles to the importation and printing of missionary tracts were compounded by press censorship. Elder Philip Maycock, president of the Turkish Mission from 1897 to 1899, described the irrational and rather comic nature of censorship when he related,

A chemist landed, so the story goes, at one of these ports and a strict examination of his trunk-packed library was at once begun. Volume after volume passed the severe test until at last the special textbook on chemistry was opened and the eye of the unlearned, yet loyal, censor caught that scientific sign for water H_2O. This was more than his brain could decipher and a council of all his wise associates was immediately called for the purpose of unraveling the hidden mystery. At last one, like Daniel of old, was found who could interpret the hieroglyphics to their entire satisfaction. The council accepted the interpretation of H_2O as an impious sling at the sultan [Abdülhamid II], for they said it meant "Hamid the second is nothing."[51]

Maycock later learned of a story about a hymnbook that was seized because "the censor found in it a belligerent command, "Hold the fort, for I am coming."[52]

The lack of official government recognition of the Mormon sect also led to difficulties in establishing social services such as educational institutions. Article 129 of the Ottoman "Education Regulation" of 1869 required public inspection of all foreign schools, their curricula, and their teachers. Teachers in nongovernmental institutions had to acquire certificates from the ministry of education in Istanbul or the ministry's local representative. Officially certified schools were also required to prove that they were not giving lessons that were "contrary to custom and [state] policy and ideology."[53] This regulation was established to place limits on the formation of foreign educational institutions. In 1876, *Basiret*, one of the most influential and widely read newspapers in Istanbul, reflected government thinking that

American, British, and German missionary schools were "founts of the foreign poison of Protestant proselytism."[54]

In the last decades of the nineteenth century, the government frequently sent directives to the provinces to insure the licensing of missionary schools and churches, but these regulations were essentially unenforceable. In 1886, the minister of education, Münif Pasha, advocated closer inspection of non-Muslim schools since these schools were not under ministry control and the government had no way of knowing their "curricula, textbooks, and moral character and behavior of the teachers."[55] The government was especially concerned to prevent Muslim children from attending foreign schools where the potential existed for their conversion out of Islam. Religious authorities (ulema) were given the duty to warn the Muslim population against sending their children to these schools.

On December 27, 1891, a Military Reform Commission memorandum advised the government to ignore pressure from foreign governments and immediately close unlicensed schools and churches.[56] In 1892, the governor of the province of Damascus reported that there were 159 unlicensed schools organized in buildings other than schoolhouses. He also noted that attempts to increase the numbers of Ottoman primary schools, while extraordinary, still did not fulfill the needs of the population, and the missionary schools filled these gaps.[57] The missionaries not only educated non-Muslim children without cost, but also clothed and fed them and, reportedly, paid their parents.[58] Although Ottoman authorities continually warned missionaries that their schools were illegal, and occasionally closed them, noncompliance by foreign missionaries with the regulations continued to be the norm in the final decades of the empire.

In addition to difficulties in publishing and establishing education institutions, the Mormons struggled with other obstacles that stemmed from lack of official recognition. In 1889, L. O. Littlefield reported from Antep that although many people came to investigate Mormon teaching, and some even maintained that they had converted, very few would be baptized since it could lead to imprisonment, banishment, increased taxation, or persecution.[59] In 1890, Ferdinand Hintze further noted that the government did not recognize an individual outside of his denomination. Since the Mormons were not recognized, they could not guarantee protection to those who might wish to convert. Hintze remained hopeful, however, since he had "conversed with many who are looking forward to some change whereby they may be liberated from their present state of bondage and be made free in the Lord Jesus Christ."[60]

The Mormon missionaries were subjected to particular scrutiny and suspicion as a result of their work in the Armenian community. In 1890, Frederick Stauffer reported that after arriving in Maraş he was arrested by the police and his books were examined on suspicion that he was inciting the Armenians. He was brought to Aleppo where he was held, but the court eventually set him free. When he asked the reason for his arrest, the judge "replied that there was nothing, merely some Government matters that could not be told."[61] Stauffer was in custody for seventeen days, set free without fine or punishment, and ended up paying five dollars of his own money for traveling expenses. In 1894, the new president to the Turkish Mission, Edward W. Robinson, was accused of aiding and abetting Armenian separatist activities. The Ottomans were suspicious because he lived in a room within the Armenian community in Aleppo. He was accused of being an Armenian spy, but after having been brought before the Pasha he was eventually released and able to leave Aleppo for Antep.[62]

It became clear to the missionaries that the problems they were encountering in Aleppo resulted not only from lack of recognition and from their work with the Armenian community but from orders originating in Istanbul. In 1898, Elder Lund reported that the governor of Aleppo had received word from Istanbul not to recognize the Mormons as a religious body. The Mormons had been considering the establishment of a colony to support local converts, but the governor was also instructed to prevent such a settlement. Lund realized that the best they could do was to find money to buy looms and raw material to support a weaving business for their Armenian converts. In this way the converts would be freed from the prejudices of their current employers.[63]

By 1899, the Mormons had established branches in a few towns, but they were far apart and lightly staffed. They had two Sunday schools and an Improvement Association, attended by both sexes, at Antep and Aleppo. Day schools were also in operation at Antep and Zara and "were doing good work."[64] Mormon missionaries were primarily based in Antep and traveled as itinerant preachers to these various branches. Unlike Protestant sects where female missionaries predominated, the Mormons did not generally send women on missions into the field. Local converts ran the branches, though, and some of the female converts occasionally took positions as teachers in the schools. There was one rare example of a wealthy female convert who sought permission to sell her property in Palestine so that she might undertake a mission to Budapest. The results of her request are unknown.[65]

In 1899, Mr. Boyadjian, the president of the Bible House in Istanbul who represented the Protestants, suggested to Ferdinand Hintze that the Mormons could apply for recognition as a member of the Protestant community. Hintze rejected the offer since the Mormons were not Protestants but a distinct church with its own doctrine.[66] It is not clear why Mr. Boyadjian would make such an offer. It is unlikely that he canvassed the various denominations or received approval to allow inclusion of the Mormons.

Without recognition, obstacles and harassment continued to plague the missionaries. When Hintze was preaching in Antioch in March, 1899 he reported that many were coming to hear him against the advice of the police. The governor of the province also sent a telegram to Antioch saying that it was necessary to halt the spread of Mormonism. Hintze did not stop preaching and instead requested that the American consul in Alexandretta, Horace Lee Washington, call on the governor and inform him that "the Mormon Church was a recognized organization in America."[67] The governor reiterated that the Ottoman government did not recognize the Mormons as a church. "He said there were orders from the Sultan to stop Mormonism and particularly not to let any Mormon missionaries go to Antioch."[68] By June of 1899, Mr. Straus, the American ambassador in Istanbul, was demanding that the Ottoman government give the Mormon elders the same recognition as other missionaries. The governor of Aleppo continued to maintain that the Mormons were not to hold any meetings or run any schools until they received official recognition.[69]

By 1900, the mission was finally meeting with some success. Ferdinand Hintze reported back to Salt Lake City that, after struggling for fourteen years, the Mormons had obtained printing privileges. Hintze immediately printed twenty-nine thousand tracts, translated twenty-eight sections of the *Doctrine and Covenants* into Turkish, and began translating the *Book of Mormon*. The Church had more than one hundred members and, if more elders were sent, the prospects were good for more conversion.[70] Hintze received his release to return to Utah, and Albert Herman (1900–1904) succeeded him as president of the mission. Herman had five missionaries working in the empire, including J. Alma Holdaway in Aleppo and Thomas P. Page in Antep. The brothers Henry and Charles Teuscher preached from Aleppo southward to Damascus, Baalbeck, Homs, and Palestine. Herman's mandate was to travel to the various mission branches to preach and visit with members.[71] Mormon missionaries often lived this peripatetic lifestyle where they traveled alone to a city, staying only for a few days or weeks before moving to the next city. They did not acquire a large number of converts by this method, but instead hoped to build the foundation for others who would follow them.[72]

Ottoman authorities were suspicious of the Mormon itinerant lifestyle. In 1903, authorities placed Albert Herman under police supervision and monitored his correspondence. Postal officials discovered nine letters that Herman had addressed to the various missionaries and to the administrative heads of the Mormon centers in Liverpool and Salt Lake City. Some of the information in the letters was rather mundane. There was a list, for example, of monthly and yearly expenses for Herman and for their centers in Antep, Aleppo, and Zara, as well as the costs for renting a factory for rug production. Another letter petitioned for more missionaries and listed various locations that needed representation. On a rather personal note, Herman discussed the desires of the missionaries. He wanted to visit "a place near the Black Sea coast in the north of Turkey near Mount Ararat that is very charming."[73] But he was worried because these places were without leadership. Holdaway reportedly was desperate to go to Jerusalem but could not leave his post until someone was appointed to take his place. Yet the missionaries were still in good humor. According to Herman, their joy was increased when they heard the sounds of the bells ringing in their churches.[74]

Ottoman authorities were aware that Herman was traveling around the interior of Asia Minor. And Herman was aware that he was under suspicion. "The government is suspicious of me. They issued a judgment that…my Book of Mormon was against the state."[75] Herman and the missionaries were certainly touched by the disastrous economic conditions of the Armenians, particularly those in Aleppo who could not find work. They sought funds to aid the community, collecting contributions while at the same time encouraging men and women to meet in churches in the evenings to hear the

Mormon doctrines. Ottoman authorities sent instructions to the governor in Antep that the Mormons should cease their meetings because they were clearly contrary to Ottoman custom. In fact, Ottoman authorities believed that Herman was a spy working in support of Armenian revolutionary movements based in Europe. Their suspicions seemed to be confirmed when they found a list of names of members of the sect who were giving money to aid the Armenians. The Ottomans advised that "it is necessary from the political and administrative point of view to forbid them in every way from taking money from people for the Armenian committees in Europe."[76]

Mormons believed that the suspicions about Albert Herman had been perpetrated by false accusations from jealous Protestants who were trying to convince Ottoman officials to expel the missionaries. Herman went directly to American ambassador Leishman in Istanbul who in turn petitioned the Sublime Porte to guarantee the security and rights of the missionaries.[77] But frustrations and problems continued as the result of lack of official recognition. According to J. Wilford Booth's 1904 report to Salt Lake City, "We are and we have been for several years trying to secure recognition from the government, with privileges of holding schools and open meetings, and of preaching the Gospel with more liberty, and we trust in due time of the Lord this will be given to us."[78] Unbeknownst to Booth, during the period of the first Mormon mission from 1884 through 1909 the Mormons would never achieve official recognition from the Ottoman government.

STICKS AND STONES—SLANDER AND PHYSICAL ATTACKS

When the Mormons entered the region in 1884, indigenous churches and Protestant missions immediately became concerned that these newcomers would poach from their membership. Antagonism and hostility toward the Mormon missionaries continued throughout the twenty-five years of the first Turkish Mission. Immediately upon arriving in Istanbul, Jacob Spori reported, "European preachers…already spread some nonsense about us, which, however, found not the credit they expected."[79] These attacks often took place in articles in missionary publications. On March 14, 1885, for example, Spori reported, "The reverends of the American Bible Society published a most slanderous article in their paper, to which, for the present, I have only answered with a polite letter asking for an interview to clear up some of the mistakes.... I think the lies and slanders can easily be refuted."[80] In May, Spori avoided a scandal when the reverends tried to entrap him into transgressing social customs.

> A few days ago I was asked to give an interview to some young la-
> dies from a Scutari Institute, as some of them speak French. Directly
> warned by a feeling I said: "I shall be happy to meet these ladies, only
> they must bring their fathers, brothers or teachers with them." It was a
> trap from our old friends the reverends.[81]

Spori described Mormon-Protestant relations as a "torpedo" since everything was under the surface. Whereas initially attacks against them were published in newspapers and could be refuted, within a few months the Methodists and others were secretly spreading slander and lies.[82]

In 1889, Janne Sjodahl reported in more detail on Protestant accusations against the Mormons. They first accused the Mormons of having many wives, and then the stories became embellished. Rumors spread that there were two Mormon missionaries in Haifa who were looking to marry five hundred wives, and they would pay a lot of money for these women. Sjodahl confirmed the impact of these stories when one day he encountered a man who asked for a few wives and some money to help him emigrate.

> Such startling requests the "Mormons" will have to listen to, and thank
> their "Christian" friends for helping the natives in circulating the
> yarns.... God only knows how long this complicated system of false-
> hood known as Christianity shall play its role upon this earth. But this
> we do know, that when He rules who had the right, then only shall
> truth prevail.[83]

The Protestants spread other false stories about the Mormons. In April 1889, Charles U. Locander reported from Adana that Turkish and Armenian papers had printed specious stories about Mormons who had fled America and "landed on these hospitable shores and dared, under the very shadow of the Ottoman Crescent, to elude its officers."[84] These Mormons were now allegedly traveling through Anatolia and spreading "their polluting doctrine," but Ottoman officers would track them down and they would be expelled from the empire.[85] Locander noted that Protestant attacks went beyond defamatory articles and actually placed the missionaries in physical danger. "These labors, though tiresome (as we are called from 6 a.m. to 10:30 p.m., besides being followed in the streets when going to meals) are yet a source of much satisfaction; and a few stones thrown at our windows and scoffling [sic] in the street, and even an occasional burlesque song about 'Mormonlar' (the 'Mormons') have not done much to scare us off."[86] The negative accusations spread by various Protestant sects appeared to backfire, however, and instead created more interest in the Mormon sect. Locander reported that over one hundred Greeks, Catholics, Romans, orthodox Armenians, Muslims, Protestants, and nonconformists attended their gatherings.[87]

Mormon missionaries did not sit back and accept such slander. In 1890, Frederick Stauffer recounted how the Mormons were challenging Protestant accusations directly by attending their churches and engaging the priests and congregations in conversations. "The result of our conversation was to turn many from their old prejudices against the 'Mormons,' which they had engendered by reading newspapers which had been filled with slander against us during the past eight or ten months."[88] These small victories did not put an end to the accusations from Protestant mission officials. In 1898, Ferdinand Hintze described the acrimonious accusations and jealousy that he confronted in Antep because he was attracting crowds from twenty-five to one hundred persons.

> Now such a condition could, of course, not exist without opposition. Soon the professors from the Central Turkish college [sic] of Antep, an institution belonging to the American mission in Turkey, saw the danger to their crafts. They immediately issued five circulars on Mormonism, purporting to prove by the Bible that Mormonism is false, and winding off with all the vile stories about the Mormons long since exploded. Polygamy horribly described, blood atonement, the Mountain Meadow Massacre, etc. They claimed it was necessary to show the sources of Mormonism in order to prove its falsity, also that Joseph Smith was a lazy, low money digger.[89]

Professor Gregorian frequently visited the Mormon missionaries to ask for their publications so he could refute their teachings. He produced a number of articles that utilized Mormon doctrines of polygamy and blood atonement, as well as the famous Mountain Meadow Massacre, as weapons to delegitimize the sect in the minds of potential converts.[90] By 1898, the time of these accusations, polygamy had been outlawed for eight years, blood atonement was not a part of mainstream practice, and the main figure in the Mountain Meadow Massacre had been tried and convicted with no further arrests of the main authorities of the Mormon Church.[91]

Physical attacks and general harassment perpetrated by Protestant opposition became more voracious during the year 1898. According to Ferdinand Hintze, a harrowing event occurred after a Sunday morning meeting in Antep.

> So severe was the onslaught that it looked like a cyclone of persecutions. On the streets we were followed by curious, shouting mobs, occasionally stoning us, and all the time whistling and yelling Mor-r, Mor-r-r-, rolling out the r in a real comical way. Now Mor [*sic*] means purple in Turkish so they yelled, savy, mavy Mor-r-r (Yellow, blue Purpe-l-l) [*sic*]. This, of course, was fun for the Antep hoodlums, hundreds followed us in the streets. Men, women and children in the gates and on the flat housetops taking in the sight afforded. Why it was a real circus to them to see what they thought to be the much married Mormons...until we had, at last, to call in the police to protect us.[92]

Elder Anthon H. Lund expanded on this particular event by exposing the role of an unnamed professor in the college in Antep who published a series of papers that turned the people against the Mormons. This professor was apparently very learned and well respected by the Armenians and so was able to incite the people. The Mormons believed that the professor's accusations caused the stoning and rough handling on the streets. After the police were called and several arrests were made, the Protestant ministers finally promised that they would no longer harass the Mormons. The Mormons insisted, however, on meeting with the local Ottoman commander who promised them protection and said, "Those who have a new message to bring unto the world have always been persecuted."[93]

As they traveled far and wide, Mormon missionaries continued to encounter harassment that they believed emanated from the accusations of the professors at the Central Turkey College. In June of 1898, while preaching in Malatya, Brothers Hintze and Nisham were accused of being spies and detained for five days. Ottoman officials took one look at the size of Hintze's daybook and judged that "he must be something more than an ordinary man or else he would not write so much."[94] Letters from the professors of the college had apparently warned of the coming of the Mormons and aroused suspicions among the people, which led to Hintze and Nisham's detention. Local Protestants asked for protection from the government since the Mormons were considered "disturbers of the peace."[95] Later that same year, two Armenian converts, Brothers Vezerian and Nadjerian, were arrested in Diyarbekir, allegedly for carrying drugs. They were dentists so this may not have been so unusual. The brothers told the authorities that they were Mormons, but the officials in Diyarbekir did not know about the sect and requested information from Istanbul. The matter was then referred to the Armenian patriarch who apparently told the police that Mormonism was not a sect and must be a secret organization. The American consul in Aleppo, however, informed the authorities in Diyarbekir that there was indeed a religion called Mormonism and the Armenian brothers were Mormons of good character. Ottoman authorities refused to release them since "the two Armenian Mormons were Ottoman subjects."[96] In October, they were sentenced to four months in jail. After serving their sentence, Vezerian and Nadjerian were returned to Aleppo. Dr. Armanag Hagopian, former president of the Antep branch, provided bail to have them released and, finally, the government set them free on December 14, 1898.[97]

An Armenian teacher instigated physical attacks, which took place during a holiday in Antioch in 1899, when thousands of people were picnicking in the hills. Philip S. Maycock reported that people began to shout and hurl stones at the missionaries as they preached to the crowd. Ottoman police officers tried, unsuccessfully, to restrain the crowd, and then attempted to guide the Mormons to the safety of their homes. The crowds increased, along with slanderous shouts and more hurling of stones. Since the Mormons were in the charge of the police, the crowds spread the news that the missionaries were now under arrest and being taken to jail. Maycock informed Salt Lake City that this event showed the barbarity of fellow Christians who profess to follow the precepts of good will toward men. It was also not the first time that the Mormons were protected by Muslims who prevented the Christians from committing "barbarous excesses."[98]

Protestant methods of proselytizing did not go unnoticed by Mormon missionaries. The Mormons were, in fact, quite critical of the commercialism that financed Protestant activities and concerned over the impact of that commercialism on converts. In contrast to the Protestant sects, the Mormons operated under tremendous financial constraints. The community in Salt Lake City was not wealthy, and the missionaries were generally self-supporting, so they were unable to rely on the kind of financing generated by Protestant fundraising activities. The Mormons had more difficulty in purchasing property or finding the funds to support social and educational services for their converts.

While in Smyrna (Izmir) in 1889, Ferdinand Hintze described a coffee shop called "The Rest" that belonged to the American Congregational Mission Society and an English mission board where one could relax and read religious newspapers. The walls were decorated with scriptural passages about Christ and the Bible.

> Here we have the work reduced to a business principle. Of course, cafes are in great demand in the orient [*sic*], but I can hardly conceive the idea that this is the way to preach the Gospel. But perhaps looking at it a little different it may be better comprehended. Their doctrines being man-made [*sic*]. Why should not also their methods of expounding them be man-made as well?[99]

In 1889, Janne Sjodahl asserted that Christian missionaries had abandoned their work for the sake of monetary gain, and that the impact of money had tarnished missionary relations with the indigenous population. Protestant missionaries were well paid and surrounded themselves with worldly goods. As a result, the locals connected missionary work and conversion with profit. Protestant commercialism had an impact on Mormon missionaries since the local people were incredulous and could "hardly comprehend that a man can sacrifice his property and travel thousands of miles and come out here preaching the Gospel without remuneration."[100]

In 1890, a Mormon newspaper, the *Deseret Weekly*, reported on the success of Protestant missions among the Armenian population. There has been a "great religious revival in connection with the Turco-American Mission in Antep, in Armenia, and...it has resulted in the addition of five hundred and thirty four new members to the Protestant Church."[101] The correspondent believed that this revival was fueled by monetary considerations. According to the article, the Protestant missionaries hired only servants who converted to the faith. The missionaries also invited the target population to social events and promised them even more entertainments if they attended church and registered as "enquirers." If they attended church regularly, they would also receive free medical care and be released from military duties. Pecuniary considerations were so much a part of the conversion business that "Christ is being sold by the great bulk of missionaries out there, as He once was by Judas, and for much less than thirty pieces of silver."[102] Missionaries should not be surprised when people inquired, "Suppose we are willing to accept your doctrines, how much do we get for it? What profit is there in it?"[103]

COLONIZATION AND THE DEDICATION OF THE LAND OF ISRAEL

The Mormon missionaries to the Middle East, like their Protestant counterparts, were compelled by the belief in the fulfillment of the biblical prophesy of the coming millennium and the ingathering of the Jews in Palestine. They were theologically connected as agents in implementation of these events.[104] From the very beginnings of their religion, Mormon emissaries traveled to the Holy Land in order to determine ways in which they might participate and assist in the realization of this historic event.

In April 1840, Apostle Orson Hyde, a member of the Quorum of Twelve, the ruling body of the Mormon Church, was called upon to travel to the Holy Land with the instruction to determine the potential for establishing a mission.[105] Upon reaching Jerusalem in the autumn of 1842, he ascended the Mount of Olives, blessed the land, and dedicated it as the place where the Jews would gather.[106] Hyde's attempts at proselytizing did not meet with much success and he determined that this was not the time for Mormon missionaries to work in the Middle East.[107] His arrival in Palestine occurred at the end of a period known as the Egyptian Crisis, a particularly inauspicious time. This crisis was a conflict over control of Greater Syria, fought for more than a decade between Mehmet Ali, the Ottoman governor of Egypt, and the Sultans Mahmud II (1808–1839) and Abdülmecid (1839–1861). The retreat of the Egyptian army in 1840 ended the conflict but created a substantial power vacuum in the region that led to two decades of civil unrest.[108] Hyde's mission to Palestine was undertaken against this backdrop of political and civil instability and it is reasonable to assume that he did not feel the time was ripe for missionary activities due to the unstable conditions.

The instability of the times did not lead the Mormons to abandon their belief in their role in fulfilling biblical prophesy. In 1845, the Quorum of Twelve Apostles issued a proclamation concerning the Mormons' role in the return of the Jews to Palestine. In the proclamation, the Church declared that the Jews were commanded by God to return to Jerusalem and rebuild the city and their temple. The Mormons now held "the keys of the priesthood and kingdom which are soon to be restored unto them."[109]

Mormon reengagement in the Middle East revived only after they established themselves in Utah Territory, and gained their own level of stability. In October 1872, another group of missionaries led by President George A. Smith, and Lorenzo Snow and Albert Carrington were ordered by Brigham Young to "dedicate and consecrate the land [of Palestine] to the Lord, that it may be blessed with fruitfulness, preparatory to the return of the Jews in fulfillment of prophesy and the accomplishment of the purpose of our Heavenly Father."[110] They landed in Jaffa in the spring of 1873 and proceeded to Jerusalem, where they held services on the Mount of Olives and rededicated Palestine as the land for the gathering of the Jews and the rebuilding of Jerusalem. President Smith reported back to Utah that the day of the return of the Jews was not far distant and the prophesies of the restoration of Israel would soon be fulfilled.[111] This group also surveyed the land in order to determine if conditions were ready for missionary work. They concluded that, although conditions had improved in the thirty years since Orson Hyde's visit, the time was still not ripe for missionary work.[112] The Ottoman Empire was in a financial crisis due to the 1873 crash of the international stock market. Years of drought and floods had also led to famine in the Anatolian countryside, resulting in depopulation and migration. The depression nearly bankrupted the empire, and increased taxation led to civil unrest.[113] In the early 1870s, Russia and Austria-Hungary fought for control of the Ottoman's Balkan territories in a war that would last most of the decade. Stability did not return until the Treaty of Berlin was concluded in July of 1878, which led to the end of Ottoman rule in the Balkans.[114]

The end of the Balkan crisis, the establishment of a constitutional regime in 1876 and the rise to power of Abdülhamid II led to more peaceful conditions, and only then did the Mormons consider once again sending missions to the empire. The Mormons were well aware that Jews from around the world were beginning to settle in Palestine. In 1876, the French Jewish financier, Baron de Rothschild, met with Elder John Taylor and asked him what was necessary for Jewish settlement in Palestine. Elder Taylor replied,

> You can do nothing unless God directs. You as a people are tied hand and foot, and have been for generations, and you can't move a peg unless God strikes off your fetters. When he says the word the things spoken of by the prophets will be fulfilled. Then, the measuring line will go forth again in Jerusalem, then your Messiah will come, and all those things spoken of by the prophets will be fulfilled.[115]

The missionaries frequently wrote back to Salt Lake City newspapers about the ways in which their labors fulfilled biblical prophesy and the coming millennium. In 1889, Ferdinand Hintze expressed his belief that their work would bring the knowledge of the Lord to Asiatic nations that were in ignorance of the coming of Jesus.[116] In the same year, Janne Sjodahl noted that many theologians did not currently believe in the literal reestablishment of the Jews in Palestine and that, instead, biblical prophesy should be understood spiritually. He disagreed because the Jews were indeed gathering and building cities in Jerusalem. It was only a matter of time before the temple was rebuilt. Biblical prophesy was "hardly a matter of belief any longer; it is a matter of fact, every day demonstrated before our very eyes."[117] Sjodahl also believed that Sultan Abdülhamid II's concession to a French company to build railroads from Jaffa to Jerusalem and from Haifa to Damascus confirmed that the gathering of the Jews was near.

> A Jew once told me that the railway would be the forerunner for the Messiah and one of the means by which the children of Israel should return from their exile. He referred to … the Jews scattered among the nations, bringing their offerings to Jerusalem on various conveyances— "on horses, and wagons, and mules, and on kirkaroth." This word "kirkaroth" has been variously translated, commonly into meaning

"swift runners" or "swift camels." It is, however, coined from *kar*, a furnace, and *karkar* to sway and might be rendered swaying furnaces. The Prophet evidently tried to coin a word for a railway train which he saw in his vision, but for which object the language then had no word.[118]

An article in the *Deseret Weekly* in 1890 commented that Jewish settlements, which covered the plains in and around Jerusalem, were fulfillment of prophesy. There were approximately forty thousand Jews out of a population of seventy thousand in Jerusalem. Jewish agricultural colonies were established throughout Palestine with the assistance of the Rothschild family.

> In connection with the numerous and active efforts being made by various religious agencies throughout the country for the evangelization of the people and the conversion of the Jews, these facts must encourage every lover of God's ancient people to hope that His set time to favor Zion is fast approaching.[119]

Reports on Jewish settlement and the fulfillment of biblical prophesy continued to dominate the newspapers in Salt Lake City for the duration of the Mormon missions in the Middle East.[120]

The Mormons were not intent on simply standing by and observing fulfillment of prophesy. Ferdinand Hintze believed that the Mormons were active participants and, in 1889, he raised the idea of establishing a colony in order to bring about the "true restoration of Man."[121] By colonizing Palestine, the Mormons would be the "means of restoring and redeeming Palestine prior to the gathering of the Jews."[122] The missionaries could then circumvent the obstacles placed in their path by Ottoman nonrecognition, and by opposition from the Protestant churches.[123] The Ottoman government also made it difficult for poor members of the Mormon Church to emigrate from the empire. The United States did not facilitate immigration to Utah, either. Hintze's proposal for a colony was favorably received by the church hierarchy in Salt Lake City. Apostle George Q. Cannon pointed out that great resistance in the United States already existed to Mormon immigration, and it would only increase if they tried to bring converts from the Middle East. Authorities feared that the Mormons would bring in "polygamous hordes from Turkey and from adjacent regions, to perpetuate our own system of marriage and to fasten it upon the United States."[124] Cannon suggested that when the converts gained sufficient numbers then it would be more suitable to settle them in Palestine. Accordingly, Mormon elders should first "go from Zion to the land of Jerusalem to help lay the foundation of the work there in teaching these people the arts of true civilization, from which they have fallen through the transgressions of their fathers."[125]

The Turkish Mission was closed during the Armenian Crisis of 1895–1896 and there was no further consideration of the colony until the mission reopened in 1897.[126] Ferdinand Hintze and Anthon H. Lund were sent to Palestine to examine some Jewish colonies and search for land where they might establish their colony. Hintze noted that the costs were prohibitive. They had located six thousand acres on the banks of the Kishon River that were priced at $120,000. The Church in Salt Lake determined that it could not buy the site because of lack of funds.[127] Hintze, however, was not to be deterred. He sent a letter to Brother Maycock, president of the mission in Aleppo (1897–1899), that he was arriving after his travels in Palestine and a meeting should be arranged in Antep in early February 1898. Hintze's letter stressed that President Woodruff in Salt Lake City believed the "time had come to found a colony of Saints in Palestine."[128] Once again, however, President Woodruff and his counselors determined that "we do not think it advisable to purchase…at present; that Bro. Hintze and the brethren in Turkey continue their labors, and they watch the development of affairs in Palestine with a view to the gathering of the people."[129]

By 1898, although the most active period for planning a colony had come to an end, the idea of a colony did not die. In the following year, Joseph Wilford Booth arrived in the empire and during his seventeen years in service he continued to support the idea of a colony. The colony was necessary not only for the spiritual development of the converts but also more importantly for their economic self-sufficiency.[130] By 1905, frustrations from lack of recognition by the Ottoman government led Booth to report back to Salt Lake City that after seven years in the field he continued to wish to see "the Book of Mormon among the people in their own language…recognition from the Osmanli government for our Church, and…to see a colony established in this land for the Saints. With these I have great hopes for substantial progress of the Turkish mission."[131] A few months later, the

Church in Salt Lake again took up the discussion of whether to establish a colony of Armenian converts or, at the very least, to help those most worthy to emigrate. "The question of colonization was discussed, resulting in an action to emigrate rather than to undertake the work of colonization. And on the recommendation of President Booth it was decided to bring some of the Armenian Saints to Salt Lake City."[132] In the final year of the first Turkish Mission the Church revisited the idea of establishing a colony of saints. Brother Thomas P. Page was sent "to look over the country with a view to finding a place which could be purchased at a reasonable price suitable for colonization, in keeping with prior suggestions made by Prest. [*sic*] Booth."[133] President Booth met Brother Page on March 2, 1909, in Adana and they proceeded to travel for six weeks throughout Turkey, Syria, and Palestine in search of suitable land. After Page's return to Utah and Booth's return to Aleppo, all plans were put on hold because a constitutional revolution had deposed Sultan Abdülhamid II. Booth expressed a desire to help two hundred members of the Turkish Mission to emigrate while the possibility was opened under the new Ottoman constitution. He also advised that the mission be closed "until the people should more readily manifest a willingness to receive the Gospel."[134] Shortly thereafter, the branches in the Ottoman Empire were organized so that they could survive independently, and the missionaries were released from their labors to return home. The Turkish mission was closed because the political situation was deemed too risky for further missionary activity. Converts in the empire had to find their way without additional aid from the United States.

Joseph Wilford Booth, upon his return to Utah in 1909, gave the following interview to the *Deseret Evening News* that summed up the Mormon experiences, successes, failures, and hopes for the future. He recounted how just before the Ottoman counterrevolution of April 1909 there were dangerous conditions throughout the empire and no one could foresee the future. Battleships from England, France, the United States, and other countries were patrolling along the coast, but their presence did not ease tensions within the country. The missionaries of the Turkish Mission still maintained hope that their mission would be permanent and their desire for establishing a colony would be realized. On the morning of the fifteenth of April 1909, however, everything changed as a massacre began in the city of Adana and quickly spread to neighboring towns and villages and then into the province of Aleppo. Booth estimated that twenty thousand people had been killed. Most of those killed were Armenians, but there was a smaller percentage of Muslims. As a result of these events, the elders in Salt Lake City recalled the missionaries and left some two hundred converts, most in the four branches of Aleppo, Antep, Maraş, and Zara, and others scattered throughout Syria and Asia Minor. Some fifty brethren were assisted to immigrate to Utah and they hoped that those remaining would soon follow. In Booth's account he recalled the history of Mormon missions to Palestine and the belief that the fulfillment of biblical prophesies was at hand.

> On Oct 24, 1841, the late Apostle Orson Hyde dedicated the land of Palestine to the Lord for the gathering of "Judah's scattered remnants." Since that date three other apostles, viz. Lorenzo Snow (1873), Anthon H. Lund, (1898) and Francis M. Lyman (1902) have visited the holy land and each one knelt, as did Elder Hyde, on the sacred summit of Mount Olives, and called upon the God of Abraham, Isaac and Jacob, to remember his covenant with them.... The predictions of the Scripture concerning the Jews and their regaining Palestine are now being fulfilled in the most remarkable manner.... Now, we are asked if all this is worth the while? Yes, yes, many times over, not only for the souls already brought into the light of truth, but the way has been opened for thousands yet to hear and learn of the great latter-day restoration. The Book of Mormon is there, being read in a language common to the people.... Thus the hearts of thousands are being prepared even in our absence to receive the truth when the mission shall be reopened in the due time of the Lord.[135]

Mormon missionaries would not return until after World War I when, in 1921, Joseph Wilford Booth took up residence for his third and final mission. The question of establishing a colony was raised again, and further investigations were made in Syria and Palestine throughout the 1920s. Although the idea of a colony was never outrightly dismissed, it was continually postponed. When mission headquarters was moved from Aleppo to Haifa and European Mormons began to carry out missionary work, a more realistic solution seemed to be at hand.[136]

CONCLUSION

The first Mormon Turkish Mission (1884–1909) was a rather brief journey of proselytizing in the Ottoman Empire and establishing their claim to the Holy Land and biblical prophesy. Along the way they encountered many challenges similar to those experienced by their Protestant predecessors. The Mormon missionaries were confronted with restrictions on importing, publishing, and distributing religious tracts and pamphlets, and the prohibition of preaching in public and opening schools. These obstacles primarily, but not exclusively, stemmed from Ottoman refusal to grant official recognition to the Mormon sect. One of the main reasons that the Mormons did not achieve official recognition was because they entered into missionary work at a particularly inauspicious moment in Ottoman history. Sultan Abdülhamid II's pro-Islamist policies, aimed at reinforcing Sunni orthodoxy throughout the empire, ran counter to many earlier decrees and regulations that guaranteed foreign missionaries the right to seek converts and publish and distribute their religious materials. The Mormons were confronted with a government that was not favorably inclined to accept a new religious sect into an already complex mix of religious denominations.

Protestant sects and indigenous churches continually sought to protect their communities against a real fear of Mormon poaching by undermining the work of the Mormons. Their complaints, slander, and accusations presented serious obstacles to the Mormon missionaries who had to contend with verbal and physical abuse as they carried out their mission. Accusations by Protestant sects and indigenous churches that the Mormons were a dangerous, secret group with involvement in Armenian separatist activities, also brought suspicion and police surveillance upon the missionaries. These accusations further hampered not only their labors, but also any possibility that they might achieve recognition from the Ottoman government as a separate religious sect. The obstacles intentionally put in place by the Christian communities were exacerbated by the very fact that the Mormons worked almost exclusively within the Armenian community at a moment of extraordinary political instability. The Ottomans came to believe that the Mormons were spies who intended to aid the separatist movements. The suspicions of the Ottoman government left the missionaries open to surveillance and arrest by government authorities. Ultimately, Ottoman distrust denied the Mormons the rights given other religious communities to travel and preach their message, and to be active participants in the fulfillment of biblical prophesy.

Appendix[137]:
Names and dates of the presidents of the Turkish Mission (renamed the Armenian Mission in 1924)

Jacob Spori, 1885–1887
Ferdinand F. Hintze, 1887–1889
Frederick Stauffer, 1889–1891
Joseph F. Schoenfeld, 1891–1892
Don C. W. Musser, 1892–1894
Edward W. Robinson, 1894–1895
Dr. Armanag S. Hagopian, 1895–1897, an Armenian elder, was given charge of the mission, which was closed due to political disturbances.
Philip S. Maycock, 1897–1899
Ferdinand F. Hintze (2nd term), 1899–1900
Albert Herman, 1900–1904
J. Wilford Booth, 1907–1909
Mission was closed in 1909 due to political disturbances.
J. Wilford Booth (2nd term), 1921–1928

Notes

1.   Author's Note: The author wishes to thank the director and staff of the Başbakanlık Osmanlı Arşivi in Istanbul, and William W. Slaughter and the staff of the archives and library of the Church of Jesus Christ of Latter-day Saints in Salt Lake City, Utah. This article would not have been possible without their generous assistance. I also wish to extend my appreciation to the editors of this book for their invaluable suggestions. A special thanks is extended to Kent Schull for his insightful comments and for making his research available for this chapter. Portions of this research were supported by a fellowship from the Fulbright Institute for International Education. I also extend my gratitude to the directors and staff of the Fulbright Commission in Turkey.

2.   Selim Deringil quotes Edward Said in *The Well-Protected Domains: Ideology and the Legitimation of Power in the Ottoman Empire, 1876–1909* (London: I. B. Tauris, 1998), 113.

3.   See, for example, David P. Charles, "The Day the 'Brave sons of Mohamed'

Saved a Group of Mormons," *BYU Studies, Special Issue on Islam* (2001): 237–254, and "'You Had the Alps, but We the Mount of Olives': Mormon Missionary Travel in the Middle East (1884–1928)," *Mormon Historical Studies* 1:1 (1999): 93–126; James A. Toronto, "Early Missions to Ottoman Turkey, Syria, and Palestine," in *Out of Obscurity: The LDS Church in the Twentieth Century*, 339–362 (Salt Lake City, UT: Deseret Book Company, Sperry Symposium Series, 2000); Daniel C. Peterson, *Abraham Divided: The LDS Perspective on the Middle East* (Salt Lake City, UT: Aspen Books, revised edition 1995); Daniel J. Pingree, "'And Your Name Will be Remembered....' The History of John Alexander Clark's Turkish Mission," *The Thetean* 24 (1995): 31–50; Denton Y. Brewerton, "Istanbul and Rexburg: Jacob Spori's Mission Field," *Ensign* 10:6 (June 1980): 26–32; Rao H. Lindsay, "The Dream of a Mormon Colony in the Near East," *Dialogue: A Journal of Mormon Thought* 1:4 (Winter 1966): 50–67.

4. Seçil Karal Akgün, "Mormon Missionaries in the Ottoman Empire," *Turcica* 28 (1996): 347–357, and "The Turkish Image in the Reports of American Missionaries in the Ottoman Empire," *Turkish Studies Association Bulletin* 13 (1989): 91–105.

5. For a discussion of the literature on missionary activity and imperialism see Ussama Makdisi, "Reclaiming the Land of the Bible: Missionaries, Secularism, and Evangelical Modernity," *The American Historical Review* 102:3 (June 1997): 680–713. The quotation is on page 681.

6. James A. Field, *America and the Mediterranean World 1776–1882* (Princeton: Princeton University Press, 1969), 76–77.

7. Barbara Welter, "She Hath Done What She Could: Protestant Women's Missionary Careers in Nineteenth-Century America," *American Quarterly* 30:5 Special Issue: Women and Religion (Winter 1978): 624–625; Heather J. Sharkey, "Empire and Muslim Conversion: Historical Reflections on Christian Missions in Egypt," *Islam and Christian-Muslim Relations* 16:1 (January 2005): 44; Ömer Turan, "Protestant Missionary Activities in Turkey during the Late Ottoman and Early Republican Periods," in *The Great Ottoman Turkish Civilisation*, ed. Kemal Çiçek et al., vol. 1, 513 (Ankara: Yeni Türkiye Yayınları, 2000); Field, *America and the Mediterranean World*, 77; and Rao H. Lindsay, "A History of the Missionary Activities of the Church of Jesus Christ of Latter-day Saints in the Near East, 1884–1928" (Master's thesis, Brigham Young University, 1958), 1.

8. Hans-Lukas Kieser, "Muslim Heterodoxy and Protestant Utopia. The interactions between Alevis and missionaries in Ottoman Anatolia," *Die Welt des Islams* 41:1 (March 2001): 92; Richard W. Cogley, "The Fall of the Ottoman Empire and the Restoration of Israel in the 'Judeo-centric' Strand of Puritan Millenarianism," *Church History* 72:2 (June 2003): 304; Makdisi, "Reclaiming the Land of the Bible," 684–685.

9. The New Testament book of Revelations 13:12 defined the chronology of the coming events. The reign of the anti-Christ (either the Catholic Pope in Rome

or the Ottoman Sultan) would last for 1,260 years. The year 606 AD was calcu-
lated as the beginning of the rise of the Pope to universal ruler, and, incorrectly,
the date of the beginning of the Ottoman Empire. The millennium would com-
mence in 1866 (1,260 years from 606 CE) and usher in one thousand years of
just rule leading to the Day of Judgment. Field, *America and the Mediterranean
World*, 78–82; Andrew N. Porter, "Evangelicalism, Islam, and Millennial Expectation in the Nineteenth Century," *International Bulletin of Missionary Research* 24:3 (July 2000): 111–116; Makdisi, "Reclaiming the Land of the Bible,"
686.

10. Ruth Kark, *American Consuls in the Holy Land, 1832–1914* (Detroit, MI:
Wayne State University Press, 1994), 75–81. Embassies were established in Constantinople (Istanbul), Alexandria, Beirut, Smyrna (Izmir), Salonika, Bursa,
Aleppo, Cyprus, and Crete. See also Akgün, "The Turkish Image," 92, and also
her "Mormon Missionaries," 350.

11. Leland J. Gordon, "Turkish-American Treaty Relations," *The American Political
Science Review* 22:3 (August 1928): 711–714.

12. Çağrı Erhan, "Ottoman Official Attitudes Towards American Missionaries,"
in *The United States & the Middle East: Cultural Encounters*, ed. Abbas Amanat and Magnus Thorkell Bernhardsson (New Haven: Yale Center for International and Area Studies, 2002), 324–325.

13. Gordon, "Turkish-American Treaty Relations," 711–714, and Erhan, "Ottoman
Official Attitudes," 321–322.

14. See "Hatt Şerif of Gülhane," in *The Middle East and North Africa in World Politics: A Documentary Record*, vol. 1, ed. J. C. Hurewitz (New Haven: Yale University Press, 1975), 115 and 317.

15. C. G. Walpole, trans., *The Ottoman Penal Code, 28 Zilhijeh 1274* (9 August
1858) (London: William Clowes and Sons, Ltd., 1888), 59.

16. The Treaty of Berlin effectively ended the Russo-Turkish War of 1877–1878.
Paul Halsall, ed., "Treaty between Great Britain, Austria-Hungary, France,
Germany, Italy, Russia and Turkey. (Berlin). July 13, 1878," in *Modern History
Sourcebook: The Treaty of Berlin, 1878 Excerpts on the Balkans* (New York: Ford-
ham University, July 1998), http://www.fordham.edu/halsall/mod/1878berlin.
html.

17. Deringil, *Domains*, 114. See also Jeremy Salt, "A Precarious Symbiosis: Ottoman Christians and Foreign Missionaries in the Nineteenth Century," *International Journal of Turkish Studies* 3:2 (Winter 1985–86), 56.

18. For recent works on Ottoman attempts to strengthen and spread Sunni Islam
during the Hamidian period see Deringil, *Domains*, 115–16; Isa Blumi, "Contesting the Edges of the Ottoman Empire: Rethinking Ethnic and Sectarian Boundaries in the Malësore, 1878–1912," *International Journal of Middle
East* Studies 35:2 (May 2003): 237–56; Karen M. Kern, "Rethinking Ottoman Frontier Policies: Marriage and Citizenship in the Province of Iraq," *Arab*

Studies Journal 15:1 (Spring 2007): 8–29; Thomas Kuhn, "Ordering the Past of Ottoman Yemen, 1871–1914," *Turcica* 34 (2002): 189–220; Eugene L. Rogan, *Frontiers of the State in the Late Ottoman Empire: Transjordan, 1850–1921* (Cambridge: Cambridge University Press, 1999), and his *"Aşiret Mektebi*: Abdülhamid II's School for Tribes (1892–1907)," *International Journal of Middle East Studies* 28:1 (February 1996): 83–107. See also various articles in Thomas Kuhn, ed. "Borderlands of the Ottoman Empire in the Nineteenth and Early Twentieth Centuries," *MIT Electronic Journal of Middle East Studies*, 3 (Spring 2003).

19. Deringil, *Domains*, 114.
20. When the Mormons referred to Istanbul, they used the term Constantinople. The author has elected to use Istanbul for the sake of clarity and consistency throughout this volume.
21. Hagop Vartooguian sent his invitation to John Henry Smith, the president of the Mormon European Mission. Mr. Vartooguian and his wife and two children were soon baptized and became the first converts of the Mormon Turkish Mission. Toronto, "Early Missions," 340–341.
22. These collections are in the Library of the Church of Jesus Christ of Latter-day Saints, hereafter LDS-Library. LDS-Library, "The Turkish Mission," by Elder Jacob Spori, *Millennial Star*, January 12, 1885, collected in *Journal History*, December 31, 1884.
23. Deringil, *Domains*, 112–113.
24. Başbakanlık Osmanlı Arşivi (hereafter, BOA), Hariciye Nezareti Siyasi Kısmı Belgeleri (HR.SYS) 44-38, November 3, 1871. The press in the United States was filled with discussions of the tense relations between the Mormons and the U.S. government. President Millard Fillmore appointed Brigham Young as governor and placed other Mormons in government positions in the territory. President Franklin Pierce, although aware that Mormon appointees were complicit in covering up crimes in the territory, closed his eyes to press complaints against the Mormons. When James Buchanan was sworn in as president on March 4, 1857, many expected him to take immediate military action against the "rebellion" of Brigham Young and his followers. Buchanan's administration was under heavy criticism from the press over his failure to deal decisively with Mormon control over the territory. *New York Daily Times*, May 19, 1857, and May 27, 1857.
25. BOA, HR.SYS 44-38, November 3, 1871.
26. This was the first time a man had been tried in Utah territory for adultery based on a polygamous relationship. The indictment was brought under a Utah territorial statute enacted on March 6, 1852, during the governorship of Brigham Young. That statute held that the Court had the discretion to punish both parties who committed adultery by imprisonment between three and twenty years and/or a fine of between three hundred and one thousand dollars. The courts

could not prosecute the crime of adultery, however, without a complaint by the husband or wife. Laws of Utah, chapter 22, section 31. *New York Times*, November 10, 1871.

27. Harriet Hawkins was married to Thomas for twenty-two years, had borne him seven children, and was forty years of age at the time of the trial. Press reports noted that "the evil spirit of polygamy…took possession of this man" and he introduced into his family Elizabeth Mears and afterward Sarah Davis, who had borne him three children. According to Harriet's testimony, her husband assured her that he was "doing religious duties" and that "she had had her day, and he must have a younger woman." The defense was based on Hawkins having taken two additional wives in accordance with the Mormon doctrine of plural marriage, which was a fundamental principle of the faith and a divine revelation. Since the Church sanctioned polygamy, the defense argued that Hawkins was not guilty of criminal intent. The jury considered the matter for ten minutes and returned a verdict of guilty. In the view of the press, it was not the individual as much as the system that was on trial in this case. *New York Times*, November 10, 1871. On March 14, 1882, the U.S. Congress enacted the "Bill Suppressing Mormonism." According to this legislation, a person contracting a polygamous marriage, or already in such a marriage, would be punished with a fine and prison term. Polygamists would also not be eligible to vote or hold public office in any territory or state in the United States. Children born before enactment of this bill were considered legitimate. See *Bill Suppressing Mormonism. Essential Documents in American History* 1, no. 1 (2009): 1, compiled by Norman P. Desmarais and James H. McGovern.

28. The U.S. press reported the details. Immediately after the verdict Daniel H. Wells, an apostle of the Church, mayor of Salt Lake City, and the former chief justice of the State of Deseret, was indicted and arrested for the 1857 murder of Richard Yates and a man named Buck. Hosea Stout and George Kimball, the son of Heber C. Kimball, were also indicted for the murder. A warrant was sent out for the arrest of Orson Hyde, one of the twelve apostles, on the same charge, but he eluded authorities. Warrants were also issued for Brigham Young and his son Joseph for ordering the killing of Richard Yates. At the moment of the trial and issuing of the warrants, Young and his vice-regent, George H. Smith, were apparently in Provo where they were drilling armed troops. *New York Times*, October 29, 1871, and November 10, 1871.

29. BOA, HR.SYS 44-38, November 3, 1871.

30. The original petition for statehood was submitted in 1862.

31. BOA, HR.SYS 59-33, January 21, 1888. It should be noted that polygamy was outlawed in 1890, and Utah Territory was admitted into the Union on January 4, 1896.

32. Arnold H. Green and Lawrence P. Goldrup, "Joseph Smith, An American Muhammad? An Essay on the Perils of Historical Analogy," *Dialogue: A Journal*

of Mormon Thought 6 (Spring 1971): 54; M. Guy Bishop, "The Saints and the Captain. The Mormons Meet Richard F. Burton," *Journal of the West* 33:4 (October 1994): 29.

33. Alan Duben and Cem Behar, *Istanbul Households: Marriage, Family and Fertility, 1880–1940* (Cambridge: Cambridge University Press, 1991), 148–158. Duben and Behar's research was confined to Istanbul and it is reasonable to assume that these statistics do not hold for rural areas of the Ottoman Empire. Further research needs to be undertaken to determine the prevalence of polygamous marriages in the countryside.

34. *Tasvir-i Efkar*, no. 10, no. 11 (1279), 1863. The two phrases are "ne bela bir zene mahsur olmak" and "taze zevk eylemeden dur olmak."

35. My appreciation to Kent Schull for making this article available and for suggesting the interpretation of "orientalizing of the occident."

36. LDS-Library, "Round About Beyrouth," by F. F. Hintze, on board the Moeris, Mediterranean, March 28, 1889, *Deseret Evening News*, April 25, 1889, collected in *Journal History*, March 28, 1889.

37. LDS-Library, "Islam," by J.M.S. (Janne Mattson Sjodahl), *Deseret Weekly*, March 15, 1890.

38. These collections are in the Archive of the Church of Jesus Christ of Latter-day Saints, hereafter LDS-Archive. LDS-Archive, MS3390, *Diary of Fred A. Huish*, Antep, October 16 and October 18, 1893.

39. Ibid., December 7, 1893.

40. Ibid., Aleppo, March 10, 1894.

41. Stanford J. Shaw and Ezel Kural Shaw, *History of the Ottoman Empire and Modern Turkey, Volume II, Reform, Revolution and the Republic: The Rise of Modern Turkey 1808–1975* (Cambridge: Cambridge University Press, 1997), 203–205.

42. Kieser, "Muslim Heterodoxy," 96–98, 103. See also Erdal Açıkses, "An Assessment of the Missionary Activities in the Ottoman Empire: Examples from Two Centers," in *The Great Ottoman Turkish Civilisation*, ed. Kemal Çiçek et al., vol. 1, 591–592 (Ankara: Yeni Türkiye Yayınları, 2000).

43. Erhan, "Ottoman Official Attitudes," 333–334.

44. Ibid., and Roderic H. Davison, *Reform in the Ottoman Empire 1856–1876* (Princeton: Princeton University Press, 1963), 278.

45. Davison, *Reform*, 278, and Erhan, "Ottoman Official Attitudes," 334–335.

46. Erhan, "Ottoman Official Attitudes," 334–336.

47. LDS-Library, "The Turkish Mission," by Elder Jacob Spori, *Millennial Star*, January 12, 1885, collected in *Journal History*, December 31, 1884.

48. Lindsay, "A History of Missionary Activities," 28–29.

49. BOA, Meclis-i Vükela (MV) 28-50, 26 Cemaziye'l-ahir 1305/10 March 1888; MV 26-33, 4 Recep 1305/17 March 1888; Bab-ı Ali Sadaret Mektubi Kalemi Mühimme Kalemi (Odası) Belgeleri (A.MKT.MHM) 492-32, 6 Recep 1305/19 March 1888.

50. Lindsay, "A History of Missionary Activities," 55; LDS-Library, *Journal History*, July 14, 1899.

51. Ibid. See also, LDS-Library, MS 12235, *Diary of Philip S. Maycock*, March 16, 1898.

52. LDS-Library, "A Letter from Turkey," by Philip Maycock, Antep, Syria, *Deseret Evening News*, June 3, 1899, collected in *Journal History*, May 2, 1899.

53. Benjamin C. Fortna, *Imperial Classroom: Islam, the State, and Education in the Late Ottoman Empire* (Oxford: Oxford University Press, 2002), 91–93.

54. Davison, *Reform*, 278.

55. Fortna, *Imperial Classroom*, 96–98. Non-Muslim inspectors with knowledge of European languages were appointed initially, but because this was considered a particularly sensitive position, within a year the policy was changed to require the appointment of Muslims only. By the early 1890s inspectors were almost exclusively Muslim.

56. Davison, *Reform*, 278.

57. Abdülhamid II attempted to limit the influence of foreign educators by building a system of primary and secondary schools that would ensure centralized authority over education. It has been estimated that during his long reign some ten thousand schools were opened. Fortna, *Imperial Classroom*, 98–99, and Deringil, *Domains*, 117–118.

58. Deringil, *Domains*, 116; Açıkşes, "An Assessment of the Missionary Activities," 588. These accusations were not new. Armenian patriarchs had been making the same accusations since as early as 1844.

59. LDS-Library, "Correspondence," by L. O. Littlefield, *Millennial Star*, August 1, 1889, collected in *Journal History*, August 1, 1889.

60. LDS-Library, "Elder Hintze's Mission," by F. F. Hintze, *Deseret Weekly*, March 15, 1890.

61. LDS-Library, "Turkish Mission," Frederick Stauffer, Antep, Alleppo [*sic*] Villayet [*sic*], October 30, 1890, *Journal History*, October 30, 1890.

62. Lindsay, "A History of Missionary Activities," 60–61.

63. LDS-Library, *Journal History*, December 29, 1898.

64. LDS-Library, *Journal History*, March 23, 1899.

65. BOA, Yıldız Sarayı Mütenevvi Maruzat Evrakı (Y.MTV) 242–243, 9 Muharrem sene 321/7 April 1903.

66. Charles, "The Day the 'Brave sons of Mohamed' Saved a Group of Mormons," 243–244.

67. LDS-Archive, MS1594, *Diary of Andrew Lund Larson*, March 5–March 9, 1899.

68. Ibid.

69. Ibid., August 18–September 15, 1899.

70. LDS-Library, "The Missionary Fields. The Turkish Mission," by F. F. Hintze, *Deseret Evening News*, February 17 1900, collected in *Journal History*, January 27, 1900.

71. Lindsay, "A History of Missionary Activities," 80–90.

72. Toronto, "Early Missions," 344–345, and Lindsay, "A History of Missionary Activities," 87.

73. BOA, Y.MTV 242-43, 9 Muharren sene 321/7 April 1903. Melek Çolak discusses various aspects of this document in "Osmanlı İmparatorluğunda Mormonlar," *Tarih ve Toplum* 210 (Haziran 2001): 23–27.

74. BOA, Y.MTV 242-43, 7 April 1903.

75. Ibid.

76. Ibid.

77. Lindsay, "A History of Missionary Activities," 91.

78. LDS-Library, "The Turkish Mission," by Pres. J. Wilford Booth, *Journal History*, March 24, 1904.

79. LDS-Library, "The Turkish Mission," by Elder Jacob Spori, *Millennial Star*, January 12, 1885, collected in *Journal History*, December 31, 1884.

80. LDS-Library, "The Turkish Mission," by Elder Jacob Spori, *Millennial Star*, April 6, 1885, collected in *Journal History*, March 14, 1885.

81. LDS-Library, "Abstract of Correspondence. From Constantinople," by Jacob Spori," *Millennial Star*, May 18, 1885. For early opposition to their work see Agnes M. Smith, "The First Mormon Mission to Britain," *History Today* 37 (July 1987): 26–28.

82. LDS-Library, "Turkish Mission, From Constantinople," *Millennial Star*, October 21, 1885, collected in *Journal History*, September 26, 1885.

83. LDS-Library, "From the Orient," by Janne M. Sjodahl in Haifa, Palestine, February 13, 1889, *Deseret Weekly*, March 23, 1889.

84. LDS-Library, "In Turkey," by Charles U. Locander, Adana, Turkey, April 9, 1889, *Deseret Weekly*, May 18, 1889.

85. Ibid.

86. Ibid.

87. Ibid.

88. LDS-Library, "Turkish Mission," by Frederick Stauffer, Antep, Alleppo Villayet [*sic*], collected in *Journal History*, October 30, 1890.

89. LDS-Library, "Editor *Deseret News*," by F. F. Hintze, Antep, March 28, 1898, *Deseret News*, collected in *Journal History*, March 28, 1898. The *Deseret News* was the official publication of the Mormon Church. See also, LDS-Archive, MS 12235, *Diary of Philip S. Maycock*, January 21–March 15, 1898. The American Board of Commissioners for Foreign Missions established the Central Turkey College in Antep in 1876. Its primary objective was to educate young men for the Christian ministry who would take the lead in the reformation of the empire. *New York Times*, January 27, 1874, and January 5, 1879.

90. LDS-Archive, MS1594, *Diary of Andrew Lund Larson*, March 7 to March 14, 1898.

91. Bishop, "The Saints and the Captain," 34. Blood atonement was a ritual of early Mormon history in which followers, under divine inspiration, targeted sinners and apostates for purification by death. The Mountain Meadow Massacre took place at a site in southwestern Utah between September 7 and 11, 1857, when a group of Mormon men and Native Americans massacred one hundred and twenty men, women, and children of the Baker-Fancher party who were traveling from Arkansas and Missouri to California. John D. Lee, an adopted son of Brigham Young, confessed to being the leader of the attack and was executed by firing squad on March 23, 1877. Brigham Young, however, continued to insist that Native Americans had perpetuated the slaughter. It was only under pressure from the U.S. government that Young excommunicated and executed Lee. This event caused widespread mistrust of the Mormon Church in the United States and included, at the time, accusations that violence and blood atonement were a part of the faith. Caroline Fraser, "The Mormon Murder Case," review of *Blood of the Prophets: Brigham Young and the Massacre at Mountain Meadows*, by Will Bagley, and *Red Water*, by Judith Freeman, *The New York Review of Books* (November 21, 2002): 18–23.

92. LDS-Library, "Editor *Deseret News*," by F. F. Hintze, *Deseret News* March 28, 1898. See also, LDS-Archive, MS1594, *Diary of Andrew Lund Larson*, March 20, 1898.

93. LDS-Library, "In the Turkish Mission," by Apostle Anthon H. Lund, *Deseret Evening News*, May 17, 1898, collected in *Journal History*, March 31, 1898.

94. LDS-Archive, MS1594, *Diary of Andrew Lund Larson*, July 1, 1898; MS 12235, *Diary of Philip S. Maycock*, June 24, 1898.

95. Ibid.

96. Ibid., August 20 to September 8, 1898. See also, LDS-Archive, MS12235, *Diary of Philip S. Maycock*, August 15–August 29, September 14–September 19, 1898, and October 13–October 16, 1898.

97. LDS-Archive, MS1594, *Diary of Andrew Lund Larson*, December 5 through December 17, 1898.

98. LDS-Library, *Journal History*, April 29, 1899.

99. LDS-Library, "Smyrna. Journey to and Description of This Turkish City," by F. F. Hintze, *Deseret Evening News*, August 15, 1889, collected in *Journal History*, July 24, 1889.

100. LDS-Library, "From the Orient," by Janne M. Sjodahl in Haifa, Palestine, February 13, 1889, *Deseret Weekly*, March 23, 1889.

101. LDS-Library, "Making Converts in the Orient," *Deseret Weekly*, August 23, 1890.

102. Ibid.

103. Ibid.

104. Field, *America and the Mediterranean World*, 323–327. Joseph Smith was their American Moses leading them westward to their Zion in the Great Salt Lake

Basin. The Mormons called their river "Jordan." They named their towns
Enoch, Ephraim, Hebron, Jericho, Jerusalem, Little Zion, Manasseh, Moab,
Ophir, and Salem. Their mountains were Canaan, Carmel, Gog and Magog,
Nebo and Pisgah.

105. Peterson, *Abraham Divided*, 322–323.
106. "The Turkish Mission," by President J. Wilford Booth, published in *Millennial Star*, March 24, 1904, collected in *Journal History*, March 24, 1904.
107. Correspondence and other documents from the Mormon archives refer to the region as the Near East, which was the terminology used during this period. For purposes of clarity, I will use the more contemporary usage of the Middle East.
108. Erik J. Zücher, *Turkey: A Modern History* (London: I. B. Tauris, 2nd edition, 2003), 38–40, 54; and Beshara Doumani, *Rediscovering Palestine: Merchants and Peasants in Jabal Nablus, 1700–1900* (Berkeley: University of California Press, 1995), 44–49.
109. Peterson, *Abraham Divided*, 321–322.
110. Lindsay, "A History of Missionary Activities," 5.
111. Peterson, *Abraham Divided*, 326.
112. Lindsay, "A History of Missionary Activities," 6; and Peterson, *Abraham Divided*, 327.
113. Zücher, *Turkey*, 76–77.
114. Caroline Finkel, *Osman's Dream: The History of the Ottoman Empire* (New York: Perseus Books, 2005), 479–484.
115. Peterson, *Abraham Divided*, 258–259. The Latter-day Saints believed that the British Mandate over Palestine after World War I and the Balfour Declaration supporting a homeland for the Jews in Palestine were the fulfillment of prophesy.
116. LDS-Library, "In Turkey," by F. F. Hintze, *Deseret Weekly*, January 26, 1889.
117. LDS-Library, "Jerusalem," by J.M.S., *Deseret Weekly*, May 11, 1889.
118. LDS-Library, "Around Jerusalem," by J.M.S., *Deseret Weekly*, May 11, 1889.
119. LDS-Library, "Jerusalem Awakening," *Deseret Weekly*, January 25, 1890.
120. LDS-Library, "Jews in Jerusalem," *Millennial Star*, November 18, 1889; "Letter from Asia," by F. F. Hintze, *Deseret Evening News*, January 3, 1889; "Elder Hintze's Mission," *Deseret Weekly*, March 15, 1890; "Proselytizing in the East," by F. F. Hintze, *Deseret Evening News*, December 12, 1890; "Letter from Palestine," by Don C. Musser, *Deseret Weekly*, January 14, 1893; "In the Holy Land," by F. F. Hintze, *Deseret Evening News*, February 21, 1898; "To the Editor," by F. F. Hintze from Haifa, Palestine, *Deseret News*, May 17, 1898.
121. Lindsay, "The Dream of a Mormon Colony," 53–54.
122. Ibid.
123. Ibid., 52.
124. Ibid., 53.

125. Ibid. Cannon's view that the United States might oppose immigration of converts from the Ottoman Empire was well founded. Press reports in the United States reflected this concern. The *New York Times* reprinted an interview by C. E. Penrose in the *Pall Mall Gazette* in London in which he insisted that despite the persecution of the saints in Utah they would continue to increase in strength and numbers "until America, the 'land flowing with milk and honey,' is completely gained over to our principles." Thousands of Mormon converts were sailing from Liverpool and settling in western states and territories. They gained footholds in Dakota, and other states in northern territory, and the Mexican Congress gave the Mormons land in Sonora, Chihuahua. It was clear, according to the article, that the first convictions and imprisonment of a few polygamists had not halted the rate of increase of polygamy. *New York Times*, September 28, 1885.

126. The *New York Times* reported on September 17, 1894 that a number of professors in the American schools in Antep and Maraş had been arrested and imprisoned for being in league with Armenian revolutionaries, and for teaching sedition against the Ottoman government. A *New York Times* report of October 18, 1894, noted that the missionaries had been taken to Aleppo, questioned, and exonerated. Reports over the next year, however, noted that the situation in Antep remained precarious. See *New York Times*, December 22, 1895. By March 1896, press reports were calling attention to missionaries who had been killed during the massacres. See *New York Times*, March 16, 1896.

127. Lindsay, "The Dream of a Mormon Colony," 54–57. The American Consul in Jerusalem reported that land throughout Palestine was becoming valuable as a result of the planned building of railroads from Haifa to Damascus and the increasing importance of Palestine in the world economy. He described how "Twelve acres sold in 1890 for $35 per acre, sold in 1892 for $2178; seven acres sold in 1886 for $363 per acre, sold in 1892 for $6534; two acres, sold in 1886 for $1200 per acre, sold in 1892 for $3000; half an acre, sold in 1881 for $200, sold in 1892 for $3700; one acre, sold in 1872 for $40, sold in 1892 for $12,000; two-thirds of an acre, sold in 1866 for $100, sold in 1891 for $3600; one acre, sold in 1865 for $1000, sold in 1891 for $24,000." LDS-Library, "Real Estate in Palestine," *Deseret Weekly*, June 10, 1893.

128. LDS-Archive, MS1594, *Diary of Andrew Lund Larson*, December 7, 1897.

129. LDS-Library, *Journal History*, July 7, 1898.

130. Lindsay, "The Dream of a Mormon Colony," 58–59.

131. LDS-Library, "The Turkish Saints Celebrate—Progress in Syria," by Pres. J. Wilford Booth, *Millennial Star*, August 24, 1905, collected in *Journal History*, July 25, 1905.

132. LDS-Library, *Journal History*, October 5, 1905.

133. LDS-Library, *Journal History*, June 23, 1909.

134. Ibid.

135. LDS-Library, "The Close of the Turkish Mission," by J. Wilford Booth, *Deseret Evening News*, January 1, 1910, collected in *Journal History* December 22, 1909.
136. Lindsay, "The Dream of a Mormon Colony," 65–66.
137. "Turkish Mission," *Encyclopedia History of the Church of Jesus Christ of Latter-day Saints* (Salt Lake City: Andrew Jenson, 1941), 888–890.

1. Merzifon College, graduation ceremony, beginning of the twentieth century. *Courtesy of the American Board Library, Istanbul.*

2. Rufus Anderson. *Courtesy of the American Board Library, Istanbul.*

3. Burj Bird, The Old Mission House (Beirut). *Courtesy of the American Board Library, Istanbul.*

4. (Right) Cyrus Hamlin. *Courtesy of the American Board Library, Istanbul.*

5A. (Below) Joseph Wilford Booth served three missions to the Mormon Turkish or Armenian missions and died during his third mission. *Courtesy LDS Church Archives, Salt Lake City.*

5B. (Below Right) Mary Rebecca (Reba) Moyle Booth served in the Mormon Turkish or Armenian missions with her husband on his second and third missions. *Courtesy LDS Church Archives, Salt Lake City.*

6. Mary Mills Patrick. *Courtesy of the American Board Library, Istanbul.*

7. American Press, bindery and machine room, Beirut. *Courtesy of the American Board Library, Istanbul.*

8. Team of translators for the Bulgarian translation of the Bible sponsored by the British and Foreign Bible Society and printed in 1871. From left to right: Khristodul Kostovich Sichan-Nikolov, American Board missionary Elias Riggs, Methodist Episcopal Church missionary Albert Long, Petko Rachov Slaveykov. Undated photograph, ca. 1860s. *Courtesy of the Hilandar Research Library, Ohio State University.*

9. Egyptian Christian family having worship, ca. 1923; "The father is employed by the American Bible Society." Dwight H. and Lucille B. Fee Papers. *Courtesy of the Presbyterian Historical Society, Presbyterian Church (U.S.A.) (Philadelphia, PA).*

10. "Miss Finney at Sombat telling Bible story as women sort the wheat. Evangelical home—house clean—people mentally alert, ca. 1921–1923." Dwight H. and Lucille B. Fee Papers. *Courtesy of the Presbyterian Historical Society, Presbyterian Church (U.S.A.) (Philadelphia, PA).*

PART 2

RIPPLES OF CHANGE:
THE CONSEQUENCES OF MISSIONARY ENCOUNTERS

The Gospel of Science and American Evangelism in Late Ottoman Beirut

Marwa Elshakry

In the eighteenth and nineteenth centuries, Protestant re-vivalist and millenarian movements swept the shores of the Atlantic. Wesleyan Methodism captured the imagination of English enthusiasts, while their overseas brethren witnessed two "Great Awakenings." Numerous prophecies foretold the triumph of Christ's spiritual rule over the earth and the conversion of all the world's peoples, particularly the Jews, who were expected to return to the Holy Land and there embrace a reformed faith on the path to salvation. With the coming of the Savior and the destruction of all the Men of Sin, a "thousand years of peace, brotherhood and justice" were expected.[1]

Inspired by the spirit of "disinterested benevolence" of Jonathan Edwards and Samuel Hopkins—and by visions of America's "manifest destiny" in the world—American Protestant disciples set out to prepare the road for Christ's return and to sow the seeds of peace, justice, and brotherhood among the heathen and unreformed.[2] In 1810 a fraternity known as the "Brethren" at the Calvinist Divinity College (later the Andover Theological Seminary) founded what would quickly become one of the largest interdenominational missionary societies in the northeastern United States: the American Board of Commissioners for Foreign Missions (ABCFM).[3] From the start, theirs was a project with global ambitions: "Prophesy, history and the present state of the world," announced the board in 1812, "seem to unite in declaring that the great pillars of the Papal and Mahommedan impostures are now tottering to their fall.... Now is the time for the followers of Christ to come forward boldly and engage earnestly in the great work of enlightening and reforming mankind."[4]

By mid-century the ABCFM had established numerous missionary outposts across the Mediterranean, Asia, Africa, and the Americas. "Through various channels of influence," wrote the Reverend James Dennis, an early member of the station at Beirut, "missions are pouring vitalizing forces into the social, national, commercial and religious life of foreign peoples." The aim was to create "new men" abroad or, as Dennis wrote, "the embryonic norms of a new society and a new life."[5] Hoping to mold "new national lives and characters," American evangelists promoted spiritual and worldly reform in foreign lands through an ambitious amalgam of pedagogy, philanthropy, and politics that critics have since referred to as "colonial evangelism."[6]

Commentators and scholars have long debated the relationship between Christian missions and imperialism in the Middle East. From the start, there were those who suspected that a colonial agenda lurked behind the missionaries' religious aspirations. As early as the 1890s, contemporary writers and journalists linked the evangelists with foreign occupiers such as the British in Egypt and the Sudan, or the French in Algeria and Northwest Africa.[7] Some twentieth-century Arab nationalist historians followed suit and described them as the shock-troops of imperialism.[8] Others, however, especially in the Anglophone world, have portrayed Christian, and particularly Protestant, missionaries in a more favorable light, not as collaborators with foreign imperialists but as mentors of Arab nationalism itself—both the carriers of new ideas from Europe and agents in the revival and modernization of the Middle East.[9] Missionaries to the Middle East are thus hailed as playing a role in a surprisingly diverse number of rather worldly endeavors, whether as sponsors of the late nineteenth century revival of the Arabic language and *belles-lettres* known as the *Nahda*, or "Arab Renaissance," or as promoters of a new spirit of Arab secularism and nationalism.[10] Historians have since tempered such broad claims while nevertheless according the missionaries a key role in the transformation of Syrian society and identity.[11] Even as missionaries failed ultimately in their mission to save souls—their success in terms of numbers of actual converts to the Protestant church was never very impressive—they were nevertheless said to have helped win the battle for the "conversion to modernities" in the Middle East.[12] What is at stake in this long-standing argument, of course, is the very concept of "conversion" itself—a question that bedeviled missionaries, their patrons, and subjects alike, and one which this article ultimately addresses.

Recently historians have moved the debate beyond the role of missionaries in the genesis of Arab nationalism and modernization and have argued instead for the need to pay closer attention to the influence of the missionaries' religious world-views on their ambitions and objectives "in the field." In this way the ambiguities and tensions in the position of those who combined evangelical fervor with a parallel commitment to a broader, civilizing mission have been underlined. Some have argued that Christianization itself was a process of colonizing hearts and minds.[13] Others have highlighted how the missionaries' aims gradually changed over time, showing that an exclusively religious concern with conversion was complicated by a growing commitment to secular and civilizing ventures[14]—something which may be said to have paralleled developments in postmillennial Protestant thought and the rise of the "social gospel" movement in the United States itself.[15] The very nature of missionary work, after all, shifted considerably over the long nineteenth century (and after), branching out into various international institutions, from liberal arts universities to NGOs, and contributing to the shaping of American foreign policy in the region.[16]

In the mid- to late nineteenth century this tension between spiritual conversion and this-worldly reform crystallized around a subject somewhat neglected to date in the scholarly literature on missions, though crucial to the missionaries' own endeavors: the promotion of natural science.[17] As was the case in India and China during this period, science (and medicine) became critical weapons in the missionaries' spiritual arsenal[18]—albeit ones which, in the age of Darwin, had a propensity to backfire.[19] Far from viewing science as engaged in constant "warfare" with theology, many missionaries in Beirut regarded the natural and allied sciences as integral to their broader spiritual commitments and theological vision and saw in them a means to promote the path to salvation and to advance the reformation of minds and daily habits.[20] Healing and training in the medical arts and sciences, for example, might offer one way to fulfill the promise of conversion, whether by acting in the role of Christ in healing the body (and soul) and extracting somatic (and spiritual) evils or by striking at "degraded superstitions" found in "the prevalence of quackery and magic in the healing arts."[21] Public experiments and demonstrations of electricity and pneumatics embodied the virtues of disciplined

understanding and allowed the missionary to stage a public testimonial to
the power of truth.[22] Training in engineering works, meanwhile, were seen
as providing practical skills and acting as a spur to the technological progress
of nations, free trade and commerce, and, ultimately, to just governance and
universal brotherhood.[23]

Behind this vision, too, lay, for some, an appeal to natural theology, whereby
arguments about God's existence, character, and being were made through re-
course to empirical and rational proofs of design in nature.[24] As many missionaries in Syria argued, this rational approach to nature also exemplified the
superiority of Protestant rationality over the superstitious and irrational character of the Eastern churches and of Islam. Science provided the means. As
one missionary put it in 1813, "the more the mind of the Christian is enlarged
and strengthened by scientific pursuits, the better he is fitted to understand,
believe, and defend the truths of the Bible."[25] In this way, the spiritual authority of the true faith was bolstered by the cultural authority of science.

Of course this view of "science" was itself under constant threat from heterodox or sceptical positions, especially in the second half of the nineteenth
century.[26] During what some historians have termed "the spiritual crisis of
the Gilded Age" the older reconciliation of Baconian, inductive, and Scottish
Common Sense philosophy fell apart as the challenges posed by historical
biblical criticism and philosophical naturalism led to a rapid fragmentation
of Protestant opinion.[27] With the rise of uniformitarian geology and Darwinian evolution in particular, debates over the proper relation of science to
faith grew more heated, both at home and abroad.

The repercussions were felt in Syria.[28] While some missionaries promoted
scientific education and training as one of the paths to God, others increasingly saw it as a dangerous and ineffectual diversion, a waste of resources, and
possibly worse. Bitter arguments among missionaries and their supporters
over these issues were played out between Beirut and New England and would
eventually come to a head at the Syrian Protestant College in 1882—the year
of Charles Darwin's death—with a public controversy over the theory of evolution by natural selection. As missionaries divided over the question of Darwinism, others began publicly to challenge Protestant claims to the superior
rationality of their faith. Appealing to the virtues of rational argumentation
could now suddenly be used as easily against Christianity as for it, as errant
missionary disciples and Muslim theologians wasted no time pointing out.

The highly visible character of the whole affair was no accident. By staging public experiments and scientific demonstrations, founding scientific societies and debating clubs and authoring and sponsoring new forms of print-press publications, from science journals to calendars and almanacs, missionaries had deliberately opened new avenues for public discussion and debate about science and its particular knowledge-claims. The most important of these activities—and the one with the greatest consequences—was undoubtedly their use and sponsorship of the printing press. Yet by the 1880s the mission press house in Beirut was only one of many in the Ottoman port city and the empire at large.[29] Mission publications on science had thus been readily taken up by a growing public sphere of readers and authors who collectively constituted a new cross-confessional and interregional community of knowledge.

This was by no means the single-handed creation of the missionaries. A highly influential postwar generation of historians of secular nationalism and intellectual life in the Middle East has depicted these mission preachers, educators, and public spokesmen as external forces for change and key figures in a long line of agents of Western modernization that stretched forward from Napoleon's *savants* in Egypt.[30] In fact (not unlike Napoleon's expeditionary force), missionaries in Syria were not so much reeling in a recalcitrant periphery for the forces of modernity as finding themselves enmeshed in a broader and ongoing process of Ottoman social and cultural transformation.[31] Few works that deal with the social dimension of mission work in the Middle East, however, have taken seriously this local context and engagement. This article redresses that oversight and argues that missionary propagation of science was shaped ultimately by the pressure of local demands. Responding to these, in turn, transformed the missionaries' views on the nature of conversion and over time helped to convert them to a different sense of themselves and their own mission.[32]

I

The Holy Land—the lands that stretched from the Mesopotamian valleys to the Nile basin—captured the nineteenth-century missionary imagination.[33] In the words of Pliny Fisk, one of the first American missionaries to reach Jerusalem in 1819 under the auspices of the ABCFM (and a recent graduate of

Andover), these lands were "rendered sacred in the eyes of every Christian, by a thousand religious associations," for the Holy Land was venerated by American evangelists not only for its sacred past, but also for its promised future.[34]

Spurred by their belief in Christ's imminent return, the first generation of American missionaries began their work in Jerusalem. Faced with growing suspicion and hostility from local ecclesiastical authorities there, they soon moved to Beirut. Yet their work was not much easier in the port city. Their memoirs and letters make much of their difficulties with local bureaucrats, and of the obstinacy of those they hoped to convert. Still, they stuck to the task of preaching from public pulpits and distributing Arabic-language Bibles—something that earned them the name *biblishiyyun* or "Bible-men" among locals. In 1824, even their efforts to bestow scripture were curtailed. Accused of disturbing the peace, and distributing "blasphemous literature," Fisk and fellow Bible-man and Andover graduate Isaac Bird, were arrested by Ottoman authorities (though saved, in the end, through English consular protection). The ABCFM remained undeterred: "It may be thought," missionaries were instructed, "that the present troubles in the Turkish Empire will interpose a serious obstacle to missionary efforts. Suffer not your minds to be discouraged by this apprehension.... Is the opinion of the mere politician to be the rule of duty for the Christian church?"[35]

The "martyrdom" of one of their early converts under the Maronite Patriarchate showed just how difficult efforts to proselytize could be.[36] The assault on Beirut in 1826 by a fleet of Greek ships (during the Greek war of independence) further unsettled the enterprise, and two years later American missionaries sought refuge in Malta. The Egyptian occupation of Syria in 1831 came as an unexpected boon.[37] By the time it ended (in 1842) the ABCFM "mission to Syria and the Holy Land" had some twenty-eight persons stationed in three outposts.[38] It was further helped in 1850 when Sultan Abdülmecid issued an "Imperial Protestant Charter of Rights" which guaranteed Protestants all the rights and privileges of other sects in the empire.[39] In 1853 he issued another edict decreeing it unlawful to persecute those who adopted the Protestant faith.[40]

Despite these advantages, direct conversion still proved difficult, and missionaries increasingly turned to strategies of "indirect conversion" through schooling. From the very start, they had stressed the need for general education to accompany their proselytizing efforts, believing that it was "education which forms the Mohommetan and Pagan, the Jew and Christian."[41] Teaching their charges to read and write, moreover, was particularly important given the value missionaries placed on the power of individual communion with God through the reading of scripture.

Over time, however, mission schools did far more than promote literacy and the rudiments of an elementary education. It was not long before their curricula grew to include a range of subjects from moral and natural philosophy to geography and astronomy. This approach proved remarkably successful: The number of students enrolled at Beirut and the surrounding mountain villages rose steadily, from about six hundred in 1827 to over five thousand in 1884.[42]

The strategy was, as one missionary put it, to "bait the hook with arithmetic." The Beirut High School for Boys (a boarding school), for example, opened in 1835 with the express aim of introducing the sciences in association with Christian doctrine. Alongside English, Arabic, and arithmetic, students were instructed in geography, astronomy, natural and moral philosophy, and logic; they also had regular readings in the Bible and attended mandatory church services (mostly prayer). Missionaries believed that such instruction would also work to "enlighten" the minds of their students "respecting the prevailing and soul-destroying errors of this country."[43]

Education in the natural sciences was promoted as one way to aid pupils on the path to God: Geography, for instance, was said to demonstrate to students the providential control of God in nature—in adapting the climate to inhabitants or vice versa—and was seen to inculcate an appreciation for the goodness of His divine will and order, as well as to excite the sense of religious awe and wonder so central to the spirit of evangelical thought.[44] Eli Smith, a long-serving missionary in Syria who taught geography and astronomy at the mission high school, expressed his enthusiasm for the spiritual potential of these subjects. Having just closed a short course of lectures on astronomy for the first time in 1835, Smith noted how, despite some of the students' initial reservations toward the "new" [i.e., Copernican] astronomy, "some of them, in the end, could not restrain their admiration at His power and wisdom."[45] In this way, winning students over to an irrefutably rational Copernican cosmology hinted at the eventual promise of conversion itself: Over time, with perseverance, and through an appeal to the rationality and truth of their message, students might be similarly won over to the true faith.

Missionaries in Syria made much of the pioneering nature of this task: "It was perhaps the first time," wrote Smith, that "the Copernican system was taught in the country." He noted he had "many objections to encounter" at first, but "all who heard me soon become advocates, and by their reports and arguments made considerable talk in the city." Whether or not the missionaries were the first to introduce Copernican astronomy in Syria, "talk" was precisely the sort of thing they wanted for it was clear that they were hoping to attract widespread interest and elicit a broad public discussion. As early as 1837, missionaries at the school began to stage public experiments in natural science for exactly that reason. After experiments on pneumatics and electricity were carried out (with apparatus sent to the school from the board), missionaries reported back happily that not only were these numerously attended "by the first people in Beyroot" to witness such wonders, but that they had, as a result, also "excited much interest."[46]

Yet by mid-century the Syria mission station had still made very few converts and had, in fact, earned a reputation back home for directing too much of its energy to the opening and running of schools. Although enrollments were high, not one student from the Beirut High School for Boys had been won over to the true cause: "It is a painful truth that we do not see those manifestations of spiritual life attending our labors, which we desire," lamented one missionary at Beirut in 1841. "These youth are in a state of moral death. We have not satisfactory evidence that a single one of them is a child of God.... Why, we often enquire, why is no one from this school converted to Christ?"[47]

Questions of this imbalance in missionary priorities became a subject of considerable concern for board members in 1837, when the board discovered it had a deficit of some sixty thousand dollars. Rufus Anderson, the secretary of the ABCFM, pledged to cut costs and to reconsider issues of mission strategy.[48] Board funds, maintained Anderson, could only be justified on the grounds of effective efforts at conversion. In 1837, he was among the first to complain that mission schools were not "intended to educate natives for the law, nor for medicine, nor for civil office, except so far as this will directly promote the legitimate object of the mission."[49]

The work of missionaries in Syria soon came under scrutiny. In 1840, shortly after promises of a "mass conversion" of the Druzes of Mount Lebanon had begun to unravel, Anderson announced: "Upon reading the report for last year we have been surprised to find how little there is encouraging, as it appears to our mind, in the prospect of many of the missions."⁵⁰ Anderson was convinced that missionaries in Syria were on the wrong path and, under his tenure, the ABCFM soon began to instruct missionaries there to establish and promote schools that fitted more properly religious rather than "merely expedient" aims. Funds were now made available to schools only insofar as they proved a "direct auxiliary" to the preaching of gospel.⁵¹ In 1842, as a direct result of Anderson's new policy, the board closed the Beirut High School; and, in 1846, following a tour of inspection in the Levant, Anderson recommended the opening of a theological seminary which was to be located at 'Abeih, a village some distance from Beirut, as he feared the corrupting influences of the increasingly "Frankish" city. (He had been alarmed to learn that many high school graduates had found employment in 1841–1842 with the British and French forces that landed there to oust Ibrahim and the Egyptians. This was not, in his view, what missionary funding was intended to support.)

At 'Abeih, religious instruction and theological training were emphasized.⁵² But even Anderson recognized the virtues of a relatively broad curriculum in the work of religious conversion: "To how great an extent have all useful ideas perished from the minds of pagan nations," he wrote in an 1850 tract on *Mission Schools*.

> Their history, chronology, geography, astronomy, their philosophical notions of mind and matter, and their views of creation and providence, religion and morals are exceedingly destitute of truth.... So that, happily, even the simplest course of elementary instruction in schools could not be otherwise than a direct attack upon their false religions.⁵³

Science was for Anderson, however, a peripheral concern:

> The whole course of education, from beginning to end, should be Christian, planned with a view to raising up, through the blessing of God, an efficient body of native helpers in the several departments of missionary labor—to be teachers of schools, catechists, tutors and professors in the seminaries, and, above all, preachers of the gospel, pastors of the native churches, and missionaries to the neighbouring heathen districts and countries.⁵⁴

Throughout his long term as secretary of the board (from 1832 to 1866) Anderson remained suspicious of the missionaries' more this-worldly efforts. After a further visit to Syria in 1856, he warned his colleagues there to guard against turning their stations into "book-making" or "educating" ones, reminding them once again that "the governing object of every mission and of every missionary should not be to liberate, to educate, to enlighten, to polish, but to *convert* men."[55] Anderson and the New England-based board of trustees hammered away at this point. Funds for mission organizations could only be entrusted to works aimed at converting men, not civilizing them. "Civilization is not conversion," announced a circular published in 1856 by the ABCFM on *The Divine Instrumentality for the World's Conversion*. "Iron rails, steam engines, electric wires, power looms and power presses, however powerful, are no part of Christianity and can never turn men from the power of Satan unto God"; for "the world will never be converted by the arts of civilized life ... nor by the introduction of true science or an improved literature."[56]

But as Anderson well knew, missionaries in the field did not agree. "The directors of missions and missionaries themselves," he later admitted, "have not yet come to a full practical agreement as to the principles that underlie the working of missions, nor as to the results to be accomplished by them."[57] In fact, missionaries in Syria continued to successfully defend and build upon their commitment to a broader vision of pedagogy. Just one year after the seminary at 'Abeih opened, they combined forces with local scholars in Beirut to inaugurate the short-lived *Syrian Society of Arts and Sciences*, or *al-Jam'iya al-Suriya li iktisab al-'ulum wa al-funun*, a society open to members of all religious backgrounds and which aimed at "the awakening of a general desire for the acquisition of the sciences and arts, irrespective of disputed questions relative to religious rites and doctrines."[58] With a sizeable library, the society also owned a lecture hall where papers were delivered monthly and read in Arabic. Aiming to foster "a general desire for attainments in the sciences and acquisitions of knowledge," it hosted lectures on such topics as "On the Delights and Utilities of Science," "A Discourse on the Instruction of Women," and "On the Principles of the Laws of Nature."[59]

Even at the 'Abeih seminary, the course of instruction grew well beyond its initial focus on religious studies and Bible training. Within a few years, in fact, its curriculum began to look suspiciously similar to that of the earlier Beirut High School for Boys: alongside regular instruction in theology, Arabic, and English, students were instructed in mathematics, geography, astronomy, history, and natural philosophy. The emphasis on science was something missionaries were clearly (even if cautiously) proud of: "It is, we suppose," announced the 'Abeih station report of 1849, "the only institution in Syria where the true principles of science are taught," adding quickly:

> At the same time we desire never to lose sight of the fact that it was established with express reference to the training up of preachers of the everlasting gospel.... We feel the danger of merging too much the religious in the literary and scientific...and seek grace to make this seminary more and more a religious institution and to teach the sciences as entirely subservient to Christianity.[60]

Anderson's pedagogical conservatism did not prevail in the end for a number of reasons. For one, it ignored the social and political obstacles to conversion, including excommunication and ostracism, something missionaries on the ground complained of frequently in their reports to the board.[61] But, more importantly, his policies also ignored the possibilities prompted by the increased local demands for education—and the missionaries' own anxieties about the competition to meet and supply these.

Beirut was a prosperous and growing city as capitalism helped transform the Eastern Mediterranean.[62] Its bureaucracy, infrastructure, and commercial sector were rapidly expanding, particularly after the resolution of the civil conflicts in Mount Lebanon. After 1860, the numbers of schools also increased dramatically, and American missionaries found themselves competing for custom not only with other Protestants but also with Jesuit, Syrian Catholic, Greek Orthodox, Maronite, Druze, and local Muslim and Ottoman schools.[63] "All the various groups are vying with each other in finding Boarding Schools for their children and youth," warned missionaries there, "and if Protestant Christianity is to maintain a foothold here, it must do its part in the great work of education."[64]

American missionaries worried, in particular, about the increase in Catholic activity following the arrival of French forces in Beirut in 1861. "The Jesuits and other Roman Catholic missionaries are rapidly multiplying their institutions in various parts of the country," warned some, "and holding out attractions to draw into them, not only all those who are awaking to more enlarged and liberal views and aspirations, but even the children and youth of Protestants." Protestant-Catholic rivalry had been evident in Beirut from the early decades of the century, but after 1860, their competition intensified. For the local ABCFM mission station, it was "in fact no longer a question whether or not education is to be obtained, but simply who are to be the teachers."[65]

As local missionaries knew from their earlier experience with the Beirut High School, science was the great draw—and Anderson's reforms never took root precisely because he failed to acknowledge this. The transformation of Jesuit schools—with the expansion of their curricula and with their acquisition of the latest scientific apparatus—confirmed that students would flock to the schools that offered up-to-date scientific and technical training. Thus while missionaries boasted about their pioneering efforts in the diffusion of modern science, they were in fact largely responding to local demand and the widespread interest in new forms of technical and professional knowledge in the empire. Moreover, imparting scientific truth, they argued, might itself also help to testify to the superior rationality of the Protestant faith by demonstrating to the more "superstitious" Eastern—and particularly Catholic—creeds that only a truly rational and reformed faith could foster a proper and systematic enquiry into the natural world.

Before long, all these factors came into play to push the missionary pedagogic crusade in a new and even more ambitious direction. Competition with the Jesuits and confidence in the value of their scientific curriculum led leading figures of the American mission station at Beirut to argue for the need for their own permanent institution of higher learning "to give a thorough scientific and professional education to the youth of Syria."[66] This implied breaking with the board's more narrow definition of mission school pedagogy, and when it came, the break was a real one.

II

In 1860 the idea of establishing a college for boys at Beirut was discussed with members of the ABCFM. It was quickly agreed that any future college should be administered separately since, as Anderson later put it, "the American Board could not undertake so large a literary work in any one mission."[67]

Setting aside denominational distinctions, senior missionaries proceeded to collect funds from a wide array of Protestant organizations. Daniel Bliss, who had joined the Syria mission station in 1855, was released from his connection with the mission to raise funds for the new college. Hoping to secure "the liberal cooperation of all friends and patrons of a sound Christian education in the East," he began in Civil War America and Great Britain in 1861.[68]

In their fund-raising campaigns at Protestant churches across the American Northeast, Bliss and his sometime companion and fellow-missionary (and author of the best-selling *The Land and the Book*), William Thomson, stressed the "remarkable awakening in the Orient" and the rise of a "great anxiety for education, especially in scientific knowledge" taking hold among the "Arab races." It was, they claimed, left to the American people alone—as "their freedom from all political entanglements" gave them a decisive advantage and duty over all others—to assist them in rousing from centuries' old "mental and spiritual torpor." They spoke of the dangerous inroads being made in Beirut by "Popish educators," with their "showy but deceptive" education and complained of the dangers of the situation—something which would no doubt have struck a chord with American audiences of the time, who were themselves in the midst of a strongly anti-Catholic mood after the influx of Irish immigrants beginning in the 1840s.

As Jessup stated in 1863 in a letter he circulated in papers and evangelical dailies throughout the Northeast: "*Syria will have a College of some sort. If our religious influence is not thrown in to found and control it, irreligious men will do it, and we shall have an infidel breeding institution growing up as the bane and curse of Syria forever.*"[69] Within two years they raised over one hundred thousand dollars, and in December 1863, a New York–based board of trustees was established. The following year, the Syrian Protestant College at Beirut was officially chartered.[70] Circulars were distributed—in Arabic and in English—throughout Greater Syria shortly thereafter to announce the new boarding school.[71] According to the prospectus, there were to be six departments at the college: Arabic language and literature; mathematics, astronomy, and engineering; chemistry, botany, geology, and natural science; modern languages; medicine; and law and jurisprudence.[72]

In December of 1866, the Syrian Protestant College, known to local Syrians as *al-Madrasa al-Kulliya al-Injiliya*, or "The Evangelical College School," opened to admit eighteen students of various faiths. The college (now known

as the American University of Beirut) would prove to be one of the missionaries' most ambitious—and successful—enterprises. It expanded rapidly.
Within five years, it had nearly one hundred boarders drawn from throughout the empire and two dozen missionary instructors and local tutors. By the
turn of the century, it had forty acres of land, over a dozen buildings, forty
teachers, and some six hundred students of all faiths who came from as far
afield as Albania, Anatolia, Egypt, and the Sudan.[73]

The secret behind the college's success was without question its strong interest in technical and professional education and its commitment to the diffusion and translation of science in Arabic. For a moderate charge, students
received instruction in all the latest scientific disciplines, from engineering
and astronomy to medicine and natural science.[74] A medical school or department was founded in 1867, and those students who enrolled at the college but decided not to engage in medical studies were listed as pupils of the
"Literary Department." In 1872 a preparatory department was also added.[75]
All students thus spent the first few years studying algebra, geometry, natural
philosophy, and Bible studies—in Arabic—together with Arabic grammar,
English, French, and Latin. Those in the Medical Department spent four additional years studying a variety of medical and clinical subjects, while those
in the Literary Department had lessons in a variety of literary and scientific
subjects, from natural and moral philosophy to zoology and physiology.[76]

The college's overall emphasis on science represented a significant shift
from Anderson's earlier educational priorities (Anderson, incidentally,
retired from the ABCFM the year the college opened). Missionaries at the
college remained committed to the "general cause of science," and believed
that their wide-ranging curriculum would serve as an agent of social and political reform. Daniel Bliss, who served as the college's first president (until
1903), declared in 1862 that the work of the college should be to "cast in just
as much good seed as possible, and thus prepare material for constructing
good government and good society."[77]

Yet it would be quite wrong to think that evangelism had in any way faded
in the minds of the missionaries involved. Faculty and members of the Board
of Managers (formed from among resident American and British missionaries as well as local Protestant merchants of Syria and Egypt) insisted that
the school be "conducted on strict evangelical principles." Established outside the ABCFM proper, the college nevertheless shared many of its aims. Its

constitution made clear that the college would be "conducted on principles strictly Protestant and evangelical."[78] Alongside their literary and scientific or medical studies, students had regular lessons in scripture and daily readings in the Bible and were introduced to topics in mental philosophy and moral science, so as "to enforce the great fact upon the mind of the student that a pure morality and a rational religious faith are in accordance with the constitution of the human mind, and a necessity to its highest well-being."[79]

Although the college was administrated separately from the board, missionaries at the college maintained it was nevertheless a "child of the Syria Mission."[80] When George Post retired from his office at the Syria mission to take up a position as professor of surgery, *materia medica*, and botany, he was described by the Syria station as bringing "to the college the same earnestness of Christian purpose that made him so valuable as a missionary. It is as a *Christian* institution that the college is of special interest to other gentlemen connected with it."[81] Indeed, for Post, the new Protestant College, free from the constraints of ABCFM finances, promised to be an even more effective vehicle for enlightening men and saving souls than the mission station itself had been: Upon joining the ranks of the college faculty, Post wrote that he felt he had entered "a new era" in his life, one that "provided him with a broader or higher sphere of influence."[82]

Those in charge of the Beirut mission would also come to see the College as a partner in their work. In 1870, when the Syria mission was transferred to the Presbyterian Church Board of Foreign Missions (as a result of the unification of the Old and New School Presbyterian Churches), the PCBFM praised the college for serving as a "prominent agency in promoting the cause of missions in Syria."[83] Within three years of taking over the mission, the new organization closed down the ʿAbeih seminary, declaring that such theological training was already covered by the work of the college.[84]

Missionaries at the college and beyond clearly saw the boarding school as a vehicle for moral and spiritual improvement along what they considered to be evangelical lines. Rules of personal and moral conduct were strictly applied both inside and outside the classroom, and children were encouraged, if not required, to learn the lessons of regular habits of study and devotion. For missionaries, religious conversion implied a more sweeping transformation of morals and manners. A convert was encouraged not merely to adopt the doctrines of the faith, but also to reform his or her character, moral conduct, and daily habits, as well as to develop a sense of mental discipline and personal industriousness. Schooling was seen by many as the best way to achieve this.

The curriculum at the Syrian Protestant College was intended to attract not only those local Christian sects among whom American missionaries had thus far had some measure of success, but also local Muslims and others who had so far remained aloof. Blaming stubborn Muslim feelings of "pride in the superiority of their own religion," James Dennis, with whom this article began, complained in an 1872 *Sketch of the Syria Mission* of the difficulties American missionaries faced in converting them, and suggested science as the way forward. "They rarely attend our preaching, rarely visit us for religious conversation," he wrote. "Contact with Moslem minds, so difficult through other means, is in a measure possible through education. Scripture truth may be inculcated in connection with science, and this when youthful minds are most susceptible to impressions." For missionaries like Dennis, science—as a means of exercising the "reasoning powers" of the mind—would expose these absurdities, and thus prepare the way for the acceptance of another faith: "Mohammedanism, as a system, is vulnerable through science.... To an educated mind there are in it puerilities, absurdities, glaring inconsistencies."[85] When in 1877, for example, the college opened its astronomical observatory, Bliss wrote in his annual report of his hope that "this Observatory will... prove useful in the direct education of students and in attracting the attention of natives to the superiority of Western knowledge, thus helping to dispel ancient deep-rooted superstitions."[86]

Bliss, like other missionary instructors at the college, saw such instruction moreover as a vehicle for the "awakening of intellects" and the reformation of minds. As early as 1873, he published a primer on "Primary Lessons in Rational Philosophy"—composed with the assistance of "native tutor" Ibrahim al-Hurani—for use in his course on logic and moral philosophy at the college. "Reason," began Bliss, "is what distinguishes men from brutes," and the science of reason he counted as among the most important subjects of study at schools and "the best means to exercise, strengthen and improve minds."[87]

Many missionary instructors at the college also hoped that a sound and reasoned study of the natural world—or enquiry into the Book of Nature alongside the Book of God—would win them over to the soundness of their religious views. In Syria, this approach went back to the 1840s, when

Cornelius Van Dyck (later an important figure at the college) recommended translating William Paley's *Natural Theology* into Arabic.[88] Natural science textbooks subsequently translated or compiled for the college relied on a similar approach. As early as 1841, for instance, the Arabic press was publishing local translations of natural history textbooks, such as Faris Shidyaq's *Sharh al-tabi'a al-hayawan* (A Treatise on the Nature of Animals). These often became the vehicles for an appeal to the wonders of the Divine Providence and order in nature. As'ad al-Shadudi's 1873 textbook on elementary natural philosophy, to take one example, began with a thorough endorsement of the natural sciences as one of the means of uncovering "the wisdom of creation and the perfection of God's natural laws and system."[89] Four years later, another graduate and "native tutor," Ya'qub Sarruf, translated an account of providence and design in nature by a Reverend Walker for use as a text in the college.[90] In short, natural theology—with its appeal to the wisdom, beauty, and design in nature along with its emphasis on a rational and purposeful view of the natural order—proved if not an effective strategy for conversion, then at least a force of edification.

III

Pedagogical translations such as these formed part of a growing range of missionary activities designed to publicize and diffuse the findings and methods of Western science. Missionaries also continued to attract large audiences through public demonstrations, talks, and discussions. In 1872, for example, a series of public lectures were given to "audiences...so large that many were unable to enter." (They included one by Van Dyck on "Astronomy," illustrated by diagrams with the use of the "Oxy-hydrogen" light, and another by Johannes Wortabet, a professor of surgery, on "Anatomy," with the use of a "manakin" and diagrams.) But, as elsewhere, it was the printing press that proved to be the missionaries' most successful vehicle for reaching a wider audience. As early as the 1830s and 1840s, missionaries in Beirut had received scores of letters requesting Arabic books on geography, astronomy, history, and theology.[91] And by mid-century the mission press at Beirut (founded in 1834) was one of a number of Arabic presses in the city. Indeed Beirut soon became the center of the print revolution in the Arab lands: twenty-five periodicals, for example, were founded there between 1852 and

1880, compared with thirteen in Cairo and ten in Alexandria.[92] "The demand for books in Syria is constantly increasing," commented the Syria Mission in its 1868 Annual Report. "The cry comes from Egypt and Palestine, from Assyria and Northern Africa, and even from Peking, the capital of China, 'Give us Arabic books!'"[93]

Taking advantage of this demand, members of the faculty began to publish a wide variety of materials, from books and journals to calendars and almanacs. In 1867, for example, the mission press at Beirut issued an almanac, *al-Manakh* (the climate), which missionaries claimed "was *probably* the first almanac ever *printed* in Arabic." It contained a verse of scripture for every day in the year as well as "lists of the sovereigns and governments of the world…geographical, historical, and philosophical information…tables of eclipses, religious miscellany and hymns, time-tables of the Prussian, French and Austrian steamers, and the prospectus of the Syrian Protestant College."[94] At the same time, missionary-authored science primers appeared and were added to the college curriculum. Modeled on American school textbooks of the time, in both content and form, they were translated with the help of native tutors who assisted the regular faculty in their teaching duties and served as on-site translators in classroom discussions and lectures.[95] These texts proved popular within the college and were also utilized in many local Muslim and Christian schools.

Missionaries at the college, moreover, also published (and patronized) a variety of Arabic medical, literary, and scientific journals and weekly papers.[96] A weekly, *al-Nashra al-Usbu'iya* (The Weekly News), the official press organ of the college, was founded in 1870; in 1874, George Post started a "Medical Journal," and in 1882 he also founded, along with Van Dyck, *al-Tabib* (The Physician).[97] These periodicals relied heavily on translations from Anglo-American sources, played an important role in the transmission of Western science to an Arabic-readership, and emphasized, among other things, the moral and material benefits of modern methods of hygiene and medical practice.

In this respect, undoubtedly the most important journal of all was *al-Muqtataf* (The Digest), a "journal of science and industry" begun in 1876 by college tutors Ya'qub Sarruf and Faris Nimr.[98] "We used to regret," the editors wrote, recounting how the idea for a science journal occurred to them, "that our Arabic language lacked a magazine which could simplify the arts and sciences." The aim of the journal, as the editors put it, was to announce the virtues of modern science to an Arabic-reading public—an ambitious attempt to encourage scientific and technical progress in the Arab East. "It is our sincere hope that this journal will meet with the approval of the public and will encourage the reader to acquire scientific knowledge and to strengthen industry."[99]

The magazine enjoyed a long and prolific career (it lasted in Egypt until the revolutionary days of 1952), and quickly became the principal vehicle for the translation and discussion of Western science in the Arab provinces of the empire.[100] The first few issues of the journal were slim compilations of the latest European and American scientific and technical advances, and edited in accordance with a self-consciously evangelical viewpoint by Sarruf and Nimr. At the start, each month's issue totaled no more than twenty-four pages and contained one or two original—typically unsigned—articles, while the rest were usually summaries of other publications, culled by the editors from such fashionable late nineteenth-century journals as *The American Artisan*, *Scientific American*, the *American Journal of Science*, *Nature*, *Popular Science Monthly*, the *Nineteenth Century*, and *The Times*. Summaries of the proceedings of professional societies—such as the Royal Society of London, the Royal Asiatic Society, the Royal Geographic Society of Egypt, the Eastern Scientific Society, and the Cairo Scientific Society—were later also included.[101] Familiar European and American medical and scientific thinkers of the day—from Laplace to Pasteur—were thus regularly featured in the journal.

Although later counted among the leading publications of the *Nahda* or "Arab Renaissance," the magazine was published by the American mission press and shared, at least initially, the vision and aims of American mission culture. It was veteran college tutor Cornelius Van Dyck, for instance, who had helped Sarruf and Nimr realize their project, and it was he who suggested the name *al-Muqtataf*, a kind of "Readers' Digest"—or, literally, "Selections"—recommending that they take "selections" from the Western science journals that could be found in the college library. Van Dyck even arranged to have the American mission press publish the magazine and helped to secure a permit from the Ottoman Syrian director of publications, Khalil al-Khuri.[102]

Nor was Van Dyck its only supporter in the college. Senior faculty as well as board and missionary members were initially quite proud of the journal, and the magazine was even passed around for admiration at board meetings at home.[103] Instructors at the college referred their students to it, and many saw it as an example of the superior enlightenment provided by Protestant culture and learning. "I was conducting my Bible-class to a group of young men last evening when the eclipse commenced," wrote Henry Jessup in February 1877, the day after a full umbral lunar eclipse, at which point Jessup used the opportunity to read to them "from the magazine published by two young native tutors in the college, an exact account of the beginning, middle and end of the eclipse...published a month ago."[104]

The eclipse itself, in fact, provided further demonstration of why *al-Muqtataf*, and Protestant promotion of science in general, were considered such valuable missionary tools. According to Jessup, in a letter sent to the PCBFM, it was "a magnificent phenomenon...a total obscuration of the full moon, lasting for 96 minutes." Yet in contrast to the calm, quiet, and, above all, rational appreciation of the eclipse at the college, pandemonium was said to have reigned outside the college gates: "Deep darkness came down on the land," wrote Jessup, "and the superstitious population with common consent set themselves to frighten it away." Copper kettles and drums were beaten, guns fired, and rockets sent off as shouts filled the air, while "the muezzins ascended the minarets and screamed 'There is no god but Allah,' and the devout Musslemen chanted prayers for protection." Amid the furor came shouts of "Allah Curse the Russians!" (the event took place during the Russo-Turkish war of 1876–1878)—"as though the eclipse were a Russian invention for the overthrow of the Turks," was Jessup's dry commentary. "Superstition, ignorance of God and ignorance of his works keep these poor people in bondage of fear and terror," wrote Jessup, noting with satisfaction that "of the millions of subjects of the Sultan of Turkey," it was only "our little Protestant communities" who could both appreciate and comprehend the phenomenon. "It is a comfort to know," he added, "that there is some light." Indeed, according to Jessup, the students were proud to know that "some of their own people" (that is, the editors of the journal) could have made such an accurate prediction.

The journal's prediction of lunar eclipses did more than impress missionaries and their students. It also impressed *al-Muqtataf*'s wider readership. "A group of us gathered together," wrote one enthusiastic reader of the new journal, schoolmaster Yawaqim Mas'ud, "and we had a general meeting on the night of the eclipse you gave notice of in the second and fourth issue of your journal," referring to an earlier partial eclipse in September 1876, whose timing the journal had also predicted for its readers. "There were over a hundred people there, and before they left, we announced to them that there was to be an eclipse. Astonishment appeared on their faces and many did not believe it and, as long tales were being spun, some people began to bet." More and more people soon joined the crowd and sat and waited for the event, until "suddenly the light of the moon became dimmer and the eclipse took place amidst great excitement. Those who were asleep got up to watch the event, and gunshots were fired. People were saying, 'It's true! They were right!'" referring to the science magazine and its editors, "'How can we disbelieve them then?'"[105]

Not all local opinion was so easily won over, however. During its very first year—and in response to claims then circulating locally for a geocentric view of the universe—*al-Muqtataf* published, along with the latest astronomical calculations from the college's observatory, a series of articles on the solar system and on Newton.[106] The Christian Orthodox Archimandrite of Antioch, Gabriel Jabbara, promptly sent a letter to the editors demanding an explanation—if not a recantation. "A clear refutation of the rotation of the earth," he wrote, "has already been published in several issues of *al-Jinan*." (An 1876 article by Nasir al-Khuri in *al-Jinan*—an earlier Beirut-based journal of the arts and sciences founded in 1860 by Butris al-Bustani—had claimed that the earth remained constant as the sun revolved around it, "as revealed in scripture."[107]) The Revealed Books, warned the Archimandrite, include not only all fundamental beliefs and commandments from God, but also "a clearly written account of the true state of the natural world and all its elements." He then proceeded to list ten biblical references that proved the fixity of the earth. These included such claims as: "Genesis demonstrates clearly to us that during the Great Flood it rained for 40 days and 40 nights, so that water covered the entire surface of the earth." It follows from this, he concluded, that if the earth rotated, the water could not have remained upon its surface and the Flood would not have occurred.[108]

The editors responded by prefacing the Archimandrite's letter with a short, didactic essay on "The Natural Sciences"—in which they clearly laid out their own theological views, emphasizing the compatibility of science with a true and reasoned faith. "Without wishing to single any one out," they began, "we will here set out to explain our intentions sincerely, so as to not perpetuate any misunderstanding on the part of our readers." There is a misguided view among those people, they wrote, "who link the sciences with disbelief and corruption." On the contrary, the natural sciences were the closest of the sciences to Creation, and a means of recognizing the power and will of God—"the designer of all designs"—in nature. "Therefore those who prevent people from pursuing these sciences, stand against God and all that He has revealed." (It was precisely this attitude, they added, which had led to the decline of scientific, technical, and industrial advancement in the Arab East.[109]) Those who claim that all the sciences of the natural world can be gleaned from the Revealed Books, moreover, not only belittle science, but also change the very meaning and purpose of revelation itself. True science, they believed, has never and will never be found to oppose true faith.[110]

A few months later they received support from an unexpected source. 'Abd Allah al-Fikri, a Muslim astronomer in the service of Riaz Pasha, the then Minister of Education at the court of the Khedive Isma'il, responded to the Archimandrite's assertions by backing the editors and insisting on the harmony of the natural sciences with Muslim religious law (shari'a). "When Riaz Pasha, the esteemed Minister of Education in Egypt," explained the editors in a preface to his response, "read in the eighth issue of our journal an article referring to the fixity of the earth, he told our deputy that this opinion was clearly wrong and corrupt, both religiously and scientifically." Riaz Pasha then wrote to the astronomer and civil servant at the ministry, 'Abdallah al-Fikri, asking him to compose a short piece comparing some of the discoveries of astronomy with the laws of the shari'a. "When we received it," wrote the editors, "we were overwhelmed by its logic and perfect analysis." They decided to summarize some of its main points, they continued, so as to demonstrate the compatibility of the astronomical sciences with Islam and "by way of answering the requests of our many readers who have asked about this."[111]

Referring to the eleventh-century philosopher al-Ghazali and his *Tahafut al-falasifa* (Incoherence of the Philosophers), al-Fikri pointed out the dangers of declaring an absolute (i.e., a mathematical) proof to be against received religious pronouncements since, as al-Ghazali was said to have pointed out, "to compare religion with matters that involve mathematical and engineering proofs would only harm religion and weaken its aims." Quoting from a recently published Turkish treatise on astronomy, al-Fikri laid out a short dialogue between a *faqih* (a legal scholar or jurisprudent) and an astronomer. In this, the faqih tells the astronomer: "I see you are following the new astronomy, despite the fact that it disagrees with the laws of *shariʿa*, the Book [of God] and *sunna*. I thought you were certain of your faith and discerning in your affairs," concluding: "So how is it that you chose to separate yourself from your faith and leave the circle of believers?" The astronomer then replies:

> God save us! How can you declare someone an unbeliever when he believes in God and His Prophet and the Day of Judgment, and when he believes in all of God's Creations, whether the sun is the centre of the universe and the earth revolves around it or not—whatever it is, it is God Almighty's Creation.

As for the supposed disagreement between the "new astronomy" and the shariʿa, continues the astronomer: "When I returned to what the Quranic verses and Prophetic sayings (*ahadith*) have commented on regarding astronomy, I found they did not really contain any pronouncements which contradict those certain proofs which are in favor of the new astronomy." Al-Fikri ended his objections by concluding that if a scientific truth that was thought to contradict revelation is proved beyond a doubt by absolute, mathematical proofs, revelation must be reinterpreted through *taʾwil* (a kind of analogic interpretation).[112]

It is hard to conceive of a more vivid illustration of the way science and the press were between them transforming and redefining the epistemological communities of Ottoman society. Here was a Muslim civil servant in Egypt coming to the public defense of Christian editors of a Syrian mission journal against a local Christian cleric. Like the missionaries themselves, al-Fikri was essentially arguing for the compatibility of science with a true, rational faith—only for al-Fikri it was an argument, ultimately, about the rationality of Islam, and for both, the promotion of science was linked to the efforts to reform and modernize their state and society.

Yet, just as science was creating new communities of knowledge that cut across religious boundaries, it was also leading to new factions and frictions. Local and foreign—particularly French—political and ecclesiastical authorities spoke frequently of the dangerous inroads being made by Protestant

educational and scientific works, and saw in these a continual effort aimed at
the "propagation of Protestantism."[113] The leaders of the established Christian
churches of Syria, moreover, continued to regard the mission-press journal
al-Muqtataf with suspicion and saw in its message a very Protestant design.

There was further debate, for instance, with Catholic critics following
al-Muqtataf's onslaught against magic and the supernatural. After the editors had published numerous articles against the obscurantism implied by
a belief in magic, hypnotism, animal magnetism, and supernaturalism of all
kinds, the Jesuit journal *al-Bashir* (The Herald) accused the editors of deny-
ing the existence of all spiritual entities and publicly proclaimed them here-
tics.[114] Once more, graduates of the college and the teaching staff, along with
interested outsiders, Christian and Muslim alike, felt compelled to defend
the journal.[115] This dispute lasted for several years, until 1884, when Khalil al-
Khuri, the Ottoman censor, issued an ultimatum to the contending journals,
ordering that they quit their attacks upon one another.[116] Other controver-
sies, such as over the nebular hypothesis and evolution, continued between
the two journals well into the new century.

IV

Yet the controversy which had the greatest effect upon the journal—and on
American missionaries' own faith in the promotion of science—came not
from outsiders at all but, ironically, from within the ranks of the Protestant
College itself. In the summer of 1882 Edwin Lewis, a Harvard graduate and
professor of geology and chemistry at the college, delivered the annual commencement speech and made what turned out to be the grave error of paying
tribute to Charles Darwin. Delivered in Arabic under the title of *al-Ma'rifa
al-'ilm wa'l-hikma* (Knowledge, Science and Wisdom), Lewis's speech was essentially a reflection on the nature (and limits) of "science," or *'ilm*. In that respect, it was typical of many of the college missionaries' efforts to partake in
a broad project of translation—turning *'ilm*, the broadest word in Arabic for
"knowledge"—into "science." Lewis, however, also used the opportunity to
cite Darwin as an outstanding example of contemporary scientific achievement through devotion to empirical study, or as he put it, "an example of the
transformation of knowledge (*ma'rifa*) into science (*'ilm*) by long and careful

examination."[117] Senior missionary colleagues at the college immediately objected.

Lewis had, of course, been aware of Darwin's controversial status, which was why he emphasized that a true reading of his views demonstrated no fundamental challenge to personal faith. The administrators and professors of the college, nevertheless, saw the speech as a poor "apology of Bible truth" and as an acceptance of "yet unproven theories." "Dr Lewis," announced the board of trustees during a special meeting in December, "appeared so distinctly to favor the theories of Darwin, that several of his associates and of the Managers of the College were constrained to express alarm at the utterance of such views by a Professor of the Institution."[118] "Lewis," wrote President Bliss later to his sons, "gave the impression that he was a Darwinian and that man descended from the lower animals. Dr. Dennis was up in arms—replied to Lewis' oration (the oration was printed in M. Faris' journal) and wrote very strongly to Mr. Dodge, so did Post and so did I."[119]

The fact that Lewis's speech was published in *al-Muqtataf*—along with numerous responses to it, mostly favorable—made matters all the worse. Writing to President Bliss on its publication, David Stuart Dodge asked, "How did it get in there? Is not this a point to be examined? Has [Lewis's] influence so perverted our young Tutors that their journal is to throw its influence in that direction?"[120] Dennis, who was then director of the college's theological school, sent a letter to the journal hoping to bring it round to the administration's position. Published in the November 1882 issue of *al-Muqtataf*, Dennis wrote of how he "regretted the many references made by Lewis to Darwin and his theories." Darwin's theory, he cautioned, should not be confused with a theory of the progression of species under divine providence (*al-irtiqa' bi-quwat ilahiya*).[121]

It was in the journal, too, that Lewis published a rejoinder. He cautioned against too swift a denunciation of Darwin's theory of evolution, and once again he emphasized the ultimate harmony of religion and science. "It is clear," he wrote, "that the scientific method, correctly applied, does not make men turn away from their religion." Revelation and natural science, he added, both worked to strengthen men's faith. "By studying nature we learn about the way God established it, but through revelation we learn who and what God is."[122] In this respect, like Asa Gray, whose lectures at Harvard he attended, Lewis argued that Darwin and design could be united.[123] Indeed, throughout the affair, Lewis maintained that he was merely behaving in strict accordance with those natural theological views the college had always up-held. Nevertheless, strong opposition remained and shortly afterward it was determined that he should resign.[124]

After the Lewis affair senior missionaries at the college and board mem-bers in New York felt it was necessary to exercise greater care in the hiring of instructors, and to reaffirm their Christian commitment to the teaching of science in accordance with scripture. The minutes of the board of trustees meeting in January of 1883 read as follows:

> The Trustees desire to urge upon the Board of Managers the neces-sity of using the utmost caution in selecting candidates for any post of instruction in the College, not merely as members of Evangelical Churches, but in full sympathy with the spiritual and missionary aims of the College…. No effort should be spared to make this Institution what it was originally established to be—a fountain of sound and scrip-tural teaching in science, morals and religion … inculcating right views & phases of modern scientific inquiry.[125]

All faculty members were now required to sign a religious manifesto—a Declaration of Principles which was drafted by Dennis in conjunction with the Evangelical Alliance (an international Protestant coalition group)—and to pledge themselves "to the inculcation of sound and reverent views on the relation of God to the natural universe as its Creator and Supreme Ruler." They were to give instruction, moreover, "in the spirit and method best cal-culated to conserve the teachings of revealed truth, and to demonstrate the essential harmony between the Bible and all true science and philosophy." Only those who met with these principles and the religious "spirit of the col-lege" were declared eligible to hold teaching positions.[126]

Several faculty resignations followed. These included *al-Muqtataf*'s men-tor, Cornelius Van Dyck, and his son William. Cornelius Van Dyck felt his colleagues had misinterpreted Lewis and behaved improperly in suspending students; while William, who had always been dedicated to science above all else (to the extent that his employers had hesitated to employ him at all), felt that the college was moving, as he put it, in "a dangerous direction." (William Van Dyck had also been among the first to introduce students at the college to Darwin in 1880, when he brought with him copies of the *Origin of Species* and *The Descent of Man* for use in his class on zoology. He had also corresponded briefly with Darwin in 1882.[127]) Several others resigned from the college's medical department with similar objections. In fact, the medical school was depleted.[128] Senior missionary and board members were not much bothered, however: "Let us stand clear on the records—'Resignations' springing from such grounds there be welcomed. Better run at half-speed— 'slow her clear down'—than make sixteen knots with the aid of atheistic, materialist or non-religious boilers."[129]

Student protests and even a few skirmishes erupted on campus.[130] But despite the resignations and protests, administrators and senior faculty at the college held to their position. Faculty and board members demanded that all dissenting students sign an apology before returning to their classes or else face expulsion. In a letter they drafted to the faculty, the dismayed students wrote: "It never occurred to the thoughtful people of Syria nor to the sons of the college, your students, that good people such as yourselves, who belong to the country of freedom, America, would pass such a verdict." Within the year, some fifteen medical students, including the future journalist, historical novelist, and science popularizer Jurji Zaydan, had been suspended.[131]

V

With the Lewis affair, missionary attitudes toward science came under new scrutiny, and within a few years, the debate they had helped initiate in Beirut had expanded enormously, both geographically and socially. Unhappy with the turmoil of previous years and bitter about the college's longstanding reluctance to promote them from the position of "native tutors" to the rank of faculty, Sarruf and Nimr, the editors of *al-Muqtataf*, left Beirut in 1884. That year Sarruf inveighed against those who were "fanatical against some of the sciences taught in their institutions" and who "selected teachers based upon their religious beliefs and not their academic competence." Institutions of higher learning, he warned bitterly, were destined to fail unless "they renounce religious fanaticism and permit their teachers and pupils to embrace whatever religious beliefs they choose, expecting nothing from them but teaching and learning."[132] Upon their retirement, Dodge wrote to Bliss: "I do not feel troubled by Nimr and Surroof as far as the College is concerned, but

those young men will turn miserably unless grace prevents." "'Going down
into Egypt,'" he wrote, "has never proved very wholesome."[133] In fact, Sarruf
and Nimr's journal, *al-Muqtataf*, attained even greater popularity after the
editors' move, and it became one of the most popular Arabic science journals
of the nineteenth and twentieth centuries.

Sarruf and Nimr had set up their base in Cairo—since 1882 under British
rule—where they hoped official censorship would be lighter than in the Ottoman lands, and where they anticipated little of that religious and especially
Christian "fanaticism" which had proved so oppressive in Beirut. In Egypt
they continued to proselytize for Darwin: in fact, after 1885, *al-Muqtataf*
proved to be one of the most influential organs for the promotion of Darwinian, and increasingly social Darwinian, thought across the Arab world.[134]

The spectrum of publicly espoused positions on the relation between religion and science soon ranged from their fellow college graduate and radical
materialist Shibli Shumayyil's translation of Ludwig Büchner's commentaries
on Darwin to the Grand Mufti of Egypt, Muhammad 'Abduh's positive
mention of Darwin in his *tafsir al-Qur'an*, or exegesis of the Qur'an, and
the Tripolitan Sufi *shaykh* Husayn al-Jisr's 1887 treatise, entitled *al-Risala
al-Hamidiya fi haqiqat al-diyana al-Islamiya wa haqiqat al-shari'a al-Muhammadiya* (A Hamidian Treatise on the Truthfulness of Islam and Muhammadan Law). At one extreme, Shumayyil used the new evolutionary science
as a means of promoting his materialistic view of the natural and man-made
world, claiming that all religions were nothing but reworkings of primi-
tive instincts and that, therefore, all theocratic autocracies (and here he was
clearly speaking of the Ottoman empire) rested on backward and retrograde
impulses, incompatible with the international development and progress of
mankind. Abduh II, by contrast, saw Darwin's theory as a means to prove the
alignment of Islam with rational thought and hence with all true science.[135]
This was a view that al-Jisr also advocated, and one that was clearly favored
by Sultan Abdülhamid II, who awarded him an Imperial prize in 1891. Islam,
al-Jisr wrote bluntly, "does not contradict science." So long as the principles
of a theory of evolution by natural selection could be found to be compatible
with a faith in God, reasoned al-Jisr, then there could be said to be little
conflict between evolution and Islam. Whether or not you believe that all
of His creatures were created at once or gradually in evolutionary stages, he
wrote, and so long as you believed that there is no creator but God, then, he

concluded, you would not be barred from interpreting scripture in such a fashion, and your faith as a Muslim could be said to remain uncorrupted. To be sure, al-Jisr also warned against making hasty conclusions, for he felt that "absolute proofs" in favor of evolution had not yet been found. In the case that they should be, however, he provided the means and arguments in favor of such a scriptural reconciliation. (Al-Jisr, of course, like many theistic and other evolutionists in Europe and elsewhere, drew the line at the evolution of man from some lower form, which he felt—not unlike the theory of evolution's co-founder, Alfred Russel Wallace—was unarguably the result of a special creation.) Nevertheless, for al-Jisr—who had been in Beirut during the turbulent events of 1882 while serving as the director of the newly founded Ottoman-Muslim school *al-Madrasa al-Sultaniya* (the Sultan's School), and who frequented the Protestant College's library while there—such a cautious argument in favor of a potential reconciliation allowed him, much like 'Abduh, to assert the superior rationalism of Islam to other, as he saw it, more dogmatic faiths, particularly Christianity.[136]

American missionaries, meanwhile, would move on, after 1884, to publish ever more aggressively against the new evolutionary biology, using their journal *al-Nashra al-Usbu'iya*, in particular, for this purpose: It was there that native tutor and editor Ibrahim Hurani would pen a series of objections to Shumayyil's treatise, later bound and published as *Manahij al-hukm fi nafy al-nushu' wa'l-irtiqa'* (The Procedure for a Judgement Refuting Evolution).[137] And as late as the 1890s, American missionaries were still sponsoring works in natural theology—such as their edition (also earlier serialized in *al-Nashra al-Usbu'iya*) of the Melkite Fransis Marrash's *Shihadat al-tabi'a fi wujud Allah wa'l-shari'a* (Nature's Testimony to God and Divine Law).[138] Yet it was to *al-Muqtataf*, and not to the missionaries, that most Arabic men of letters turned for their knowledge of science for much of the late nineteenth and early twentieth centuries.

Viewed in the long term, American evangelical efforts to promote Protestantism through science constituted a highly uncertain strategy for conversion. Their patronage of scientific works in education and publishing did indeed mean that missionaries were able to spread their message more and more widely throughout the late nineteenth century, gaining them access to audiences they might not have otherwise had. But eventually they lost control over the very same public space they had hoped would work in their favor, as what constituted a theologically sound view of science became increasingly contested, both within the fold and outside it.

Some had originally hoped that science would pave the way to God, that its rationality would testify to the superiority of Protestantism over the benighted superstitions of the East. However, missionaries—both at home and in the field—fought among themselves as to whether natural science helped or hindered their cause. The argument for rationality, meanwhile, was used variously by those who embraced science for their own ends—and often at cross-purposes to those of the missionaries themselves.

Behind all these developments lay the ever-expanding cultural authority of science as Syrian Protestants, Catholics, Orthodox, and Muslims alike staked out different claims in its name. A focus on its appropriations among missionaries, their patrons, and subjects thus allows us to appreciate the synergistic and not merely antagonistic relation between science and religion as well as to understand the complex—and highly indeterminate—social and cultural dynamics involved in the process of conversion itself. For many of the missionaries' own converts and disciples (men like Sarruf and Nimr) would come, at the hands of their patrons, to see science—and not a reformed faith—as a means of disentangling Ottoman society and polity from Eastern superstitions and sectarianism. In the end, it was science that, for them, proved to be the true gospel.

Acknowledgments

The research for this article was made possible through the support of the Center for Middle Eastern Studies at the University of California, Berkeley, and the British Academy. Special thanks are also due to the librarians and archivists at the American University of Beirut. A previous version of this article was published in *Past and Present*, no. 196 (August 2007): 173–214.

Notes

1. Oliver Wendell Elsbree, "The Rise of the Missionary Spirit in New England, 1790–1815," *New England Quarterly* 3 (1928): 295–299. On the first Great Awakening (c. 1720–1740), see Frank Lambert, *Inventing the "Great Awakening"* (Princeton: Princeton University Press, 2001); on the second (c.

1795–1835), see Barry Hankins, *The Second Great Awakening and the Transcendentalists* (Westport: Greenwood Press, 2004). See also Mark A. Noll, *The Rise of Evangelicalism: The Age of Edwards, Whitefield and the Wesleys* (Leicester: Apollos, 2004).

2. See Carl J. C. Wolf, ed., *Jonathan Edwards on Evangelism* (Westport: Greenwood Press, 1958); Samuel Hopkins, *A Treatise on the Millennium*, repr. of 1793 edition (New York: Arno Press, 1972). On manifest destiny, see Anders Stephanson, *Manifest Destiny: American Expansion and the Empire of Right* (New York: Hill and Wang, 1995). American mission work began in the mid- to late eighteenth century with efforts to convert—and civilize—Native Americans through local mission societies set up in the 1790s; in 1802 congressional appropriations known as the "Civilization Fund" also made money available to religious groups "to provide civilization among the aborigines." Francis Paul Prucha, ed., *Americanizing the American Indian: Writings by the "Friends of the Indian," 1880–1900* (Lincoln: University of Nebraska Press, 1978), 19.

3. Although Congregational in origin, the ABCFM quickly grew to include Presbyterian, Dutch-Reformed, and other denominational members. See Clifton Jackson Phillips, *Protestant America and the Pagan World: The First Half Century of the American Board of Commissioners for Foreign Missions, 1810–1860* (Cambridge, MA: East Asian Research Center, Harvard University, 1969), 20; James A. Field Jr., *America and the Mediterranean World, 1776–1882* (Princeton: Princeton University Press, 1969), 89.

4. "Address to the Christian Public," Nov. 1811, from *First Ten Annual Reports of the American Board of Commissioners for Foreign Missions* (Boston: Crocker and Brewster, 1834), 28.

5. James S. Dennis, *Christian Missions and Social Progress: A Sociological Study of Foreign Missions*, 3 vols. (New York: Fleming H. Revell, 1897–1906), III: 3–4.

6. See, for instance, T. O. Beidelman, *Colonial Evangelism: A Socio-Historical Study of an East African Mission at the Grassroots* (Bloomington: Indiana University Press, 1982). Cf. John L. Comaroff and Jean Comaroff, *Of Revelation and Revolution: Christianity, Colonialism and Consciousness in South Africa* (Chicago: University of Chicago Press, 1991), 7–11; Andrew Porter, *Religion versus Empire? British Protestant Missionaries and Overseas Expansion, 1700–1914* (Manchester: Manchester University Press, 2004).

7. See, for example, *al-Mu'ayyid* 1 (1890): 50–54; *al-Manar* 1 (1898): 898–899; *ibid.*, (1899): 141–142. See also Mahmud Samrah, "Christian Missions and Western Ideas in Syrian Muslim Writers, 1860–1918" (PhD diss., University of London, 1958), 33–42; Robert Truett Gilliam, "A Muslim Response to Protestant Missionaries: The Case of al-Manar" (master's thesis, American University of Beirut, 2000), 12–16; Mahmoud Haddad, "Syrian Muslim Attitudes Toward Foreign Missionaries in the Late Nineteenth and Twentieth Centuries," in

Altruism and Imperialism: Western Cultural and Religious Missions in the Middle East, ed. Eleanor H. Tejirian and Reeva Spector Simon (New York: Middle East Institute, Columbia University, 2002).

8. Mustafa Khalidi and 'Umar Farrukh, *al-Tabshir wa'l-isti'mar fi al-bilad al-'Arabiya* [Missions and Imperialism in the Arab World] (Beirut: al-Maktaba al-'Asriya, 1953); Ibrahim Khalil Ahmad, *al-Mustashriqun wa'l-mubashirun fi al-'alam al-'Arabi* [Orientalists and Missionaries in the Arab and Muslim World] (Cairo: Maktabat al-Wa'i al-'Arabi, 1964); 'Imad Sharaf, *Haqa'iq 'an al-tabshir* [The Truth about Missions] (Cairo: al-Mukhtar al-Islami, 1975); 'Abdul Rahman Hasan al-Midani, *Ajnihat al-makr al-thalatha wa khawafiha: al-tabshir, al-istishraq, al-isti'mar* [The Three Wings of Duplicity: Missions, Orientalism and Imperialism] (Damascus: Dar al-Qalam, 1975). For a review of some of these works, see Robert Truett Gilliam, "A Muslim Response to Protestant Missionaries," 92–95; Heather J. Sharkey, "Arabic Antimissionary Treatises: Muslim Responses to Christian Evangelism in the Modern Middle East," *International Bulletin of Missionary Research* 28:3 (July 2004): 98–104.

9. Philip K. Hitti, *Lebanon in History from the Earliest Times to the Present* (London: St. Martin's Press, 1957), ch. 31; Albert Hourani, *Arabic Thought in the Liberal Age, 1798–1939* (Oxford: Oxford University Press, 1962), 55; Kamal S. Salibi, *The Modern History of Lebanon* (London: Weidenfeld and Nicolson, 1965), ch. 7; George Antonius, *The Arab Awakening: The Story of the Arab National Movement* (London: H. Hamilton, 1945), 35–43; Elie Kedourie, *The Chatham House Version and Other Middle Eastern Studies* (New York: Praeger, 1970), 289; Elie Kedourie, "The American University of Beirut," in his *Arab Political Memoirs and Other Studies* (London: Cass, 1974), 70.

10. On the former, see citations above, n.9; on the latter, see, for example: Adnan Abu-Ghazaleh, *American Missions in Syria: A Study of American Missionary Contribution to Arab Nationalism in 19th Century Syria* (Brattleboro, VT: Amana Books, 1990); Nazik Saba Yared, *Secularism and the Arab World* (London: Saqi, 2002), 18–19.

11. Abdul Latif Tibawi, "Some Misconceptions about the *Nahda*," *Middle East Forum* 47 (1971): 15–22; Fruma Zachs, *The Making of a Syrian Identity: Intellectuals and Merchants in Nineteenth Century Beirut* (Leiden: Brill, 2005), ch. 4.

12. On the idea of "conversion to modernities," see Peter Pels, "The Anthropology of Colonialism: Culture, History, and the Emergence of Western Governmentality," *Annual Review of Anthropology* 26 (1997): 171–174; Peter van der Veer, ed., *Conversion to Modernities: The Globalization of Christianity* (New York: Routledge, 1996), introduction. For critical reflections on the idea of conversion, see also Talal Asad, "Comments on Conversion," in *ibid.*; Gauri Viswanathan, *Outside the Fold: Conversion, Modernity and Belief* (Princeton: Princeton University Press, 1998), ch. 3.

13. Paul Sedra, "Modernity's Mission: Evangelical Efforts to Discipline the Nine-teenth Century Coptic Community" in *Altruism and Imperialism*, ed. Tejirian and Simon; cf. Beidelman, *Colonial Evangelism*, 4.

14. Ussama Makdisi, "Reclaiming the Land of the Bible: Missionaries, Secularism and Evangelical Modernity," *American Historical Review* 102 (1997): 683.

15. On postmillennialism and the social gospel movement, see Walter Rauschen-busch, *A Theology for the Social Gospel* (New York: Abingdon Press, 1917); Charles Howard Hopkins, *The Rise of the Social Gospel in American Protes-tantism, 1865–1915* (New Haven: Yale University Press, 1940); *The Social Gos-pel in America, 1870–1920: Gladden, Ely, Rauschenbusch,* ed. Robert T. Handy (New York: Oxford University Press, 1966); J. B. Quandt, "Religion and So-cial Thought: The Secularization of Postmillennialism," *American Quarterly* 25 (1973): 390–409.

16. See, for example: James Eldin Reed, "American Foreign Policy, The Politics of Missions and Josiah Strong, 1890–1900," *Church History* 41 (1972): 230–245; Alexander Schölch, "Britain in Palestine, 1838–1882: The Roots of the Bal-four Policy," *Journal of Palestine Studies* 22 (1992): 39–56; Eleanor H. Tejirian, "Faith of Our Fathers: Near East Relief and the Near East Foundation—From Mission to NGO," in *Altruism and Imperialism*, ed. Tejirian and Simon. Also relevant is Betty Anderson, "Defining Liberal Education at the American Uni-versity of Beirut: Education, Protestantism, and Service to Nation" (paper pre-sented at University of Erlangen-Nürnberg, Erlangen, 2005).

17. See, however, Sujit Sivasundaram, *Nature and the Godly Empire: Science and Evangelical Mission in the Pacific, 1795–1850* (Cambridge: Cambridge Univer-sity Press, 2005), esp. ch. 2.

18. The literature on missions and medicine is considerably more substantial. See, for instance, C. Peter Williams, "Healing and Evangelism: The Place of Med-icine in Late Victorian Protestant Missionary Thinking," in *The Church and Healing*, ed. W. J. Sheils (Oxford: Studies in Church History, 1982); Megan Vaughan, *Curing Their Ills: Colonial Power and African Illness* (Cambridge: Cambridge University Press, 1991), ch. 3; Paul S. Landau, "Explaining Surgi-cal Evangelism in Colonial Southern Africa: Teeth, Pain and Faith," *Journal of African History* 37 (1996): 261–281; John L. Comaroff and Jean Comaroff, *Of Revelation and Revolution: The Dialectics of Modernity on a South African Fron-tier* (Chicago: University of Chicago Press, 1997), ch. 7; Rosemary Fitzger-ald, "'Clinical Christianity': The Emergence of Medical Work as a Missionary Strategy in Colonial India, 1800–1914," in *Health, Medicine and Empire: Per-spectives on Colonial India*, ed. Biswamoy Pati and Mark Harrison (Hyderabad: Orient Longman, 2001).

19. See, for instance: Lynette Thistlethwayte, "The Role of Science in the Hindu-Christian Encounter," *Indo-British Review* 19 (1991): 73–83. Cf. Neil Gunson,

"British Missionaries and Their Contribution to Science in the Pacific Islands," in *Darwin's Laboratory: Evolutionary Theory and Natural History in the Pacific*, ed. Roy MacLeod and Philip F. Rehbock (Honolulu: Univeristy of Hawaii Press, 1994), 283–316.

20. For the origins of the idea of the war of science with theology, see John William Draper, *A History of the Conflict between Religion and Science* (New York: D. Appleton, 1875); Andrew Dickson White, *A History of the Warfare of Science with Theology in Christendom*, 2 vols. (New York: D. Appleton, 1896).

21. Quote from Daniel Bliss [for more on which, see below], Amherst College Library Archives and Special Collections, Bliss Family Papers, 1850–1981, box 5, addendum 1, folder 1, 1863 notebook, 110.

22. On the moral authority of experimenters and the role of public experiments, see Simon Schaffer, "Self Evidence," *Critical Inquiry* 18 (1992): 327–362; Steven Shapin, "The House of Experiment in Seventeenth Century England," *Isis* 79 (1988): 373–404.

23. On commerce and Christianity, see Andrew Porter, "'Commerce and Christianity': The Rise and Fall of a Nineteenth-Century Missionary Slogan," *Historical Journal* 28 (1985): 597–621.

24. For diverging nineteenth-century evangelical views on natural theology, see Aileen Fyfe, *Science and Salvation: Evangelical Popular Science Publishing in Victorian Britain* (Chicago: University of Chicago Press, 2004), 6–8. See also Jonathan R. Topham, "Science, Natural Theology and Evangelicalism in Early Nineteenth Century Scotland," in *Evangelicals and Science in Historical Perspective*, ed. David N. Livingstone, D. G. Hart, and Mark A. Noll (Oxford: Oxford University Press, 1999).

25. *Missionary Herald* ix (July 1813): 72; Rao Lindsay, "Nineteenth-Century American Schools in the Levant: A Study of Purposes" (PhD diss., University of Michigan, 1964), 33, 41.

26. On the development of American Protestant views of science from the early to mid-nineteenth century, see Theodore Dwight Bozeman, *Protestants in the Age of Science: The Baconian Ideal and Ante-Bellum American Religious Thought* (Chapel Hill: University of North Carolina Press, 1977). On the question of orthodoxy and heterodoxy in nineteenth-century science, see Alison Winter, "The Construction of Orthodoxies and Heterodoxies in the Early Victorian Life Sciences," in *Victorian Science in Context*, ed. Bernard Lightman (Chicago: University of Chicago Press, 1997), 24–50.

27. See Paul Carter, *The Spiritual Crisis of the Gilded Age* (DeKalb: Northern Illinois University Press, 1971); D. H. Meyer, "American Intellectuals and the Victorian Crisis of Faith," *American Quarterly* 27 (1975): 583–603; Michael Karmen, "The Science of the Bible in Nineteenth Century America: From 'Common Sense' to Controversy, 1820–1900" (PhD diss., Notre Dame University, 2004).

28. The term "Syria" is here used—much as missionaries of the time used it—to refer to Greater Syria, or, roughly, what is now Lebanon, Syria, Jordon, Palestine,
and Israel.

29. See Ami Ayalon, *The Press in the Arab Middle East: A History* (New York: Oxford University Press, 1995), 31–39.

30. The *locus classicus* for this view is Hourani's *Arabic Thought in the Liberal Age*.

31. This coupling of missionaries with modernity is itself rather ironic, given the
eschatological nature of their understanding of time and history. For a critical
discussion of the uses—and abuses—of the term *modernity* outside the Anglo-
American and Continental European world, see Frederick Cooper, *Colonialism in Question: Theory, Knowledge, History* (Berkeley: University of California
Press, 2005), ch. 5.

32. See, for instance, Comaroff and Comaroff, *Revolution and Revelation*, II: 28.

33. John Davis, *The Landscape of Belief: Encountering the Holy Land in Nineteenth-
Century American Art and Culture* (Princeton: Princeton University Press,
1996), 29.

34. Pliny Fisk, *The Holy Land an Interesting Field of Missionary Enterprise: A Sermon* (Boston, 1819), 24.

35. Gregory M. Wortabet, *Syria and the Syrians: or, Turkey in the Dependencies*, 2
vols. (London: J. Madden, 1856), I: 47–49. Quote from Abdul Latif Tibawi,
*American Interests in Syria, 1800–1901: A Study of Educational, Literary and Re-
ligious Work* (Oxford: Clarendon Press, 1966), 22.

36. The Maronite As'ad Shidyaq's conversion to Protestantism was said to have
aroused the ire of Patriarch Youssef Hobaich who was residing in Qannu-
bin at the time. According to missionary accounts, Shidyaq, who was sum-
moned to see the patriarch but refused to recant his new faith, was confined to
a cell, where he stayed until he died (c. 1830). Missionaries claimed this as the
first martyrdom of one of their converts in Syria. See Jonas King, *The Oriental
Church, and the Latin* (New York: John A. Gray & Green, 1865), 3–5; Butrus
al-Bustani, *Qissat As'ad al-Shidyaq* [The Story of As'ad al-Shidyaq] (Beirut: Dar
al-Hamra, 1992). Also relevant is Ussama Makdisi, "The Two Deaths of As'ad
al-Shidyaq" (paper presented at Birkbeck College, London, 2002), and *Artillery of Heaven: American Missionaries and the Failed Conversion of the Middle
East* (Ithaca: Cornell University Press, 2008).

37. Tibawi, *American Interests in Syria*, 61.

38. "Mission to Syria and the Holy Land," *Missionary Herald* 39 (Jan. 1843): 6–7.

39. "Translation of the Firman of His Imperial Majesty Sultan 'Abd-el-Mejid,
Granted in Favor of his Protestant Subjects," trans. Reverend H. Dwight, *Journal of the American Oriental Society* 3 (1853): 218–20.

40. "Translation of the Firman Granted by Sultan 'Abd-al-Mejeed to his Protestant
Subjects," trans. Reverend H. Dwight, *Journal of the American Oriental Society*

4 (1854): 443–444. See also Joseph L. Grabill, *Protestant Diplomacy and the Near East: Missionary Influence on American Policy, 1810–1927* (Minneapolis: University of Minnesota Press, 1971).

41. *Missionary Herald* 5 (Dec. 1810): 517.

42. By 1862, there were 1,925 students in American mission schools, and 2,840 in 1876: Lindsay, "American Schools in the Levant," 95–101.

43. "American Board of Commissioners for Foreign Missions; Syria and the Holy Land. Journal of Mr. W. M. Thomson on a Visit to Safet And Tiberias," *Missionary Herald* 33 (Nov. 1837): 445.

44. Lindsay, "American Schools in the Levant," 40.

45. "Favorable Location of Beyroot. Progress of Missionary Labors," *Missionary Herald* 31 (Mar. 1835): 93.

46. "American Board of Commissioners for Foreign Missions; Syria and the Holy Land. Journal of Mr. W. M. Thomson on a Visit to Safet And Tiberias," *Missionary Herald* 33 (Nov. 1837): 444–445.

47. "Report of the Syria Mission for the year 1841," *Missionary Herald* 38 (June 1842): 227.

48. For more on Anderson and his mission strategy, see Paul William Harris, *Nothing but Christ: Rufus Anderson and the Ideology of Protestant Foreign Missions* (Oxford: Oxford University Press, 1999).

49. ABCFM, *Annual Report*, 1837, 137.

50. Rufus Anderson, "A Sermon on the Present Crisis in the Missionary Organizations of the American Board of Commissioners for Foreign Missions," *Christian Examiner and General Review of* 29 (Sept. 1840): 57–59. By then, missionaries in Syria were claiming that the Druzes' earlier interests in conversion (first reported in 1835–1836) seemed to be motivated largely by the desire for exemption from military service—which under Muhammad 'Ali's new conscription laws was incumbent upon Muslim subjects only—and by hopes for English protection and patronage (for the Americans at that time were also acting under English consular protection). See "Letter from Mr. Smith, Beyroot," *Missionary Herald* 38 (Sept. 1842): 362.

51. The only function of mission schools, insisted Anderson time and time again, was to 'train native pastors and preachers'. ABCFM, *Annual Report*, 1841, 44–47. Whenever possible, too, the Lancastrian method of education—established by Joseph Lancaster (1778–1838), and whereby more advanced students taught less advanced ones—was to be encouraged, for it was hoped that the operation of mission schools and churches might eventually be left in the hands of local personnel as a means of cutting back on expenditures.

52. Rufus Anderson, *Report to the Prudential Committee of a Visit to the Missions in the Levant* (Boston, 1844), 34.

53. Rufus Anderson, *Missionary Schools (From the Biblical Repository)* (New York, n.d.), 16.

54. Ibid., 24.

55. *Minutes of the Special Meeting of the Syrian Mission Held in September and October, 1855, On Occasion of the Visit of One of the Secretaries of the American Board of Commissioners for Foreign Missions* (Boston, 1856), 9, emphasis in original.

56. ABCFM, *The Divine Instrumentality for the World's Conversion* (Boston: Missionary House, 1856), 4, 10; Lindsay, "American Schools in the Levant," 154–156.

57. Rufus Anderson, *History of the Missions of the American Board of Commissioners for Foreign Missions to the Oriental Churches*, 2 vols. (Boston: Congregational Publishing Society, 1872), v.

58. From the 1847 constitution, in Edward Salisbury, "Syrian Society of Arts and Sciences," *Journal of the American Oriental Society* 3 (1853): 477–486. The majority of its members were nevertheless Christian. See Filib Tarrazi, *Tarikh al-sihafa al-'Arabiya* [A History of the Arabic Press] 4 vols. (Beirut: al-Matba'a al-Adabiya, 1913–1933), IV: 112; Zachs, *Making of a Syrian Identity*, 137–145. The Society lasted only some five years, or from 1847 to 1852. It is possible that Eli Smith, one of the founding members, established the society on the model of the 1844 Syro-Egyptian Society of London. Smith was in regular correspondence with several of the council members of the latter society—including As'ad Ya'qub Khayyat and John Gordon Scott—and had copies of the society's circulars in his possession. The two societies also had many common goals: "Great efforts are making for the general diffusion of knowledge," read the *Prospectus of the Plan and Objects of the Syro-Egyptian Society*, "and though various benefits have been conferred, those who are acquainted with the modern condition of Egypt and Palestine and Syria are well aware how much remains to be done before they can be ranked among the civilized nations of the earth." Houghton Library Archives, Harvard University, ABC 60, Eli Smith Papers, folders 46, 72 and 144. The *Syrian Society* expressed similar sentiments. "The existence and prosperity of this society is an indication most interesting to the philanthropist and the scholar," read a report in the 1853 *Journal of the American Oriental Society*, "that the culture of Western nations is exerting a great and happy influence upon minds in Syria, and even gives promise for the naturally fine intellect of the Arab race in the mould of modern civilization." Edward Salisbury, "Syrian Society of Arts and Sciences," 477.

59. These were delivered by Cornelius Van Dyck, Butrus al-Bustani, and Salim Nawfal, respectively. Other papers included: Nasif al-Yaziji's "On the Sciences of the Arabs"; Johannes Wortabet's "The Measure of the Progress of Knowledge in Syria at the Present Time and Its Causes"; Mikha'il Mudawwar's "On the Origins of Commerce and Its Vicissitudes." See "Syrian Society of Arts and Sciences," 478; Butrus al-Bustani's *A'mal al-jam'iya al-Suriya* [Proceedings of the Syrian Society] (Beirut, 1852).

60. "'Abeih Station Report for 1849," *Missionary Herald* 66 (Aug. 1850): 262–263.

61. Until 1853—when Protestantism was declared an official civil and ecclesiastical community by imperial decree—missionaries alleged that would-be converts had been deterred by the prospect of existing outside any clear ecclesiastical, legal, or political protection in the empire. As late as 1880, however, missionaries were expressing similar anxieties, complaining that the 1853 firman seemed to have been seen as "merely provisional" in the eyes of local authorities. See Presbyterian Church Board of Foreign Missions (PCBFM), Correspondence and Reports, vol. 5, no. 42, W. W. Eddy to Reverend Ellinwood, 3 May 1880.

62. The combination of the 1838 Anglo-Turkish Convention and the *Tanzimat* reforms introduced by Sultan Abdülmecid in the 1840s triggered a period of rapid socioeconomic transformation and commercial growth. See Jens Hanssen, *Fin de Siècle Beirut: The Making of an Ottoman Provincial Capital* (Oxford: Oxford University Press, 2005), 32–37.

63. According to an 1883 paper read in Arabic to the Scientific Society in Beirut (a later descendent of the 1847 Society of Arts and Sciences), it was reported that in the *sanjaq* of Beirut alone, there was a ratio of some 250 students to every 1,000 people (nearly six times the number of other districts throughout Lebanon). Henry Diab and Lars Wahlin, "The Geography of Education in Syria in 1882: With a Translation of 'Education in Syria' by Shahin Makarius," *Geografiska Annaler* 65 (1983): 105–128.

64. ABCFM Correspondence and Reports, vol. 545, "Documents, Reports and Letters, 1860–1871," no. 110, "Reasons for the establishment of a Syrian Protestant College," n.d.

65. Ibid.

66. Ibid.

67. Anderson, *History of the Missions of the American Board of Commissioners for Foreign Missions to the Oriental Churches*, vol. 2, 387–388. For the Prudential Committee's full response and recommendations, see Amherst College Library Archives and Special Collections, Bliss Family Papers, 1850–1981, box 5, addendum 1, folder 1.

68. American University of Beirut (AUB) Library Archives, Syrian Protestant College (SPC) Minutes of the Board of Trustees, bk 1 (4 Oct. 1866), 59.

69. Amherst College Library Archives and Special Collections, Bliss Family Papers, 1850–1981, box 5, addendum 1, folder 1, 1863 notebook, 59–94, emphasis in original.

70. Both the Syrian Protestant College and Robert College in Istanbul were chartered in New York that year. AUB Library Archives, SPC Minutes of the Board of Trustees, bk 1 (18 Apr. 1863), 3–4.

71. ABCFM Correspondence and Reports, vol. 545, "Documents, Reports and Letters, 1860–1871," no. 36, "Annual Report of the Beirut Station, 1866."

72. ABCFM Correspondence and Reports, vol. 545, "Documents, Reports and Letters, 1860–1871," no. 110, "Prospectus and Programme of the Syrian Protestant Collegiate Institute Beirut," 2.

73. *Catalogue of the Syrian Protestant College* (Beirut, 1902–1903).

74. Tuition for the college was initially set at 5 Turkish liras, and the cost of full board was 12 Turkish liras (or the equivalent of about $25 and $80 at the time). See "Education in Syria," *Hours at Home: A Popular Monthly of Instruction and Recreation* 11 (1870), 328. Many students were aided moreover through board funds, although the majority were encouraged to secure means toward their own support so as to foster "self-reliance." AUB Library Archives, MSS AUB 33, Record of the Secretary of the Board of Managers of the Syrian Protestant College, 1864–1903, 23 Jan. 1868, 89.

75. In the preparatory department, students (admitted from the age of ten) engaged in regular Bible study plus ancient, modern, and scripture history and took lessons in Arabic, English and Latin, French or Greek, arithmetic, algebra and geometry, geography, geology, chemistry, physics, botany, zoology, physiology, and astronomy over a period of four years.

76. Students in the Medical Department took lessons in chemistry and anatomy (in year 1); materia medica, physiology, and zoology (year 2); surgery, obstetrics, and pathology, alongside clinical work (years 3 and 4). In the Literary Department students studied Arabic, English, French, scripture criticism (*tafsir al-kitab al-muqadis*), and mathematics (in year 1); history and natural philosophy (regularly after year 2); Latin, chemistry, botany, and zoology (year 3); geology and physiology, logic, and moral philosophy (year 4).

77. *Missionary Herald* 63 (Sep. 1862): 220; Lindsay, "American Schools in the Levant," 184.

78. Minutes of the Board of Trustees, bk 1 (4 May 1864), 23, 27.

79. SPC *Annual Reports* (Beirut, 1963), Daniel Bliss to the Board, 27 June 1871, 18.

80. ABCFM Correspondence and Reports, vol. 545, "Documents, Reports and Letters, 1860–1871," no. 36, "Annual Report of the Beirut Station, 1866."

81. *Fifty-ninth Annual Report of the American Board of Commissioners for Foreign Missions* (Cambridge, MA: Riverside Press, 1869), 32–33, emphasis in original.

82. PCBFM Correspondence and Reports, vol. 5, no. 47, George Post to the Board, June 1880. For more on Post, see Lutfi Sa'di, "The Life and Works of George Edward Post (1839–1910)," in *The Founding Fathers of the American University of Beirut*, ed. Ghada Yusuf Khoury (Beirut: American University of Beirut Press, 1992), 151–177.

83. AUB Library Archives, SPC Minutes of the Board of Trustees, bk 1 (1 Nov. 1870), 98.

84. PCBFM Correspondence and Reports, vol. 5, no. 26, F. A. Wood to the Board, 23 March 1877. Instead, a theological department at the college was set up

under the supervision of James Dennis to accommodate the needs of theology students, though they also enrolled in the regular course of study available through the literary department. AUB Library Archives, SPC Minutes of the Board of Trustees, bk 1 (31 January 1873), 116.

85. James S. Dennis, *A Sketch of the Syria Mission* (New York: Mission House, 1872), 21–22.

86. SPC, *Annual Reports*, Daniel Bliss to the Board, 19 July 1877, 36. The observatory was supplied with a full set of instruments for meteorological observations (which were then also shared with Istanbul via two daily telegrams).

87. Bliss, *al-Durus al-awliya*, 1–2.

88. At the meeting held on 2 October 1848, however, it was decided to publish a translation of Azariah Smith's treatise on cholera instead. In 1868, Van Dyck also suggested Paley's *Evidences of Christianity* for translation: Tibawi, *American Interests in Syria*, 126, 184. For more on Van Dyck, see Lutfi Sa'di, "Al-Hakim Cornelius Van Allen Van Dyck," *Isis* 27 (1937): 20–45.

89. As'ad Ibrahim al-Shadudi, *Kitab al-'arus al-badi'a fi 'ilm al-tabi'a* [The Magnificent Bride of Natural Science] (Beirut: American Mission Press, 1873), i.

90. Ya'qub Sarruf, *al-Hikma al-Ilahiya* [Divine Wisdom] (Beirut: American Mission Press, 1877); see also Sarruf, "*al-'Ilm wa'l-madaris al-jami'i*" [Science and Higher Education], *al-Muqtataf* 2 (1884), 87, 200.

91. See Houghton Library Archives, Harvard University, ABC 50, Eli Smith Arabic Papers (1821–1857), box 1.

92. See Ayalon, *The Press in the Arab Middle East*, 28–49.

93. ABCFM, *Annual Report*, 1868, 47.

94. Ibid., 48, emphasis in original. On the broader cultural importance of calendars for the diffusion of ideas among "common readers," see James M. Brophy, "The Common Reader in the Rhineland: The Calendar as Political Primer in the Early Nineteenth Century," *Past and Present*, no. 185 (Nov. 2004): 119–157.

95. See, for example, Cornelius Van Dyck's *Usul al-kimiya* [Principles of Chemistry] (Beirut: American Mission Press, 1869); George Post's *Nizam al-halaqat fi silsilat dhawat al-fiqarat* [Vertebrates and the Great Chain of Being] (Beirut: American Mission Press, 1869) and his *Mabadi 'ilm al-nabat* [Principles of Botany] (Beirut: American Mission Press, 1871); As'ad Ibrahim al-Shadudi's 1873 work on natural science mentioned above, *Kitab al-'arus al-badi'a fi 'ilm al-tabi'a*; and Daniel Bliss's 1873 text on rational philosophy, also mentioned above, *al-Durus al-awliyya fi-al-falsafa al-'aqliyya*. For a full listing of these, see Suha Tamim, *A Bibliography of A.U.B. Faculty Publications, 1866–1966* (Beirut: American University of Beirut Press, 1967).

96. AUB Library Archives, SPC Minutes of the Board of Trustees, bk 2 (26 Jan. 1882), 49.

97. AUB Library Archives, SPC Minutes of the Board of Trustees, bk 1 (2 Dec. 1874), 128.

98. The subtitle changed from "a journal of science and industry" in 1876 to "a journal of science, industry, and agriculture" in 1888; "and medicine" was added in 1893. For more on Sarruf, see "*al-Duktur Ya'qub Sarruf*" [Dr Ya'qub Sarruf], *al-Muqtataf* 71 (1927); Muhammad Kurd 'Ali, "*al-'Alama al-Duktur Ya'qub Sarruf*" [Professor Ya'qub Sarruf], *Majallat al-majma al-'ilmi al-'Arabi* 1 (1928), 57; Fuad Sarruf, *Ya'qub Sarruf* (Beirut: American University of Beirut Press, 1960), 12; Henry H. Jessup, *Fifty Three Years in Syria*, 2 vols. (New York: Fleming H. Revell, 1910), i, 430; Nadia Farag, "Al-Muqtataf, 1876–1900: A Study of the Influence of Victorian Thought on Modern Arabic Thought" (PhD diss., University of Oxford, 1969), 17–20. For more on Nimr, see "*al-Duktur Faris Nimr*" [Dr Faris Nimr], *al-Muqtataf* 120 (1952); Farag, "Al-Muqtataf," 20, 42–47.

99. "*al-Muqaddima*" [Introduction], *al-Muqtataf* 1 (1876), 1.

100. On the journal's move to Egypt, see below.

101. For a complete list of the journal's sources, see Farag, "Al-Muqtataf," 119–131.

102. By 1877 the library was said to hold some two thousand volumes of "Cyclopedias and Governmental reports of a Legal, Political, Historical, Educational and Scientific nature," as well as scores of other books and periodicals in Arabic, English, French, and Turkish. See SPC, *Annual Reports*, Daniel Bliss to the Board, 19 July 1877, 37.

103. See, for example: MSS AUB 1, box 5, 1/3, folder 3, Letters from Dr. Stuart Dodge to Daniel Bliss, 1880–1883, letter dated 24 November 1881.

104. PCBFM, Correspondence and Reports, vol. 4, no. 21, H. H. Jessup to the Board, 28 February 1877.

105. "*al-Khusuf al-juz'i*" [The Partial Lunar Eclipse], *al-Muqtataf* 1 (1876): 117.

106. See, for example: "*al-Nizam al-shamsi*" [The Solar System], *al-Muqtataf* 1 (1876); "*Khusuf al-qamar*" [The eclipse of the Moon], ibid.; "*Dawaran al-ard*" [The Rotation of the Earth], ibid.

107. Nasir al-Khuri, "*'Amal falakiyya*" [On Astronomy], *al-Jinan* 20 (1876). For more on Bustani, see Jurji Zaydan, *Tarajim mashahir al-Sharq* [Biographies of Famous Men of the East](Cairo: Matba'at al-Hilal, 1911), 25–32; "*Butrus al-Bustani*," *al-Muqtataf* 8 (1883), 1–7; Abdul Latif Tibawi, "The American Missionaries in Beirut and Butrus al-Bustani," in *Middle Eastern Affairs* 3 (1963); Butrus Abu-Manneh, "The Christians between Ottomanism and Syrian Nationalism: The Ideas of Butrus al-Bustani," *International Journal of Middle East Studies* 11 (1980); Albert Hourani, "Bustani's Encyclopaedia," in the *Journal of Islamic Studies* 1 (1990).

108. "*Thabut al-ard wa raddat ilayna hadha al-risala*" [A Letter on the Fixity of the Earth included with our Answer to it], *al-Muqtataf* 1 (1876): 265–267 and 268–270. See also Farag, "Al-Muqtataf," 63–67.

109. Here they referred their readers to an earlier article of theirs on "*Tabzir al-Sharq wa tadbir al-Gharb*" [The prodigality of the East and the ingenuity of the West], *al-Muqtataf* 1 (1876).

110. *"al-'Ulum al-tabi'aya"* [The Natural Sciences], *al-Muqtataf* 1 (1876).
111. *"al-'Ulum al-tabi'aya wa'l-nusus al-shari'aya"* [The Natural Sciences and the Principles of the *shari'a*], *al-Muqtataf* 1 (1876). This article also appeared in the Cairo journal *Rawdat al-madaras* 7 (1876). The latter was founded in 1870 by the Egyptian Bureau of Schools. Devoted to the "diffusion of knowledge," it was distributed free of charge to all students in government schools; see Timothy Mitchell, *Colonising Egypt* (Berkeley: University of California Press, 1988), 92.
112. *"al-'Ulum al-tabi'aya wa'l-nusus al-shari'aya,"* *al-Muqtataf* 1 (1876).
113. Archive diplomatique de Nantes: Ministère des Affaires Étrangères: Constantinople Série E: 709: "Ottoman and American Schools," carton 173, dossier 4. See also complaints in *Les Missions Catholiques* 9 (1873), 570–571.
114. Virtually every issue of the journal, in its early years, contained some denunciation of magic and its "tricks," see Nadia Farag, "Al-Muqtataf," 63–67.
115. See *"al-Sihr ghish"* [Magic Is a Scam], under *"Akhbar wa-ikhtashafat wa-ikhtira'at"* [News, Findings and Discoveries], *al-Muqtataf* 3 (1878): 333; and *"Iman al-Muqtataf wa kufr al-Bashir"* [*al-Muqtataf*'s Faith and *al-Bashir*'s Disbelief], *al-Muqtataf* 8 (1883): 714–717, where they cite the Tipolitan shaykh Husayn al-Jisr and others in their support.
116. Khalil al-Khuri, *al-Muqtataf* 9 (1884): 47. Al-Khuri only issued a warning, citing "personal invective and incitement to public disturbances" as the charge. See Donald Cioeta, "Ottoman Censorship in Lebanon and Syria, 1876–1908," *International Journal of Middle East Studies* 10 (1979): 182.
117. Edwin Lewis, *"al-Ma'rifa al-'ilm wa'l-hikma"* [Knowledge, Science and Wisdom], *al-Muqtataf* 7 (1882): 158–167.
118. Minutes of the Board of Trustees, bk 2 (1 Dec. 1882), 51–55.
119. Amherst College Library Archives and Special Collections, Bliss Family Papers, 1850–1981, box 1, folder 7, Daniel Bliss to Howard and Willie Bliss, Beirut, 28 February 1883.
120. MSS AUB 1, box 5, 1/3, folder 3, Letters from Dr. Stuart Dodge to Daniel Bliss, 1880–1883, letter dated 29 September 1882.
121. James Dennis, *"al-Madhab al-Darwini"* [The Darwinian School of Thought], *al-Muqtataf* 7 (1882): 233–236.
122. Edwin Lewis, *"al-Madhab al-Darwini"* [The Darwinian School of Thought], *al-Muqtataf* 7 (1882): 287–290.
123. See Harvard University Archives, HU 20.41 mfp, 1804–1888/9, reel 4, 1863/4–1873/4.
124. Lewis already enjoyed something of a controversial status prior to the 1882 affair. He had been routinely chastised by senior missionary colleagues regarding the excessive time he devoted to music instruction at the college at the expense, it was claimed, of his regular instruction in the medical school, and for his breaches in temperance (he had wine at a "public entertainment" in 1882, something which shocked Daniel Bliss, David Stuart Dodge, and others). See

MSS AUB 1, box 5 and box 14; Farag, "The Lewis Affair and the Fortunes of *al-Muqtataf*," *Middle Eastern Studies* 8 (1972): 73–83. See also Donald Leavitt, "Darwinism in the Arab World and the Lewis Affair at the Syrian Protestant College," *Muslim World* 71 (1981): 85–98; Shafiq Juha, *Darwin wa azmat 1882* [Darwin and the Crisis of 1882] (Beirut: American University of Beirut Press, 1991).

125. AUB Library Archives, SPC Minutes of the Board of Trustees, bk 2 (28 Jan. 1883), 56–72.

126. SPC "Declaration of Principles," *Certificate of Incorporation and Constitution* (passed 1864, amended 1882); MSS AUB 1, Bliss Papers, Letters with Various Faculty Members, box 14, folder 1, Letters from James Dennis, 1883–1910, 5 February 1884.

127. Lewis had an exchange with Darwin in January of 1882, and then, shortly afterwards, sent him a copy of a paper "On the modification of a race of Syrian street dogs of Beirut," which Darwin helped publish in the Zoological Society proceedings. See The Darwin Correspondence Online Database, calendar number 13645, C.R. Darwin to W.T. Van Dyck, 25 January 1882; 13710, W.T. Van Dyck to C.R. Darwin, 27 February 1882; 13757 C.R. Darwin to W.T. Van Dyck, 3 April 1882 (Darwin died sixteen days later).

128. Sarruf and Nimr were also temporarily promoted to the newly created position of "adjunct professors," so as to allow for some instruction (in Arabic) to continue at the medical school while nevertheless managing to exclude the two young instructors from having any control over college affairs, which was left to other governing full faculty and board members.

129. MSS AUB 1, box 5, 1/3, folder 3, Letters from Dr. Stuart Dodge to Daniel Bliss, 1880–1883, letter dated 1 August 1882.

130. See "*al-Madrasa al-Kulliya al-Tabiʿaya*," [The Syrian Protestant College Medical School], *al-Muqtataf* 7 (1882): 192; "*al-Duktur Lewis*" [Doctor Lewis], *al-Muqtataf* 9 (1884): 183; Stephen B. L. Penrose, *That They May Have Life: The Story of the American University of Beirut 1866–1941* (New York: Trustees of the American University of Beirut, 1941), 47–48; Abdul Latif Tibawi, "The Genesis and Early History of the Syrian Protestant College," *Middle East Journal* 21 (1967): 208.

131. Jurji Zaydan, *Mudhakkirat Jurji Zaydan*, trans. by Thomas Philipp as *The Autobiography of Jurji Zaydan* (Washington D.C.: Three Continents Press, 1990), 58–62.

132. Yaʿqub Sarruf, "*al-ʿIlm waʾl-madaris al-jamiʿi*" [Science and Higher Education], *al-Muqtataf* 9 (1884): 468.

133. MSS AUB 1, box 6, 2/1, folder 1, Letters from Dr. Stuart Dodge to Daniel Bliss, 1880–1885, letter dated 13 February 1885.

134. See Marwa Elshakry, "Darwin's Legacies in the Arab East: Science, Religion and Politics, 1870–1914" (PhD diss., Princeton University, 2003), ch. 2.

135. See "*Tafsir al-Qur'an al-hakim*" [Exegesis of the Qur'an], *al-Manar* 1 (1898): 234–235; 2 (1899): 232–236; and 4 (1901): 268.

136. Shibli Shumayyil, *Sharh Bukhnar 'ala madhab Darwin* [Büchner's Exposition of Darwinism] (Alexandria: Matba'at Jaridat al-Mahrusa, 1884); Husayn al-Jisr, *al-Risala al-Hamidiya fi haqiqat al-diyana al-Islamiya wa haqiqat al-shari 'a al-Muhammadiya* [A Hamidian Treatise on the Truthfulness of Islam and Muhammadan Law] (Cairo, 1905), 222.

137. Ibrahim Hurani, *Manahij al-hukm fi nafy al-nushu' wa'l-irtiqa'* [The Procedure for a Judgement Refuting Evolution] (Beirut, 1884).

138. Fransis Fath Allah al-Marrash, *Shihadat al-tabi'a fi wujud Allah wa-al-shari'a* [Nature's Testimony to God and Divine Law] (Beirut: American Mission Press, 1891).

Petko Slaveykov, the Protestant Press, and the Gendered Language of Moral Reform in Bulgarian Nationalism

Barbara Reeves-Ellington

WHEN THE BULGARIAN ORTHODOX COMMUNITY OF STARA ZAGORA opened a girls' school in the summer of 1863, former teacher turned newspaperman Petko Slaveykov expressed his surprise that the community had found two female teachers to teach the young girls. He knew of one female teacher in Tŭrnovo and a half one in Tryavna, he quipped, but not even a half one could be found elsewhere.[1] Slaveykov's remark suggests that he was mildly amused by the notion of female teachers and unaware of the contributions that women were beginning to make to an incipient movement to organize schools where ethnic Orthodox Bulgarian girls could be educated beyond the basic literacy options offered in convents and churches. Bulgarian historians hail Slaveykov as a leading advocate for female education in the decade before Bulgarian independence from Ottoman rule in 1878, yet, they have neglected his early writings about women and failed to explain the process through which he came to promote the idea of education for women.[2] This chapter brings a gendered lens to an analysis of Slaveykov's writings and offers an appreciation of the changes in his writing over time. It moves the historical narrative about him from a narrow nationalist historiographical reading to a fuller, transnational interpretation through an examination of his relationship with American Protestant missionaries.

A perceptible change in Petko Slaveykov's worldview about women can be traced to his decision in 1864 to work with American Protestant missionaries in the Ottoman capital. In the company of missionaries, Slaveykov became acquainted with New England views about women and community education, which he used to counter Ottoman proposals for a universal empire-wide education system. Wrestling with competing ideas about women that were entering the Ottoman Empire through its multilingual press, he gradually clarified his views to embrace an American ideal of educated Christian womanhood in the service of the family, the community, and the nation that American missionaries had introduced in their school and publications. By promoting women as teachers of the Orthodox faith and the Bulgarian language, Slaveykov rearticulated a gendered message of moral reform that contributed to shaping one particular strand of Bulgarian nationalism in the late 1860s.

This topic is situated at a crossroads where three distinct areas of scholarly specialization intersect—the study of Bulgarian nationalism in the decades before independence from Ottoman rule (*Vŭzrazhdane*), the study of American missionaries among the Bulgarians, and the study of Ottoman civil reform (Tanzimat).[3] Scholarship on American missions in Ottoman Bulgaria has acknowledged the work of missionaries who produced a modern Bulgarian translation of the Bible and founded the prestigious Robert College for young men. It has also debated the "imperialist" connections of "Protestant propaganda" and commented on the failure of missionaries to attract large numbers of Orthodox Christians to Protestantism during a period of increasing Bulgarian Orthodox nationalism. But it has overlooked the ways in which missionaries promoted social change through education for women and neglected the larger Ottoman context in which American-Bulgarian interactions took place.

Women's education was a major element of the strategy of American missionaries to convert Bulgarian Orthodox Christians to Protestantism. A mission school for girls in Stara Zagora served as the catalyst for the opening of a Bulgarian school in the town that provoked Slaveykov's witticism about half-teachers.[4] The mission magazine *Zornitsa* (*Day Star*, 1864–1871) was the first Bulgarian-language periodical to target women and girls. The magazine advocated female education from its very first issue and promoted the idea that educated women were essential to spiritual regeneration and national progress through their work as mothers and teachers. Slaveykov gradually adapted these ideas in his writings.

Slaveykov did not convert to Protestantism, nor was he a captive to Protestant ideas. He read widely and was widely read by Bulgarians throughout the Ottoman Empire during the 1860s. He saw the usefulness of new ideas to the Bulgarian reform movement during a period of increasing Bulgarian nationalism against Greek cultural hegemony and Ottoman civil reform. He reconfigured an American Protestant ideal to his own purposes to thwart Ottoman educational reforms that, in his view, threatened the Bulgarian nation-in-the-making.

This chapter brings a new dimension to our understanding of the American Protestant–Bulgarian Orthodox encounter in Ottoman Europe by illuminating the ways in which American Protestant ideals shaped the thinking of one of the most prominent newspapermen of the Bulgarian National Revival. In the first section, I sketch Slaveykov's early years against a background of social and political changes in Ottoman Europe. In the second section, I explain the significance of the missionary encounter for Slaveykov. In the third section, I introduce American Protestant ideas about women and education and show how they were promoted among Bulgarian Orthodox Christians. Finally, I analyze Slaveykov's writings about women from 1863 to 1870 to show how he grappled with the paradoxes of Enlightenment thought coming into Ottoman Europe and rearticulated American ideas as women became important to his views of Bulgarian nationalism.

Slaveykov Emerges as a Political Actor during the Tanzimat

Petko Rachov Slaveykov was born in 1827 into a family of entrepreneurial artisans in Tŭrnovo, a town in the northeastern sector of the Ottoman province of Rumeli (present-day Bulgaria).[5] Like most sons of the growing Bulgarian artisanal and commercial classes in the early to mid-nineteenth century, Slaveykov received his elementary education in cell schools attached to churches or monasteries and his post-elementary education at a Greek school, in his case the Vaskidovich school in Svishtov. Because Greek was the language of churches, schools, and commerce in the Orthodox community, educated Bulgarians read and spoke Greek, but this began to change in the 1840s as ethnic Bulgarians began to challenge Greek cultural hegemony.

Within the Ottoman administrative system, all subjects were organized within religious communities (*millets*).[6] Bulgarian Christians were members

of the Orthodox Christian community headed by the Greek Patriarch, who
exercised spiritual and temporal control of the community. The diffusion of
Greek-language education following Greek independence from the Ottoman Empire in 1830 served to unite Greeks throughout the Ottoman Empire
with the citizens of independent Greece in an endeavor known as the "great
idea" (*megalee idea*), a plan to incorporate Greeks and non-Greeks into a
greater Greek state with a territorial range of the old Byzantine Empire.[7] Relations between Greeks and Bulgarians began to sour in the mid-1840s when
the "great idea" became incompatible with budding Bulgarian national aspirations.[8]

Urban, educated Bulgarians began a movement that increasingly gathered steam to organize Bulgarian-language schools, publish Bulgarian books
and periodicals, and demand church services in Bulgarian. Through expanding commercial and educational contacts throughout the Ottoman Empire and across Europe, a wealthy urban Bulgarian commercial class evolved
that could support a nascent print culture and the beginnings of a modern
school system.[9] Through these new institutions, urban, educated Bulgarians
began to develop a sense of national consciousness. Slaveykov was among
those Bulgarians who worked to promote Bulgarian language and education.[10] Yet, he was far removed from the center of action in the Ottoman
capital of Istanbul, where a small group of prominent Bulgarians took advantage of imperial Ottoman reforms to gain recognition for Bulgarian national identity.

Ottoman imperial reform facilitated the increasing expression of Bulgarian nationalism. Beginning in the mid-nineteenth century, Ottoman statesmen pursued a program of secularizing civil reform (*Tanzimat*, 1839–1876)
through which they aimed to create a modern state, with a modern citizenship. Their reforms ordered a restructuring of the imperial administrative system, proclaimed freedom of religion, legislated equality of Muslims
and non-Muslims, and promoted a homogenizing concept of Ottomanness
(Osmanlılık) for all Ottoman subjects, regardless of religious and ethnic affiliation. Of particular importance to the Christians of the Ottoman Empire were the imperial edicts of 1839 (Gülhane fermanı, or Hatt-ı Şerif) and
1856 (Islahât fermanı, or Hatt-ı Hümâyun) that guaranteed to all Ottoman
subjects throughout the empire security of life, honor, and property, freedom of religion, and equality before the law. The reforms guaranteed to both

Muslims and non-Muslims access to Ottoman professional schools and equal opportunity for appointment to government posts. They also began to diminish the temporal powers of the Patriarch by establishing a direct relationship between Ottoman subjects and the state. Orthodox Christians could bypass the patriarchate and petition the Ottoman government to recognize their demands.

During the period from 1848 to 1850, Bulgarians in Istanbul succeeded in their demands for change. The Patriarch confirmed the appointment of a Bulgarian-speaking bishop and the Ottoman government authorized a printing press for a Bulgarian-language newspaper and construction of a church building in Istanbul that would be recognized as a Bulgarian church.[11] These actions confirmed the existence of an identifiable Bulgarian community in the Ottoman capital, where the Bulgarian church became the focus of nation-building and the Bulgarian newspaper *Tsarigradski vestnik* (*Istanbul Herald*, 1848–1862) provided the beginnings of a print culture through which Bulgarians could shape an imagined community within the Ottoman Empire and beyond its borders.[12]

For the greater part of twenty years (1843 to 1863), Petko Slaveykov was far removed from this center of power. He worked as a peripatetic teacher, finding employment where he could and writing articles critical of the Greek ecclesiastical hierarchy. He was a lay representative to the provisional council of the Greek Orthodox Church that met to debate reform from October 1858 to January 1860, but he was unable to remain in the capital. That changed when American missionaries invited him to join them in their work to translate the Bible into Bulgarian. The first stage in that move came in October 1860 when Slaveykov met Methodist Episcopal Church missionary Albert Long, who invited him to work on the translation of several evangelical tracts.[13]

SLAVEYKOV MOVES TO ISTANBUL TO WORK WITH MISSIONARIES

By February 1864 Slaveykov had joined Long, American Board missionary Elias Riggs, and Bulgarian translator Khristodul Kostovich in Istanbul. He initially expected to work as a colporteur (a back-packing traveling salesman) of the British and Foreign Bible Society.[14] Instead he worked to revise translations of the scriptures previously completed under commission of the British and Foreign Bible Society by Neofit Rilski (New Testament) and Konstantin Fotinov (Old Testament).[15]

Slaveykov's association with American missionaries was important for three reasons. First, the translation work with the missionaries offered him full-time, permanent employment and provided him and his family financial security. Second, the work necessitated his presence in Istanbul, which gave him easier access to a printing press and put him in the center of the Bulgarian movement for religious and educational reform. Third, the missionaries introduced Slaveykov to new ideas about women and education that he incorporated into his own evolving views about the contributions that women could make to an emerging Bulgarian nation.

Financial insecurity had plagued Slaveykov before he met Long. Members of his family and his biographers have noted his financial problems during his peripatetic career before he moved to Istanbul.[16] His family was embarrassed by his impecuniary position. After his work with the missionaries was completed and he was obliged to leave the capital, Slaveykov was often short of resources and was not infrequently reduced to begging small amounts of money from acquaintances. His salary in Istanbul enabled him to live comfortably as he engaged in the newspaper business.

Albert Long initially offered Slaveykov a monthly salary of 1,000 grosh to translate evangelical tracts. This sum was twice the annual salary of 6,500 grosh that Slaveykov was offered the following year to teach in the town of Tryavna.[17] The records of the British and Foreign Bible Society indicate that Slaveykov received approximately one hundred British pounds annually for his work on Bible translation and revision.[18] Slaveykov's connections to the American missionaries were therefore a crucial component of his personal financial stability in Istanbul during the years 1864 to 1871. The British and Foreign Bible Society inadvertently financed his newspaper activities.

Istanbul was not only the publishing center of the empire. The city also contained the largest population of ethnic Bulgarians of any town in the empire and was the center of Bulgarian cultural and political life.[19] In Istanbul, Slaveykov published the newspapers *Gayda* and *Makedoniya* through which he achieved a broader audience for his views. *Makedoniya* in particular enjoyed wide circulation.

The Bulgarian newspaper business before independence was a difficult one.[20] Censorship was a constant problem. The Ottoman censor shut down

Gayda several times and *Makedoniya* five times, the final time in 1872 when Slaveykov was briefly imprisoned.[21] The majority of Bulgarian periodicals launched in the thirty years from 1848 to 1878 folded within twelve months, and newspaper circulations rarely exceeded several hundred. Publication and subscription costs were high, distribution channels were irregular, and the pool of available readers was in any case small. Editors complained that readers frequently neglected to pay subscriptions.[22] It is all the more impressive, therefore, that *Makedoniya* ran for six years (it was the third-longest-running newspaper before Bulgarian independence in 1878) and its circulation reached 3,600. In contrast, the émigré revolutionary newspapers *Svoboda* (*Liberty*) and *Nezavisimost* (*Independence*), both edited by Lyuben Karavelov in Bucharest, had a circulation of approximately 400 among the Bulgarian émigré population.[23]

Slaveykov enjoyed a large Bulgarian reading public, both inside and outside the Ottoman Empire, and he used his newspapers first and foremost as vehicles to promote his views on religious reform, which he called the church question, and education.[24] It was precisely the reform position of *Makedoniya* on the church question that led to accusations in some quarters that *Makedoniya* was a Protestant paper and that Slaveykov worked in the service of the Protestants.[25] Slaveykov's ideas on church reform, which had been circulating in the Balkans for fifty years or more among leading Greek and Serbian intellectuals as a more democratic form of religion, were certainly ideas that American missionaries shared and supported, but Slaveykov never for a moment considered converting to Protestantism. Although he provided space in *Makedoniya* for articles by Albert Long and several Bulgarian Protestant pastors, Slaveykov strenuously denied such accusations throughout his journalistic career. That he felt compelled to deny them is indicative of his close association with the missionaries. He made a personal profession of his faith in the pages of *Makedoniya* in November 1868. "As a Bulgarian and a son of our holy orthodox church, as in the past, so in the future," he wrote, "we shall respect and hold sacred the following principle: Holding fast to the faith of our fathers and preserving religious unity is the first, greatest, and most important need of our nation."[26] Slaveykov decried apostasy, urging his readers to remain united in the faith because religious unity was the only tie that held them together. In his view, their patriotic duty had three elements. The first was to the Ottoman Empire, the second was to religious unity, and the third was to national education.

Slaveykov was a strong proponent of education, particularly Bulgarian-language education. His connections to the missionaries influenced his choice of education for his children. His eldest son, Ivan, briefly (1865) attended the British Protestant school on the island of Malta.[27] Ivan and younger son Racho subsequently attended Robert College, the American institution in Istanbul founded by former missionary Cyrus Hamlin.[28] In the early 1880s, Slaveykov sent his younger daughter, Penka, to Home School (subsequently the American College for Girls in Constantinople), founded by the Woman's Board of Missions of the American Board of Commissioners for Foreign Missions.[29] Slaveykov's choice of schools was in part influenced by his financial position at the time his children attended them but was also reflective of his openness to new ideas and opportunities. In particular, his ideas about women's education evolved during his work with American missionaries.

AMERICAN MISSIONARIES PROMOTE FEMALE EDUCATION

From their earliest arrival in the Ottoman Empire in the 1820s, American missionaries organized girls' schools and promoted female education as a strategy to attract Ottoman Christian populations to Protestantism.[30] At the close of the Crimean War, missionaries of the American Board of Commissioners for Foreign Missions and the Methodist Episcopal Church extended their missions into Ottoman Europe (which they called European Turkey), targeting Bulgarian Orthodox Christians as the focus of their endeavors. American Board missionary Elias Riggs and Methodist Episcopal Church missionary Albert Long were particularly impressed by Bulgarian efforts to reform the Greek Orthodox Church and promote a national education. They believed that they could take advantage of those efforts to promote Protestant religious and educational ideas through schools, the press, and didactic reading materials.

Although the Bulgarian-speaking population was largely illiterate, Long noted that young people were learning to read.[31] He believed that the missionaries could help meet their need for reading material and attract them to Protestantism. "When these children grow up with our books in their hands," he wrote, "then will come the great harvest."[32] Long hoped to bring ordinary Bulgarians to Protestantism as they learned to read. Like evangelical Christians in the United States, he wanted to use the printed word to connect religious teachings and social transformation by linking Protestant ideals to the everyday experiences of his readers.[33]

In addition to translating evangelical tracts, Long began to publish a Bulgarian-language monthly magazine, *Zornitsa* (*Day Star*, 1864–1871). Slaveykov was a member of the editorial team. *Zornitsa* was a significant presence in the Bulgarian press in the 1860s. Its illustrated format was innovative. It was inexpensive, widely distributed, and widely read among the small but growing literate population. It was the longest-running Bulgarian magazine before Bulgarian independence from Ottoman rule in 1878. Perhaps most important, it was the only periodical in the 1860s that specifically appealed to women and children.[34] What is striking about *Zornitsa* is its targeting of women and young girls. Almost every issue of *Zornitsa* contained articles that emphasized the important contributions of women as mothers to society. Long asserted that "the future of the Bulgarian nation depends more on the current generation of Bulgarian women, and not so much on their men." Appealing to his female readers, he wrote, "Bulgaria wants mothers...sober-minded, God-fearing, educated mothers are wanted for the coming generation of Bulgarians."[35] By appealing to Bulgarian women and girls as mothers who would nurture the Bulgarians of the future, the articles in *Zornitsa* elevated the task of child-rearing to the level of a national project that depended on educated women. Martha Riggs's series of articles for women, "Letters for Mothers," first published in *Zornitsa*, reinforced the importance of the maternal task. Only educated Christian women could responsibly fill the task. In her view, only "great women" could bring forth "great sons" and contribute to shaping the character of a civilized Christian nation.[36]

In the early nineteenth century, evangelical Protestants in the United States gradually developed a new view that women were more spiritual than men.[37] Instead of being perceived as inherently sinful, women were seen as models of piety and virtue who could exert a beneficial moral influence on their husbands and children. This new view had a religious and a secular expression. A Christian mother's love and nurture was the pathway through which her children would be assured of personal salvation even if the children did not experience religious conversion. A Christian mother's instruction would shape the character of her children and hence the character of future generations. Maternal influence was grounded in the home but domesticity extended into the nation as women's child-rearing tasks shaped future American citizens.[38]

Evangelical Christians argued that nations prospered only in societies where women were educated, respected, and capable of exerting such influence. They believed that the United States was at the pinnacle of civilization as a Protestant republic because Christian American women exerted such influence at home, in the community, and across the nation. This form of domestic discourse equated Christianity with Protestantism and became linked to the Euro-American mission to domesticate and Christianize the non-Protestant, non-European peoples within the expanding borders of the United States and around the globe.[39] In the evangelical view, if national progress was a function of the status of women in society, it followed that, wherever women remained uneducated and disrespected, nations failed to progress and prosper. Missionary magazines were replete with images of "heathen" women: Indian women who practiced infanticide, Chinese women who practiced foot-binding, and Native American women who, according to missionaries, suffered under inappropriate divisions of labor were all stock stereotypes in the missionary press. Missionaries argued that their status could be raised through conversion to Protestant Christianity. Missionaries in Istanbul and Ottoman Europe took the view that Bulgaria would not prosper as a nation unless Bulgarian women were educated and Orthodox Christians were converted to Protestantism.

American Board missionaries opened their first girls' school for Bulgarians in Stara Zagora in January 1863. This school and the pages of *Zornitsa* introduced Bulgarians to the American domestic ideal of the educated Christian woman who shaped communities and formed the national character through her role as a mother. The ideal appealed to Bulgarian women because they recognized themselves in the image of the educated Christian mother.[40] To Long's disappointment, however, they were not attracted to Protestantism. Instead, they used the language of educated motherhood to organize in women's associations. Bulgarian Orthodox women took the lessons of maternal influence to erect a platform on which they could enter the public sphere to promote the idea of female education and urge the leaders of local community councils to provide greater educational opportunities for their daughters.

This was an important change in Bulgarian culture. Despite some efforts to improve education for girls in Bulgaria, the press did not seriously promote the idea of female education before 1864. Bulgarian women reconfigured the

American domestic ideal in their women's associations, a move that surprised many male journalists, including Petko Slaveykov, who quickly saw the utility of the women's actions and began to support the ideal of women's education in his writing. Slaveykov rearticulated the language of educated motherhood within the larger discourse of Bulgarian nationalism to promote the idea that Bulgaria was a progressive nation because it educated its womenfolk and valued the contributions of its educated mothers. The change over time in Slaveykov's writings about women can be traced through his newspapers *Gayda* and *Makedoniya*.

SLAVEYKOV DEVELOPS A GENDERED LANGUAGE OF BULGARIAN NATIONALISM

Slaveykov's early writings in *Gayda* were little witticisms designed to appeal to his male readers. In the newspaper's first year, we find quips of the sort "Good wine and a beautiful woman are two pleasant poisons"; "Woman is a devil of the home—a plaything for the stupid, a calamity for the wise"; "Capriciousness and stupidity are the only companions of a woman's beauty"; or "Women are like riddles, once you've solved them they don't interest you any more."[41] Although Slaveykov's pieces about women always appeared under the rubric "from the women's paper," the men in his audience were more likely to be amused. Nothing in these early writings connected women with education, religion, or national progress.

A perceptible change in Slaveykov's contributions to his "women's" column came in August 1864, shortly after he began working with Long and Riggs.[42] His writings expressed a more serious, reflective side. In this new mode, Slaveykov translated articles that contained the binary opposites of the Enlightenment in his attempt to rationalize the difference between men and women. He noted that male was the norm, female was different; men were ruled by the head, women by the heart; men had the power of intellect and reason, whereas women had the power of sentiment and compassion; men shone in the marketplace, women shone in the home; men made laws, women shaped morals.[43]

By the third year of *Gayda*, Slaveykov began to borrow articles from the Protestant press.[44] These pieces argued that women, teachers, and priests exerted the most influence in society; yet, added Slaveykov, in few nations did women, teachers, and priests distinguish themselves in learning and virtue. Bulgaria was no exception in his view.

Finally, Slaveykov turned his attention to the education of girls. In his view, girls' education was a sorely neglected subject that demanded even more attention than the education of boys. For girls would become householders much earlier than their male cohorts, bearing responsibility for running a home, managing servants, assuring the happiness of their husbands, and "most important, educating children and preparing their future." Slaveykov based his appeal for female education on the need for mothers to educate their children. Bulgarians took great care to preserve their property, wrote Slaveykov, and they should take the same care to give their daughters a good upbringing, "to adorn them with moral and religious goodness."[45]

Slaveykov's writings on women gradually began to change shortly after he accepted the position to work with the missionaries. Slaveykov was closely associated with *Zornitsa*, which he read, edited, and sent to his wife in Tryavna.[46] Yet, he did not automatically mimic what he read there. He had not yet fully articulated the Protestant evangelical position that women's status in society correlated with national progress and prosperity. He gradually came to this position during the Bulgarian debates on national education prompted by discussions of Ottoman government plans for universal reform of education within the empire.

Educational reform had long been a concern of the Ottoman government.[47] Traditionally, schooling was a matter for religious communities (*millets*). In an effort to create a modern Ottoman citizenship and a greater sense of Ottoman belonging (*Osmanlılık*) among the subjects of the sultan, Ottoman statesmen recommended a universal Ottoman education. Following a review of Christian and Muslim educational institutions in the Danubian province from 1865 to 1867, governor Midhat Pasha proposed that Christian and Muslim schools be closed and replaced by Ottoman state schools.[48] His proposals included elementary-level education for students in their native languages; instruction beyond the elementary level would be in Ottoman Turkish.

Ottoman proposals did not sit well with some prominent members of the Bulgarian community in Istanbul. They were concerned that post-elementary multiethnic secular classrooms where instruction was provided in Turkish would eventually lead to loss of both faith and language—the dual pillars of Bulgarian nationalism—among Bulgarians. Petko Slaveykov published several translated articles in which he discussed the idea of nationality as an idea expressed by a group of people living within distinct geographical borders and unified by faith and language.[49] In his view, it was an idea that had succeeded in Italy, Germany, and Greece. According to Slaveykov, if Bulgarians were to preserve their nationality, they had to preserve their faith, for their faith was their only inheritance from their ancestors. The school question was no different from the church question: They had to rid themselves of the "perilous foreign influence in our institutions of education."[50] His objective, he wrote, was to warn fellow Bulgarians not only against Greek control of religion, but also against Ottoman experiments in education.

As Ottoman government attempts to gain control over education continued, the school question became for Slaveykov "the most important, the most sacred" because it concerned "the moral and religious instruction of our sons and grandsons, to whom we shall transfer the pledge we received from our fathers." In Slaveykov's view, religious instruction must be the foundation of Bulgarian education; and it must be provided by Bulgarian priests, no matter their level of training or education.[51]

In his public writings through 1867, Slaveykov continued to see no role for the educated Christian mother in the transfer of religious knowledge and no place for women as educators, for religious faith was passed on from father to son. But he was about to begin to perceive things differently as he developed his ideas on the concept of nationality. Accompanying Slaveykov's article on the idea of nationality was an article entitled "Women with Regard to the Nation."[52] Women had shown as much courage as had men in patriotic wars, he noted, but nature had not created women to wield the sword. Love, he wrote, was the fundamental essence of women; and love for the fatherland united everything that was sacred, divine, noble, and lofty. Slaveykov bemoaned families who failed to educate their daughters, content to let them think only of toys and games, singing and dancing. Girls needed to be educated for domestic life, he wrote; but the home was only a small part of the state. Mothers who could see no further than the narrow confines of their homes would raise sons to become slaves or rebels. Only "great mothers" could raise "great sons," he wrote, adopting the concept of maternal influence.

Slaveykov went on to note that, in all advanced lands, women participated in resolving the big questions of the day. Neither an Englishwoman, nor an

American woman, nor a Polish woman, nor a German woman, nor a French woman, he wrote, was ignorant of the affairs of her people or her fatherland. Even Greek and Italian women had begun to take an interest in their fatherlands. But was there even one woman in Bulgaria, he asked, who could put the general interest above the latest fashion? The answer to this question, he continued, was an indication of the level of understanding of the concept of nation among Bulgarians. The sense of the national, he wrote, was "still in diapers" among men, but women had no concept of it, for "some are still like butterflies on the wind, and others like senseless dolls, but none are mothers of the nation."[53] While Slaveykov had been eager to raise "the woman question," his articles about women had found no place for women in the issues that had most provoked him—the church question and the school question. In developing his ideas on the concept of nationalism, the place for women became apparent to him. Great mothers raised great sons. Women needed to be educated beyond a preparation for the domestic hearth because Bulgarians had a nation to build, and it was everyone's concern to be involved in the affairs of the nation. Slaveykov compared Bulgarian women with other women of Europe and America and found them lacking. Not one, he wrote, could put the national interest first. In the enlightenment stakes, Bulgaria was, he wrote, "behind."[54] Slaveykov rapidly moved from a critical stance on women to a position of advocacy. Men were accustomed to the degradation of women and considered every attempt to raise them from degradation as a violation of the rights of men. For their part, long-suffering women accepted their pitiful situation as their natural lot in life. Woman was, he wrote, "pushed aside, restricted, imprisoned, deprived of rights, uneducated, and the eternal slave of man—her tormentor in that respect."[55] Slaveykov acknowledged that his remarks might seem strange to some of his male readers. He urged them toward a more serious consideration of his comments, however. Only then would they discover that the lamentable condition of family life among Bulgarians, the state of their industry, the moral instruction of their children, and in general the lack of prosperity were all a direct result of the deplorable situation of women and the neglect of their education. By late 1868, Slaveykov had come fully to the evangelical viewpoint. He promised his readers a series of articles on the topic.

Slaveykov's series, which ran in *Makedoniya* from December 1868 through April 1869, was also published in a separate edition under the title *On the*

Question of Women.[56] Slaveykov explained to his readers that the topic engaging him was one of the most crucial of the age. He recognized the profound purpose of women and their important role in the affairs of human prosperity. The articles, which he selected and translated, indicate that he had a wide variety of sources at his disposal. He began with what he called a historical viewpoint on a "new phenomenon," women's demands for equality with men, an idea born, he suggested, among the Saint Simonists in France.[57] Even the famous John Stuart Mill had taken up his "strong, male pen" to defend the idea. Moreover, in America, newspapers and societies popularized the idea. Even in Russia women were demanding universities. While exploring these new ideas, however, Slaveykov reverted to the tensions and contradictions that informed his earlier writing. Indeed, he reworked some of his earlier writings from *Gayda*, portraying women as beguiling temptresses.[58] He promised his readers, nonetheless, that he would present women from a different point of view.[59]

Slaveykov argued that the nineteenth century had cleared away old ideas, dispersed the glow of true education, and illuminated the contributions of women to the general capital of human development. As his first example, Slaveykov mentioned the women of America, who were fine teachers, in whose hands rested even the education of boys. He informed his readers that women worked as physicians in Switzerland. Moreover, in America and England, the great question of the day was whether women should get the vote.[60] The prosperity of individuals, indeed whole nations, rested on education, he wrote; it therefore followed that the greatest efforts of nations had to be made on behalf of education.[61] In his view, the clearest index of the development of a nation was the education of the female sex. Subsequently, the first objective of Bulgarians was to raise and educate their female children to be good and worthy mothers, for their daughters were "the hope for the future of our fatherland." He went on to say that, however much Bulgarians did for the education of their sons, they should do twice as much for their daughters, not only because this would facilitate the education of the nation but also because it would have salutary effects on the morality of the nation.

Slaveykov wrote one more article in this vein to support the education of girls, claiming that the moral and intellectual education of the nation depended on the moral and intellectual education of women. An educated woman could be of use to her husband, her family, her homeland, and her fatherland. Mothers played a crucial role in the rearing and education of their children and, therefore, of the nation. They must take up the task, aided by fathers and teachers. If mothers were worthy, families, schools, churches, society, and the state would flourish. Slaveykov urged his readers to teach their daughters the finest customs, industriousness, and thrift, and "to love, exalt, and embellish and be proud of everything Bulgarian."[62] If they did so, then these virtues would be transmitted to men.

At the end of 1870, Slaveykov appealed to women to take up the task of educating the nation. According to him, fathers and teachers would play a secondary role. This view represents quite a change from Slaveykov's previous insistence that priests should educate children and the nation. The irony is that, by the end of 1870, Bulgarian women had been organizing publicly for nearly two years on behalf of the idea of educating the nation. Between January 1869 and December 1870, Bulgarian Orthodox women organized themselves across Ottoman Europe in thirty women's associations. Slaveykov was not in the vanguard of promoting women to the work of the nation. Instead, his writings reflected a movement that was well underway among literate urban women. Slaveykov was surprised by the emergence of the Bulgarian women's associations.[63]

Within a very short space of time, Slaveykov had done a complete turn-around on his apparent view of the situation of Bulgarian women and the equality of the sexes among Bulgarians. As a nation, Bulgarians had been backward; now they were among the most advanced as regards the woman question. Instead of decrying woman's duplicity and cunning, Slaveykov now praised Bulgarian women's patience and diligence—qualities he called their "natural advantages." Sexual equality and women's industriousness were, he decided, the reasons that Bulgarian women had access to the public sphere and were thus free to perform the duties that love of the fatherland imposed on them. Slaveykov argued that the gentle sex deserved acknowledgment, respect, and encouragement for the path they had embarked on independently. They also deserved help. Their work would be of great use to the fatherland, wrote Slaveykov; their field of work was broad.[64]

Finally Slaveykov insisted that the issue of women's education become a national issue, no longer a question solely for civic-minded Bulgarians or patriotic women's associations, but for the one national Bulgarian institution—the Bulgarian Orthodox Church. Slaveykov immediately called on the

Bulgarian Exarchate, which was established by imperial Ottoman decree in 1870, to take up the task of female education. It was, he wrote in a lead article, a task for the nation.[65] Accordingly, the Exarchate should set aside funds in its budget to provide for schools of higher education to train girls as teachers.

In appealing to the Exarchate, Slaveykov once again reiterated that women wielded great influence over their husbands and children. Mothers were those responsible for the good or bad morals of a nation, and mothers were the most suitable individuals to preserve the national language and the national spirit. As teachers, women could spread learning all over the fatherland, thereby preparing better mothers for future generations, for, "from worthless mothers come forth worthless generations."[66] And if Bulgarian women could be educated and count on the respect of their men-folk, then Bulgarians would enjoy "the true civilization of the Gospel."[67] In promoting the cause of nationalism through a newly established national Bulgarian Orthodox Church, Slaveykov had come full circle to the Protestant position that a Christian civilization depended on an understanding of the scriptures, which required an educated Christian womanhood.

Slaveykov's message became more urgent after promulgation of the Ottoman reforms of education, which included female education and teacher-training courses for girls. In the face of universal, multiethnic education within the empire, with instruction in the Turkish language, Slaveykov and other educated Bulgarians feared total loss of their nationality. They had previously struggled to promote Bulgarian schools against fierce competition from Greek-language schools. In 1869, they faced the possibility of Turkish-language schools. If Bulgarian children did not learn their faith and language at school, Slaveykov asked, where would they learn them? Originally, he had recommended that priests should educate children. In the end, he decided that instruction of future Bulgarians was the job of mothers. In 1870 Slaveykov called on the Exarchate to fund female education, and he called on Bulgarian women to do their duty by educating future generations. By then, several other newspapers had picked up the message to proclaim the connection between education for women and national progress.

By 1871 Slaveykov's world in Istanbul was coming to an end. His work with the missionaries to revise the Bulgarian translation of the Bible was complete. In 1872, *Makedoniya* was closed down for the last time by the Ottoman censor after Slaveykov published a severe critique of his opponents in the church question.[68] Slaveykov lost not only his public platform but also his regular income. His work with the missionaries finished, his fight for the cause of a reformed independent church lost, and his newspaper *Makedoniya* banned by the Ottoman authorities, Slaveykov in middle age reverted to the career of peripatetic teacher. He settled in Stara Zagora, which is where he was when the town was burned to the ground during the Russo-Turkish War of 1877–1878 that gained independence for Bulgaria.

Conclusion

Working with American Protestant missionaries in Istanbul, Petko Slaveykov gradually came to appreciate a new gender model for Bulgarian society, one that reinforced women's position as preservers of the national religion and culture while simultaneously arguing for an understanding of women as harbingers of progress. What American-Bulgarian interactions reveal is the importance of religion in women's contribution to nation formation and the perception of educated women as symbols of national development as well as tradition.

Slaveykov incorporated an American gender ideal in his writings about women, women's education, and women's contribution to nation formation. He did not simply mimic American texts but struggled to develop his own thinking as he worked to promote the idea of a Bulgarian nation initially against Greek religious and cultural hegemony and subsequently against imperial Ottoman reforms. The issue of female education became critical in the context of an ethnic movement for national recognition based on the elements of religion and language in the face of American religious reform and Ottoman secularizing reform. Slaveykov's particular strand of evolving Bulgarian nationalism lost out to a revolutionary strand in the Bulgarian uprising of 1876 and the subsequent Russo-Turkish War that ultimately gained recognition of an independent Bulgarian state. It nevertheless offers an illustration of American Protestant–Bulgarian Orthodox encounters against a background of Ottoman reform in the short window of opportunity between 1860 and 1876.

NOTES

1. *Gayda*, 13 July 1863, p. 19. Tŭrnovo and Tryavna are towns in north-central present-day Bulgaria, which before 1878 were part of the Ottoman province of Rumeli, or Rumelia. All translations from the Bulgarian are mine. I use the Romanization system of the United States Board on Geographic Names.

2. Margarita Cholakova, *Bulgarsko zhensko dvizhenie prez Vuzrazhdaneto, 1857–1878 (The Bulgarian Women's Movement During the National Revival, 1857–1878)* (Sofia: Albo, 1994); Krassimira Daskalova, "Obrazovanie na zhenite i zhenite v obrazovanieto na vuzrozhdenska Bulgaria" ("Education of Women and Women in the Education of Bulgaria during the National Revival"), *Godishnik na Sofiyskiya universitet Sv. Kliment Okhridski* 85 (1992): 5–18; Krassimira Daskalova, *Ot syankata na istoriyata: Zhenite v bulgarskoto obshtestvo i kultura (From the Shadows of History: Women in Bulgarian Society and Culture)* (Sofia: Bulgarian Group for the Historical Study of Women and Gender, 1998); Virdzhiniya Paskaleva, *Bulgarkata prez vuzrazhdaneto (The Bulgarian Woman during the National Revival)* (Sofia: Otechestven front, 1984); Aleksandra Pundeva-Voynikova, *Bulgarkata prez epokhata na Vuzrazhdaneto (The Bulgarian Woman during the National Revival Era)* (Sofia: Bulgarian Women's Union, 1940).

3. The literature in all three areas is voluminous. For American missionaries among the Bulgarians, see James F. Clarke, *Bible Societies, American Missionaries and the National Revival of Bulgaria* (New York: Arno Press, 1971); Dennis Hupchick, ed., *The Pen and the Sword: Studies in Bulgarian History by James F. Clarke* (Boulder, CO: East European Monographs, 1988); Ivan Ilchev, "Robert Kolezh i formiraneto na bulgarska inteligentsiya, 1863–1878g" ("Robert College and the Formation of a Bulgarian Intelligentsia, 1863–1878"), *Istoricheski pregled* 1:1 (1981): 50–62; Tatyana Nestorova, *American Missionaries Among the Bulgarians (1858–1912)* (Boulder, CO: East European Monographs, 1987); Petko Petkov, "Amerikanski misioneri v bulgarskite zemi, XIX do nachaloto na XX v" ("American Missionaries in Bulgarian Lands from the Nineteenth to the Beginning of the Twentieth Century"), *Istoricheski pregled* 46:5 (1990): 18–32; Manyo Stoyanov, "Nachalo na protestantskata propaganda v Bulgaria" ("The Beginning of Protestant Propaganda in Bulgaria"), *Izvestiya na instituta za istoriya* 14–15 (1964): 45–67. For the Bulgarian National Revival (*Vŭzrazhdane*), see Roumen Daskalov, *Kak se misli Bulgarskoto vuzrazhdane (Interpreting the Bulgarian National Revival)* (Sofia: Lik, 2002); Nikolay Genchev, *Bulgarskoto vuzrazhdane (The Bulgarian National Revival)*, Fourth ed. (Sofia: Ivan Vazov press, 1995). For the Tanzimat, see Roderic H. Davison, *Essays in Ottoman and Turkish History, 1774–1923: The Impact of the West* (Austin: University of Texas Press, 1990); Roderic H. Davison, *Reform in the Ottoman Empire, 1856–1876*

(New York: Gordian Press, 1973); Fatma Müge Göçek, *Rise of the Bourgeoi-sie, Demise of Empire: Ottoman Westernization and Social Change* (New York: Oxford University Press, 1996); Şerif Mardin, *The Genesis of Young Ottoman Thought: A Study in the Modernization of Turkish Political Thought* (Princeton: Princeton University Press, 1962); Milen V. Petrov, "Tanzimat for the Country-side: Midhat Paşa and the Vilayet of Danube, 1864–1868" (PhD diss., Prince-ton University, 2004); Donald Quataert, "The Age of Reforms, 1812–1914," in *An Economic and Social History of the Ottoman Empire, 1300–1914*, ed. Halil İnalcık and Donald Quataert (Cambridge: Cambridge University Press, 1994), 759–944.

4. Velichka Koycheva, "Protestantskoto misionerstvo v Stara Zagora i Bulgarskata obshtestvenost prez 50-te–70-te godini na XIX vek" ("Protestant Missionaries in Stara Zagora and Bulgarian Society from the 1850s to the 1870s"), *Izvestiya na myzeite ot yugoiztochna Bulgaria* 5 (1982): 145–154; Barbara Reeves-Elling-ton, "A Vision of Mount Holyoke in the Ottoman Balkans: American Cultural Transfer, Bulgarian Nation-Building and Women's Educational Reform, 1858–1870," *Gender & History* 16:1 (2004): 146–171.

5. For biographical details, see Nikolay Genchev and Krassimira Daskalova, eds., *Bulgarskata vuzrozhdenska inteligentsiya* (*The Intelligentsia of the Bulgarian Na-tional Revival*) (Sofia: State Press Dr. Petur Beron, 1988), 595–597.

6. Benjamin Braude and Bernard Lewis, eds., *Christians and Jews in the Ottoman Empire: The Functioning of a Plural Society* (New York: Holmes & Meier, 1982).

7. Paschalis M. Kitromilides, "'Imagined Communities' and the Origins of the National Question in the Balkans," *European History Quarterly* 19:2 (1989): 149–192.

8. Nadya Danova, "Bulgarski studenti na ostrov Andros" ("Bulgarian Students on Andros Island"), *Istoricheski pregled*, no. 1 (1996): 32–69; Nadya Danova, *Kon-stantin Georgiev Fotinov v kulturnoto i ideyno-politicheskoto razvitie na Bal-kanite prez XIX vek* (*Konstantin Georgiev Fotinov in the Cultural, Ideological, and Political Development of the Balkans in the Nineteenth Century*) (Sofia: Bul-garian Academy of Sciences, 1994); Nadya Danova, "Les Etudiants Bulgares a l'Universite d'Athenes" (paper presented at the Colloque International: Univer-site, Ideologie et Culture, Athens, Greece, 1989).

9. On urban and economic development, see Raina Gavrilova, *Bulgarian Urban Culture in the Eighteenth and Nineteenth Centuries* (Selinsgrove: Susquehanna University Press, 1999); Michael Pailaret, *The Balkan Economies c 1800–1914: Evolution without Development* (Cambridge: Cambridge University Press, 1997).

10. Slaveykov was influenced to join the anti-Greek movement by two events in the early 1840s: the imprisonment on Mount Athos of the Bulgarian priest Neofit Bozveli by the Greek Patriarch, and his reading of Father Paissiy Kh-ilendarski's manuscript "Slavo-Bulgarian History." In Bulgarian historiography,

Khilendarski's history is accepted as the clarion call of the Bulgarian National Revival. The history circulated in manuscript copy during his lifetime; its impact was delayed almost a century, however, until such men as Petko Slaveykov read it. The first printed version of the history was published in 1844. See Thomas Butler, *Monumenta Bulgarica: A Bilingual Anthology of Bulgarian Texts from the 9th to the 19th Centuries* (Ann Arbor: Michigan Slavic Publications, 1996), 333–344.

11. Julietta Velitchkova Borin, "Les projets d'education bulgares au XIXe Siecle: Affirmation nationale et transferts culturels" (PhD diss., Ecole des Hautes Etudes en Sciences Sociales, 1998); Thomas A. Meininger, *The Formation of a Nationalist Bulgarian Intelligentsia, 1835–1878* (New York: Garland, 1987); Peter Nikov, *Vuzrazhdane na bulkarskiya narod: Tsurkovno-natsionalni borbi i postizheniya (The National Revival of the Bulgarian People: The Struggle for Recognition of a National Church)* (Sofia: Nauka i izkustvo, 1971).

12. On the significance of language and religion to Bulgarian nationalism, see Maria Todorova, "Language as Cultural Unifier in a Multilingual Setting: The Bulgarian Case during the Nineteenth Century," *East European Politics and Societies* 4:3 (1990): 439–450; Toncho Zhechev, *Bulgarskiyat Velikden ili strasti bulgarski (Bulgarian Easter, or Passions Bulgarian)*, 6th ed. (Sofia: Prof. Marin Drinov, 1995).

13. Letter, A. Granitski to Petko Slaveykov, 21 October 1860, Papers of Petko Rachov Slaveykov, Bulgarian Historical Archive (BHA), Collection 43, item II.C. 10282; Letter, Albert Long to Ivan Slaveykov, 18 November, 1895, inventory no. 149 PRS, box 18.5 (II) 2a, Slaveykov Museum, Sofia.

14. Letter, Petko Slaveykov to N. H. Palauzov, 19 January 1865, in Sonya Baeva et al., eds., *Petko R. Slaveykov: Suchineniya (Petko R. Slaveykov: Writings)*, vol. 8 (Sofia: Bulgarski pisatel, 1982), 79–83.

15. For a history of Bible translation into Bulgarian, see Clarke, *Bible Societies*.

16. Letter, Donka Slaveykova to Ivan Slaveykov, 2 January 1875, Papers of Petko Rachov Slaveykov, BHA, item II.C. 774; Letter, Donka Slaveykova to Ivan Slaveykov, 8 March 1876, Papers of Ivan Petkov Slaveykov, BHA, item II.C. 1691. Meininger, *The Formation of a Nationalist Bulgarian Intelligentsia*, 298; Sonya Baeva, *Petko Slaveykov: Zhivot i tvorchestvo, 1827–1870 (Petko Slaveykov: Life and Literature, 1827–1870)* (Sofia: Bulgarian Academy of Sciences, 1968), 101; Konstantin Gulubov, *Petko Slaveykov: Life, Work, Literature* (Sofia: Nauka i izkustvo, 1970), 95; Racho Slaveykov, *Petko Rachov Slaveykov, 1827–1895–1927: A Sketch of His Life and Memories of Him* (Sofia: Hemus, 1927), 26–47.

17. Letter, Albert Long to Petko Slaveykov, 20 August 1861, Papers of Khristo Daskalov, BHA, item II.C. 713; Letter, Tryavna notables to Petko Slaveykov, 5 October 1862, Papers of Petko Rachov Slaveykov, BHA, item II.A. 2321.

18. British and Foreign Bible Society Papers, Foreign Accounts Current, 1858–1871, Volume 8, E1/2/2/8, Cambridge University, Cambridge, UK. It is difficult to

ascertain exactly how much Slaveykov was paid as his salary was not listed separately from other salaries. The salaries of Riggs and Long were also paid partly through the British and Foreign Bible Society.

19. Nikolay Nachov, *Tsarigrad kato kulturen tsenur na bulgarite do 1877g* (*Constantinople as a Bulgarian Cultural Center before 1877*) (Sofia, 1925); Zhechev, *Bulgarian Easter.*

20. Meininger, *The Formation of a Nationalist Bulgarian Intelligentsia*, 282–301; Monika Skowronski, "Die distribution Bulgarischer Volksbucher im 19. und 20. Jahrhundert (bis 1944)," in *Sudosteuropaische Popularliteratur im 19. und 20. Jahrhundert* (Munchen: Munchner Vereinigung fur Volkskunde, 1993), 137–158; Johann Strauss, "Who Read What in the Ottoman Empire (19th–20th Centuries)?" *Arabic Middle Eastern Literatures* 6:1 (2003): 39–76.

21. On censorship and circulation numbers, see Sonya Baeva, "Dnevnik Makedoniya" ("The Makedoniya Journal"), in *Literaturen Arkiv P.R. Slaveykov*, ed. Petur Dinekov, Georgi Dimov, and Sonya Baeva (Sofia: Bulgarian Academy of Sciences, 1959), 80–146; Manyo Stoyanov, *Bulgarska vuzrozhdenska knizhnina* (*Literature of the Bulgarian National Revival*) (Sofia: Nauka i Izkustvo, 1957). The longest running newspaper was *Tsarigradski vestnik* (*Istanbul Herald*, 1848–1862). The second-longest-running newspaper was the pro-Ottoman paper *Turtsiya* (1864 to 1873).

22. For example, "From the Editor," *Makedoniya*, 20 December 1871, p. 201; "To the Readers," *Pravo*, 23 August 1869, p. 100.

23. Historian Keta Mircheva estimates that as few as twenty copies of the revolutionary papers crossed the Danube to be read by Bulgarians in the Ottoman Empire. Keta Mircheva, "The correspondence network of the newspapers *Svoboda* and *Nezavisimost*—Imagined and real geography," paper presented at the conference *Imagined Texts of the Bulgarian National Revival*, Institute of Literature, Bulgarian Academy of Sciences, Sofia, November 25–26, 1999.

24. *Gayda* was satirical and humorous in tone but there was no mistaking Slaveykov's barbs against the Greek ecclesiastical hierarchy. The masthead of *Makedoniya* made no effort to conceal Slaveykov's intentions to call the people living under Greek influence in Macedonia back into the Bulgarian fold. Slaveykov expressed his intentions for *Makedoniya* clearly in *Gayda*, 1 September 1866. *Makedoniya* became the organ of the reform wing of the Bulgarian movement for an independent church. See Meininger, *The Formation of a Nationalist Bulgarian Intelligentsia*, 297; Stoyanov, *Bulgarska vuzrozhdenska knizhnina*, 445.

25. Manyo Stoyanov, "Petko R. Slaveykov i protestantskata propaganda v Bulgaria" ("Petko R. Slaveykov and Protestant Propaganda in Bulgaria"), *Rodina* 3, no. 3 (1941): 90–98.

26. *Makedoniya*, 25 November 1868, p. 174.

27. Letter, Petko Slaveykov to Irina, 22 March 1865, in Baeva et al., *Petko R. Slaveykov*, 140–141.

28. Named after the New York businessman and philanthropist Christopher Robert, Robert College was founded by Cyrus Hamlin, former missionary with the American Board, in 1863. The college was formally opened in a new building on July 4, 1872, by former secretary of state William Seward. See Cyrus Hamlin, *Among the Turks* (New York: Robert Carter and Brothers, 1878); Cyrus Hamlin, *My Life and Times*, 4th ed. (Boston: Congregational Sunday-School and Publishing Society, 1893); George Washburn, *Fifty Years in Constantinople and Recollections of Robert College* (Boston: Houghton Mifflin, 1911). Racho's further education, after Slaveykov left mission employment, continued in Russia, as did the education of Slaveykov's other sons, Rayko and Khristo. Russian diplomats were suspicious of Slaveykov's association with American missionaries and sought avenues to gain "moral influence" over him. Financing the education of his sons was suggested as one possible avenue by Todor Minkov, Bulgarian director of the South Slav Boarding School in Nikolaev, Russia. Report from V. F. Kozhevnikov to E. P. Novikov, Tŭrnovo, 28 November 1862, in K. Khristov et al., *Russiya i bulgarskoto natsionalno-osvoboditelno dvizhenie, 1856–1876 (Russia and the Bulgarian National Liberation Movement, 1856–1876)*, vol. 1, Part 2 (Sofia: Bulgarian Academy of Sciences, 1987), 276–284. and Letter, T. Minkov to Aleksandur Sergeevich, 18 December 1865, in Z. Markova et al., *Russia and the Bulgarian National Liberation Movement, 1856–1876: Documents and Materials*, vol. 2 (Sofia: Bulgarian Academy of Sciences, 1987), 241–243.

29. Home School was founded by the Woman's Board of Missions in 1870. Through the endeavors of President Mary Mills Patrick, the college eventually became independent of the mission. See Mary Mills Patrick, *The American College for Girls, Scutari, Constantinople* (Gloucester: John Bellowes, 1898); Mary Mills Patrick, *A Bosporus Adventure: Istanbul (Constantinople) Woman's College, 1871–1924* (Stanford: Stanford University Press, 1934); Mary Mills Patrick, *Under Five Sultans* (New York: Century Company, 1929).

30. Constantia Kiskira, "'Evangelising' the Orient: New England Womanhood in the Ottoman Empire, 1830–1930," *Archivum Ottomanicum* 16 (1998): 279–294; Barbara Merguerian, "Mt. Holyoke Seminary in Bitlis: Providing an American Education for Armenian Women," *Armenian Review* 43 (1990): 31–65; Reeves-Ellington, "A Vision of Mount Holyoke," 146–171; Frank Andrews Stone, "Mt. Holyoke's Impact on the Land of Mt. Ararat," *Muslim World* 66, no. 1 (1976): 44–57.

31. On Bulgarian literacy, see Krassimira Daskalova, *Gramotnost, Knizhnina, Chitateli, Chetene (Literacy, Literature, Readers, Reading)* (Sofia: Lik, 1999).

32. Letter, Albert Long to John P. Durbin, 10 October 1862, Missionary Files, United Methodist Church Archive-General Commission on Archives and History (UMCA-GCAH), Madison, New Jersey.

33. Candy Gunther Brown, *The Word in the World: Evangelical Writing, Publishing, and Reading in America, 1789–1880* (Chapel Hill: University of North Carolina Press, 2004).

34. Petko Slaveykov began to publish the short-lived *Pchelitsa* for children and *Ruzhitsa* for women only in 1871. The first Ottoman Turkish-language women's journal, *Terakki-i Muhadderat* (*Progress of Muslim Women*), first appeared as a supplement to *Terakki* (*Progress*) in 1869. On the Ottoman press for women, see Elif Ekin Aksit, "Girls' Education and the Paradoxes of Modernity and Nationalism in the Late Ottoman Empire and the Early Turkish Republic" (PhD, State University of New York at Binghamton, 2004); Elizabeth Brown Frierson, "Unimagined Communities: State, Press, and Gender in the Hamidian Era" (PhD diss., Princeton University, 1996).

35. *Zornitsa*, January 1866, p 4.

36. Martha Riggs's "Letters" were originally published in Greek in 1842. In Bulgarian, they were initially published in serialized form in *Zornitsa* from January 1864 to December 1967 and subsequently in three separate editions, in each case anonymously. See Martha Jane Riggs, *Pisma za mayki ili rukovodstvo za mayki v dobroto otkhranvanie na detsata im* (*Letters to Mothers, or A Manual for Mothers on the Good Nurturing of Their Children*) (Tsarigrad: A. Minasian, 1870).

37. Ruth H. Bloch, "American Feminine Ideals in Transition: The Rise of the Moral Mother, 1785–1815," *Feminist Studies* 4, no. 2 (1978): 101–126.

38. Anne L. Kuhn, *The Mother's Role in Childhood Education: New England Concepts, 1830–1860* (New Haven: Yale University Press, 1947); Mary P. Ryan, *The Empire of the Mother: American Writing about Domesticity 1830–1860* (New York: Haworth Press, 1982); Kathryn Kish Sklar, *Catharine Beecher: A Study in American Domesticity* (New York: W. W. Norton, 1971).

39. On the simultaneous development of the American discourse of domesticity with the ideology of manifest destiny, see Amy Kaplan, "Manifest Domesticity," *American Literature* 70, no. 3 (1998): 581–606. On the ways in which domestic discourse shaped the experiences and practices of American women missionaries in the nineteenth century, see Patricia Grimshaw, *Paths of Duty: American Missionary Wives in Nineteenth-Century Hawaii* (Honolulu: University of Hawaii Press, 1989); Jane Hunter, *The Gospel of Gentility: American Women Missionaries in Turn-of-the-Century China* (New Haven: Yale University Press, 1984); Amanda Porterfield, *Mary Lyon and the Mount Holyoke Missionaries* (New York: Oxford University Press, 1997); Dana Robert, *American Women in Mission: A Social History of Their Thought and Practice* (Macon: Mercer University Press, 1996); Mary Zwiep, *Pilgrim Path: The First Company of Women Missionaries to Hawaii* (Madison: University of Wisconsin Press, 1991).

40. Several prominent urban educated Bulgarian women rearticulated the ideas in *Zornitsa* to justify the foundation of women's associations in the late 1860s.

See Barbara Reeves-Ellington, "Gender, Conversion, and Social Transformation: The American Discourse of Domesticity and the Origins of the Bulgarian Women's Movement, 1864–1876," in *Converting Cultures: Religion, Ideology and Transformations of Modernity*, ed. Dennis Washburn and A. Kevin Reinhart (Leiden: E. J. Brill, 2007), 115–140.

41. *Gayda*, 10 August 1863, 40; 19 October 1863, 80; 2 November 1863, 88; and 16 November 1863, 94. Slaveykov was a prolific journalist and also a poet. My analysis focuses on his journalism, not his poetry.

42. *Gayda*, 10 August 1864, 40, and 23 August 1864, 48.

43. *Gayda*, 17 April 1865, 165–166, and 24 April 1865, 173–174.

44. "Obraovanieto na zhenite" ("The Education of Women"), *Gayda*, 15 June 1866, 200; "Muzh i zhena" ("Man and Woman"), *Gayda*, 1 July 1866, 216; and "Zhenite, uchiteli i dukhovenstvoto" ("Women, Teachers, and the Priesthood"), *Gayda*, 15 August 1866, 261. These pieces first appeared in Bulgarian in the monthly magazine *Lyuboslovie*, printed in Izmir from 1844 to 1846. They appeared, respectively, in April 1846, February 1844, and January 1846. Edited by Konstantin Fotinov, *Lyuboslovie* was essentially a product of the American Board mission station in Izmir. See James F. Clarke, "Konstantin Fotinov, *Liuboslovie* and the Smyrna Bulgarian Press," in *The Pen and the Sword: Studies in Bulgarian History by James F. Clarke*, ed. Dennis P. Hupchick (Boulder, CO: East European Monographs, 1988); Danova, *Konstantin Georgiev Fotinov*, 321–327.

45. "Vuzpitanieto na devoykite" ("The Instruction of Girls"), *Gayda,* 1 August, 1866, 227.

46. Letter, Slaveykov to Irina, 7 January 1868, in Baeva et al., *Petko R. Slaveykov*, 144.

47. Benjamin C. Fortna, *Imperial Classroom: Islam, the State, and Education in the Late Ottoman Empire* (Oxford: Oxford University Press, 2002); Andreas M. Kazamias, *Education and the Quest for Modernity in Turkey* (Chicago: University of Chicago Press, 1966); Selçuk Akşin Somel, *The Modernization of Public Education in the Ottoman Empire, 1839–1908: Islamization, Autocracy and Discipline* (Leiden: Brill, 2001).

48. Diana Karabinova, "A Late Attempt to Find an Integrative Approach through Common Secular Education: Midhat Pasa as Governor of the Danube Province (1864–1868)," in *International Congress on Learning and Education in the Ottoman World*, ed. Ali Caksu (Istanbul: Research Centre for Islamic History, Art and Culture, 1999), 237–246.

49. See, for example, his articles on nations and nationalities in *Makedoniya*, 13 May 1867, 12 August 1867, 23 September 1867, and 2 December 1867.

50. "Uchilishtniya vupros" ("The School Question"), *Makedoniya*, 11 November 1867, 201.

51. "Obshtestvenoto obrazovanie" ("Public Education"), *Makedoniya*, 20 May 1867, 101.

52. "Zhenite v otnoshenieto na narodstvoto" ("Women with Regard to the Nation"), *Makedoniya,* 2 December 1867, 1–2.

53. Ibid.

54. "Za prosveshtenieto" ("On Enlightenment"), *Makedoniya,* 12 November 1868, 166.

55. "Edna duma i za zhenite" ("And a Word about Women"), *Makedoniya,* 7 December 1868, 5.

56. P. R. Slaveykov, translator and compiler, *Po vuprosa za zhenite* (*On the Question of Women*) (Tsarigrad: Makedoniya, 1869).

57. "Neshto za zhenite" ("Something about Women"), *Makedoniya,* 1 February 1869, 38.

58. "Za zhenite" ("About Women"), *Makedoniya,* 8 February 1869, 41–42; 15 February 1869, 45–46; and 22 February 1869, 50–51.

59. "About Women," *Makedoniya,* 15 March 1869, 62.

60. Ibid.; "Pravdinite na zhenite" ("The Rights of Women"), *Makedoniya,* 23 October 1869, 183.

61. "Zhenata: Vazhnostta i v kruga na obshtestvoto i neynoto vuspitanie v Bulgariya" ("Woman: Her Importance in the Public Sphere and Her Education in Bulgaria"), *Makedoniya,* 26 July 1869, 137.

62. "Vuzpitanieto na zhenite i naroda" ("Education of Women and the Nation"), *Makedoniya,* 21 September 1870, 291.

63. "Zhenskite druzhestva u nas" ("Our Women's Associations"), *Makedoniya,* 23 August 1869, 151.

64. *Makedoniya,* 22 February and 19 April 1869; *Pravo,* 24 March 1869.

65. "Raboti za predstavitelite" ("Work for the Representatives"), *Makedoniya,* 31 July 1870, 251.

66. Ibid.

67. "V zashtitata na zhenite" ("In Defense of Women"), *Makedoniya,* 9 November 1871, 179.

68. "Dve kasti i dve vlasti" ("Two Castes and Two Powers"), *Makedoniya,* 25 July, 1872, 69–70.

American Missionaries, the Arabic Bible, and Coptic Reform in Late Nineteenth-Century Egypt

Heather J. Sharkey

Q. Do they accept the Bible?

A. When our mission was first established it was almost an unknown book to them, but they believed it to be the Word of God. It has been widely distributed among them and is now read in Arabic in their church but in such a way as to have no power.

—Mrs. Mary B. Reid, *Egypt: Questions and Answers for Use of Junior Societies* (Pittsburgh: Women's General Missionary Society of the United Presbyterian Church of North America, 1900); "Price 4 cents."

Introduction

In a history of Protestant evangelicalism in Britain, the historian David Bebbington identified four elements that have stood at the heart of evangelical religion since the nineteenth century. He called these elements "conversionism, the belief that lives need to be changed; activism, the expression of the gospel in effort; Biblicism, a particular regard for the Bible; and crucicentrism, a stress on the sacrifice of Christ on the cross."[1] Historians of evangelicalism in the United States have embraced this definition to describe the American experience as well.[2] This essay proposes to take the third element of evangelical religion—what Bebbington called "Biblicism"—as a

point of departure for studying the work of American Presbyterian missionaries, who beginning in 1854, sought to propagate in Egypt a kind of evangelical Christianity based on firsthand knowledge of the Bible. Missionaries
soon realized that, to expand Bible knowledge, they needed to expand Bible reading. Thus they directed their efforts not only toward developing a
system of mission schools for children, but also toward devising informal
literacy programs for adults. At the same time, by helping to sell and distribute cheap Bibles, either as bound volumes or as "portions" (i.e., as Bible
segments or selections printed as booklets), they contributed to a booming
Anglo-American trade that had its place within a burgeoning global market
of Christian evangelical literature.[3]

Because this volume is devoted to the study of American missionaries in
the nineteenth-century Middle East, it is important to emphasize two points
at the outset. First, American Presbyterian efforts to promote the Bible in
Egypt entailed close cooperation with British evangelicals, who included Anglicans, Scottish and Irish Presbyterians, and others. Missionary Bible publishing in Egypt was indisputably a joint Anglo-American affair. Second, a
study of the American missionaries' efforts to promote Bible knowledge in
Egypt cannot be confined to the nineteenth century. Policies pursued by the
American missionaries in the mid-nineteenth century persisted, with minor
adaptations, for a hundred years. Indeed, a strong line of continuity con-
nects the American mission's Bible-based literacy efforts in 1856—two years
after the American mission in Egypt was founded—to efforts that it undertook in 1956, when Egypt and the region were grappling with the Suez crisis.
This article will therefore attempt to draw out these Anglo-American connections on the one hand, and nineteenth-to-twentieth-century continuities
on the other. It will also try to show how a study of Arabic Bible culture and
of Bible distribution in Egypt provides some clues to how Protestant missions worked at the grassroots—that is, how Egyptians themselves became
involved in the evangelization of the Nile Valley.

BIBLES FOR SALE

In 1897, the Rev. Andrew Watson of the American Presbyterian mission in
Egypt reflected on the status of the Coptic Orthodox Church as it had been

in 1854, when the American missionaries first arrived in the country. "Christian in name, Christian in form," he wrote, "it was well typified by the mummified human body taken out of the tombs."[4] Watson's attitude was typical of the American missionaries, who believed that the Coptic Orthodox Church was a "dead church" in need of resuscitation, and who set out to stimulate what they hoped would be a Coptic reformation in Egypt.[5]

The Americans believed that the best way to stimulate Coptic revival was to spread knowledge of the Bible and to supplant Coptic-language liturgies with prayers, sermons, and religious discussions conducted in Arabic, the living language of the Egyptian people. Noting in the mid-nineteenth century that many Coptic Orthodox churches lacked a copy of the Bible and that many priests were barely literate, Americans also set out to train a new generation of Egyptian church leaders who would be "Bible scholars." In this way, the missionary J. R. Alexander suggested, the Americans could help Copts to overcome what he described as centuries of Muslim persecution by "fir[ing] some of the younger men with a hope and a zeal that their fathers did not know."[6] Within ten years of their arrival in Egypt, American efforts had led to the establishment of a new Protestant church—the Egyptian Evangelical Church (*al-kanisa al-injiliyya al-misriyya*)—which in decades to follow would draw the vast majority of its members from the Coptic community. Within ten years the Americans were also developing girls' and boys' schools in Alexandria and Cairo. In 1860, after having bought a riverboat that had been owned by Sa'id Pasha, the viceroy of Egypt,[7] they began to set out on tours into Upper Egypt, where they sold Bibles and preached to Copts (in market squares or in Orthodox churches) as occasions arose.

In 1864, as the U.S. Civil War was still raging, the American missionary Gulian Lansing published an account of one of these Bible-selling tours in Upper Egypt. (The account was entitled *Egypt's Princes*, in a reference to Psalm 68:31, "Princes shall come out of Egypt; Ethiopia shall haste to stretch out her hands unto God.") Lansing had set out on his voyage in 1860 with a British man whom he had befriended in Alexandria: This was Lord Haddo, who during the voyage received news of his father's death in Britain and of his own succession to the title of Earl of Aberdeen.[8] Lord Haddo, or Lord Aberdeen, as he became called, was a born-again Christian who had a deep regard for the conditions of the laboring poor in England and Scotland and

who had come to Egypt to recover his health. Aberdeen left some records of
the Nile voyage as well, and a friend later compiled these after his death into a
volume entitled, *Memoir of Lord Haddo*.[9]

From *Egypt's Princes* and the *Memoir of Lord Haddo*, we can glean that
Lansing and Aberdeen had three other travel companions—though these individuals are given short shrift in both accounts. First, there was Aberdeen's
unnamed "good wife," who according to Lansing, kept the account books
for her husband's Bible sales and who sold penny tracts to Coptic children
during the voyage.[10] Second, there was a man described simply as "Faris," a
converted Maronite priest who had been sent to Egypt by the missionaries in Beirut[11]; his work in this venture testifies to the links that connected
the American Presbyterians in Egypt to their counterparts in Beirut, despite
the fact that the two missions represented different denominations within
American Presbyterianism. (Faris al-Hakim, as he is more fully known in
other sources, also drew the attention of American observers for another reason: In 1861, Muslim authorities imprisoned and bastinadoed him for trying
to help a Coptic woman—or more accurately, a woman who had converted
to Islam upon marrying a Muslim man—recant and return to the Christian
community. His case prompted the American missionaries to call upon their
consular authorities, who in turn called upon Washington, D.C., with the
result that Abraham Lincoln wrote a letter to Sa'id Pasha asking for intervention and clemency in Faris's case.[12]) Finally, the third travel companion,
who helped them in distributing the Bibles, was a former Coptic Orthodox
priest turned Protestant whom Lansing and Aberdeen called "Father Makh-
iel."[13] This would have been Mikha'il Yusuf al-Bilyani (1819–1883), who became the first ordained Evangelical Presbyterian pastor in 1867 and a leader
in the Evangelical Church.[14]

The Bibles and tracts that Lansing and Aberdeen sold came from different sources. In order to prepare for his "Coptic evangelizing scheme,"[15] Aberdeen acquired supplies from two London sources: he got Arabic Bibles from
the British and Foreign Bible Society, and Arabic Bible portions ("such as
the Parables and Miracles") from the Society for the Promotion of Christian
Knowledge (SPCK). The compiler of his memoir added that, "On reaching
Malta on the voyage out, he had added to his store from the depot there. In
addition, when arrived at Cairo, he bought large numbers of Bibles and tracts
from the American Mission store. All these he had stowed in his boat; and

moreover ordered a further large supply to be forwarded, to meet him after advancing a certain way up the river."[16] Lansing, meanwhile, noted that some of his supplies came from London, but that some were published by the American mission in Beirut; he also mentioned that a Beirut edition of the Arabic Psalms was especially popular among the Copts, who committed the whole thing to memory.[17]

At each stop along the Nile, Aberdeen not only sold books, but also pitched a tent that he used to "explain the Scriptures, and exhort, and encourage enquirers."[18] For his part, Lansing persuaded the Coptic Orthodox bishop of Luxor to let him deliver Arabic sermons in addition to the bishop's regular mass. The Arabic sermon was a Protestant missionary innovation, though as S. S. Hasan notes, by the early twentieth century Coptic Orthodox churches had integrated this practice into their worship.[19]

On this journey, Lansing and Aberdeen only approached Coptic men, whom they could identify by their black turbans; they did not try to approach or sell Bibles to Muslims, though they were glad to sell Bibles to Muslims who approached them.[20] They may have been cautious about selling to Muslims because they feared that Muslims might treat the Bible with disrespect; Lansing claimed that this had been the case with his own Muslim boatmen, who fiddled with the Bible's pages and handled the books as if they were rough cargo.[21] In a similar vein, J. R. Alexander, who joined the American mission in 1874, later wrote that when the American missionaries first arrived in Egypt, Muslims who got hold of a Bible "frequently tore its leaves and threw them down on the ground in contempt."[22]

According to Lansing, Copts showed a tremendous interest in the Bibles he was selling. He claimed that in Biba, just south of Beni Suef, one man "almost snatched the book, saying, 'I'll take it and spend my evenings reading it!' and he kissed it and pressed it to his bosom with evident delight."[23] Lord Aberdeen kept records that give a sense of the sales: for example, in Minya during two days in November 1860, Aberdeen and his assistants sold one full Bible, 108 New Testaments, 34 Pentateuchs, and 150 "smaller books" or Bible portions. (These figures do not include the sale of penny tracts.) They had so many sales at each stop of the riverboat that by the time they reached Sohag, they had exhausted their supply of Bibles and sent a request upriver to Cairo for more.[24]

Lansing and Aberdeen did report some resistance to their Bible-selling—not from Muslims and not from ordinary Copts, but rather from Coptic

Orthodox church authorities. Lansing claimed that the Coptic Patriarch
Cyril IV, fearing that the Protestants would win followers, ordered Copts
in a place called Bosh, near Beni Suef, to desist from buying Arabic Bibles.[25]
(This is a striking detail, because as Paul Sedra has pointed out, Cyril IV has
been typically regarded by Orthodox Coptic historians as the church's first
modernizer, who enacted reforms that "spoke to all the concerns evangelicals had raised, and employed all the techniques evangelicals had endorsed,
in their writings."[26] Yet at this juncture, Lansing interpreted Cyril's alleged
opposition to Arabic Bible-buying as a sign of mounting concern over Protestant success in winning Coptic followers.) Later, Andrew Watson recorded in his chronicle of the American mission that in 1867, Cyril's succes-
sor, Demetrius II, organized a Bible-burning in Assiut—specifically, a bon-
fire of the Van Dyck Arabic edition of the Bible that had been imported
from the American mission press in Beirut.[27] Iris Habib al-Misri, the distinguished late twentieth-century chronicler of the Coptic Orthodox Church
(who was, incidentally, a graduate of the American mission girls' college in
Cairo[28]), made no mention of the book-burning episode in her 584-page
English-language abridgement of *Qissat al-kanisa al-qibtiyya* (which is al-
Misri's multivolume opus on the history of the Coptic Orthodox Church).
She did acknowledge, however, that in 1867 Demetrius II set out on a three-
month pastoral tour of Upper Egypt "to expound and defend the Orthodox
doctrines" in the face of American missionary incursions.[29] American missionaries, by contrast, described this episode as part of a campaign of Protestant persecution which the Khedive Ismail was happy to abet. Charles R.
Watson, the son of Andrew Watson and the future founder of the American University in Cairo, was among the Americans who took this view. The
younger Watson wrote in 1905 that, "This persecution was not an accidental
outbreak of fanatical jealousy and hate. It was a deliberate plan in which the
government lent its authority and influence to make effective the efforts of
the Coptic Church to wipe out Protestantism forever" and to rid Egypt of
American influence.[30]

It is hard to imagine, today, that a Coptic patriarch presided over a public burning of Arabic Bibles in 1867, but it is also hard to appreciate the threat
that Orthodox authorities were perceiving in this period, when both Protestant and Catholic missions were trying to poach from the Coptic flock.
What is clear, in any case, is that American and British evangelicals left a

mark on Egyptian Christianity. By the early twentieth century, the Coptic Orthodox Church had fully embraced the Arabic Bible and the culture of Bible-reading, and was arguably developing evangelical strains of its own.[31] This was certainly the impression held by the Rev. W. L. McClenahan, who contributed the following item to an American mission newsletter in 1913: "Let the Mission give thanks for a real revival which is going on in the Coptic Church at Suez. Evangelistic meetings have been held nightly for two or three months. They are attended by large audiences. The teaching and the form of service are quite 'Protestant.'"[32]

Christian Literacy and Bible Work at the Grassroots

While a deep regard for the Bible may be the hallmark of all evangelical communities, the United Presbyterian Church of North America, which sponsored the mission in Egypt, was especially committed to the idea that all men, women, and children in the church should have a firm grasp of biblical knowledge. The Rev. William J. Reid, a United Presbyterian pastor in Pittsburgh, clarified this idea in a manual of church doctrine that was published in eight successive editions after 1881 and that addressed the question, "What must we do to be saved?" To have a "saving faith," Reid advised, "we must study the Bible diligently, and listen attentively and regularly to the preaching of the word." Besides baptism and the profession of belief, he added, "Another qualification of the members of the church is *knowledge.* ... The ultimate standard of knowledge is the Scriptures. No one who is ignorant of the doctrines of grace, as revealed in the Bible, has a right to a place in the church."[33] Writing in 1894, a United Presbyterian pastor and historian named J. B. Scouller attributed the church's emphasis on knowledge to Calvinist values that demanded intelligent Bible-reading, that is, "not ... learning for its own sake, but [learning as an] auxiliary to the advancement of religious truth." Scouller claimed that these values had guided the forebears of the United Presbyterians in America when they "built their schoolhouse near the church, and very often hired the schoolmaster before they hired their pastor."[34] The American Presbyterians in Egypt appear to have followed a similar impulse, by making education and Bible-based literacy a mission priority and by starting schools in towns like Luxor and Assiut before they had functioning Evangelical churches in place.[35]

The Americans in Egypt were not unique among missions of that era in promoting education as a vehicle for Bible study, embracing print technologies for the development of Christian literatures, or using schools for acculturating children. Nevertheless, their approach to literacy and literary work in Egypt was quite distinctive. For unlike their closest peer among the Protestant missions in Egypt—namely, the British Church Missionary Society (CMS)—which focused its efforts on urban communities and on formal schooling for children in Cairo and Alexandria, the American Presbyterians promoted literacy even among urban working classes and Upper Egyptian peasants. They did so by seeding *ad hoc* voluntary programs that called upon Egyptians to teach each others how to read. The result was that, in late nineteenth-century Egypt, many Copts appear to have learned to *read* the Bible without ever learning how to *write*. The Rev. Menes Abdel Noor, an Egyptian Evangelical pastor in Cairo, recalled in 2005 that this had been the case with his own paternal grandmother in Upper Egypt. His grandfather (a railway employee whose family disowned him for turning from Coptic Orthodoxy toward Protestantism) taught his grandmother how to read (the Bible), yet she never learned how to write.[36] By teaching themselves and each other how to read and understand the Bible, members of the fledgling Coptic Evangelical community deserve credit for evangelizing themselves in a way that missionary archives have failed to record.

After Lansing, missionaries did not go on major Bible-selling tours up the Nile. Instead, they increasingly delegated their work to Egyptian Protestant men who were hired as colporteurs.[37] According to the *Oxford English Dictionary*, this word "colporteur" had meant simply a hawker or peddler of books in the early nineteenth-century English language, yet by the late nineteenth-century the word had developed a more specific connotation suggesting "one employed by a society to travel about and sell or distribute Bibles and religious writings."[38] Although the colporteur's main task was to sell Bibles, scattered references in missionary accounts suggest that colporteurs also gave sermons, "won converts," and helped others to read and understand the Bible more fully.[39] Moreover, many of these men appear to have been in steady contact with the American Presbyterian mission, the CMS and other British missions, and the Egyptian Evangelical Church. Consider the case, for example, of "Mr. Gabra Hanna," who is mentioned briefly in a chronicle of the American mission that was published in 1958. Gabra Hanna was an ordained pastor in the Egyptian Evangelical Church, which means that he would have studied with the American Presbyterians at their seminary in Cairo. Sometime after the Anglo-Egyptian conquest of the Sudan in 1898, but before British authorities granted the first American and British missionaries permission to enter Khartoum in 1901, Gabra Hanna arrived in the Sudan working as a colporteur for the British and Foreign Bible Society.[40] While Gabra Hanna's Bible work illustrates the convergence of American, British, and Egyptian actors in the history of Nile Valley evangelization, it also challenges standard accounts in Sudanese history, which date the start of Protestant missions in the Sudan to 1901, when the first American and British missionaries arrived together in Khartoum.[41] It means, in other words, that the pioneer of Protestant missions was neither British nor American, but Egyptian—it was Gabra Hanna, the Evangelical pastor and Bible-seller.

By the late nineteenth century, both the London-based British and Foreign Bible Society (founded 1804) and the New York-based American Bible Society (founded 1816)[42] were working closely with the American Presbyterians and their Egyptian Evangelical counterparts. Indeed, in 1876, the American Presbyterian missionary, Dr. S.C. Ewing, became the American Bible Society's subagent for Egypt—a position that he held until 1897. Other American missionaries took on this role for the American Bible Society, until 1910, when the position was passed to an Egyptian Evangelical named Mikha'il Bakhit, who began to supervise a network of some twenty-five Egyptian colporteurs.[43]

In their annual report for the 1883–1884 year, American missionaries noted that they (or more accurately, their colporteurs), had sold 7,622 volumes of scriptures on behalf of the American and British Bible societies, as well as many smaller tracts.[44] Records show that in 1888 American Presbyterians applied for, and received, a grant from the British and Foreign Bible Society to pay for the salaries of twelve Egyptian Bible Women, whom the Americans trained to make house-to-house visits to women.[45] These grants were part of the British and Foreign Bible Society's special program for "promoting the knowledge of the Bible and (as a consequence) the circulation of Holy Scripture among females in the East."[46] Sarah Lane, a historian of the British Bible society, observed that, in nineteenth-century England, Bible Women may have helped to foster a savings ethic among the working classes, because Bible Women refused to give anything for free, but instead

encouraged even the poorest to buy Bibles on installments or by "subscription." Lane also noted that Bible Women in England appear to have contributed to the rise of English literacy among females. She explained, "Frequently
a lady collector would spend time reading the Bible with the subscribers, for
there were many of the poor who were illiterate. On receiving their own Bible, these people then often wanted to learn to read themselves."[47] The same
dynamic may have been working among Bible Women in Egypt. Yet in
Egypt, Bible Women did much more than read the Bible. An American missionary recorded that as the years went on, some of these Bible Women developed specialties, so that, for example, "one would be in great demand at
mournings, another to settle quarrels."[48] One could therefore argue, as another historian of Bible Women in England has done, that these Egyptian Bible Women were engaged in a kind of female ministry to females.[49]

One striking point that stands out about late nineteenth-century Egyptian Bible Women, and that distinguishes them from their counterparts in
England, is that "several of the most faithful among them" were blind. (Most
of these blind Bible Women would have been victims of ophthalmia, which
was widespread in Egypt during that period.) Blind Bible Women relied on
a new form of publishing—Arabic Braille print—in order to read, and carried Braille portions of the Bible with them as they made their rounds from
house to house.[50]

These examples from the Arabic Bible networks of late nineteenth-century Egypt suggest that anyone seeking to understand the role of Egyptian
men and women in Christian missions during this period must focus on the
Bible distributors. For they clearly did much more than sell Bibles, and they
reached into places—ranging from small villages to dense city neighbor-
hoods—where Americans and Britons rarely ventured.

BIBLE DISTRIBUTION UP TO WORLD WAR I

If one takes this story into the closing years of the "long nineteenth century"
and goes up to World War I, then some other trends in the Egyptian Bible
trade become salient.

By 1900, the British and Foreign Bible Society and the American Bible
Society were both working in Egypt, but were essentially dividing their turf.
The British agent had his "depot" in Alexandria and concentrated on Bible

distribution in the Delta, whereas the American agent had a depot in Assiut and concentrated on Upper Egypt. They both operated in Cairo. This
said, their markets sometimes converged even outside Cairo, largely because
Anglicans and CMS missionaries had close ties to the British Bible society
whereas the American Presbyterians and Egyptian Evangelicals had close
ties to the American society.[51] And so, for example, a British Anglican archdeacon named T. E. Dowling, who served as a "season chaplain" to British
tourists in Aswan, wrote in 1909 that he had sold both American and British
Bibles to members of the Coptic Orthodox community in that town. Dowling also noted, incidentally, that since not every Egyptian could afford a Bible, or even a portion thereof, "Selim Hanna Effendi, the Coptic Postmaster
at Assouan, and my efficient interpreter, [had] presented thirty copies of
the [American Bible Society's] Arabic edition" to some of the poorest people in the town.[52] Once again, an Egyptian was taking initiative in the work
of propagating the Christian gospel. Like Lord Aberdeen before him, Selim
Hanna, the Coptic postmaster in Aswan, was pursuing a one-man mission of
piety.

In 1905, the British and Foreign Bible Society took an important step by
moving its depot from Alexandria to Port Said, which was the largest coaling
station for ships in the world. James Moulton Roe, the society's chronicler,
wrote in 1965 that "From the Society's standpoint Port Said...was an ideal
entrepôt from which bulk consignments of Scriptures could be redistributed
by the extensive coastal shipping routes to all parts of the Eastern Mediterranean, and to East Africa, as well as to Palestine and by rail to Upper Egypt."
Indeed, the society's bureau in Egypt was responsible for arranging Bible
sales in Syria, Palestine, Cyprus, Malta, Arabia, Abyssinia, and Sudan; it was
also connected to the society's Eastern Central Africa Subagency, which was
based in Zanzibar. But sometimes its representatives in Port Said sold Bibles
to passing sailors: In this way, in 1905, for example, it sold many volumes in
Russian and Polish. It procured supplies from three sources—the Bible Society in London, the American mission press in Beirut, and the Russian Bible
Society in St. Petersburg.[53] By 1913, the society's monumental "Bible House"
in Port Said held a stock of over 160,000 books, representing fifty to sixty different languages. While Arabic Bibles represented the largest market for the
Port Said Bible depot, Roe wrote that its sales were not as high as one might
expect given the size of the Arabic-speaking populations.[54] Roe attributed

low sales to pervasive illiteracy. "The number of illiterates among the native population of Egypt, Syria, and Palestine in 1905," he wrote, "was estimated at not less than 97 per cent. When only three out of every hundred encountered by a colporteur could read the books he tendered, the work of selling them was inevitably a slow and tedious business."[55]

One other development of this period is worth noting. In 1905, an interdenominational group of American and British missionaries launched the Nile Mission Press in Cairo.[56] The Nile Mission Press did not publish Bibles; rather, it focused on the development of what we could call an auxiliary evangelical literature—that is, a Christian literature of novels, children's stories, biographies, and more, all of which aimed to inspire or convince. Although the Nile Mission Press had headquarters in Tunbridge Wells, England, it also had, from 1915, a supporting agency in New York, which sought to raise American funds on its behalf. The name of this New York agency was telling: It was called the American Christian Literature Society for Moslems, or ACLSM.[57] Lord Aberdeen, upon sailing up the Nile in 1860, had described his Bible work as a scheme for evangelizing Copts. But by 1915, as the mere existence of the ACLSM indicated, times had changed, and Anglo-American missions in Egypt were pressing themselves upon Muslims as a matter of official policy. Moreover, Christian literature was growing, its target audiences were widening, and so were its global ambitions. Consider, after all, that by 1925 the Nile Mission Press in Cairo was distributing its evangelical literature to Muslims living as far afield as Canada, Ecuador, South Africa, and China.[58] And distributing, not selling, is the important word. For while Muslims *sometimes* bought Christian evangelical publications, many became the recipients of free copies.[59] Missionaries realized that Muslims were not as eager to buy Bibles and Christian tracts as the Copts in Upper Egypt had been, so that giving seemed the easiest way to pass on the message.

Conclusion

American Presbyterian missionaries emphasized Bible-reading from the moment they reached Egypt in 1854, and as the years went on, they took pride in the high literacy rates that were found among the small Egyptian Evangelical community. In 1927, for example, one missionary pointed proudly to the "latest literacy figures" in Egypt, which reported that among those over age five, 17.5 percent of Muslim males and 2.1 percent of Muslim females were literate; that 30 percent of Coptic Orthodox males and 8.7 percent of Orthodox females were literate; but that 40.8 percent of Protestant males and 18.9 percent of Protestant females were literate.[60]

Yet while rates of literacy were relatively high among Egyptian Evangelicals, the size of the community was rather small: an official church tally counted precisely 21,679 members by 1939. The vast majority was of Coptic origin; only 150 or so had entered the church from Islam.[61] Before World War I, missionaries had already noted that fewer Copts were joining the Evangelical church than they had been doing in the late nineteenth century; one missionary speculated in 1912 that this was a consequence of a Coptic "counter-reformation."[62] By the late 1930s, not only were the Evangelical churches failing to draw new members, but in the words of an American mission report, they were also losing extant members "to the ancestral Church or to the world."[63] Notwithstanding these developments, the American missionaries continued to pursue literacy projects, including some that sought to eradicate illiteracy and others that sought to expand literacy skills among adults. In the 1930s and 1940s, for example, the American mission supported efforts to open public lending libraries in village churches, and to develop a literature for married women and mothers.[64] In the 1940s and 1950s, they devised literacy campaigns that followed a pedagogical model associated with Frank Laubach, a former American missionary to the Philippines.[65] While these mid-twentieth-century, Laubach-style campaigns had a catchy motto—"Each One Teach One"—the idea behind the pedagogy in Egypt was, in fact, little changed from the late nineteenth century, when the American missionaries had urged newly educated Copts to teach their friends and relatives to read.[66] (After 1948, American missionaries took their Each One Teach One method for Arabic to Gaza, where they helped the United Nations to establish literacy training programs for Palestinian refugees.[67])

The year 1956 seems to be an appropriate moment of closure in this story. Two developments in the history of missionaries and the Bible in Egypt stand out.

First, the year 1956 was a turning point in Egyptian Bible distribution. In the aftermath of the Suez crisis, the regime of Gamal Abdel Nasser deported British missionaries, including the agent of the British and Foreign Bible Society. The Egyptian government also froze the Bible society's bank assets. But since the American Bible Society had completely merged its Egyptian distribution network and funds with the British society in 1937, the Egyptian government's policy, in effect, froze the American Bible operation as well. Within a year, however, the Egyptian government agreed on a modus vivendi: The British and Foreign Bible Society would stay out of Egypt, while the American Bible Society would assume full custodianship of the British society's assets and responsibility for distribution in Egypt.[68]

Second, and also in 1956, the American woman missionary Davida Finney, together with a few dynamic young pastors from the Egyptian Evangelical Church, launched a new literacy campaign in the village of Deir Abu Hinnis, near Minya. Their goal was to help all 5,200 Christian villagers, Orthodox and Protestant alike, become literate by the end of a year. But before they could even start, they had to end a longstanding feud that had riven the Protestant and Orthodox sections of the community; they also had to ensure that the Coptic Orthodox priest and the Coptic Evangelical pastor would assume joint leadership roles within the movement.[69] This project in Deir Abu Hinnis was symbolically important in two respects. First, it signaled the growth of Protestant-Orthodox ecumenism on the ground in Egypt. This development was confirmed on a global scale in the late 1950s and early 1960s when the Coptic Orthodox Church began to participate more actively in the largely Protestant World Council of Churches, based in Geneva.[70] Second, this project signaled the passing of the torch for social services from the American Presbyterian mission to the Coptic Evangelical Organization of Social Services (CEOSS)—an organization, founded in 1952, which is today one of the largest faith-based NGOs in Egypt.[71] While American missionaries continued to work on Egyptian literacy projects in the 1960s, they did so under the authority of, and by invitation from, CEOSS and the Egyptian Evangelical Church.[72] Meanwhile, after 1956, CEOSS undertook Arabic Bible publishing and distribution. Thus between 1957 and 1979, CEOSS distributed more than 20,800 Arabic Bibles, either by selling them or distributing them as prizes to Christian children who memorized scriptures. During this period, CEOSS also sold more than 93,000 New Testaments and Bible portions, as well as a series of Bible study guides for newly literate adults.[73]

In 1958, two years after the literacy project began in Deir Abu Hinnis, Rev. Adib Galdas, the village's Evangelical pastor, reflected on the project's aims and impact. According to Davida Finney, who translated his words into English, Galdas observed,

> When the Literacy Committee came to Deir Abu Hinnis, its members sometimes asked people why they were so eager to learn to read. The answer always was, "because I want to read the Bible." The Committee members thought that perhaps many people said this in order to please them. Later on, when hundreds had learned to read, the Committee members were astonished to see men, women and children poring over a Bible in their hands as they sat in the doorway of their homes or on the sand. Everywhere they went they saw the same sight. For centuries our Christians had not been able to read their Holy Book. Now it lay open in their hands and they could read it for themselves. When they went to church, carrying this precious book in their hands or in their pockets, they could open it quickly at the right place when the preacher announced where he would read. They were now truly like other men everywhere, just as able to share in the church service and in the worship of God.

Galdas added,

> Our villagers are a simple people, not yet divorced from their inherited belief in God. I want with all my heart to help them learn about God's purposes and love as revealed in the Bible so that they will not be swept into worldliness as their material condition improves.[74]

Certainly John G. Lorimer (a retired American missionary who served in Egypt from 1952 to 1970) was impressed by the biblical knowledge that many Egyptian Christians commanded. Lorimer recalled that when he used to visit rural Evangelical churches in the 1960s, pastors would sometimes start to recite a Bible verse during worship, whereupon the men and women in the congregation would call out and finish the verse: such was the extent of their biblical knowledge.[75]

However, biblical knowledge and the modern culture of Bible reading did not make its only marks on the converted, that is, on those who embraced the evangelical, reformed Christianity that American and British missionaries were trying to spread. As Sasson Somekh has shown, a growing knowledge of the Arabic Bible left clear marks on modern Arabic literature, including works produced by Christian and Muslim writers alike. (Somekh pointed, for example, to the poetry of Mahmoud Darwish, a Palestinian Muslim, whose motifs of crucifixion borrow from the New Testament version of Jesus's life, and not from the Quranic account.) Somekh stressed the importance, above all, of the Van Dyck Bible that was produced by American missionaries in Beirut—the same version that Americans and Britons were distributing in late nineteenth- and early twentieth-century Egypt.[76]

In sum, beginning in the 1860s, Protestant missionaries, colporteurs and Bible Women, and pious Egyptian Christians helped to make the Arabic Bible more readily available to Egyptian men, women, and children. They thereby helped to change the culture of Bible-reading, affecting not only *who* read the Bible, but *how* and even *where* they did so.[77] One could argue that the expansion of Arabic Bible reading helped, in turn, to democratize Christian worship in Egypt. Ordinary men and women in congregations began to know the Bible so well that they could keep pastors and priests on their toes. Laypeople became biblical experts, and this in turn, helped laypeople to exercise power as leaders in the church. Adapting the ideas of Benedict Anderson, who argued that the culture of print capitalism helped to create new imagined communities in the form of modern nationalisms,[78] I suggest that the burgeoning evangelical culture of Arabic print may have helped to create new imagined communities of Christians. It fostered not only specific Coptic Orthodox, Protestant, and Catholic imagined communities, but also, in the long run, imagined ecumenical, that is, trans-sectarian, communities. In the Egyptian case, a culture of Arabic Bible reading may have contributed to a kind of "Coptism"[79] or "Copticity" that transcends Orthodox, Protestant, and Catholic identities, though without completely eliminating the sectarian rivalries that sometimes preoccupy Egyptian Christians even today.

Notes

1. David Bebbington, *Evangelicalism in Modern Britain: A History from the 1730s to the 1980s* (London: Routledge, 1989), 3.

2. See, for example, Mark A. Noll, *American Evangelical Christianity: An Introduction* (Oxford: Blackwell Publishers, 2001), 13; and John Wolffe, "Evangelicals and Pentecostals: Indigenizing a Global Gospel," in *Global Religious Movements in Regional Context*, ed. John Wolffe (Aldershot, UK: Ashgate, 2002), 18.

3. On the roots of this movement in Britain, see Leslie Howsam, *Cheap Bibles: Nineteenth-Century Publishing and the British and Foreign Bible Society* (Cambridge: Cambridge University Press, 1991).

4. Andrew Watson, *The American Mission in Egypt, 1854 to 1896*, 2nd edition (Pittsburgh: United Presbyterian Board of Publication, 1904), 58. On the history of the American Presbyterians in Egypt from 1854 to 1967, see Heather J. Sharkey, *American Evangelicals in Egypt: Missionary Encounters in an Age of Empire* (Princeton: Princeton University Press, 2008).

5. J. R. Alexander, for example, called the Coptic liturgy "a dead language in a dead church." J. R. Alexander, "A Great Adventure in the Valley of the Nile," *The Biblical Review* 10:3 (July 1925): 355. Rena Hogg, a second-generation missionary in Egypt, described the Coptic Orthodox church as an "embalm[ed]" or "mummied" [*sic*] church. Rena L. Hogg, *A Master-Builder on the Nile, being a record of the life and aims of John Hogg, D.D., Christian Missionary* (Pittsburgh: United Presbyterian Board of Publication, 1914), 96–97. On the earlier efforts of a British mission, the Church Missionary Society (CMS), to promote reform among Copts through education, see Paul D. Sedra, "John Lieder and His Mission in Egypt: The Evangelical Ethos at Work among Nineteenth-Century Copts," *The Journal of Religious History* 28:3 (2004): 219–239; and Paul Sedra, "Textbook Maneuvers: Evangelicals and Educational Reform in Nineteenth-Century Egypt" (PhD diss., New York University, 2006).

6. Alexander, "A Great Adventure in the Valley of the Nile," 335, 372; J. R. Alexander, *A Sketch of the Story of the Evangelical Church of Egypt* (An address delivered by the Rev. J. R. Alexander, D.D., before the Missionary Association, at its meeting in Assiut, January 5, 1930, on the 75th Anniversary of the Founding of the American Mission in Egypt) (Alexandria: Whitehead Morris Limited, 1930), 8.

7. Earl E. Elder, *Vindicating a Vision: The Story of the American Mission in Egypt, 1854–1954* (Philadelphia: The United Presbyterian Board of Foreign Missions, 1958), 34.

8. Rev. Gulian Lansing, *Egypt's Princes: A Narrative of Missionary Labor in the Valley of the Nile*, 2nd edition (Philadelphia: William S. Rentoul, 1864).

9. Rev. E. B. Elliott, ed., *Memoir of Lord Haddo, in His Latter Years, Fifth Earl of Aberdeen*, 5th rev. ed. (London: Seeley, Jackson and Halliday, 1869).

10. Lansing, *Egypt's Princes*, 211.

11. Ibid., 21.

12. Watson, *The American Mission in Egypt*, 127–135; Lansing, *Egypt's Princes*, 341–342.

13. Elliott, *Memoir of Lord Haddo*, 256–257; Lansing, *Egypt's Princes*, 34–35.

14. James Brown Scouller, *A Manual of the United Presbyterian Church of North America, 1751–1881* (Harrisburg, PA: Patriot Publishing Company, 1881), 616–626.

15. Elliott, *Memoir of Lord Haddo*, 256.

16. Ibid., 256–257.

17. Lansing, *Egypt's Princes*, 38, 305.

18. Elliott, *Memoir of Lord Haddo*, 261–262.

19. S. S. Hasan, *Christians versus Muslims in Modern Egypt: The Century-Long Struggle for Coptic Equality* (Oxford: Oxford University Press, 2003), 73.

20. Lansing, *Egypt's Princes*, 39, 256, 315, 331; Elliott, *Memoir of Lord Haddo*, 262.

21. Lansing, *Egypt's Princes*, 157–158.

22. Alexander, "A Great Adventure in the Valley of the Nile," 356.

23. Lansing, *Egypt's Princes*, 31.

24. Elliott, *Memoir of Lord Haddo*, 259–260.

25. Lansing, *Egypt's Princes*, 31.

26. Sedra, "John Lieder and His Mission in Egypt," 235–236.

27. Watson, *The American Mission in Egypt*, 206. Regarding the Van Dyck Bible, see John Alexander Thompson, *The Major Arabic Bibles* (New York: American Bible Society, 1956), 20–27.

28. Christine Sproul, "The American College for Girls, Cairo, Egypt: Its History and Influence on Egyptian Women—A Study of Selected Graduates" (PhD diss., The University of Utah, 1982), 109–110.

29. Iris Habib el Masri, *The Story of the Copts* (n.p.: The Middle East Council of Churches, 1978), 523; Iris Habib al-Misri, *Qissat al-kanisa al-qibtiyya* (Vols. 1–4, Cairo: Maktabat Kanisat Mar Jirjis, 1960; Vols. 5–9, Cairo: Maktabat al-Mahabba, n.d.).

30. The Rev. Charles R. Watson, "Fifty Years of Foreign Missions in Egypt," in *Foreign Missionary Jubilee Convention of the United Presbyterian Church of N.A., celebrating the Fiftieth Anniversary of the Founding of Missions in Egypt and India* (Philadelphia: The Board of Foreign Missions of the UPCNA, 1905), 83, 87–88.

31. Indeed, Bible instruction for children became a platform of the Coptic Orthodox Sunday schools, which the layman Habib Jirjis helped to promote beginning in 1918. Hasan, *Christians versus Muslims in Modern Egypt*, 74. On the history of Protestant and Catholic efforts to woo Orthodox Copts, see Sharkey, *American Evangelicals in Egypt*. For the earlier history of Catholic overtures, see Alastair Hamilton, *The Copts and the West, 1439–1822: The European Discovery of an Egyptian Church* (Oxford: Oxford University Press, 2006).

32. Presbyterian Historical Society, Philadelphia (henceforth PHS) UPCNA RG 209-20-14: The American Mission in Egypt, Circular Letter, No. 1, November 1913.

33. William J. Reid, *United Presbyterianism*, 8th edition (Pittsburgh: United Presbyterian Board of Publication, 1900), 14, 49. The first edition appeared in 1881.

34. James B. Scouller, *A History of the United Presbyterian Church*, vol. 11, The American Church History Series, gen. ed. Philip Schaff et al (New York: Christian Literature Company, 1894).

35. See Lansing, *Egypt's Princes*.

36. Conversation with the Rev. Menes Abdel Noor, Cairo, May 23, 2005.

37. PHS, *Annual Report of the United Presbyterian Mission in Egypt, 1883–4*, 28.

38. "Colporteur," *Oxford English Dictionary*, Second Edition Online, 1989.

39. A particularly "keen soul winner," for example, was George Kaoustos (also known by the Muslim name, Ali Salih), who was described as the son of a Greek publican and Muslim woman-servant from the Delta town of Bilbeis. He studied in a CMS school, had a conversion experience and joined the Egyptian Evangelical Church, and then worked in the Delta with the Egypt General Mission (a British interdenominational mission, founded in Belfast) before eventually becoming a colporteur for the British and Foreign Bible Society in Khartoum. George Swan, *"Lacked Ye Anything?": A Brief Story of the Egypt General Mission*, Revised edition (London: Egypt General Mission, 1932), 57–59; James Moulton Roe, *A History of the British and Foreign Bible Society, 1905–1954* (London: The British and Foreign Bible Society, 1965), 386–387.

40. Elder, *Vindicating a Vision*, 102.

41. See, for example, Richard Hill, "The Government and Christian Missions in the Anglo-Egyptian Sudan, 1899–1914," *Middle Eastern Studies* 1:2 (1964): 113–134; J. Spencer Trimingham, *The Christian Approach to Islam in the Sudan* (London: Oxford University Press, 1948); and Charles R. Watson, *The Sorrow and Hope of the Egyptian Sudan: A Survey of Missionary Conditions and Methods of Work of the Egyptian Sudan* (Philadelphia: Board of Foreign Missions of the United Presbyterian Church of North America, 1913). One of my own earlier articles reflected these assumptions about missionary chronology: Heather J. Sharkey, "Christians among Muslims: The Church Missionary Society in the Northern Sudan," *Journal of African History* 43 (2002): 51–75. Gabra Hanna is also mentioned in the following recent work: Roland Werner, William Anderson, and Andrew Wheeler, *Day of Devastation, Day of Contentment: The History of the Sudanese Church across 2000 Years* (Nairobi: Paulines Publications Africa, 2000), 232.

42. Peter J. Wosh, *Spreading the Word: The Bible Business in Nineteenth-Century America* (Ithaca: Cornell University Press, 1994). As early as 1824, the American Bible Society had sent a supply of Arabic Bible portions to Alexandria; in 1838 the society sent some portions to the American consul in Alexandria, to be

distributed by a "Mr. Wolf" of a mission to the Jews. But there appears to have
been no systematic distribution by the American Bible Society until after the
American Presbyterians started their mission in Egypt. W. P. Strickland, *History of the American Bible Society* (New York: Harper and Brothers, 1849), 266,
276.

43. Marcellus Bowen, *The Bible in Bible Lands: History of the Levant Agency* (New
York: American Bible Society, 1917), 16–17, 37.

44. PHS, *Annual Report of the United Presbyterian Mission in Egypt, 1883–4*, 28.

45. Later, in 1889, the American mission secured another grant from the British
and Foreign Bible Society to support some Bible Women in the Cairo district
of Shoubra. PHS RG 209-21-27: Egypt Mission, British & Foreign Bible Association Letters, John Sharp, British & Foreign Bible Society, to Rev. Dr. Watson of the American Mission Cairo, dated London, October 16, 1888; Robt. H.
Weakley of the British and Foreign Bible Society, Egyptian Agency, to Rev. Andrew Watson of the American Mission, dated Alexandria, March 29, 1889.

46. PHS RG 209-21-27: Egypt Mission, British & Foreign Bible Association Letters, John Sharp, Secretary, British & Foreign Bible Society, to Sec. American
Mission in Egypt, dated London, August 15, 1888, mimeographed handwritten
letter.

47. Sarah Lane, "Forgotten Labours: Women's Bible Work and the BFBS," in *Sowing the Word: The Cultural Impact of the British and Foreign Bible Society, 1804–2004*, ed. Stephen Batalden, Kathleen Cann, and John Dean (Sheffield, UK:
Sheffield Phoenix Press, 2004), 60–61.

48. Elizabeth Kelsey Kinnear, *She Sat Where They Sat: A Memoir of Anna Young
Thompson of Egypt* (Grand Rapids, MI: William B. Eerdmans Publishing Company, 1971), 64.

49. Roger H. Martin, "Women and the Bible Society," in *Sowing the Word*, ed.
Batalden et al., 45, 52.

50. Kinnear, *She Sat Where They Sat*, 64–65. On the history of Arabic Braille, see
El Sayed A. Fattah, "Beirut Conference on Perso-Arabic Braille," *Proceedings of
the World Assembly of the World Council for the Welfare of the Blind* (1954), 75–78.

51. CMS missionaries sold Bibles on behalf of the British Bible society at their
bookstore in Cairo. An American mission report of 1921 stated that Evangelical
congregations in Upper Egypt sent annual contributions to support the work
of the American Bible Society. Roe, *A History of the British and Foreign Bible
Society*, 177; PHS, *Minutes of the Fifty-first Annual Meeting of the Egyptian Missionary Association, Cairo, February 10th to 18th, 1921*, p. 11. A major British supporter of the British Bible society in Cairo was the CMS missionary Douglas
Thornton (1873–1909) who, besides supporting book-selling, also tried to improve Bible education in Coptic (Orthodox) schools; see W. H. T. Gairdner,

D. M. Thornton: A Study in Missionary Ideals and Methods (New York: Fleming H. Revell Company, 1909), 45, 104.

52. Archdeacon Dowling, *The Egyptian Church* (London: Cope & Fenwick, 1909), 2.

53. On the work of the St. Petersburg Bible society, see Stephen K. Batalden, "The BFBS Petersburg Agency and Russian Biblical Translation, 1856–1875," in *Sowing the Word*, ed. Batalden et al., 169–196.

54. Roe, *A History of the British and Foreign Bible Society*, 175-179.

55. Ibid., 179.

56. Abdul-Fady (Arthur T. Upson), *High Lights [sic] in the Near East: Reminiscences of Nearly 40 Years' Service* (London: Marshall, Morgan & Scott, Ltd. 1936), 42.

57. PHS UPCUSA RG 81-27-20: COEMAR, American Christian Literature Society for Moslems, Correspondence, 1915–1940.

58. PHS UPCNA RG 209-1-04: J. W. Acheson Papers, "A Summary of N.M.P. Annual Report for 1925" (Nile Mission Press), attached to a letter from Acheson to Edie dated March 16, 1925.

59. The mission was distributing some free Bibles to Muslims in 1932, from a special fund, even as a budgetary crisis was otherwise forcing the mission to cut programs. PHS UPCNA RG 209-3-28: Earl R. Jamieson Papers: Jamieson to W. B. Anderson, dated Fayoum, October 15, 1932.

60. H. E. Philips, *The Question Box: A Catechism on Missions in Egypt* ([Pittsburgh?]: The Publicity Committee of The Egyptian Mission of the United Presbyterian Church of North America, 1939), 27.

61. Philips, *The Question Box*, 24.

62. PHS (MS T3788p), Forrest Scott Thompson, "The Present Crisis in the History of the American Mission in Egypt," typescript, c. 1912, preliminary outline; British and Foreign Bible Society, *One Hundred and Fifty-Third and Fifty-Fourth Reports of the British and Foreign Bible Society for the Years Ending December 31st 1957 and 1958* (London: Bible House, 1958), 84; and Cambridge University Library, Bible Society Archives, E1/3/7/5/6: Property: North Africa—BSA Egypt, including memoranda and correspondence from the British and Foreign Bible Society entitled, "Special Situation, UK/Egypt 1956-1957," December 1956–March 1959.

63. PHS UPCNA RG 209-21-24: Egypt mission, miscellaneous historical papers: "Should the American Mission dissolve its organization and merge itself into the Evangelical Church and its Organizations?" Unsigned typescript with handwritten insertions, 47 pages, dated American Mission Assiut, March 24, 1939.

64. Davida Finney, *Tomorrow's Egypt* (Pittsburgh: Women's General Missionary Society, 1939), 123; PHS UPCNA RG 209-2-51: Davida Finney Papers: Davida Finney to Dr. W. B. Anderson, dated Assiut, February 6, 1933, with attachment

consisting of short descriptions of the books published by the Joint [American Mission & Evangelical Church synod] Committee in 1930–32, prepared by Rev. Tawfik Saleh, Secretary of the Committee; PHS UPCNA RG 209-2-52: Davida Finney Papers, Finney to Glenn Reed, dated Cairo, April 9, 1942.

65. Frank C. Laubach and Robert S. Laubach, *Toward World Literacy: The Each One Teach One Way* (Syracuse: Syracuse University Press, 1960); Frank C. Laubach, *Teaching the World to Read: A Handbook for Literacy Campaigns* (New York: Friendship Press for the Committee on World Literacy and Christian Literature of the Foreign Missions Conference of North America, 1947).

66. PHS UPCNA RG 209-2-54: Davida M. Finney Papers, 1946–1957: Papers on the mission literacy campaigns and the Laubach method.

67. PHS UPCNA RG 209-2-53: Davida Finney Papers, Finney to Friend of the Laubach Campaign, dated Cairo, December 12, 1950; Garraud of UNWRA to Finney, dated Beirut, August 17, 1951; and Finney to Glenn [Reed], dated Cairo, June 15, 1951. PHS UPCNA RG 209-6-07: F. Scott Thompson Papers, "With the Quaker Relief Unit in Gaza," memoir by John A. Thompson (son of F. Scott Thompson), undated.

68. RG 209-2-10: Ewing M. Bailey Papers, E. M. Bailey to Dr. Black, dated Cairo, November 19, 1956.

69. Adib Galdas, *A Village Reborn: The Transformation of the People of a Village in Central Egypt after They Had Learned to Read in an All-Village Literacy Campaign: Told by Adib Galdas of Deir Abu Hinnis to Davida Finney* (New York: The Committee on World Literacy and Christian Literature, 1958), 6–7.

70. Aziz S. Atiya, *A History of Eastern Christianity* (London: Methuen & Co., 1968), 120–121; Hasan, *Christians versus Muslims in Modern Egypt*, 78, 97–98. There is some disagreement about when the Coptic Orthodox Church actually "joined" the World Council of Churches. It accepted an invitation to participate upon the organization's establishment in 1948, but only began to send observers in 1954 and official delegations in the early 1960s. Presumably that is why S. S. Hasan claims that its membership started in the early 1960s. See World Council of Churches, *Official Report of the First Assembly of the World Council of Churches* (New York: Harper & Brothers, 1949), 234. I am grateful to Stanley H. Skreslet for the last reference.

71. David W. Virtue, *A Vision of Hope: The Story of Samuel Habib* (Oxford: Regnum, 1996); Conversation with Dr. Nabil Abadir, Director of the Coptic Evangelical Organization of Social Services, Cairo, May 26, 2005.

72. Marjorie Dye, Davida Finney, Adib Galdas, and Samuel Habib, *Literacy—The Essential Skill: A Handbook for Literacy Workers* (New York: The Committee on World Literature Christian Literature, 1964).

73. Marjorie Dye, *The CEOSS Story* (Cairo: Dar al-Thaqafa, 1979), 35–38.

74. Galdas, *A Village Reborn*, 27–28.

75. Conversation with John G. Lorimer, Pasadena, California, August 29, 2004.

76. Sasson Somekh, "Biblical Echoes in Modern Arabic Literature," *Journal of Arabic Literature* 26 (1995): 186–200; Thompson, *The Major Arabic Bibles*, 20–27; and PHS RG 209-20-21: "The Arabic Bible," including two items: (1) Letter from Paul Erdman, Managing Editor, The American Press of the Board of Foreign Missions of the Presbyterian Church in the U.S.A., to Mrs. A. Birdwood of Tel el Kebir, Egypt, dated Beirut, Syria [*sic*], Sept. 24, 1930; and (2) "A Chapter in Bible History: First Font Reference Arabic Bible," by Franklin E. Hoskins, dated Beirut, Syria, August 1912, typescript carbon copy.

77. Rogerson speculates on the impact of modern Bible distribution on the culture of English-language Bible reading in J. W. Rogerson, *An Introduction to the Bible* (London: Penguin Books, 1999), 16–18. For a comparative study on the culture of Arabic literacy and reading, see Ami Ayalon, *Reading Palestine: Printing and Literacy, 1900–1948* (Austin: University of Texas Press, 2004).

78. Benedict Anderson, *Imagined Communities: Reflections on the Origin and Spread of Nationalism*, revised edition (London: Verso, 1991).

79. On the idea of modern "Coptism," see Paul Sedra, "Class Cleavages and Ethnic Conflict: Coptic Christian Communities in Modern Egyptian Politics," *Islam and Christian-Muslim Relations* 10:2 (1999): 219–235.

COMPARING MISSIONS

Pentecostal and Presbyterian Orphanages on the Nile

BETH BARON

MISSIONARIES TO THE MIDDLE EAST ARE OFTEN CHARACTERIZED AS modernizers in much of the scholarly literature. Forced to disavow their intended goal of converting Muslims due to Islamic injunctions against apostasy, missionaries turned, we are told, to civilizing and modernizing the local inhabitants, and they restricted their proselytizing to local Christians and Jews. They thus traded their short-term evangelical goals for long-term "enlightenment," building schools, hospitals, clinics, and refuges. While missionaries' letters home voice a strong desire to convert local Muslims, scholars have tended to see these writings as a part of strategy to cultivate donors. They argue that supporters back home had to be told that the missionaries were saving souls, particularly Muslim ones. Had they known that missionaries had become secular educators and health care providers, they would never have sent funds, particularly when some could barely afford to send their own children to schools and doctors.

The notion that missionaries were secularists in disguise has gained traction in part due to the emphasis in the scholarly literature on institutions of higher education. That missionary colleges and universities turned out secular intellectuals has reinforced the claim that missionaries were modernizers rather than failed proselytizers. However, most missionaries were not engaged in higher education but rather in preaching, teaching, healing, and distributing Bible literature, among other activities, and worked with broad sectors of the population rather than elites.

The claim that missionaries in the Middle East were modernizers has also grown out of an emphasis in the literature on mainstream Protestants (in particular Congregationalists and Presbyterians) rather than fundamentalists. Missionaries, who have been painted with broad brushstrokes, came in many shapes and sizes, and reflected a spectrum of Christian thought. They included Americans, British, Dutch, French, German, Italians, Swiss, and Scandinavians, and were affiliated (or not) with various Protestant denominations and Catholic orders. Protestant sects themselves diverged, with Presbyterians in Egypt and Lebanon, for example, coming from branches that had split over slavery and other issues.

Missionaries worked their programs out in practice in sites such as orphanages, where they had intimate contact with locals. This chapter juxtaposes the histories of two orphanages started by American missionary women in Egypt in the early twentieth century. The two orphanages would seem to have parallel histories, yet they diverged in important ways. Margaret (Maggie) Smith established the Fowler Orphanage for girls in Cairo in 1906 as part of a network of educational and health institutions sponsored by the mission of the United Presbyterian Church of North America (UPCNA). Five years later, Lillian Trasher established the Assiout Orphanage as an independent institute, later on affiliating it with the Assemblies of God Church.[1]

By throwing Pentecostals into the mix, it is not my intention to create a binary—Presbyterians as modern and Pentecostals as not. In fact, fundamentalist churches arose in the early twentieth-century United States as a product of modernity as well as in reaction to it. By juxtaposing Lillian Trasher's experiment with that of Margaret Smith, and putting Pentecostal missionaries on the radar of scholars, I hope to raise questions about the modernizing agendas of Protestant missionaries as well as their supposed homogeneity. Missionaries across the board embodied multiple tendencies and their evangelizing combined contradictory elements, with locals taking away what they wanted from the contact.

A Home in Cairo: The Presbyterian-Quaker Partnership

American Presbyterians started, in their words, to "occupy" towns and cities in Egypt in the 1850s. Having arrived after the Church Missionary Society of England had abandoned the field, they claimed it as their own. Under unwritten missionary rules extant in the nineteenth century, establishing colonies or outposts in vacant areas effectively marked them as theirs to evangelize. The British occupation from 1882 offered privileges—patronage, passes, and protections—and drew competitors. Some of them provided services that complemented those of the UPCNA: distributing Bibles, setting up a Christian printing press, establishing branches of the YMCA and YWCA, and starting the American (Christian) University in Cairo. Eventually an interdenominational council was inaugurated to coordinate activities and present a united front to the Egyptian government.

During their hundred years in Egypt, the Presbyterians dominated the missionary field, intermarrying among a number of families who served for multiple generations and creating a bureaucracy to oversee their activities. To reach the broader population, the missionaries offered an array of educational and medical services at a time when such social services were limited. The members of the Egyptian Missionary Association, which in its heyday numbered well over a hundred men and women, met twice a year to discuss business: they voted on membership and tenure; heard recommendations of committees that met throughout the year; bargained over finances and apportioned funds; and confirmed assignments in schools, hospitals, and homes. The association reported back to the board, or boards in the United States—the male Missionary Board and the Women's General Missionary Society (WGMS)—upon whom they depended for recruits and resources. One of the distinguishing features of the UPCNA's missionary activity was the longevity of its women's missionary arm, which took responsibility for a number of schools and eventually the entire medical mission.[2] The link between the home and foreign front was crucial in sustaining the enterprise.

The Presbyterian missionaries in Egypt had a sense of mission and of history. They left a trove of material for future generations, including diaries, journals, letters, newspaper clippings, pamphlets, minutes from biannual meetings, annual reports, photographs, missionary magazines, and other assorted documents. Much of this archival material is stored at the Presbyterian Historical Society in Philadelphia, with some of the published material available elsewhere, particularly at theological libraries with earlier Presbyterian roots. The bulk of material is in English, with the occasional Arabic document finding its way into the records; there are also extensive summaries and translations of material from the Arabic press which relate to mission work but have relevance far beyond it.

Many Presbyterian missionaries spent years in the field, learning Arabic in intensive and carefully monitored programs. Their knowledge of Arabic and interest in living among potential converts rather than apart from the people gave them an access to society that many other foreign observers lacked. Their biases are quite clear and must be considered when reading through reports and other literature produced for varying purposes. The sheer volume of material and its diversity can be overwhelming.

The orphanage founded by American Presbyterians in Egypt must be seen in the context of a network of social services. These services were meant to be self-sustaining, not charities, and fees were charged, sometimes on a sliding scale. Those served by the missionaries met them in the guise of teachers, nurses, matrons, doctors, and Bible readers. The missionaries were there to convert Egyptians of all backgrounds—Muslims, Jews, and Orthodox Christians (Copts)—and in so doing "save" them. The orphanage was not the central institution of the mission, or even a main one, but was one of its most successful enterprises.

The Presbyterian orphanage must also be seen in the context of the history of orphanages in Egypt.[3] Orphanages arose in nineteenth-century Egypt as part of the expansion of Ottoman-Egyptian state welfare. The idea of gathering together abandoned and orphaned children under one roof, separating them from relatives, and segregating them from other indigents while providing for their needs and giving them industrial work was novel. When the British occupied Egypt in 1882, they forced the state to cut back on welfare services, closing schools and refuges and privatizing social services. Catholic and Protestant missionaries found an easy opening.

Margaret Smith was the organizing spirit behind the Fowler Orphanage. She arrived in Egypt in 1872 as a single missionary, joining the growing American group, which included Anna Thompson. Smith and Thompson spent sixty years in close proximity in Egypt. Thompson described her petite friend as "humble and unpretending," although admitting she also could be "indomitable."[4] Earl Elder concurred, "Mission tradition has it that it was Miss Margaret Smith, a timid, new missionary, who when the mission association came into being, stuck by her guns and asserted her right and along with it that of all unmarried women to sit as a member of the association."[5]

Yet unlike Anna Thompson, who left a long paper trail including diaries, letters, and other papers, Smith's literary output was limited. Her activities can
be followed mostly through her reports and the records of her colleagues and
friends in the mission.[6]

After completing the requisite Arabic course, Smith, like many single female missionaries, took up teaching and directed the girls' school in Harat
al-Saqqa'in, an assignment she had for thirty-two years. The school grew to
become one of the largest in Egypt, attracting daughters of the elite, including the children of 'Urabi Pasha, the nationalist leader exiled for his role
in the 1882 revolt that led to the British occupation. Smith also organized
women Bible readers within the quarter who visited homes to read to illiterate women.[7] The story of these women, and how they were perceived, remains an untold story.

For years, Smith had dreamt of starting a home for homeless children.
Street children had become a preoccupation of British officials and Western residents, and few institutions served them. Smith found patrons in Esther and John Fowler, an American Quaker couple from Ohio who visited
Cairo in 1895 and were disturbed by the numerous street children they encountered. Impressed by Smith's missionary school, they raised over eight
thousand dollars in funds for an orphanage upon their return home. That
amount was insufficient to buy a property and sustain a home but was a start,
and the Fowlers began negotiating with the Board of Foreign Missions on
an agreement. The board was not in the business of providing social services
that could not be self-supporting—schools could charge tuition and hospitals fees, but what fees could orphans pay?—and feared the expensive plan
first proposed by John Fowler. The Egyptian Missionary Association set up
a "Fowler Orphanage Committee" to develop a plan to establish and run
the orphanage, which was named for the fund-raisers. American missionaries won approval of a plan from the board only when Smith promised not to
approach the board or anyone else directly for funds. The project was to be
faith-based with funds coming in answer to prayer.[8] Smith could still write
lengthy and colorful accounts for inclusion in missionary reports and magazines, which would spur readers to contribute, and communicate with the
Fowlers or a committee of their friends established after their deaths to carry
on their work.

Once authorized by the American Board, Margaret Smith began placing orphans in existing girls' schools, paying their upkeep out of the "Fowler Orphanage Fund." The first six orphans received were placed in the Fum al-Khalig School, which Smith was directing at the time, and she was officially named superintendent of the orphanage. After a few months, a better accommodation—the home of a deceased priest whose son was sympathetic to the project and whose daughter-in-law had attended one of Smith's schools—was found close by and rented for the school and the orphanage.[9] Yet that home proved inadequate within a few years, and the missionaries began looking for a suitable property on which to build a new home, moving again in the interim.

The project of building a permanent home received a boost in 1909 when a Mrs. Arnold of Pittsburgh left a legacy of ten thousand dollars toward the cause. Smith appealed to the Women's Board (the WGMS) for support.[10] In the end, the missionaries converted the old Austro-Hungarian Hospital in 'Abbasiyya, which had been sequestered at the outset of World War I, into an orphanage. Bought for five thousand dollars, it was renovated with an additional one thousand dollars, and the 'Abbasiyya Girls' School was added.[11]

During her tenure as head of the orphanage, Smith pushed for expanded quarters, petitioned and updated the board and "Friend Fowler" on details pertaining to the new institution, pressed fellow missionaries into service, and utilized the educational and health services of the mission to help her girls. As the home grew, and Smith grew older, she required more assistance. Smith appealed to the Women's Board to name Ellen Barnes, who was already in the field assisting, a missionary.[12] Smith managed the home until 1920, when age, exhaustion, and failing eyesight forced her to hand over control to Barnes. In the interim and beyond, other women in the field helped in the home. Ellen Barnes was assisted by Annie Dinsmore through 1939, when Lucy Lightowler, who was assisted by Jane Smith, took over. From 1947 to 1949, Helen Armstrong served as head and in 1952 Elizabeth Wilson became superintendent.[13]

Prospective orphans were presented by family members or others to the committee and underwent a physical exam, toughened after one girl entered with typhus. A physician from the Tanta Mission Hospital was drafted onto the committee and called in to give check-ups and advice.[14] Those accepted for entry were also the subject of a contract outlining the terms. Within its first year, twenty-three girls had been admitted to the orphanage; since six left, the balance stood at seventeen.[15] Six months later, the total admitted stood at thirty-nine with twenty-three remaining.[16] After the move to the renovated hospital in 1915, numbers stood at sixty-three, and generally the number of girls in the orphanage fluctuated between forty and sixty.[17] But with limited space, it was hard to gain admission. In 1920 fifteen girls entered, with six applicants turned down.[18] A report filed in 1937 estimated that over two hundred girls had "graduated" from the orphanage. But many others were rejected at the outset or had only short residencies, and roughly one-quarter to one-third seemed to be expelled or left in the early years.

The orphanage opened with two Greek girls. The appeal of their widowed mother had strengthened Smith's resolve to start the project. But that pair left within a week, taken by Roman Catholic priests, who, according to the report "had a greater claim on them." Two Syrian girls, one aged three and one five, were among the youngest the first year. As Smith told the story, their mother had deserted their father, converted to Islam, married, and sent them to a Muslim school. Their father, in turn, had taken them from the school and brought them to the orphanage to be raised as Christians.[19] Many of the girls who found their way into the orphanage, for shorter or longer stays, were caught up in similar familial feuds waged between a divorced husband and wife. Some girls were fatherless, some motherless, some had lost both parents, and some had both but were caught up in the drama of divorce.

Another category of girls were those whose mothers were "living a disreputable life." How actively missionaries sought out children of prostitutes, seeing both the mothers and children as particularly vulnerable, is not clear. Smith complained when one such Syrian woman reneged on the fee mentioned in the contract that she had to pay if she did not leave her child in the orphanage until the age of eighteen.[20] Presumably the fee would have been a financial incentive not to reclaim her child. In the first year, the girls ranged from three and one-half to twelve. These were not foundlings but rather girls whose family members appealed for their entry. Only occasionally does a foundling find her way in. "[A] dear, dirty, half starved, cross-eyed baby girl was given to us to bring up for the Lord," Smith wrote in 1910. "What little she wore, even the tuft of her hair on the top of her head was cast into the fire…we call her Timmy for short."[21]

The reports are careful to note the religious backgrounds of the girls in the home. In July 1907, of the twenty-three: ten were Copts, three were Protestants, three Roman Catholic, three Greek Catholic, and four Muslims.[22] In subsequent years, the reports mention Armenians, Jews, and Syrian Catholics among the residents of the home. The agenda of converting all of the girls to Protestantism was clear. The schooling and routine of the girls carefully instilled Christian values. Their days were filled with schooling, prayer, and housework, the bulk of which was carried on by the older girls. A day school was intermittently connected to the orphanage; the girls received their early schooling there and then went on to other missionary schools for upper level education. In the 1920s, industrial work was added: the girls made silver shawls, bead bags, and garments for sale, and later dolls were added to their repertoire.[23]

Each report details the number of girls expressing an interest in joining the church, being examined, and undergoing baptism. The biggest prize for the missionaries was clearly the conversion of Muslim girls. But Smith was careful to wait until they had reached their majority (eighteen) before accepting them formally into the church. "There are now fourteen Church members besides two Moslem girls who were examined and would have been baptized if there were religious freedom; but as there is no such freedom they were asked to wait until they are older," Smith wrote in 1909.[24] The next year, all six of the "Mohammedan girls" had asked for baptism, Smith reported, but were delayed for instruction until their majority.[25] The intent of the missionaries was not lost on Egyptians. In one of the early reports, Smith noted that three girls had been withdrawn, among them "a dear little ten-year-old Mohammedan...stolen by her father and married soon after because he feared she might become a Christian" as well as "a Jewess...taken away recently—being stolen by her mother, also on account of the religion of Jesus."[26]

After the orphanage's thirty-year anniversary in 1936, Ellen Barnes provided an accounting of the girls in the home. She sought to counter the prevailing perception among Egyptians and even some missionaries that the orphans were all destined to be servants.[27] They were raised, instead, for service to the Protestant missions. The report gives the first names, professions, and marital status of many of those who went through the home. Among the graduates, forty-one were teachers, seventeen Bible women, sixteen hospital maids and nurses, and twenty-six home helpers, with some changing professions. The missionaries had prepared the girls for lives in Christian service as well as becoming Christian mothers; and collectively, the girls donated hundreds of years of service to mission institutions. Barnes wrote that "about two hundred girls have found a truly Christian home and a training which has resulted in many of these girls going out into various lines of Christian service."[28]

The report does not show what these graduates thought of their upbringing, whether their education and socialization had prepared them for life in Egypt, and if it had alienated them from their own society. (Jamila Bargach argues that missionary orphanages in Morocco often alienated local orphans from their culture.[29]) The report also does not discuss those girls who entered the institution but left, or were forced to leave, after a short period. The Fowler Orphanage, which changed its name to the Fowler Home in 1945 to sound less institutional, left its imprint on those girls who had passed through, even if briefly, on the women who worked in the home, on those who had funded and served it, and on its neighbors. Yet it was quite a different institution than the Assiout Orphanage, to which we now turn.

A VILLAGE IN ASYUT: FAITH AND PENTECOSTALS

The American Presbyterian mission to Egypt overshadowed the Pentecostal endeavor half a century later. But the Pentecostal endeavor outlasted the Presbyterian mission in large part due to one of its oldest institutions: the Assiout Orphanage. Started in 1911, the orphanage grew into a village that had its own schools, church, clinic, bakery, dairy, dormitories, and swimming pool, and was seen within the Assemblies of God Church as a testimony to the power of faith and prayer. The Assiout Orphanage became the heart of the Pentecostal missionary effort in Egypt and key to its success, producing many of its converts, preachers, and leaders.

Lillian Trasher, the founder of the orphanage and one of the most prominent Pentecostal missionaries of the twentieth century, built up a strong circle of supporters through letters that were excerpted regularly from the 1910s in such periodicals as *Word and Witness, Latter Rain Evangel, Christian Evangel, Weekly Evangel,* and *Pentecostal Evangel.* Her story reached a wide audience in 1939 when she was featured in an article by Jerome Beatty in the *American Magazine* under the title "Nile Mother." In 1951, a biography written by Lester Sumrall with the cooperation of Trasher appeared under the imprint of the Gospel Publishing House in Springfield, Missouri, as *Lillian Trasher: The Nile Mother*. That year, the movie "The Nile Mother" made its Hollywood debut and the rounds of American churches as a fund-raising vehicle. Inspired by the story, Beth Prim Howell took poetic license and wrote *Lady on a Donkey*, which appeared in 1960, published by a commercial press in New York.[30] After Trasher's death in 1961, the legend continued to flourish. In 1983, the Assemblies of God Division of Foreign Missions published excerpts from Trasher's letters, some of which had appeared in their periodicals, as *Letters from Lillian*.[31] The most recent account of her life, *Lillian Trasher: The Greatest Wonder in Egypt* (2004), is part of a children's series about Christian heroes.[32] Although the contents of these texts vary, they have generally framed her life as an affirmation of Christian faith.

In 1910, at the age of twenty-three, Lillian Trasher felt called to serve in Africa. She went out without the backing of a board or church to the Nile town of Asyut in southern Egypt. Shortly after her arrival, she responded to an appeal to attend to a dying woman. Had those who had knocked on the doors of the Pentecostal missionaries thought they would get medicine along with prayer? If so, they had confused the Pentecostals, who often turned to faith healing, with the Presbyterians, who used medical evangelizing to attract potential converts and founded a hospital in Asyut. Prayer did not save the woman, who may have been beyond the help of medicine. When her relatives handed Lillian her infant girl, Trasher saw in this, as in all things, the hand of God. She returned to the Pentecostal mission home with the baby, and when her hosts lost patience with the infant's crying, she rented a home and began the Malga' al-Aytam al-Khayri bi-Asyut, which was shortened in English to the Assiout Orphanage.

While years of planning went into the Fowler Orphanage, Lillian Trasher, who was unfettered by a board, acted spontaneously, trusting that God would provide. She chose the most marginal of people for her ministry, orphans and abandoned children, who by definition lacked family in a society that saw family as its basis and family lineage as critical to creating marital and other bonds. No such institution existed in Asyut or its environs at the time, and its beginnings were modest: "Then we took in a few children, but at first it was very hard to get them."[33] Egyptians initially suspected that she planned to take the orphans as servants or slaves to America. The thought was not that strange given Asyut's historical role as a major depot of the slave trade and the destination for caravans on the "forty days road" from the Sudan, as well as Presbyterian missionaries' past interest in helping slaves.[34]

The orphanage had a rocky start. After one child entered with bubonic plague, the home was temporarily closed. Lillian traveled to the United States to recuperate from illness and there in the summer of 1912 in North Carolina became ordained as an evangelist, something which would have been odd, perhaps, for a Presbyterian but not evidently for a Pentecostal woman.[35] She returned to Asyut, where the orphanage began to grow in size: "Every week I have to turn away four or five little ignorant children from lack of space who might be taught and led to Christ," Lillian wrote in 1913.[36] By the next year she had fifty children under her care. A Turkish woman taught them rug making, and a sixty-five-year-old missionary from Indiana helped out. Lillian decided to move the home out of the city to Abnub, a village on the east bank of the Nile where land was cheaper and the air cleaner.[37]

During World War I, Lillian Trasher stayed on in the orphanage with a staff that included Shaker Gadallah and two other native women. They struggled to feed the children in the midst of a high spike in the prices of staples. Lillian solicited funds and food in the town and surrounding villages. After the May wheat harvest when peasants were paid, Lillian rode out to villages on a donkey.[38] She was occasionally away from the orphanage for a few days at a time, staying in police stations along the way. Villagers called the itinerant Western woman the "lady on a donkey." Yet somehow she gained their trust along with gifts of food and cash. These visits to Egyptian villages gave Lillian contacts with mayors, who later asked her to take in their widows and orphans. Through this travel, she also saw how villagers lived and resolved to "civilize" the peasant children in her institution.

The orphanage doubled in size during the war, from roughly fifty to one hundred children. To accommodate the new residents, rooms were added on, in a process that became a pattern for the home. Once the children got older, they participated in the brick-making and laying process. At the end of the war an influenza epidemic that left orphans in its wake added to the numbers. "We are glad to accept the most needy cases, and have had to enlarge our house, adding four new rooms which are about filled," wrote Trasher in early 1919.[39] The boys learned trades such as carpentry and shoemaking, while the girls were taught sewing, childcare, and housework.

In March and April 1919, demonstrations in Cairo grew into a national-ist revolt. An American Presbyterian minister tried to persuade Lillian to take refuge with the other Americans and Europeans in the boys' secondary school, but she refused to leave the orphanage. After communication with Cairo was severed and the banks limited access to funds, Lillian consulted with "Auntie" Zakiya, the head matron, and decided to send all of those chil-dren with relatives in Asyut and nearby villages home. When British sol-diers reached the region, they notified Trasher that the children had to evac-uate the orphanage for safer quarters in Asyut and that she had to leave with the other Westerners on barges sent up the Nile from Cairo. The boys were moved into town into one of the American Presbyterian schools and the girls and babies into the American Presbyterian Hospital. Trasher left by boat for Cairo in the company of Pentecostal missionaries Brother and Sister Post. Restless in Cairo and blocked from returning immediately to Asyut, she de-cided to visit the United States, during which time she registered as an evan-gelist of the infant Assemblies of God Church and raised funds for the or-phanage.[40]

Trasher returned to the orphanage on the east bank in February 1920, taking in more orphans. "You cannot imagine how I feel when I have to re-fuse some," she lamented. "There are no other orphanages within hundreds of miles from here and the other orphanages in Cairo and Alexandria will not take in new ones until some of the older ones leave."[41] Rather than con-tinue to turn away children, Trasher expanded the orphanage. The enlarge-ment of the facility was made possible by a gift of $1,500 from Sultan (later King) Fu'ad (r.1917–1936) in 1921.[42] His visit to the orphanage was one in a line of Egyptian rulers and foreign royals, such as the Queen of Belgium, who sought to demonstrate their benevolence and enhance their legitimacy through charitable giving.

The Khayyats and Wissas, along with other notable families such as the Dosses and Alexans, continued to play a critical role in sustaining the or-phanage. Their Sports Club contained a box for charitable donations that Trasher periodically emptied.[43] Women such as Lily (Alexan) Khayyat and Esther (Fanus) Wissa were friends and supporters of the Assiout Orphan-age through the years. They took out subscriptions, started sewing circles, and sent gifts of wheat, beef, cooked meals, cotton, and cloth. They cele-brated births, weddings, and major life events with donations, and looked after Trasher. They invited her for meals and outings to Cairo, and sent her new dresses for herself, while she looked after the orphans. Riding out to villages on a donkey was no longer necessary: "They realize that I have given my life for their children and show their appreciation in many ways," wrote Trasher in 1924.[44]

Yet wealthy Egyptians were not the only ones who gave. Middle-strata merchants and poor workers and peasants gave money or gifts in kind—ranging from free taxi rides to stocks of soap and other essential items—when they could. The community valued Trasher's commitment to caring for orphans, offering a service that they themselves were uninterested or unwilling to provide. The orphanage charged no admission fees, accepting boys under ten and girls under twelve. Trasher wanted the children long term in order to work the transformation to body and soul that she envisioned. At some point the orphanage set basic rules for admission that required relatives "to sign a paper that they give the children to us until they are eighteen years old," at which point they would have reached their legal civil majority.[45] The orphanage accepted children with disabilities, children of lepers, and blind girls (but not blind boys, for whom there was already a home in Egypt).

"In extreme cases a child that is partly orphan is admitted," Trasher explained, by which she meant one parent was still alive.[46] However, in Islamic family law, which Copts followed on issues of inheritance, a child could not really be a "part" orphan. An orphan (*yatim*, plural *aytam* or *yatama*) was legally one whose father had died.

Infants were often brought in by fathers after their wives had died in childbirth or later from complications. Thus many of those who were deposited at the orphanage were not technically orphans but offspring of single fathers who had insufficient knowledge, will, means, or relations to raise motherless children. "I received a new baby girl last night three months old, whose mother is dead and she is nothing but skin and bones. We named her Sophie," wrote Trasher in 1925.[47] Maternal mortality rates were high at a time when women went through multiple pregnancies with limited medical interventions. "We got three newborn babies this month; their mothers died when they were born," Trasher wrote a few years later, giving their names as Amena, Objy, and Marium.[48] "Yesterday we got nothing at all in the way of money," Trasher noted in 1931, "but the Lord sent us a darling little baby boy three days old. His mother died when he was born."[49] Two years later, "Someone brought us tiny twin babies this morning. Poor little things—their mother died when they were born. They look very weak; I am afraid they will not live, but we will do our best."[50] The weakest infants were sent for care to the American Presbyterian Hospital in Asyut.

Another set of children arrived with widowed mothers who had no financial resources or willing relatives to help raise fatherless offspring. Roughly ten percent of the population of the orphanage at any given moment consisted of widows. They kept their infants with them in shared accommodations, but their weaned and older children were separated and placed in dormitories. "[I]t quite often happens that a child is received with its widowed mother, who earns her support by working in the orphanage, whilst the children receive full training along with the others," Trasher wrote.[51] These widowed women were indispensable to the orphanage: They washed clothes and dishes, and performed other menial tasks such as mending and cooking, and served as the backbone of the labor force. Although knit into the fabric of the orphanage as workers, the widows essentially remained *fellahat* (peasant women) and were divested of authority over their own children. The latter were remade into Pentecostal Christians.

The orphanage also accepted foundlings (*luqata'*, singular *laqit* or *laqita*). These infants were not legally orphans, for their parents were still presumably alive but had abandoned them for one reason or another. "About two weeks ago I had some one knock at my door about midnight and hand me a wee tiny baby, just a few hours old which they had found in the street," wrote Trasher in 1921. "We had one like this one a little while ago, but its head had been injured when it had been thrown away and it went quite blind and then it died."[52] Abandoned infants were found in various locations, often in precarious situations. "Lageah, the baby we found on the bridge, died last night," she wrote in 1927.[53] Another was found the winter of 1928 near the railroad track by a carpenter who worked at the American College. "They brought me the baby, a little boy, with not even a cloth over him; he was on a saddle pad and an old bran sack, covered with sand and dirt. He had been out in that awful cold wind for hours, quite naked, and only a few hours old." He was named Faheem Abd Alla. His last name—servant of God—was common for one whose parentage was unknown.[54] Infants were also found in wheat fields and the Nile River, evoking the story of Moses.[55] A few children were deposited directly on Trasher's doorsteps, with no identification, name, or place of origin.

Some "fallen girls" also found refuge in the orphanage with their infants. British officials in Cairo asked Trasher to give safe haven to one such unmarried mother: Her boyfriend had been killed by her father and brother, who in turn had been hanged, but the girl's mother and a younger brother still presented a physical threat to her and the child. "We would be very grateful if you could see your way to admitting this girl to your home," the authorities requested, wanting "to give her a chance to lead a decent life and avoid the risk of assassination by her family." Trasher accepted the pair, having her own motives: "Others have come like this and have been wonderfully saved."[56]

As matriarch and patriarch of this large family, Trasher was interested in sustaining bodies and saving souls. In the winter of 1926 she began to see results: "After crying and praying like the sound of many waters, they began to testify. One little Mohammedan boy got up on top of the bench and testified saying," according to Trasher, "'In my village I was a sinner but now God has saved me and if I was cut in little pieces I would not serve idols.'" Having absorbed the Protestant critique of Catholicism and Orthodox Christianity, the boy referred most probably to the presence of icons in Coptic churches. Trasher continued, "Souls are being saved and others baptized in the Holy Spirit."[57] The movement grew, and after seventeen "dry" years, the "harvest" began during a convention the following April (1927).

> Today I witnessed the greatest revival I have ever seen in my life. Three days ago [April 5] we started a revival meeting among the children. The Spirit was with us from the very first meeting, dozens getting saved and dozens seeking the baptism of the Holy Spirit.... But the most wonderful sight I ever saw in my life was when I followed the noise up to the housetop. There were dozens and dozens of little girls shouting, crying, talking in tongues, rejoicing, preaching, singing—well, just everything you can think of—praising God! Several of the children saw visions.

The revival spread from the girls, to the widows, to the boys, including older ones who lived in town and were called to the orphanage to participate.[58] A couple of days later,

The power of God is just sweeping the Orphanage like a mighty flood.... Hundreds of the children are on their faces screaming out to God for mercy, some shouting for joy and rejoicing in the marvelous, new found blessing, others talking in tongues, others standing on top of the tables, preaching, still others seeking the baptism.... Just now a little Mohammedan girl is down stairs preaching to a little cripple girl; no one is tired though they have prayed and prayed for hours.[59]

There was no count of how many had been "born again," although fifty had received "the Baptism with the Holy Spirit with the sign of speaking in other tongues," according to H. E. Randall, a Pentecostal pastor, who was on hand for the revival.[60] Some of the boys and girls raised in the orphanage began to go out to evangelize and otherwise assist in Assemblies of God missions around Asyut and elsewhere in Egypt, and another revival broke out February 3, 1933. Later, as the antimissionary movement grew, state officials removed most of the Muslim children from the orphanage.[61]

When Jerome Beatty visited the orphanage in 1939, there were 647 orphans and 74 widows.[62] The orphanage had grown into a virtual village with a number of structures. At that size, Trasher needed a hardworking, loyal staff. She recruited an array of foreign missionaries and local talent: A German nurse ran the clinic and assisted an Egyptian doctor who volunteered his time; a British missionary headed the girls' school; and an American Pentecostal missionary (Florence Christie) taught, delivered babies, and supervised the girls.[63] Christie later described Trasher as a woman who "possessed a loving, but strong personality, which people sometimes found hard to follow. I considered it a challenge. She was known to be difficult to work for also because of her high expectations and demands." There was only one "Mama." The other women, as Christie quickly learned when she saw Trasher could be jealous of the children's attention, were "Aunties."[64]

The widows, who continued to seek shelter due to their poverty, also continued to provide a crucial part of the labor in the orphanage. To their domestic chores of laundry, cooking, baking, and cleaning were added milking when the orphanage began raising Jersey cattle donated by the American Presbyterian Mission. The widows "were not allowed to care for children because they were still too much like the village they had left," noted Christie. The older girls, who were taught to be "clean and cultured," cared for the younger ones.[65] The widows were finally given separate quarters and some privacy in 1939 with the completion of a special building. When Trasher "dared to suggest" that their older children remain a few more nights in the dormitories until the rooms were finished, the widows rebelled, telling her, "We can crowd on a quilt on the floor, just anything, only don't take the children away from us again!"[66] For the widows, the orphanage provided a way out of poverty and hunger, yet it came at a price. They had little say over the upbringing of their children and experienced enforced separations.

Boys were taught artisan skills (carpentry and chair making) and girls trained in domestic tasks (infant care and sewing). Both had farming tasks, with girls feeding and collecting chicken eggs and some boys working with barn animals. The boys attended primary and secondary schools at the orphanage, and if they had the aptitude, could continue on to college. They took up the trades into which they had been apprenticed or alternatively took up careers as teachers, clerks, and pastors. Some of the boys became active in the Assemblies of God Church in Egypt, forming its core. They evangelized in villages, started schools and churches, and staffed missions scattered about Egypt.

The girls attended a general school; even if they excelled in their studies, they were not offered the option of continuing their educations. They were prepared instead for marriage. Trasher made it clear that her girls were not hired out as domestic servants, for that might have compromised their reputations and hurt their chances for marriage. Most of the girls married. Those who did not stayed on at the orphanage as helpers, with the exception of a few who felt "called" and were allowed to join female American missionaries in their work outside the orphanage.

The orphanage instilled American culture and values. The children learned English in addition to Arabic and dressed in American-style clothes that were either sent from the states or made at the orphanage (though Trasher said that the girls preferred high collars and boys long shorts, in a nod toward local customs). While cutting patterns and sewing clothes, they listened to such hymns on the gramophone as "Onward, Christian Soldiers!" "We Are Going Down the Valley," and "Joy to the World." They did not play recordings of Umm Kulthum, the most famous Egyptian singer of the century, whose records were available from the 1920s.[67] They also learned to make quilts from sewing scraps. "We feel that it is a good lesson for Egypt, as our married girls carry the idea with them to the different villages."[68]

Yet Christie did not permit American norms of gender mixing. Boys and girls had separate dormitories and schools, and separate seating in church and dining halls. With the exceptions of siblings, boys and girls were not allowed to talk to one another. When the boys were ready to leave the orphanage, they approached Trasher to ask permission to marry one of the girls. She decided if they were suitable, allowing them to meet in her presence but not to date or court one another. She did this at a time when many Egyptians challenged such conventions, calling for meeting before marriage and endorsing the ideal of companionate marriage. Trasher also did not allow the blind girls to marry, which according to Christie was a practical approach to "an already severe problem," but seemed rather draconian for those denied a choice.[69]

During World War II, when most American missionaries were evacuated from Egypt with those in Asyut heading south to Sudan, Trasher stayed put. She sent Christie to America to raise funds, which were in short supply in the midst of war, and the orphanage opened its doors to those grown children who had become refugees when cities such as Alexandria were bombed. The orphanage survived the war intact, but faced greater challenges in its wake when cholera and malarial epidemics devastated the countryside. Reinforcements of American missionaries such as Philip and Hazel Crouch helped Trasher, who was no longer young.

"It is whispered around the city of Assiut that it is always good to give an offering to the orphanage when God has been good to you!" wrote Lester Sumrall in 1951.[70] With donations from Egyptians and Americans, the Assiout Orphanage continued to expand. Trasher decided to transform the hospital into a nursery, keeping only those babies under seven months in her home and building a new hospital for sick children. Ground was broken for the new building in late 1951, in expectation that gifts would be forthcoming, and it opened the following year.[71]

Revolutionary winds transformed Egypt in 1952 when a group of officers, who were led by Gamal Abdel Nasser, toppled King Farouk (r.1936–1952) and inaugurated military rule by a Revolutionary Command Council (RCC). This in turn effectively put an end to the British presence in Egypt as well as the residence of most of the foreign missionaries they had protected.

Nasser, who was born in Alexandria in 1918, had spent many summers and some school years in Bani Murr, his father's natal village, which was adjacent to Abnub. His earlier familiarity with the institution probably helped to save it from the fate of other missionary institutions and its founder-director from expulsion.[72]

Trasher had benefited from the infrastructure and friendship of the American Presbyterian missionaries in Asyut, but their days were numbered after the revolution. The Presbyterians had been in retreat from the 1930s due to decreasing support at home and the increasing antimissionary movement in Egypt. As a result, they had gradually transferred most of their schools, hospitals, and other properties, including the Fowler Home, over to the Egyptian Evangelical Church. This process of indigenization was meant to avoid massive confiscations, and the Presbyterians phased out their mission in the 1950s.[73] In contrast to the Presbyterians, the Assemblies of God were on the upsurge in America, and their missionary fervor in Egypt was still strong. The church elected an Egyptian superintendent in the 1940s, but American Assemblies of God missionaries continued to visit and work in Egypt, albeit under new and sometimes erratic constraints.

Lillian was not downsizing or planning to leave. At the start of 1957, the orphanage headcount stood at 1,035, not including refugees from the Suez Canal region, and she pledged to take an additional twenty-five to thirty children from Port Said who had been orphaned by the 1956 Suez War.[74] The next year the orphanage built a new school to accommodate the growing numbers, and supporters sent supplies. When a new car got held up in customs, Nasser waived the duties. "I would like to tell you that your work for the orphans is very much appreciated by everyone in this country," Nasser wrote in a note that he personally signed.[75] The Egyptian press celebrated her as "Mother of a Thousand."[76]

Lillian Trasher cut short a trip to the United States in 1960 when she grew ill, not wanting to die and be buried away from her orphanage family. She returned to Egypt, where she celebrated the fiftieth anniversary of the orphanage in February 1961 and died later that year, on December 17. The Egyptian and Pentecostal press mourned the passing of a "saint," "virgin mother of thousands of Egyptians," "Nile Mother," and "Mama" Lillian. Former residents of the orphanage returned for the funeral, the largest in Asyut's history:

a six-horse carriage led the procession through the streets of the city to a plot in the orphanage cemetery where she was buried alongside her "children."

CONCLUSION

The Assiout Orphanage (renamed Trasher Orphanage after her death) and Fowler Home survived the assault on missionary structures precisely because they provided social services to a group on the margins of society. Few competed to care for those whose unclear paternity carried a stigma of shame and who had uncertain futures. Both Margaret Smith and Lillian Trasher saw a need and an opportunity. They had come to Egypt to "spread the gospel" and "word of God," and launched faith-based projects that gave meaning to their lives as single American women abroad, fulfilling spiritual and maternal ambitions at the same time. There are other marked similarities between the missionary endeavors of Smith and Trasher. Both women spent years of service in Egypt, with Trasher totaling fifty years in the field and Smith sixty; and both launched institutions that assisted orphaned and abandoned Egyptian children within years of one another that took root and flourished. Both Smith and Trasher saw the orphans as empty slates ready for conversion. That they also sought to "civilize" and "discipline" the children and teach them the rewards of hard work and hygiene did not mean that they had a secular agenda.

Yet the differences between these two institutions highlight the diversity of missionary projects and raise questions about the limits and extent of modernizing. Smith served with the American Presbyterian Mission, launched her orphanage after many years in the field and years of planning, and administered it with assistance from the Egyptian Missionary Association and boards back home. The Fowler Orphanage became a home to on average forty to sixty girls and over time hundreds of girls. Smith earned the vote in association meetings but remained within a strict hierarchical structure. Trasher started her orphanage spontaneously without the support of a board shortly after she had arrived in Upper Egypt and only later affiliated with the Assemblies of God Church. Her enterprise grew into a virtual city of orphans and widows, housing at its height some 1,400 children and widows with some 8,000 passing through the doors of the home until the time of her death.

The Presbyterians mobilized doctors from their medical mission in Tanta to help screen and treat orphans in the Fowler Orphanage. Trasher initially relied on faith healing but subsequently turned to the personnel of the American Presbyterian Hospital in Asyut for help with infants and epidemics and later opened her own orphanage hospital. The Presbyterians championed girls' education and started secondary schools and colleges for girls in Asyut and Cairo; by contrast, Trasher brought up the orphan girls to be good wives and mothers, and blocked secondary or advanced education for her girls. Moreover, at a time in which Egyptian reformers encouraged girls' higher education as well as integration of men and women, Trasher maintained a strict policy of segregation. Unlike Presbyterians, who delayed baptism until after years of education, the Pentecostals baptized believers without the test of time and encouraged revivals toward this end. They propagated a fundamentalist version of Christianity that included prophesying, talking in tongues, and being baptized in the Holy Spirit. Scenes of their revivals contrast with the well-ordered prayers and services of Presbyterians. And the home Lillian Trasher started provided a haven for children, but was overcrowded, and it mixed disciplining measures with undisciplined practices.

Trasher and her colleagues promoted a Christian fundamentalist vision of health, gender relations, and piety that countered the agendas of modernizing Egyptians and contrasted in many ways with Presbyterians. Yet she herself was a very modern figure, going abroad on her own, launching a mission independently, and traveling to raise funds. Trasher had more power within her mission than her Presbyterian counterparts, who were subservient to male leaders. She, like Margaret Smith, embodied contradictory impulses. But the intentions of evangelicals to turn their wards into Americanized Protestants, however defined, should not be confused with the outcomes and what children took away from their experiences in these institutions. Locals absorbed from these and other institutions what they wanted oftentimes in spite of missionary pressures to conform and convert.

NOTES

1.   For background on American Presbyterian missionaries in Egypt, see Heather J. Sharkey, *American Evangelicals in Egypt: Missionary Encounters in an Age of Empire* (Princeton: Princeton University Press, 2008). On the history of the

Assemblies of God Church in Egypt, see Samu'il Mishriqi, *Tarikh al-Madhhab al-Khamsini fi Misr* (Cairo: al-Majma' al- 'Amm li-Kana'is Allah al-Khamsini-yya, 1985). While Asyut is the preferred transliteration for the town, I will use the spelling for the orphanage—Assiout—that Lillian Trasher and her contemporaries used.

2.   *History of the W.G.M.S. 1883–1933* (Pittsburgh: WGMS pamphlet, 1933), 23–25.

3.   For background on the history of orphanages in Egypt, see Beth Baron, "Orphans and Abandoned Children in Modern Egypt," in *Interpreting Welfare and Relief in the Middle East*, ed. Nefissa Naguib and Inger Marie Okkenhaug (Leiden: Brill, 2008), 13–34.

4.   Elizabeth Kelsey Kinnear, *She Sat Where They Sat: A Memoir of Anna Young Thompson of Egypt* (Grand Rapids, MI: William B. Eerdmans Publishing Company, 1971), 28.

5.   Earl E. Elder, *Vindicating a Vision: The Story of the American Mission in Egypt, 1854–1954* (Philadelphia: Board of Foreign Missions of the United Presbyterian Church of N.A., 1959), 67.

6.   See also, *One Hundred Twenty Years of Service in Egypt: Anna Y. Thompson and Margaret A. Smith* (Pittsburgh: WGMS pamphlet, n.d.)

7.   Presbyterian Historical Society (hereafter PHS), RG 404, Box 1, Folder 3, entry in Margaret Smith diary, 5 Dec. 1880; *One Hundred Twenty Years*, 10.

8.   PHS, Egyptian Missionary Association (hereafter EMA), *Minutes*, July 1904, 27; *One Hundred Twenty Years*, 11–12.

9.   PHS, EMA, *Minutes*, July 1906, 13–14.

10. PHS, *Annual Report of the American United Presbyterian Mission in Egypt* (hereafter *Annual Report*), 1909, 55; EMA, *Minutes*, Feb.–March 1910, 18.

11. Elder, *Vindicating a Vision*, 134–135.

12. PHS, EMA, *Minutes*, Feb.–March 1910, 36.

13. Elder, *Vindicating a Vision*, 267.

14. PHS, EMA, *Minutes*, July 1909, 7; *Annual Report*, 1910, 64.

15. PHS, EMA, *Minutes*, Feb. 1907, 25.

16. PHS, EMA, *Minutes*, July 1907, 15.

17. PHS, *Annual Report*, 1915, 51.

18. PHS, *Annual Report*, 1920, 34.

19. PHS, *Annual Report*, 1906–1907, p.44–45.

20. PHS, *Annual Report*, 1910, 63–64.

21. PHS, *Annual Report*, 1910, 64.

22. PHS, EMA, *Minutes*, July 1907, p. 15.

23. PHS, EMA, *Minutes*, July 1920, 12; *Minutes*, Feb. 1922, 139; *Minutes*, Jan. 1925, p. 538; *Minutes*, Jan. 1931, 12.

24. PHS, *Annual Report*, 1909, 53.

25. PHS, *Annual Report*, 1910, 64.

26. PHS, *Annual Report*, 1910, 63–64.

27. PHS, RG 209, Box 2, Folder 15, Ella Barnes, Cairo, to Mr. Taylor, 6 May 1937, with "Fowler Orphanage, Abbassia, Cairo, Egypt, Record of Service, 1906–1936."

28. Ibid.; PHS, EMA, Minutes, Jan. 1937, 84–85. Quote from *Program and Needs of the Work of the American Mission in Egypt: Papers Presented to the Mission Association at Its Meeting in Assiut, January 1938* (Cairo: Nile Mission Press, 1938), 28.

29. Jamila Bargach, *Orphans of Islam: Family, Abandonment, and Secret Adoption in Morocco* (New York: Rowman and Littlefield, 2002); idem, "B-A-S-T-A-R-D Biographies: Inside an Invisible Space" (paper presented to Conference on "Family History in Islamic and Middle East Studies," Berkeley, April 2000).

30. Jerome Beatty, "Nile Mother," *American Magazine* (July 1939): 55; Lester Sumrall, *Lillian Trasher: The Nile Mother* (Springfield, MO: Gospel Publishing House, 1951); Beth Prim Howell, *Lady on a Donkey* (New York: E. P. Dutton and Company, 1960).

31. Lillian Trasher, *Letters from Lillian* (Springfield, MO: Assemblies of God Division of Foreign Missions, 1983).

32. Janet and Geoff Benge, *Lillian Trasher: The Greatest Wonder in Egypt* (Seattle: YWAM Publishing, 2004).

33. Trasher, *Word and Witness* (20 Oct. 1913), 2.

34. Muhafazat Asyut, *Asyut fi 10 Sanawat* (Cairo: Matba'at Nahdat Misr, 1962), 9.

35. Flower Pentecostal Heritage Center (FPHC), Lillian Trasher Personal Papers, File cards, 0504 074.

36. Trasher, *Word and Witness* (20 Oct. 1913), 2.

37. Veronica Seton-Williams and Peter Stocks, *Blue Guide: Egypt* (New York: W. W. Norton, 1984), 475; Hanna F. Wissa, *Assiout—The Saga of an Egyptian Family* (Sussex, UK: Book Guild, 1994), 175–176.

38. Trasher, "The Miracle of the Assiout Orphanage," *Latter Rain Evangel* (Aug. 1924): 22.

39. Trasher, *Latter Rain Evangel* (March 1919): 15.

40. Trasher, "God's Protection in Great Peril," *Latter Rain Evangel* (June 1919): 11; idem, "God's Protection through a Reign of Terror," *Latter Rain Evangel* (Sept. 1919): 16; A. H. Post, "Alexandria, Egypt," *Christian Evangel* (28 June 1919): 10.

41. Trasher, *Pentecostal Evangel* (18 July 1925): 10.

42. Trasher, *Pentecostal Evangel* (2 April 1921): 12.

43. Wissa, *Assiout*, 176; *Asyut fi 10 Sanawat*, map p. 38.

44. Trasher, *Latter Rain Evangel* (Aug. 1924): 21.

45. Sumrall, *Lillian Trasher*, 22–23.

46. Trasher, *Pentecostal Evangel* (25 Aug. 1923):12.

47. Trasher, *Pentecostal Evangel* (14 March 1925): 10.

48. Lillian Trasher, *Extracts from My Diary: A Review of God's Gracious Provisions for the Needs of the Assiout Orphanage* (Springfield: Foreign Missions Dept., 1931–1933?), 15, letter dated 31 Jan. 1928.

49. Trasher, *Pentecostal Evangel* (21 March 1931): 15.

50. Trasher, *Letters from Lillian*, 20, letter dated 13 March 1933.

51. Trasher, *Pentecostal Evangel* (25 Aug. 1923): 12.

52. Trasher, *Pentecostal Evangel* (25 June 1921): 13.

53. Trasher, *Extracts from My Diary*, 11, letter dated 22 Nov. 1927.

54. Trasher, *Extracts from My Diary*, 17–18, letter dated 24 Feb. 1928.

55. Florence Christie, *Called to Egypt* (Seal Beach, CA: Florence V. Christie Church School Services, 1997), 42.

56. Trasher, "Thou God Seest Me," *Pentecostal Evangel* (13 Dec. 1930): 11.

57. "A Big Revival in Egypt," *Pentecostal Evangel* (27 March 1926): 11.

58. Trasher, *Letters from Lillian*, 17–18, letter dated 7 April 1927; idem, "Mighty Revival at Assiout Orphanage, Egypt," *Pentecostal Evangel* (7 May 1927): 10; idem, "More About the Revival in Assiout, Egypt," *Pentecostal Evangel* (14 May 1927): 10.

59. Trasher, "Great Pentecostal Outpouring in North and South Africa," in *Latter Rain Evangel* (May 1927): 13, letter dated 9 April 1927.

60. H. E. Randall, "Assiout Orphanage Revival—A Wonderful Work of God," *Pentecostal Evangel* (4 June 1927): 6.

61. Trasher, "Another Wonderful Revival at Assiout, Egypt," *Pentecostal Evangel* (18 March 1933): 8; idem, "Continued Revival in Assiout, Egypt," *Pentecostal Evangel* (8 April 1933): 11.

62. Beatty, "Nile Mother," 55.

63. Noel Perkin, "Down in Egypt," *Pentecostal Evangel* (1 May 1937): 9–11.

64. Christie, *Called to Egypt*, 54.

65. Ibid., 45–46.

66. Trasher, "The Widow's Haven," *Pentecostal Evangel* (15 July 1939): 10.

67. Trasher, *Work of Faith*, 29, letter dated 8 March 1935; Virginia Danielson, "Artists and Entrepreneurs: Female Singers in Cairo during the 1920s," in *Women in Middle Eastern History: Shifting Boundaries in Sex and Gender*, ed. Nikki R. Keddie and Beth Baron (New Haven: Yale University Press, 1991), 297–301.

68. Trasher, *Work of Faith*, 26, letter dated 13 Dec. 1934.

69. Christie, *Called to Egypt*, 53.

70. Sumrall, *Lillian Trasher*, 38.

71. Trasher, "'Growing Pains' at Assiut," *Pentecostal Evangel* (2 Dec. 1951): 7.

72. Seton-Williams and Stocks, *Blue Guide: Egypt*, 476.

73. Heather J. Sharkey, "Missionary Legacies: Muslim-Christian Encounters in Egypt and Sudan during the Colonial and Postcolonial Periods," in *Muslim-Christian Encounters in Africa*, ed. Benjamin Soares (Leiden: Brill, 2006), 57–88.

74. Trasher, "News from Lillian Trasher," *Pentecostal Evangel* (10 March 1957): 23.
75. FPHC, Lillian Trasher Personal Papers, 1094 247, Gamal Abdel Nasser to Lillian Trasher, Cairo, 13 Oct. 1959; Lill to Jen, Assiout, 20 Oct. 1959.
76. Raymond T. Brock, "Mother of a Thousand," *Pentecostal Evangel* (26 June 1960): 11.

BIBLIOGRAPHY

INTRODUCTION

Ahlstrom, Sydney E. *A Religious History of the American People.* New Haven: Yale University Press, 1972.

Al-Sayegh, Fatma Hassan. "American Women Missionaries in the Gulf: Agents for Cultural Change." *Islam and Christian-Muslim Relations* 9:3 (1998): 339–356.

Alexander, J. R. *A Sketch of the Story of the Evangelical Church of Egypt.* Alexandria: Whitehead Morris Limited, 1930.

Allison, Robert J. *The Crescent Obscured: The United States and the Muslim World, 1776–1815.* Chicago: The University of Chicago Press, 1995.

Amanat, Abbas, and Magnus T. Bernhardsson, eds. *U.S.-Middle Eastern Historical Encounters: A Critical Survey.* Gainesville: University Press of Florida, 2007.

Anderson, Betty S. "Liberal Education at the American University of Beirut." In *Liberal Thought in the Eastern Mediterranean*, edited by Christoph Schumann, 99–120. Leiden: Brill, 2008.

Antier, Jean-Jacques. *Charles de Foucauld.* Trans. Julia Shirek Smith. San Francisco: Ignatius Press, 1999.

Asad, Talal. "Muslims and European Identity: Can Europe Represent Islam?" In *The Idea of Europe: From Antiquity to the European Union*, edited by Anthony Pagden, 209–227. Cambridge: Cambridge University Press, 2002.

Ayalon, Ami. *The Press in the Arab Middle East: A History.* New York: Oxford University Press, 1995.

Bahloul, Joëlle. *The Architecture of Memory: A Jewish-Muslim Household in Colonial Algeria, 1937–1962.* Trans. Catherine Du Peloux Ménagé. Cambridge: Cambridge University Press, 1992.

Baron, Beth. *Egypt as a Woman: Nationalism, Gender, and Politics.* Berkeley: University of California Press, 2005.

———. "Talking in Tongues: Lillian Trasher, the Asyut Orphanage, and Pentecostals on the Nile." Paper presented at the Conference on "Christian Missionaries in the Middle East: Re-Thinking Colonial Encounters," North Carolina State University, Raleigh, North Carolina, May 4, 2007.

Barrett, Roby Carroll. *The Greater Middle East and the Cold War: U.S. Foreign Policy under Eisenhower and Kennedy.* London: I. B. Tauris, 2007.

Bays, Daniel H., and Grant Wacker, eds. *The Foreign Missionary Enterprise at Home: Explorations in North American Cultural History.* Tuscaloosa: The University of Alabama Press, 2003.

Beach, Harlan P., and Charles H. Fahs. *World Missionary Atlas.* New York: Institute of Social and Religious Research, 1925.

Beaver, R. Pierce. *American Protestant Women in World Mission: A History of the First Feminist Movement in North America.* Grand Rapids, MI: Eerdmans, 1980.

Bocquet, Jérôme. "Francophonie et langue arabe dans le Syrie sous mandat: l'exemple de l'enseignement missionaire à Damas." In *The British and French Mandates in Comparative Perspectives,* edited by Nadine Méouchy and Peter Sluglett, 303–319. Leiden: Brill, 2004.

Booth, Marilyn. "'She Herself Was the Ultimate Rule': Arabic Biographies of Missionary Teachers and Their Pupils." *Islam and Christian-Muslim Relations* 13:4 (2002): 427–448.

Bourmand, Philippe. "Public Space and Private Spheres: The Foundation of St Luke's Hospital of Nablus by the CMS (1891–1901)." In Murre-van den Berg, *New Faiths in Ancient Lands,* 133–150.

Bowen, Marcellus. *The Bible in Bible Lands: History of the Levant Agency.* New York: American Bible Society, 1917.

Braude, Benjamin. "Foundation Myths of the *Millet* System." In *Christians and Jews in the Ottoman Empire*, Vol. 1, edited by Benjamin Braude and Bernard Lewis, 69–88. New York: Holmes and Meier, 1982.

Carpenter, Joel A., and Wilbert R. Shenk, eds. *Earthen Vessels: American Evangelicals and Foreign Missions, 1880–1980.* Grand Rapids, MI: William B. Eerdmans Publishing Company, 1990.

Clasen, Peter (Director). *Camondo Han* (DVD). Istanbul, 2005.

Cleveland, William L., and Martin Bunton. *A History of the Modern Middle East.* Fourth edition. Boulder: Westview Press, 2009.

Courbage, Youssef, and Philippe Fargues. *Christians and Jews under Islam.* Trans. Judy Mabro. London: I. B. Tauris, 1997.

Crinson, Mark. *Empire Building: Orientalism and Victorian Architecture.* London: Routledge, 1996.

Doğan, Mehmet Ali. "Missionary Schools." In *Encyclopedia of the Ottoman Empire*, edited by Gábor Ágoston and Bruce Masters, 385–388. New York: Facts on File, 2009.

Doumato, Eleanor Abdella. *Getting God's Ear: Women, Islam, and Healing in Saudi Arabia and the Gulf.* New York: Columbia University Press, 2000.

———. "Joyful Death: The Romance of Americans in Mission to the Nestorians." Paper presented at the Conference on "Christian Missionaries in the Middle East: Re-Thinking Colonial Encounters," North Carolina State University, Raleigh, North Carolina, May 5, 2007.

Edwards, Brian T. *Morocco Bound: Disorienting America's Maghreb*. Durham, NC: Duke University Press, 2005.

Elshakry, Marwa. "The Gospel of Science and American Evangelism in Late Ottoman Beirut." *Past & Present* 196:1 (2007): 173–214.

Finnie, David H. *Pioneers East: The Early American Experience in the Middle East*. Cambridge: Harvard University Press, 1967.

Fitzmier, John R., and Randall Balmer. "A Poultice for the Bite of the Cobra: The Hocking Report and Presbyterian Missions in the Middle Decades of the Twentieth Century." In *The Diversity of Discipleship: The Presbyterians and Twentieth-Century Christian Witness*, edited by Milton J. Coalter et al., 105–125. Louisville: Westminster/John Knox Press, 1991.

Fleischmann, Ellen L. "'Our Moslem Sisters': Women of Greater Syria in the Eyes of American Protestant Missionary Women." *Islam and Christian-Muslim Relations* 9:3 (1998): 307–323.

———. "The Impact of American Protestant Missions in Lebanon on the Construction of Female Identity, c. 1860–1950." *Islam and Christian-Muslim Relations* 13:4 (2002): 411–426.

———. "'Under an American Roof': The Beginnings of the American Junior College for Women in Beirut." *Arab Studies Journal* 17:1 (2009): 62–84.

Fleischmann, Ellen. "Evangelization or Education: American Protestant Missionaries, the American Board, and the Girls and Women of Syria (1830–1910)." In Murre-van den Berg, *New Faiths in Ancient Lands*, 263–280.

———. "'I Only Wish I Had a Home on This Globe': Transnational Biography and Dr. Mary Eddy." *Journal of Women's History* 21:3 (2009): 108–130.

Freely, John. *A History of Robert College, the American College for Girls, and Boğaziçi University*. Istanbul: YKY, 2000.

Gallagher, Nancy. *Quakers in the Israeli-Palestinian Conflict: The Dilemmas of NGO Humanitarian Activism*. Cairo: American University in Cairo Press, 2007.

Garrett, Shirley S. "Sisters All: Feminism and the American Women's Missionary Movement." In *Missionary Ideologies in the Imperialist Era, 1880–1920*, edited by Torben Christensen and William R. Hutchison, 221–230. Århus, Denmark: Aros, 1982.

Geary, Christraud M., and Virginia-Lee Webb, eds. *Delivering Views: Distant Cultures in Early Postcards*. Washington, DC: Smithsonian Institution Press, 1998.

———. "Photographs as Materials for African History: Some Methodological Considerations." *History in Africa* 13 (1986): 89–116.

Gelvin, James L. *The Modern Middle East: A History*. Second edition. New York: Oxford University Press, 2008.

Geniesse, Jane Fletcher. *American Priestess: The Extraordinary Story of Anna Spaf-ford and the American Colony in Jerusalem*. New York: Nan A. Talese, 2008.

Goodwin, Godfrey. *Life's Episodes: Discovering Ottoman Architecture*. Istanbul: Boğaziçi University Press, 2002.

Goren, Haim. "The German Catholic Holy Sepulchre Society: Activities in Pales-tine." In *Jerusalem in the Mind of the Western World, 1800–1948*, edited by Ye-hoshua Ben Arieh and Moshe Davis, 155–172. Westport, CT: Praeger, 1997.

Grabill, Joseph L. *Protestant Diplomacy and the Near East: Missionary Influence on American Policy, 1810–1927*. Minneapolis: University of Minnesota Press, 1971.

Grafton, David D. *Piety, Politics, and Power: Lutherans Encountering Islam in the Middle East*. Eugene, OR: Wipf and Stock Publishers, 2009.

Graham-Brown, Sarah. *Images of Women: The Portrayal of Women in Photography of the Middle East, 1860–1950*. New York: Columbia University Press, 1988.

Guérin, Victor. *La France Catholique en Égypte*. Tours: Alfred Mame et Fils, 1894.

Hamilton, Alastair. *The Copts and the West, 1439–1822: The European Discovery of the Egyptian Church*. Oxford: Oxford University Press, 2006.

Hanioğlu, M. Şükrü. *A Brief History of the Late Ottoman Empire*. Princeton: Prince-ton University Press, 2008.

Hasan, S. S. *Christians versus Muslims in Modern Egypt: The Century-Long Struggle for Coptic Equality*. Oxford: Oxford University Press, 2003.

Hastings, Adrian. *The Church in Africa, 1450–1950*. Oxford: Clarendon Press, 1994.

Hatch, Nathan O. *The Democratization of American Christianity*. New Haven: Yale University Press, 1989.

Heuser, Frederick J., Jr. "Culture, Feminism, and the Gospel: American Presbyterian Women and Foreign Missions, 1870–1923." PhD diss., Temple University, 1991.

Heyberger, Bernard. "Individualism and Political Modernity: Devout Catholic Women in Aleppo and Lebanon between the Seventeenth and Nineteenth Cen-turies." In *Beyond the Exotic: Women's Histories in Islamic Societies*, edited by Amira El Azhary Sonbol, 71–85, 407–412. Syracuse: Syracuse University Press, 2005.

Hill, Patricia R. *The World Their Household: The American Women's Foreign Mission Movement and Cultural Transformation, 1870–1920*. Ann Arbor: University of Michigan Press, 1984.

Hocking, William Ernest, ed. *Re-Thinking Missions: A Laymen's Inquiry after One Hundred Years*. New York: Harper & Brothers Publishers, 1932.

Hogg, William Richey. *Ecumenical Foundations: A History of the International Mis-sionary Council and Its Nineteenth-Century Background*. New York: Harper & Brothers, 1952.

Hurewitz, J. C. *Diplomacy in the Near and Middle East: A Documentary Record, 1535–1914*. Princeton: D. Van Nostrand Company, 1956.

Hutchison, William R. *Errand to the World: American Protestant Thought and For-eign Missions*. Chicago: The University of Chicago Press, 1987.

Jamison, Wallace N. *The United Presbyterian Story: A Centennial Study, 1858–1958*. Pittsburgh: The Geneva Press, 1958.

Jhally, Sut (Producer), and Sanjay Talreja (Director). *Edward Said on Orientalism* (DVD). Northampton, MA: Media Education Foundation, 2002.

Kaminsky, Uwe. "German 'Home Mission' Abroad: The *Orientarbeit* of the Deaconess Institution Kaiserswerth in the Ottoman Empire." In Murre-van den Berg, *New Faith in Ancient Lands*, 191–209.

Kark, Ruth. "Millenarism and Agricultural Settlement in the Holy Land in the Nineteenth Century." *Journal of Historical Geography* 9:1 (1983): 47–62.

———. "Sweden and the Holy Land: Pietistic and Communal Settlement." *Journal of Historical Geography* 22:1 (1996): 46–67.

Kidd, Thomas S. *American Christians and Islam: Evangelical Culture and Muslims from the Colonial Period to the Age of Terrorism*. Princeton: Princeton University Press, 2008.

Kieser, Hans-Lukas. *Nearest East: American Millennialism and Mission to the Middle East*. Philadelphia: Temple University Press, 2010.

Laqueur, Walter, and Barry Rubin, eds. *The Israel-Arab Reader*. Seventh revised edition. New York: Penguin Books, 2008.

Lenczowski, George. *The Middle East in World Affairs*. Ithaca: Cornell University Press, 1952. Fourth edition, Ithaca: Cornell University Press, 1980.

Little, Douglas. *American Orientalism: The United States and the Middle East since 1945*. Chapel Hill: The University of North Carolina Press, 2002.

Lockman, Zachary. *Contending Visions of the Middle East: The History and Politics of Orientalism*. Cambridge: Cambridge University Press, 2004.

Löffler, Roland. "The Metamorphosis of a Pietistic Missionary and Educational Institution into a Social Services Enterprise: The Case of the Syrian Orphanage (1860–1945)." In Murre-van den Berg, *New Faith in Ancient Lands*, 151–174.

Lüdtke, Alf, ed. *The History of Everyday Life*. Princeton: Princeton University Press, 1995.

Makdisi, Ussama. *The Culture of Sectarianism: Community, History, and Violence in Nineteenth-Century Ottoman Lebanon*. Berkeley: University of California Press, 2000.

———. *Artillery of Heaven: American Missionaries and the Failed Conversion of the Middle East*. Ithaca: Cornell University Press, 2008.

Marr, Timothy. *The Cultural Roots of American Islamicism*. Cambridge: Cambridge University Press, 2006.

Marten, Michael. *Attempting to Bring the Gospel Home: Scottish Missions to Palestine, 1839–1917*. London: I. B. Tauris, 2006.

Masters, Bruce. *Christians and Jews in the Ottoman Arab World: The Roots of Sectarianism*. Cambridge: Cambridge University Press, 2001.

———. "Competing for Aleppo's Souls: The Roman Catholic and Protestant Missions in the Ottoman Period." *Archaeology & History in Lebanon* 22 (2005): 34–50.

————. "Missionaries." In *Encyclopedia of the Ottoman Empire*, edited by Gábor Ágoston and Bruce Masters, 384–385. New York: Facts on File, 2009.

McAlister, Melani. *Epic Encounters: Culture, Media, and U.S. Interests in the Middle East, 1945–2000*. Berkeley: University of California Press, 2001.

McCarthy, Justin. *Muslims and Minorities: The Population of Ottoman Anatolia and the End of Empire*. New York: New York University Press, 1983.

Méouchy, Nadine, and Peter Sluglett, eds. *The British and French Mandates in Comparative Perspectives*. Leiden: Brill, 2004.

Moors, Annelies. "Presenting Palestine's Population: Premonitions of the Nakba," *The MIT Electronic Journal of Middle East Studies* 1 (2001).

Mott, John R. *The Evangelization of the World in This Generation*. New York: Student Volunteer Movement for Foreign Missions, 1900.

Murre-van den Berg, Heleen. "Nineteenth-Century Protestant Missions and Middle Eastern Women: An Overview." In *Gender, Religion and Change in the Middle East: Two Hundred Years of History*, edited by Inger Marie Okkenhaug and Ingvild Flaskerud, 103–122. Oxford: Berg, 2005.

————, ed. *New Faiths in Ancient Lands: Western Missions in the Middle East in the Nineteenth and Early Twentieth Centuries*. Leiden: Brill, 2006.

Nassar, Issam. "Biblification in the Service of Colonialism: Jerusalem in Nineteenth-Century Photography." *Third Text* 20:3–4 (2006): 317–326.

Nichol, John Thomas. *Pentecostalism*. New York: Harper & Row Publishers, 1966.

Noll, Mark A. *American Evangelical Christianity: An Introduction*. Oxford: Blackwell Publishers, 2001.

————. *The Old Religion in a New World: The History of North American Christianity*. Grand Rapids, MI: William B. Eerdmans Publishing Company, 2002.

Okkenhaug, Inger Marie. *The Quality of Heroic Living, of High Endeavour, and Adventure: Anglican Mission, Women, and Education in Palestine, 1888–1948*. Leiden: Brill, 2002.

————. "Signe Ekblad and the Swedish School in Jerusalem, 1922–1948," *Svensk Missionstidskrift* 94:2 (2006): 147–161.

Oren, Michael B. *Power, Faith, and Fantasy: America in the Middle East, 1776 to the Present*. New York: W. W. Norton & Co., 2007.

Philips, H. E. *The Question Box: A Catechism on Missions in Egypt*. [Pittsburgh?]: The Publicity Committee of the Egyptian Mission of the United Presbyterian Church of North America, 1939.

Pollard, Lisa. *Nurturing the Nation: The Family Politics of Modernizing, Colonizing, and Liberating Egypt, 1805–1923*. Berkeley: University of California Press, 2005.

Porter, Andrew. *Religion versus Empire? British Protestant Missionaries and Overseas Expansion, 1700–1914*. New York: Manchester University Press, 2004.

Pruitt, Lisa Joy. *"A Looking-Glass for the Ladies": American Protestant Women and the Orient in the Nineteenth Century*. Macon: Mercer University Press, 2005.

Quataert, Donald. *The Ottoman Empire, 1700–1922*. Cambridge: Cambridge University Press, 2000.

Queen, Edward L., II. "Great Powers, Holy Powers, and Good Powers: American Protestants Tour the Holy Land, 1867–1914." Paper presented at the conference on "Great Powers in the Holy Land: From Napoleon to the Balfour Declaration," European Institute, Columbia University, April 4, 2009.

Railton, Nicholas. *No North Sea: The Anglo-German Evangelical Network in the Middle of the Nineteenth Century*. Leiden: Brill, 2000.

Reeves-Ellington, Barbara. "A Vision of Mount Holyoke in the Ottoman Balkans: American Cultural Transfer, Bulgarian Nation-Building, and Women's Educational Reform, 1858–1870." *Gender & History* 16:1 (2004): 146–171.

———. "Gender, Conversion, and Social Transformation: The American Discourse of Domesticity and the Origins of the Bulgarian Women's Movement, 1864–1876." In *Converting Cultures: Religion, Ideology, and Transformations of Modernity*, edited by Dennis Washburn and A. Kevin Reinhart, 115–140. Leiden: Brill, 2007.

———. "Women, Gender and Missionary Education: Ottoman Empire." In *The Encyclopedia of Women and Islamic Cultures*, Vol. 4, gen. ed. Suad Joseph, 285–287. Leiden: Brill, 2007.

Reid, Daniel G., ed. *Dictionary of Christianity in America*. Downers Grove, IL: InterVarsity Press, 1990.

Richter, Julius. *A History of Protestant Missions in the Near East*. Edinburgh: Oliphant, Anderson & Ferrier, 1910.

Robert, Dana L. *American Women in Mission: A Social History of Their Thought and Practice*. Macon, GA: Mercer University Press, 1996.

———. "From Missions to Beyond Missions: The Historiography of American Protestant Foreign Missions since World War II." In *New Directions in American Religious History*, edited by Harry S. Stout and D. G. Hart, 362–393. New York: Oxford University Press, 1997.

Robson, Laura. "Archaeology and Mission: The British Presence in Nineteenth-Century Palestine." Paper presented at the conference on "Great Powers in the Holy Land: From Napoleon to the Balfour Declaration," European Institute, Columbia University, April 4, 2009.

Rodgers, Daniel T. *Atlantic Crossings: Social Politics in a Progressive Age*. Cambridge: Harvard University Press, 1998.

Rostam-Kolayi, Jasamin. "From Evangelizing to Modernizing Iranians: The American Presbyterian Mission and Its Iranian Students." *Iranian Studies* (April 2008): 213–240.

Russell, Mona L. *Creating the New Egyptian Woman: Consumerism, Education, and National Identity, 1863–1922*. New York: Palgrave Macmillan, 2004.

Said, Edward. "Misinformation about Iraq." *CounterPunch*, December 3, 2002.

———. *Orientalism*. New York: Pantheon Books, 1978.

———. *Out of Place: A Memoir*. New York: Knopf, 1999.

Sanderson, Lilian Passmore, and Neville Sanderson. *Education, Religion, and Politics in Southern Sudan, 1899–1964*. London: Ithaca Press, 1981.

Seni, Nora. "The Camondos and Their Imprint on 19th-Century Istanbul." *International Journal of Middle East Studies* 26:4 (1994): 663–675.

———. *Les Camondo*. Arles: Actes Sud, 1997.

Sharkey, Heather J. "Christians among Muslims: The Church Missionary Society in the Northern Sudan." *Journal of African History* 43 (2002): 51–75.

———. "A New Crusade or an Old One?" *ISIM Newsletter* 12 (2003): 48–49.

———. "Arabic Antimissionary Treatises." *International Bulletin of Missionary Research* 28:3 (2004): 112–118.

———. "Women, Gender, and Missionary Education: Sudan." In *The Encyclopedia of Women and Islamic Cultures*, Vol. 4, gen. ed. Suad Joseph, 287–288. Leiden: Brill, 2007.

———. *American Evangelicals in Egypt: Missionary Encounters in an Age of Empire*. Princeton: Princeton University Press, 2008.

———. "Muslim Apostasy, Christian Conversion, and Religious Freedom in Egypt: A Study of American Missionaries, Western Imperialism, and Human Rights Agendas." In *Proselytization Revisited: Rights, Free Markets, and Culture Wars*, edited by Rosalind I. J. Hackett, 139–166. London: Equinox, 2008.

———. "Middle Eastern and North African Christianity." In *Introducing World Christianity*, edited by Charles Farhadian (Oxford: Blackwell, forthcoming).

Shorter, Aylward. *Cross and Flag in Africa: The "White Fathers" during the Colonial Scramble, 1892–1914*. Maryknoll, NY: Orbis Books, 2006.

Sislian, Jack. "Missionary Work in Egypt during the Nineteenth Century." In *Educational Policy and the Mission Schools: Case Studies from the British Empire*, edited by Brian Holmes, 175–240. London: Routledge & Kegan Paul, 1967.

Smylie, James H. *A Brief History of the Presbyterians*. Louisville: Geneva Press, 1996.

Stanley, Brian. *The Bible and the Flag: Protestant Missions and British Imperialism in the Nineteenth and Twentieth Centuries*. Leicester: Apollos, 1990.

———. *The World Missionary Conference, Edinburgh 1910*. Grand Rapids, MI: William B. Eerdmans Publishing Company, 2009.

Stockdale, Nancy L. *Colonial Encounters among English and Palestinian Women, 1800–1948*. Gainesville: University Press of Florida, 2007.

Stone, Frank Andrews. *Academies for Anatolia: A Study of the Rationale, Program and Impact of the Educational Institutions Sponsored by the American Board in Turkey, 1830–2005*. San Francisco: Caddo Gap Press, 2006.

Sundkler, Bengt, and Christopher Steed. *A History of the Church in Africa*. Cambridge: Cambridge University Press, 2000.

Tamcke, Martin, and Michael Marten, eds. *Christian Witness between Continuity and New Beginnings: Modern Historical Missions in the Middle East.* Berlin: LIT Verlag, 2006.

Tejirian, Eleanor H., and Reeva Spector Simon, eds. *Altruism and Imperialism: Western Cultural and Religious Missions in the Middle East.* New York: Middle East Institute, Columbia University, 2002.

Tejirian, Eleanor H. "Faith of Our Fathers: Near East Relief and the Near East Foundation—From Mission to NGO." In Tejirian and Simon, *Altruism and Imperialism*, 295–315.

Varisco, Daniel Martin. *Reading Orientalism: Said and the Unsaid.* Seattle: University of Washington Press, 2007.

———. "Framing the Holy Land as an Art: Illustrations of Arabs in 19th Century Bible Custom Accounts." Paper prepared for the conference of the Middle East Studies Association (MESA), Boston 2009.

———. "Lithographica Arabica." *Tabsir: Insight on Islam and the Middle East.* http://tabsir.net/?p=746 (Accessed May 12, 2009).

Walls, Andrew F. "British Missions." In *Missionary Ideologies in the Imperialist Era: 1880–1920,* edited by Torben Christensen and William R. Hutchison, 159–165. Århus, Denmark: Aros, 1982.

———. "The American Dimension in the History of the Missionary Movement." In *Earthen Vessels: American Evangelicals and Foreign Missions, 1880–1980,* edited by Joel A. Carpenter and Wilbert R. Shenk, 1–25. Grand Rapids, MI: William B. Eerdmans Publishing Company, 1990.

Werner, Roland, William Anderson, and Andrew Wheeler. *Day of Devastation, Day of Contentment: The History of the Sudanese Church across 2000 Years.* Nairobi: Paulines Publications Africa, 2000.

The World Bank. "Countries and Regions." http://www.worldbank.org/ (Accessed May 27, 2009).

Wuthnow, Robert. *Boundless Faith: The Global Outreach of American Churches.* Berkeley: University of California Press, 2009.

Yothers, Brian. *The Romance of the Holy Land in American Travel Writing, 1790–1876.* Aldershot, UK: Ashgate, 2007.

Zirinsky, Michael P. "A Panacea for the Ills of the Country: American Presbyterian Education in Interwar Iran." *American Presbyterians* 72:3 (1994): 187–201.

CHAPTER 1

Abu-Ghazaleh, Adnan. *American Missions in Syria: A Study of American Missionary Contribution to Arab Nationalism in 19th Century Syria.* Brattleboro, VT: Amana Books, 1990.

Ahlstrom, Sydney E. *A Religious History of the American People.* New Haven: Yale University Press, 2004.

Albaugh, Gaylord P. *History and Annotated Bibliography of American Religious Periodicals and Newspapers Established from 1730 through 1830*. 2 Vols. Worcester: American Antiquarian Society, 1994.

Anderson, Rufus. *History of the Missions of the American Board of Commissioners for Foreign Missions to the Oriental Churches*. 2 vols. Boston: Congregational Publishing Society, 1872.

———. *Memorial Volume of the First Fifty Years of the American Board of Commissioners for Foreign Missions*. Boston: The Board, 1861.

———. *Observations upon the Peloponnesus and Greek Islands made in 1829 by Rufus Anderson one of the Secretaries of the American Board of Commissioners for Foreign Missions*. Boston: Crocker & Brewster, 1830.

Andrew, John A., III. *Rebuilding the Christian Commonwealth: New England Congregationalists & Foreign Missions, 1800–1830*. Lexington: University Press of Kentucky, 1976.

Birdsall, Richard D. "The Second Great Awakening and the New England Social Order." *Church History* 39:3 (September 1970): 345–364.

Bond, Alvan. *Memoir of the Rev. Pliny Fisk, A.M., Late Missionary to Palestine*. Boston: Crocker and Brewster, 1828.

Burke, W. J. "The American Mission Press at Malta." *Bulletin of the New York Public Library* 41:7 (July 1937): 526–529.

Carwardine, Richard. "The Second Great Awakening in Comparative Perspective: Revivals and Culture in the United States and Britain." In *Modern Christian Revivals*, edited by Edith L. Blumhofer and Randall Balmer, 84–100. Urbana: University of Illinois Press, 1993.

Choules, John O., and Thomas Smith. *The Origin and History of Missions: A Record of the Voyages, Travels, Labors, and Successes of the Various Missionaries, who have been sent forth by Protestant Societies and Churches to Evangelize the Heathen...* Vol. 2. Boston: Gould, Kendall and Lincoln, 1837.

Clogg, Richard. "Ὁ Parsons καὶ ὁ Fisk στὸ Γυμνάσιο τῆς Χίου τὸ 1820." Ἐρανιστής *(Eranistes)* 5:30 (1967): 177–193.

Coakley, J. F. "Printing Offices of the American Board of Commissioners for Foreign Missions, 1817–1900: A Synopsis." *Harvard Library Bulletin* 9:1 (Spring 1998): 5–34.

The Constitution and Associate Statutes of the Theological Seminary in Andover; with a Sketch of its Rise and Progress. Boston: Farrand, Mallory, 1808.

The Constitution of the Missionary Society of Connecticut: with an address from the Board of Trustees to the people of the state, and a narrative on the subject of missions: to which is subjoined, a statement of the funds of the Society. Hartford: Hudson and Goodwin, 1800.

Cott, Nancy F. "Young Women in the Second Great Awakening in New England." *Feminist Studies* 3:1/2 (Autumn 1975): 15–29.

De Jong, James A. *As the Waters Cover the Sea: Millennial Expectations in the Rise of Anglo-American Missions 1640–1810*. Laurel, MS: Audubon Press, 2006.

Dwight, Timothy. *A Sermon Preached at the Opening of the Theological Institution in Andover, and at the Ordination of Rev. Eliphalet Pearson, LL.D. September 28th, 1808*. Boston: Farrand, Mallory, 1808.

Ehle, Carl F. *Prolegomena to Christian Zionism in America*. New York: New York University, 1977.

Field, James A. *America and the Mediterranean World 1776–1882*. Princeton: Princeton University Press, 1969.

First Ten Annual Reports of the American Board of Commissioners for Foreign Missions, with Other Documents of the Board. Boston: Crocker and Brewster, 1834.

Fitzmier, J. R. "Second Great Awakening." In *Dictionary of Christianity in America*, edited by Daniel G. Reid, 1067–1068. Downers Grove: InterVarsity Press, 1990.

Foster, Charles I. *An Errand of Mercy: The Evangelical United Front 1790–1837*. Chapel Hill: The University of North Carolina Press, 1960.

Gaustad, Edwin Scott. *A Religious History of America*. New York: Harper & Row, 1990.

Glass, Dagmar. *Malta, Beirut, Leipzig and Beirut Again: Eli Smith, the American Syria Mission and the Spread of Arabic Typography in 19th Century Lebanon*. Beirut: Orient-Institut der Deutschen Morgenländischen Gesellschaft, 1998.

Goffman, Daniel. "Izmir: From Village to Colonial Port City." In *The Ottoman City between East and West: Aleppo, Izmir, and Istanbul,* edited by Edhem Eldem, Daniel Goffman, and Bruce Masters, 79–134. Cambridge: Cambridge University Press, 1999.

Gowing, Peter G. "American Board of Commissioners for Foreign Missions." In *Concise Dictionary of the Christian Mission*, edited by Stephen Neill, Gerald H. Anderson, and John Goodwin, 18–19. Nashville: Abingdon Press, 1971.

Hall, Gordon, and Samuel Newell. *The Conversion of the World, or, the Claims of Six Hundred Millions and the Ability and Duty of the Churches Respecting Them*. Andover: Flagg & Gould, 1818.

Handy, Robert T., ed. *The Holy Land in American Protestant Life 1800–1948*. New York: Arno Press, 1981.

Hankins, Barry. *The Second Great Awakening and the Transcendentalists*. Westport, CT: Greenwood Press, 2004.

Hardman, Keith J. *Issues in American Christianity: Primary Sources with Introductions*. Grand Rapids, MI: Bakery Books, 1993.

Hutchison, William R. *Errand to the World: American Protestant Thought and Foreign Missions*. Chicago: The University of Chicago Press, 1993.

Judson, Edward. *Adoniram Judson: A Biography*. Philadelphia: American Baptist Publication Society, 1894.

Kawerau, Peter. *Amerika und die Orientalischen Kirchen: Ursprung und Anfang Der Amerikanischen Mission unter den Nationalkirchen Westasiens.* Berlin: Walter De Gruyter, 1958.

Khalaf, Samir. *Cultural Resistance: Global and Local Encounters in the Middle East,* London: Saqi Books, 2001.

Kling, David W. "The New Divinity and the Origins of the American Board of Commissioners for Foreign Missions." In *North American Foreign Missions, 1810–1914,* edited by Wilbert R. Shenk, 11–38.

Kocabaşoğlu, Uygur. "Osmanlı İmparatorluğunda 19. Yüzyılda Amerikan Matbaaları ve Yayımcılığı." In *Murat Sarıca Armağanı,* 267–285. İstanbul, Aybay Yayınları, 1988.

Lambert, Frank. *Inventing the "Great Awakening."* Princeton: Princeton University Press, 1999.

Layton, Evra. "The Greek Press at Malta of the American Board of Commissioners for Foreign Missions (1822–1833)." Ἐρανιστής *(Eranistes)* No. 53 (1971): 169–193.

Linder, Robert D. "Division and Unity: The Paradox of Christianity in America." In *Dictionary of Christianity in America,* edited by Daniel G. Reid, 1–22. Downers Grove: InterVarsity Press, 1990.

Lindsay, Rao H. *Nineteenth Century American Schools in the Levant: a Study of Purposes.* Ann Arbor: University of Michigan, 1965.

Lovett, Richard. *The History of the London Missionary Society, 1795–1895.* 2 vols. London: H. Frowde, 1899.

Masters, Bruce. *Christians and Jews in the Ottoman Arab World: The Roots of Sectarianism.* New York: Cambridge University Press, 2001.

Mathews, Donald G. "The Second Great Awakening as an Organizing Process, 1780–1830: An Hypothesis." *American Quarterly* 21:1 (Spring 1969): 23–43.

Maxfield, Charles A., III. "The 'Reflex Influence' of Missions: The Domestic Operations of the American Board of Commissioners for Foreign Missions, 1810–1850." PhD diss., Union Theological Seminary, 1995.

McCook, Matt. "Aliens in the World: Sectarians, Secularism and the Second Great Awakening." PhD diss., Florida State University, 2005.

McLoughlin, William G. *Revivals, Awakenings, and Reform: An Essay on Religion and Social Change in America, 1607–1977.* Chicago: The University of Chicago Press, 1978.

Miller, Glenn T. *Piety and Intellect: The Aims and Purposes of Ante-Bellum Theological Education.* Atlanta: Scholars Press, 1990.

Morton, Daniel Oliver. *Memoir of Rev. Levi Parsons, First Missionary to Palestine from the United States.* Burlington, VT: Chauncey Goodrich, 1830.

Noll, Mark A. *The Old Religion in a New World: The History of North American Christianity.* Grand Rapids, MI: William B. Eerdmans Publishing, 2002.

———. *A History of Christianity in the United States and Canada.* Grand Rapids,

MI: William B. Eerdmans, 2003.

Obenzinger, Hilton. "Holy Land Narrative and American Covenant: Levi Parsons, Pliny Fisk and the Palestine Mission." *Religion & Literature* 35:2–3 (Summer–Autumn 2003): 241–267.

Philliou, Christine May. "The Community of Smyrna/Izmir in 1821: Social Reality and National Ideologies." Master's thesis, Princeton University, 1998.

Phillips, Clifton Jackson. *Protestant America and the Pagan World: The First Half Century of the American Board of Commissioners for Foreign Missions, 1810–1860.* Cambridge: Harvard University, 1969.

Pierson, Hamilton W., ed. *American Missionary Memorial, Including Biographical and Historical Sketches.* New York: Harper & Brothers, 1853.

Prime, E. D. G. *Forty Years in the Turkish Empire; or, Memoirs of Rev. William Goodell.* New York: Robert Carter, 1876.

Rohrer, James R. "The Connecticut Missionary Society and Book Distribution in the Early Republic." *Libraries and Culture* 34:1 (Winter 1999): 17–26.

Roper, Geoffrey. "Arabic Printing in Malta 1825–1845: Its History and Its Place in the Development of Print Culture in the Arab Middle East." PhD diss., University of Durham, 1988.

———. "The Beginning of Arabic Printing by the ABCFM, 1822–1841." *Harvard Library Bulletin* 9:1 (Spring 1998): 50–68.

———. "Turkish Printing and Publishing in Malta in the 1830s." *Turcica*, No. 29 (1997): 413–421.

Rowe, Henry K. *History of Andover Theological Seminary.* Newton: Thomas Todd, 1933.

Sermons of Rev. Messrs. Fisk & Parsons, just before their Departure on the Palestine Mission. Boston: Samuel T. Armstrong, 1819.

Shenk, Wilbert R., ed. *North American Foreign Missions, 1810–1914: Theology, Theory, and Policy.* Grand Rapids, MI: William B. Eerdmans Publishing Company, 2004.

Squier, Miles P. "Rev. Levi Parsons." in *American Missionary Memorial, Including Biographical and Historical Sketches,* ed. Hamilton W. Pierson, 263–275. New York: Harper & Brothers, 1853.

Strong, William E. *The Story of the American Board: An Account of the First Hundred Years of the American Board of Commissioners for Foreign Missions.* Boston: Pilgrim Press, 1910.

Thorne, Susan Elizabeth. "Protestant Ethics and the Spirit of Imperialism: British Congregationalists and the London Missionary Society, 1795–1925." PhD diss., University of Michigan, 1990.

Tibawi, A. L. *American Interests in Syria: 1800–1901: A Study of Educational, Literary and Religious Works.* Oxford: Clarendon Press, 1966.

De Tocqueville, Alexis. *Democracy in America.* Washington, DC: Regnery, 2002.

Tracy, Joseph. *History of the American Board of Commissioners for Foreign Missions.* New York: M. W. Dodd, 1842.

Woods, Leonard. *History of the Andover Theological Seminary.* Boston: James R. Osgood, 1885.

———. *A Sermon Delivered at the Tabernacle in Salem, Feb. 6, 1812 on Occasion of the Ordination of the Rev. Messrs. Samuel Newell, A.M., Adoniram Judson, A.M., Samuel Nott, A.M., Gordon Hall, A.M., and Luther Rice, A.B., Missionaries to the Heathen in Asia, under the Direction of the Board of Commissioners for Foreign Missions.* Boston: Samuel T. Armstrong, 1812.

Woods, Randall B., and Willard B. Gatewood. *The American Experience: A Concise History.* Fort Worth: Harcourt College, 2000.

Worcester, S. M. "Origin of American Foreign Missions." In *American Missionary Memorial, Including Biographical and Historical Sketches,* edited by Hamilton W. Pierson, 1–28. New York: Harper & Brothers, 1853.

Yothers, Brian. *The Romance of the Holy Land in American Travel Writing, 1790–1876.* Aldershot, UK: Ashgate, 2007.

CHAPTER 2

ARCHIVES
American University of Beirut (AUB)
Harvard University Houghton Library (HHL)
Yale University Divinity School Library (YDS)
[British] Public Records Office (PRO)

SOURCES
Abu-Ghazaleh, Adnan. *American Missions in Syria: A Study of American Missionary Contribution to Arab Nationalism in 19th Century Syria.* Brattleboro: Amana Books, 1990.

Anderson, Rufus. *History of the Missions of the American Board of Commissioners for Foreign Missions to the Oriental Churches: In Two Volumes.* Boston: Congregational Publishing Society, 1872.

Aymes, Marc. "The Port-City in the Fields: Investigating an Improper Urbanity in mid-19th Century Cyprus." Paper presented at the Eighth Mediterranean Social and Political Research Meeting, Florence and Montecatini Terme, March 21–25, 2007.

Badr, Habib. "American Protestant Missionary Beginnings in Beirut and Istanbul: Policy, Politics, Practice and Response." In *New Faith in Ancient Lands: Western Missions in the Middle East in the Nineteenth and Early Twentieth Centuries,* edited by Heleen Murre-van den Berg, 211–239. Leiden: Brill, 2006.

———. "Missions to "'Nominal Christians': The Policy and Practice of the

American Board of Commissioners for Foreign Missions and Its Missionaries Concerning Eastern Churches Which Led to the Organization of a Protestant Church in Beirut (1819–1848)." PhD diss., Princeton Theological Seminary, 1992.

Beidelman, T. O. "The Organization and Maintenance of Caravans by the Church Missionary Society in Tanzania in the Nineteenth Century." *The International Journal of African Historical Studies* 15: 4 (1982): 601–623.

Benton, Loanza Goulding. *A Diary and Some Reminiscences of Loanza Goulding Benton: Mrs. William Austin Benton Missionary to Syria: 1847–1869.* Unpublished memoir. Sophia Smith Collection, Smith College Religion Collection: Box 5: Folder 56, n.d.

Bird, Isaac. *Bible Work in Bible Lands; Or, Events in the History of the Syria Mission.* Philadelphia: Presbyterian Board of Publication, 1872.

Blake, Rev. J. L. *American Universal Geography, for Schools and Academics. On the Principles of Analysis and Comparison.* Boston: Lilly, Wait &c., 1833.

Bliss, Sylvester. *Analysis of Geography; For the use of Schools, Academics, &c.* Boston: John P. Jewett & Co., 1850.

Bodenstein, Ralph, et al. "Walking Through Zokak el-Blat: A Rhythmanalysis of the Quarter?" In *History, Space and Social Conflict in Beirut: The Quarter of Zokak el-Blat,* edited by Hans Gebhardt et al. 23–33. Beirut: Ergon Verlag Würzburg in Kommission, 2005.

Booth, Marilyn. "'She Herself Was the Ultimate Rule': Arabic Biographies of Missionary Teachers and Their Pupils." *Islam and Christian-Muslim Relations* 13:4 (2002): 427–448.

Bourdieu, Pierre. *Algeria 1960.* Translated by Richard Nice. Cambridge: Cambridge University Press, 1979.

———. *Distinction: A Social Critique of the Judgement of Taste.* Translated by Richard Nice. New York: Routledge, 1984.

———. *Outline of a Theory of Practice.* Translated by Richard Nice. Cambridge: Cambridge University Press, 1977.

Bowie, Fiona, Deborah Kirkwood, and Shirley Ardner, eds. *Women and Missions: Past and Present: Anthropological and Historical Perceptions.* Oxford: Berg, 1993.

Buchanan, Rev. J. Robertson. "The Story of the Lebanon Schools and the Free Church of Scotland." n.s.: n.s., 1957.

Calvert, Karin. *Children in the House: The Material Culture of Early Childhood, 1600–1900.* Boston: Northeastern University Press, 1992.

Comaroff, John L., and Jean Comaroff. *Of Revelation and Revolution: Volume One: Christianity, Colonialism and Consciousness in South Africa.* Chicago: University of Chicago Press, 1991.

———. *Of Revelation and Revolution: Volume Two: The Dialectics of Modernity on a South African Frontier.* Chicago: University of Chicago Press, 1997.

Cooper, Frederick. *Colonialism in Question: Theory, Knowledge, History.* Berkeley: University of California Press, 2005.

Davie, May. *Atlas Historique Des Orthodoxes de Beyrouth et du Mont Liban: 1800–1940.* Balamand: Universite de Balamand, 1999.

———. *Beyrouth: 1825–1975: Un Siecle et Demi D'Urbanisme.* Beirut: Publications de l'Orde des Ingenieurs et Architectes de Beyrouth, 2001.

———. "Genèse D'une Demeur Patrimoniale: La Maison Aux Trois Arcs de Beyrouth." In *La Maison Beyrouthine Aux Trois Arcs: Une Architecture Bourgeoise du Levant,* edited by Michel Davie, 57–96. Beirut: ALBA, 2003.

Davie, Michael F., ed. *La Maison Beyrouthine Aux Trois Arcs: Une Architecture Bourgeoise du Levant.* Beyrouth: ALBA, 2003.

de Certeau, Michel. *The Practice of Everyday Life.* Translated by Steven Rendall. Berkeley: University of California Press, 1984.

Doumato, Eleanor Abdella. "Missionary Transformations: Gender, Culture and Identity in the Middle East." *Islam and Christian-Muslim Relations* 13:4 (2002): 373–376.

Fawaz, Leila Tarazi. *Merchants and Migrants in Nineteenth-Century Beirut.* Cambridge, MA: Harvard University Press, 1993.

Fleischmann, Ellen. "Evangelization or Education: American Protestant Missionaries; the American Board, and the Girls and Women of Syria (1830–1910)." In Murre-van den Berg, *New Faith in Ancient Lands,* 263–280.

———. "The Impact of American Protestant Missions in Lebanon on the Construction of Female Identity, c. 1860–1950." *Islam and Christian-Muslim Relations* 13:4 (2002): 411–426.

———. "'Our Moslem Sisters': Women of Greater Syria in the Eyes of American Protestant Missionary Women." *Islam and Christian-Muslim Relations* 9:3 (1998): 307–323.

Handy, Robert T. *Religion in the American Experience: The Pluralistic Style.* New York: Harper & Row Pub., 1972.

Hanssen, Jens. *Fin de Siècle Beirut: The Making of an Ottoman Provincial Capital.* Oxford: Clarendon Press, 2005.

Heyberger, Bernard, and Chantal Verdeil. "Spirituality and Scholarship: The Holy Land in Jesuit Eyes (Seventeenth to Nineteenth Centuries)." In Murre-van den Berg, *New Faith in Ancient Lands,* 19–42.

Hill, Patricia R. *The World Their Household: The American Woman's Foreign Mission Movement and Cultural Transformation, 1870–1920.* Ann Arbor: University of Michigan Press, 1985.

Hooker, Edward W. *Memoir of Mrs. Sarah Lanman Smith, Late of the Mission in Syria.* London: The Religious Tract Society, 1839.

Huber, Mary Taylor, and Nancy C. Lutkenhaus, eds. *Gendered Missions: Women and Men in Missionary Discourse and Practice.* Ann Arbor: University of Michigan Press, 1999.

Jansen, Willy. "Visions of Mary in the Middle East: Gender and the Power of a Symbol." In *Gender, Religion and Change in the Middle East: Two Hundred Years of History*, ed. Inger Marie Okkenhaug and Ingvild Flaskerud, 137–154. Oxford: Berg, 2005.

Jenks, Rev. William D. D. "Missionary Map." In *The Explanatory Bible Atlas and Scripture Gazetteer; Geographical, Topographical and Historical...* Boston: Charles Hickling, 1849.

Jessup, Henry Harris. *Fifty-Three Years in Syria: Volume I and II.* Originally published 1910. London: Garnet Publishing Ltd., 2002.

———. *The Women of the Arabs: With a Chapter for Children.* Edited by C. S. Robinson and Isaac Riley. New York: Dodd & Mead, Publishers, 1873.

Khalaf, Samir. "On Doing Much with Little Noise: Early Encounters of Protestant Missionaries in Lebanon." In Tejirian and Simon, *Altruism and Imperialism*, 14–44.

Khater, Akram Fouad. "'House' to 'Goddess of the House': Gender, Class, and Silk in 19th-Century Mount Lebanon." *International Journal of Middle East Studies* 28 (1996): 325–348.

Kobiljski, Aleksandra Majstorac. "Learning to Be Modern: Missionary Universities and the Formation of Secular Modernity in Lebanon and Japan, 1860s–1880s." Paper presented at Christian Missionaries in the Middle East: Re-Thinking Colonial Encounters Conference, Raleigh, North Carolina, 4–5 May 2007.

Lattouf, Mirna. *Women, Education, and Socialization in Modern Lebanon.* Lanham, MD: University Press of America, Inc., 2004.

Lindner, Christine. "Historical Perceptions of Muslim Women by American Women." Paper presented at MESA Annual Conference, Boston, MA, 20 November 2006.

———. "Negotiating the Field: American Protestant Missionaries in Ottoman Syria, 1823 to 1860." PhD dissertation, University of Edinburgh, 2009.

Makdisi, Jean Said. *Teta, Mother and Me: An Arab Woman's Memoir.* London: Saqi, 2005.

Makdisi, Ussama. "Mapping the Orient: Non-Western Modernization, Imperialism, and the End of the Romanticism." In Michie and Thomas, *Nineteenth-Century Geographies*, 40–54.

———. "Reclaiming the Land of the Bible: Missionaries, Secularism, and Evangelical Modernity." *The American Historical Review* 102:3 (June 1997): 680–713.

McDannell, Colleen. *The Christian Home in Victorian America, 1840–1900.* Bloomington: Indiana University Press, 1986.

Meriwether, Margaret L. *The Kin Who Count: Family and Society in Ottoman Aleppo, 1770–1840.* Austin: University of Texas Press, 1999.

Michie, Helena, and Ronald R. Thomas, ed. *Nineteenth-Century Geographies: The Transformation of Space from the Victorian Age to the American Century.* New Brunswick, NJ: Rutgers University Press, 2003.

Modell, John, and Tamara K. Hareven. "Urbanization and the Malleable House-
    hold: An Examination of Boarding and Lodging in American Families." In *The
    American Family in Social-Historical Perspective*, edited by Michael Gordon, 51–
    68. New York: St. Martin's Press, 1978.
Murre-van den Berg, Heleen. "'Dear Mother of My Soul': Fidelia Fiske and the
    Role of Women Missionaries in Mid-Nineteenth Century Iran." *Exchange* 30:1
    (2001): 33–48.
———. "'Simply by Giving to Them Maccaroni…': Anti-Roman Catholic Polem-
    ics in Early Protestant Missions in the Middle East, 1820–1860." In Tamcke and
    Marten, *Christian Witness Between Continuity and New Beginnings*, 63–80.
———, ed. *New Faith in Ancient Lands: Western Missions in the Middle East in the
    Nineteenth and Early Twentieth Centuries*. Boston: Brill, 2006.
———. "The Middle East: Western Missions and the Eastern Churches, Islam and
    Judaism." In *World Christianities c. 1815–1914: The Cambridge History of Chris-
    tianity Volume 8*, edited by Sheridan Gilley and Brian Stanley, 459–471. Cam-
    bridge: Cambridge University Press, 2006.
———. "Nineteenth-Century Protestant Missions and Middle Eastern Women:
    An Overview." In *Gender, Religion and Change in the Middle East: Two Hundred
    Years of History*, edited by Inger Marie Okkenhaug and Ingvild Flaskerud. Ox-
    ford and New York: Berg, 2005.
n.s. *"Minutes of the Special Meeting of the Syrian Mission, Held in the September and
    October, 1855, on Occasion of the Visit of One of the Secretaries of the American
    Board of Commissioners for Foreign Missions."* Boston: T. R. Marvin, 1856.
Ragette, Friedrich. *Architecture in Lebanon: The Lebanese House during the 18th and
    19th Centuries*. Beirut, Lebanon: American University of Beirut, 1974.
Robert, Dana L. *American Women in Mission: A Social History of Their Thought and
    Practice*. Macon: Mercer University Press, 1996.
———. "The 'Christian Home' as a Cornerstone of Anglo-American Missionary
    Thought and Practice." In *Converting Colonialism: Visions and Realities in Mis-
    sion History, 1706–1914*, edited by Dana L. Robert, 134–165. Grand Rapids, MI:
    William B. Eerdmans, 2008.
Salt, Jeremy. "Trouble Wherever They Went: American Missionaries in Anatolia
    and Ottoman Syria in the Nineteenth Century." In Tejirian and Simon, *Altruism
    and Imperialism*, 143–166.
al-Sayegh, Fatma Hassan. "American Women Missionaries in the Gulf: Agents for
    Cultural Change." *Islam and Christian-Muslim Relations* 9:3 (1998): 339–356.
Scholten, Catherine M. *Childbearing in American Society: 1650–1850*. New York:
    New York University Press, 1985.
Simon, Reeva Spector. "The Case of the Curse: The London Society for Promoting
    Christianity Amongst the Jews and the Jews of Bagdad." In Tejirian and Simon,
    Altruism and Imperialism, 45–65.
Smith, Eli. "The Papal Sects of Syria are the Maronites, Greek Catholics, Armenian

Catholics, Syrian Catholics and Latins." ABCFM microfilm Unit 5: Near East: Reel 540: 49B-69. N.s.: n.d.

Stockdale, Nancy. *Colonial Encounters among English and Palestinian Women, 1800–1948*. Gainesville: University of Florida Press, 2007.

Tarnowski, Wafa' Stephan. "Sociological Profile and Cultural Impact of American and British Women Missionaries in Lebanon (1823–1914)." Master's thesis, American University of Beirut, 1997.

Tamcke, Martin, and Michael Marten, eds. *Christian Witness Between Continuity and New Beginnings: Modern Historical Missions in the Middle East*. Berlin: LIT-Verlag, 2006.

Tejirian, Eleanor H., and Reeva Spector Simon, eds. *Altruism and Imperialism: Western Cultural and Religious Missions in the Middle East*. New York: Middle East Institute, Columbia University, Occasional Papers IV, 2002.

Thomson, William M. *The Land and the Book, or Biblical Illustrations Drawn from the Manners and Customs, the Scenes and Scenery of the Holy Land*. London: T. Nelson and Sons, Paternoster Row, 1860.

Tibawi, A. L. *American Interests in Syria: 1800–1901: A Study of Educational, Literary and Religious Works*. Oxford: Clarendon Press, 1966.

Whiting, George, and William M. Thomson. "On the Results of Past Labours in the Mission." ABCFM microfilm Unit 5: Near East: Reel 538: 53B–56B. Beirut: 10 April 1844.

Williams, Samuel H. "Rebecca Williams Hebard of Lebanon, Connecticut: Missionary in Beirut, Syria and to the Druze of Mount Lebanon, 1835–1840." pamphlet. AUB, n.d.

Wortabet, Gregory M. *Syria, and the Syrians; or, Turkey in the Dependencies. Volume I*. London: James Madden, 1856.

Yazigy, Jamil M. "American Presbyterian Mission Schools in Lebanon." Master's thesis, American University Beirut, 1964.

Zachs, Fruma. *The Making of a Syrian Identity: Intellectuals and Merchants in Nineteenth Century Beirut*. Leiden and Boston: Brill, 2005.

Zilfi, Madeline C. "Servants, Slaves, and the Domestic Order in the Ottoman Middle East." *Hawwa* 2:1 (2004): 1–33.

CHAPTER 3

Ahlstrom, Sydney E. *A Religious History of the American People*. 2d ed. New Haven, CT: Yale University Press, 2004.

Anderson, Rufus. *Missionary Paper: Promised Advent of the Spirit for the World's Conversion*. Boston: Crocker & Brewster, 1841.

———. *Report to the Prudential Committee of a Visit to the Missions in the Levant*. Boston: T. R. Marvin, 1844.

————. *Memorial Volume of the First Fifty Years of the American Board of Commissioners for Foreign Missions.* Boston: The Board, 1861.

————. *Foreign Missions: Their Relations and Claims.* New York: Charles Scribner and Company, 1869.

Arpee, Leon. *The Armenian Awakening: A History of the Armenian Church, 1820–1860.* Chicago: University of Chicago Press, 1909.

Barton, James L. "Our Evangelistic Policy." *Envelope Series* 9:3 (October 1906): 3–12.

Bond, Alvan. *Memoir of the Rev. Pliny Fisk, A.M., Late Missionary to Palestine.* Boston: Crocker and Brewster, 1828.

Constitution, Laws and Regulations of the American Board of Commissioners for Foreign Missions. Boston: Crocker & Brewster, 1835.

Daniel, Robert L. "American Influences in the Near East before 1861." *American Quarterly* 16:1 (Spring 1964): 72–84.

Dwight, Henry Otis, Allen Tupper, and Edwin Munsell Bliss. *The Encyclopedia of Missions: Descriptive, Historical, Biographical, Statistical.* 2d ed. New York: Funk and Wagnalls Company, 1910.

Eddy, David Brewer. *What Next in Turkey: Glimpses of the American Board's Work in the Near East.* Boston: The American Board, 1913.

Field, James A., Jr. *America and the Mediterranean World 1776–1882.* Princeton: Princeton University Press, 1969.

Finnie, David H. *Pioneers East: The Early American Experience in the Middle East.* Cambridge, MA: Harvard University Press, 1967.

Fisher, Sydney Nettleton. "Two Centuries of American Interest in Turkey." In *A Festschrift for Frederick B. Artz,* edited by David H. Pinkney and Theodore Ropp, 113–138. Durham, NC: Duke University Press, 1964.

Hamlin, Cyrus. "Education of a Native Ministry." In *Minutes of a Conference of Missionaries held at Constantinople, in November, 1855, on Occasion of the Visit of one of the Secretaries of the American Board of Commissioners for Foreign Missions,* 12–13. Boston: T. R. Marvin, 1856.

————. *Among the Turks.* New York: Robert Carter and Brothers, 1881.

————. *My Life and Times.* 5th ed. Boston: The Pilgrim Press Chicago, 1893.

Hankins, Barry. *The Second Great Awakening and the Transcendentalists.* Westport, CT: Greenwood Press, 2004.

Harris, Paul William. *Nothing but Christ: Rufus Anderson and the Ideology of Protestant Foreign Missions.* Oxford: Oxford University Press, 1999.

Historical Sketch of the Missions of the American Board of Commissioners for Foreign Missions, in European Turkey, Asia Minor, and Armenia. New York: John A. Gray, 1861.

Holtrop, Pieter N., and Hugh McLeod. *Missions and Missionaries.* Rochester, NY: Boydell Press, 2000.

Kaestle, Clark F., ed. *Joseph Lancaster and the Monitorial School Movement: A Documentary History.* New York: Teachers College Press, 1973.

Kocabaşoğlu, Uygur. *Kendi Belgeleriyle Anadolu'daki Amerika: 19. Yüzyılda Osmanlı İmparatorluğu'ndaki Amerikan Misyoner Okulları.* İstanbul: Arba Yayınları, 1989.

Lambert, Frank. *Inventing the "Great Awakening."* Princeton: Princeton University Press, 1999.

Makdisi, Ussama. "Reclaiming the Land of the Bible: Missionaries, Secularism, and Evangelical Modernity." *The American Historical Review* 102:3 (June 1997): 680–713.

———. "Refusing Comparison: How Middle Eastern Violence is Narrated by the American Missionary." Paper presented at a conference in honor of Professor Robert L. Tignor, "The Empire and Its Discontents," Department of History, Princeton University, September 16–17, 2005.

Manual for Missionary Candidates and for Appointed Missionaries before Entering Their Fields. Boston: The Board, 1853. Revised edition, Boston: Beacon Press, 1887.

Masters, Bruce. *Christians and Jews in the Ottoman Arab World: The Roots of Sectarianism.* New York: Cambridge University Press, 2001.

Morton, Daniel Oliver. *Memoir of Rev. Levi Parsons, First Missionary to Palestine from the United States.* Burlington, VT: Chauncey Goodrich, 1830.

Murre-van den Berg, Heleen. "Why Protestant Churches? The American Board and the Eastern Churches: Mission Among 'Nominal' Christians (1820–70)." In Holtrop and McLeod, *Missions and Missionaries,* 98–111.

Nosser, Marion A. "The Educational Policies of the American Board of Commissioners for Foreign Missions in Turkey; 1823–1923." Master's thesis, University of Chicago, 1924.

Phillips, Clifton Jackson. *Protestant America and the Pagan World: The First Half Century of the American Board of Commissioners for Foreign Missions, 1810–1860.* Cambridge, MA: Harvard University Press, 1969.

Prime, E. D. G. *Forty Years in the Turkish Empire; or Memoirs of Rev. William Goodell, D.D., Late Missionary of the A. B. C. F. M. at Constantinople.* New York: Robert Carter and Brothers, 1876.

Richter, Julius. *A History of Protestant Mission in the Near East.* New York: Fleming H. Revell Comp., 1910.

Smith, Eli. *Researches of the Rev. E. Smith and Rev. H. G. O. Dwight In Armenia.* Boston: Crocker and Brewster, 1833.

Stevens, Malcolm P., and Marcia R. Stevens. "A College on the Bosporus." *Saudi Aramco World* 35:2 (March/April 1984): 16–21.

Strong, William E. *The Story of the American Board: An Account of the First Hundred Years of the American Board of Commissioners for Foreign Missions.* Boston: Pilgrim Press, 1910.

Thain, A. R. "Cyrus Hamlin D.D., LL.D. Missionary, Statesman, Inventor: A Life Sketch." *Envelope Series* 10:2 (July 1907): 3–25.

Tracy, Joseph. *History of the American Board of Commissioners for Foreign Missions: Compiled Chiefly from the Published and Unpublished Documents of the Board*, 2nd ed. New York: M. W. Dodd, 1842.

Woods, Leonard. *History of the Andover Theological Seminary*. Boston: James R. Osgood, 1885.

Chapter 4

The American College for Girls at Constantinople. *Annual Report of the American College for Girls, 1889–1890*. Ms. Robert College Archives, New York.

The American College for Girls at Constantinople. *The President's Report to the Board of Trustees for the Year 1890–91*. London: Sir Joseph Causton & Sons. Robert College Archives, New York.

The American College for Girls at Constantinople. *Report of the Year 1909–1910*. Robert College Archives, New York.

The American College for Girls at Constantinople. *Reports for the Year 1911–1912*. Constantinople: H. Matteosian, 1912.

Beaver, R. Pierce. *American Protestant Women in World Mission: History of the First Feminist Movement in North America*. Grand Rapids, MI: Eerdsman, 1980.

Borden, Caroline. "Constantinople Home." (Two versions— published and typescript.) ABC 16.7.1 Vol. 16. ACG Folder 6, Item 2. By permission of the Houghton Library, Harvard University.

Bulletin: Constantinople Woman's College: President's Report, 1923–24. Robert College Archives, New York.

Chambers, Robert. Letter to Abbie Child, Women's Board of Missions. 22 February 1894. Robert College Archives, New York.

Charter of the Trustees of the American College for Girls at Constantinople in Turkey; also the By-Laws. Boston: Fort Hill Press, 1908.

Constantinople College: The American College for Girls at Constantinople. Bulletin. President's Report, 1912–1913. Robert College Archives, New York.

Deringil, Selim. *The Well-Protected Domains: Ideology and the Legitimation of Power in the Ottoman Empire 1876–1909*. London: Tauris, 1998.

Durant, Pauline, et al. Letter to Prudential Committee of the ABCFM, 10 May 1875. ABC 16.7.1, vol. 16. ACG Folder 2, Item 1. By permission of the Houghton Library, Harvard University.

Dwight, H. G. O. *Constantinople and Its Problems: Its People, Customs, Religions and Progress*. New York: Young People's Missionary Movement, 1901.

Fincancı, May N. *The Story of Robert College Old and New: 1863–1982*. 1983. Rev. ed., Istanbul: Redhouse, 2001.

Greenwood, Keith. *Robert College: The American Founders*. İstanbul: Boğazici University Press, 2000.

Grimshaw, Patricia. *Paths of Duty: American Missionary Wives in Nineteenth-Century Hawaii*. Honolulu: University of Hawaii Press, 1989.

Hamlin, Cyrus. *Among the Turks*. New York: Robert Carter and Brothers, 1877.

Harris, Paul William. *Nothing but Christ: Rufus Anderson and the Ideology of Protestant Foreign Missions*. New York: Oxford University Press, 1999.

Hill, Patricia R. *The World Their Household: The American Woman's Foreign Mission Movement and Cultural Transformation, 1870–1920*. Ann Arbor: University of Michigan Press, 1985.

Hutchinson, William R. *Errand to the World: American Protestant Thought and Foreign Missions*. Chicago: University of Chicago Press, 1987.

Jenkins, Hester Donaldson. *An Educational Ambassador to the Near East: The Story of Mary Mills Patrick and an American College in the Orient*. New York: Fleming H. Revell, 1925.

Murre-van den Berg, Heleen, ed. *New Faith in Ancient Lands: Western Missions in the Middle East in the Nineteenth and Early Twentieth Centuries*. Leiden: Brill, 2006.

Oren, Michael B. *Power, Faith, and Fantasy: America in the Middle East 1776 to the Present*. New York: Norton, 2007.

Patrick, Mary Mills. *A Bosporus Adventure: Istanbul (Constantinople) Woman's College, 1871–1924*. Stanford: Stanford University Press, 1934.

———. *Under Five Sultans*. New York: Century, 1929.

Porterfield, Amanda. *Mary Lyon and the Mount Holyoke Missionaries*. New York: Oxford University Press, 1987.

Pruitt, Lisa Joy. *"A Looking Glass for the Ladies": American Protestant Women and the Orient in the Nineteenth Century*. Macon: Mercer University Press, 2005.

Racheva, Penka. *Diary*. Robert College Archives, New York.

Riggs, Charles T. "Julia Rappeleye." "Near East Missionary Biographies," ts. n.d. Robert College Archives, New York.

Robert, Dana L. *American Women in Mission: A Social History of Their Thought and Practice*. Macon, GA: Mercer University Press, 1996.

Rodrigue, Aron. *French Jews, Turkish Jews: The Alliance Israélite Universelle and the Politics of Jewish Schooling in Turkey, 1860–1925*. Bloomington: Indiana University Press, 1990.

Smith, Judson. Letter to Abbie B. Child, Secretary, Women's Board of Missions Minutes. 30 April 1891. ABC 16.7.1, vol. 16. ACG Box, Folder 6. By permission of the Houghton Library, Harvard University.

Van Lennep, Mary Elizabeth. *Memoir*. Published in "Stereotype" xii, [13]–382. Micropublished in "History of Women." New Haven: Research Publications, Inc. 1975.

Vogel, Lester I. *To See a Promised Land: Americans and the Holy Land in the Nine-teenth Century*. University Park: Pennsylvania State University Press, 1993.

Williams, Katherine Pond. "Ten Years Review of the Constantinople Home." Type-script. File 1-C. Robert College Archives, Istanbul, 17 May 1881.

CHAPTER 5

PRIMARY SOURCES

BAŞBAKANLIK OSMANLI ARŞIVI (PRIME MINISTERIAL
OTTOMAN ARCHIVE), ISTANBUL, TURKEY:

Bab–ı Ali Sadaret Mektubi Kalemi Mühimme Kalemi (Odası) Belgeleri (A.MKT.
MHM)
Hariciye Nezareti Siyasi Kısmı Belgeleri (HR.SYS)
Meclis–i Vükela (MV)
Yıldız Sarayı Mütenevvi Maruzat Evrakı (Y.MTV)

OTTOMAN NEWSPAPER:

Tasvir–i Efkar, no. 10, no. 11 (1279), 1863.

ARCHIVE OF THE CHURCH OF JESUS CHRIST OF LATTER-DAY SAINTS,
SALT LAKE CITY, UTAH:

MS3390, *Diary of Fred A. Huish*
MS1594, *Diary of Andrew Lund Larson*
MS12235, *Diary of Philip S. Maycock*

THE LIBRARY OF THE CHURCH OF JESUS CHRIST OF LATTER-DAY SAINTS,
SALT LAKE CITY, UTAH:

Deseret Evening News
Deseret News
Deseret Weekly
Journal History
Millennial Star

OTHER NEWSPAPERS:

New York Daily Times
New York Times

SECONDARY SOURCES

Açıkses, Erdal. "An Assessment of the Missionary Activities in the Ottoman Empire: Examples from Two Centers." In *The Great Ottoman Turkish Civilisation*, edited by Kemal Çiçek et al., vol. 1, 584–596. Ankara: Yeni Türkiye Yayınları, 2000.

Akgün, Seçil Karal. "Mormon Missionaries in the Ottoman Empire." *Turcica* 28 (1996): 347–357.

———. "The Turkish Image in the Reports of American Missionaries in the Ottoman Empire." *Turkish Studies Association Bulletin* 13 (1989): 91–105.

Bill Suppressing Mormonism. Essential Documents in American History 1:1, compiled by Norman P. Desmarais and James H. McGovern (2009).

Bishop, M. Guy. "The Saints and the Captain: The Mormons Meet Richard F. Burton." *Journal of the West* 33:4 (October 1994): 28–35.

Blumi, Isa. "Contesting the Edges of the Ottoman Empire: Rethinking Ethnic and Sectarian Boundaries in the Malësore, 1878–1912." *International Journal of Middle East Studies* 35:2 (May 2003): 237–256.

Brewerton, Denton Y. "Istanbul and Rexburg: Jacob Spori's Mission Field." *Ensign* 10:6 (June 1980): 26–32.

Charles, David P. "The Day the 'Brave sons of Mohamed' Saved a Group of Mormons." *BYU Studies, Special Issue on Islam* (2001): 237–254.

———. "'You Had the Alps, but We the Mount of Olives': Mormon Missionary Travel in the Middle East (1884–1928)." *Mormon Historical Studies* 1:1 (1999): 93–126.

Cogley, Richard W. "The Fall of the Ottoman Empire and the Restoration of Israel in the "Judeo-centric" Strand of Puritan Millenarianism." *Church History* 72:2 (June 2003): 304–333.

Çolak, Melek. "Osmanlı İmparatorluğunda Mormonlar." *Tarih ve Toplum* 210 (Haziran 2001): 23–27.

Davison, Roderic H. *Reform in the Ottoman Empire 1856–1876.* Princeton: Princeton University Press, 1963.

Deringil, Selim. *The Well-Protected Domains: Ideology and the Legitimation of Power in the Ottoman Empire, 1876–1909.* London: I. B. Tauris, 1998.

Doumani, Beshara. *Rediscovering Palestine: Merchants and Peasants in Jabal Nablus, 1700–1900.* Berkeley: University of California Press, 1995.

Duben, Alan, and Cem Behar. *Istanbul Households: Marriage, Family and Fertility, 1880–1940.* Cambridge: Cambridge University Press, 1991.

Erhan, Çağrı. "Ottoman Official Attitudes Towards American Missionaries." In *The United States & the Middle East: Cultural Encounters*, edited by Abbas Amanat and Magnus Thorkell Bernhardsson, 321–347. New Haven: Yale Center for International and Area Studies, 2002.

Field, James A. *America and the Mediterranean World 1776–1882.* Princeton: Princeton University Press, 1969.

Finkel, Caroline. *Osman's Dream: The History of the Ottoman Empire*. New York: Perseus Books, 2005.

Fortna, Benjamin C. *Imperial Classroom: Islam, the State, and Education in the Late Ottoman Empire*. Oxford: Oxford University Press, 2002.

Fraser, Caroline. "The Mormon Murder Case." Review of *Blood of the Prophets: Brigham Young and the Massacre at Mountain Meadows*, by Will Bagley, and *Red Water*, by Judith Freeman. *The New York Review of Books*, November 21, 2002.

Gordon, Leland J. "Turkish-American Treaty Relations." *The American Political Science Review* 22:3 (August 1928): 711–714.

Green, Arnold H., and Lawrence P. Goldrup. "Joseph Smith, an American Muhammad? An Essay on the Perils of Historical Analogy." *Dialogue: A Journal of Mormon Thought* 6 (Spring 1971): 46–58.

Halsall, Paul, ed. "Treaty between Great Britain, Austria-Hungary, France, Germany, Italy, Russia and Turkey. (Berlin). July 13, 1878." In *Modern History Sourcebook: The Treaty of Berlin, 1878 Excerpts on the Balkans*. New York: Fordham University, July 1998. http://www.fordham.edu/halsall/mod/1878berlin.html.

"Hattı Şerif of Gülhane." In *The Middle East and North Africa in World Politics: A Documentary Record*, edited by J. C. Hurewitz, vol. 1, 115 and 317. New Haven: Yale University Press, 1975.

Kark, Ruth. *American Consuls in the Holy Land, 1832–1914*. Detroit, MI: Wayne State University Press, 1994.

Kern, Karen M. "Rethinking Ottoman Frontier Policies: Marriage and Citizenship in the Province of Iraq." *Arab Studies Journal* 15:1 (Spring 2007): 8–29.

Kieser, Hans-Lukas. "Muslim Heterodoxy and Protestant Utopia. The interactions between Alevis and missionaries in Ottoman Anatolia." *Die Welt des Islams* 41:1 (March 2001): 89–111.

Kuhn, Thomas, ed. "Borderlands of the Ottoman Empire in the Nineteenth and Early Twentieth Centuries," *MIT Electronic Journal of Middle East Studies* 3 (Spring 2003).

———. "Ordering the Past of Ottoman Yemen, 1871–1914." *Turcica* 34 (2002): 189–220.

Lindsay, Rao H. "The Dream of a Mormon Colony in the Near East." *Dialogue: A Journal of Mormon Thought* 1:4 (Winter 1966): 50–67.

———. "A History of the Missionary Activities of the Church of Jesus Christ of Latter-day Saints in the Near East, 1884–1928." Master's thesis, Brigham Young University, 1958.

Makdisi, Ussama. "Reclaiming the Land of the Bible: Missionaries, Secularism, and Evangelical Modernity." *The American Historical Review* 102:3 (June 1997): 680–713.

Peterson, Daniel C. *Abraham Divided: The LDS Perspective on the Middle East*. Salt Lake City, UT: Aspen Books, revised edition, 1995.

Pingree, Daniel J. "'And Your Name Will Be Remembered….' The History of John Alexander Clark's Turkish Mission." *The Thetean* 24 (1995): 31–50.

Porter, Andrew N. "Evangelicalism, Islam, and Millennial Expectation in the Nineteenth Century." *International Bulletin of Missionary Research* 24:3 (July 2000): 111–117.

Rogan, Eugene L. *Frontiers of the State in the Late Ottoman Empire: Transjordan, 1850–1921.* Cambridge: Cambridge University Press, 1999.

———. "*Aşiret Mektebi*: Abdülhamid II's School for Tribes (1892–1907)." *International Journal of Middle East Studies* 28:1 (February 1996): 83–107.

Salt, Jeremy. "A Precarious Symbiosis: Ottoman Christians and Foreign Missionaries in the Nineteenth Century." *International Journal of Turkish Studies* 3:2 (Winter 1985–1986): 53–67.

Sharkey, Heather J. "Empire and Muslim Conversion: Historical Reflections on Christian Missions in Egypt." *Islam and Christian-Muslim Relations* 16:1 (January 2005): 43–60.

Shaw, Stanford J., and Ezel Kural Shaw. *History of the Ottoman Empire and Modern Turkey. Volume II, Reform, Revolution and the Republic: The Rise of Modern Turkey 1808–1975.* Cambridge: Cambridge University Press, 1997.

Smith, Agnes M. "The First Mormon Mission to Britain." *History Today* 37 (July 1987): 24–31.

Toronto, James A. "Early Missions to Ottoman Turkey, Syria, and Palestine." In *Out of Obscurity: The LDS Church in the Twentieth Century*, 339–362. Salt Lake City, UT: Deseret Book Company, Sperry Symposium Series, 2000.

Turan, Ömer. "Protestant Missionary Activities in Turkey during the Late Ottoman and Early Republican Periods." In *The Great Ottoman Turkish Civilisation*, edited by Kemal Çiçek et al., vol. 1, 513–519. Ankara: Yeni Türkiye Yayınları, 2000.

"Turkish Mission." In *Encyclopedia History of the Church of Jesus Christ of Latter-day Saints*, 888–890. Salt Lake City: Andrew Jenson, 1941.

Welter, Barbara. "She Hath Done What She Could: Protestant Women's Missionary Careers in Nineteenth-Century America." *American Quarterly* 30:5 Special Issue: Women and Religion (Winter 1978): 624–638.

Walpole, C. G., trans. *The Ottoman Penal Code, 28 Zilhijeh 1274 (9 August 1858).* London: William Clowes and Sons, Ltd., 1888.

Zücher, Erik J. *Turkey: A Modern History.* London: I. B. Tauris, 2nd edition, 2003.

CHAPTER 6

ARCHIVES

American Board of Commissioners for Foreign Missions Correspondence and Reports, vol. 545, "Documents, Reports and Letters, 1860–1871," no. 36: "Annual Report of the Beirut Station, 1866."

American Board of Commissioners for Foreign Missions Correspondence and Reports, vol. 545, "Documents, Reports and Letters, 1860–1871," no. 110, "Prospectus and Programme of the Syrian Protestant Collegiate Institute Beirut."

American Board of Commissioners for Foreign Missions, Correspondence and Reports, vol. 545, "Documents, Reports and Letters, 1860–1871," no. 110, "Reasons for the establishment of a Syrian Protestant College."

American University of Beirut Library Archives, Minutes of the Board of Trustees, bk 1.

American University of Beirut Library Archives, Minutes of the Board of Trustees, bk 2.

American University of Beirut Library Archives, MSS AUB 1, Bliss Papers, Letters with Various Faculty Members, box 14, folder 1, Letters from James Dennis, 1883–1910.

American University of Beirut Library Archives, MSS AUB 1, box 5, 1/3, folder 3, Letters from Dr. Stuart Dodge to Daniel Bliss, 1880–1883.

American University of Beirut Library Archives, MSS AUB 1, box 6, 2/1, folder 1, Letters from Dr. Stuart Dodge to Daniel Bliss, 1880–1885.

American University of Beirut Library Archives, MSS AUB 33, Record of the Secretary of the Board of Managers of the Syrian Protestant College, 1864–1903.

Amherst College Library Archives and Special Collections, Bliss Family Papers, 1850–1981, box 1, folder 7.

Amherst College Library Archives and Special Collections, Bliss Family Papers, 1850–1981, box 5, addendum 1, folder 1.

Archive diplomatique de Nantes: Ministère des Affaires Étrangères: Constantinople Série E: 709: 'Ottoman and American Schools', carton 173, dossier 4.

The Darwin Correspondence Online Database, calendar number 13645, C. R. Darwin to W. T. Van Dyck, 25 January 1882; 13710, W. T. Van Dyck to C. R. Darwin, 27 February 1882; 13757 C. R. Darwin to W. T. Van Dyck, 3 April 1882.

Harvard University Archives, HU 20.41 mfp, 1804–1888/9, reel 4, 1863/4–1873/4.

Houghton Library Archives, Harvard University, ABC 50, Eli Smith Arabic Papers (1821–1857), box 1.

Houghton Library Archives, Harvard University, ABC 60, Eli Smith Papers, folders 46, 72 and 144.

Presbyterian Church Board of Foreign Missions Correspondence and Reports, vol. 4, no. 21.

Presbyterian Church Board of Foreign Missions Correspondence and Reports, vol. 5, no. 26.

Presbyterian Church Board of Foreign Missions, Correspondence and Reports, vol. 5, no. 42.

Presbyterian Church Board of Foreign Missions Correspondence and Reports, vol. 5, no. 47.

BOOKS AND ARTICLES

"'Abeih Station Report for 1849." *Missionary Herald* 66 (August 1850): 262–263.

"American Board of Commissioners for Foreign Missions; Syria and the Holy Land. Journal of Mr. W. M. Thomson on a Visit to Safet And Tiberias." *Missionary Herald* 33 (November 1837): 433–445.

"Butrus al-Bustani." *al-Muqtataf* 8 (1883): 1–7.

"Dawaran al-ard" [The Rotation of the Earth]. *al-Muqtataf* 1 (1876): 141–143.

"al-Duktur Faris Nimr" [Dr Faris Nimr]. *al-Muqtataf* 120 (1952): 1–13.

"al-Duktur Lewis" [Doctor Lewis]. *al-Muqtataf* 9 (1884): 183.

"al-Duktur Ya'qub Sarruf" [Dr Ya'qub Sarruf]. *al-Muqtataf* 71 (1927): 121–128.

"Education in Syria." *Hours at Home: A Popular Monthly of Instruction and Recreation* 11 (1870): 328.

"Favorable Location of Beyroot. Progress of Missionary Labors." *Missionary Herald* 31 (March 1835): 92–93.

"Iman al-Muqtataf wa kufr al-Bashir" [*al-Muqtataf*'s Faith and *al-Bashir*'s Disbelief]. *al-Muqtataf* 8 (1883): 714–717.

"al-Khusuf al-juz'i" [The Partial Lunar Eclipse]. *al-Muqtataf* 1 (1876): 117.

"Khusuf al-qamar" [The eclipse of the Moon]. *al-Muqtataf* 1 (1876): 95–96.

"Letter from Mr. Smith, Beyroot." *Missionary Herald* 38 (September 1842): 362–364.

"al-Madrasa al-Kulliya al-Tabi'ayya" [The Syrian Protestant College Medical School]. *al-Muqtataf* 7 (1882): 192.

"Mission to Syria and the Holy Land." *Missionary Herald* 39 (January 1843): 6–7.

"al-Muqaddima" [Introduction]. *al-Muqtataf* 1 (1876): 1–2.

"al-Nizam al-shamsi" [The Solar System]. *al-Muqtataf* 1 (1876): 29–32.

"Report of the Syria Mission for the year 1841." *Missionary Herald* 38 (June 1842): 224–232.

"al-Sihr ghish" [Magic is a Scam]. *al-Muqtataf* 3 (1878): 205–210.

"Tafsir al-Qur'an al-hakim" [Exegesis of the Qur'an]. *al-Manar* 1 (1898): 234–235; 2 (1899): 232–236; and 4 (1901): 268.

"Thabut al-ard wa raddat ilayna hadha al-risala" [A Letter on the Fixity of the Earth included with our Answer to it]. *al-Muqtataf* 1 (1876): 265–267 and 268–270.

"Translation of the Firman of His Imperial Majesty Sultan 'Abd-el-Mejid, Granted in Favor of his Protestant Subjects," translated by the Reverend H. Dwight. *Journal of the American Oriental Society* 3 (1853): 218–220.

"Translation of the Firman Granted by Sultan 'Abd-al-Mejeed to his Protestant Subjects," translated by the Reverend H. Dwight. *Journal of the American Oriental Society* 4 (1854): 443–444.

"al-'Ulum al-tabi'aya" [The Natural Sciences]. *al-Muqtataf* 1 (1876): 169–171.

"al-'Ulum al-tabi'aya wa'l-nusus al-shari'aya" [The Natural Sciences and the Principles of the *Shari'a*]. *al-Muqtataf* 1 (1876): 217–220.

Abu-Ghazaleh, Adnan. *American Missions in Syria: A Study of American Mission-ary Contribution to Arab Nationalism in 19th Century Syria*. Brattleboro, VT: Amana Books, 1990.

Abu-Manneh, Butrus. "The Christians between Ottomanism and Syrian National-ism: The Ideas of Butrus al-Bustani." *International Journal of Middle East Studies* 11 (1980): 287–304.

Ahmad, Ibrahim Khalil. *al-Mustashriqun wa'l-mubashirun fi al-'alam al-'Arabi wa-al-Islami* [Orientalists and Missionaries in the Arab and Muslim World]. Cairo: Maktabat al-Wa'i al-'Arabi, 1964.

American Board of Commissioners for Foreign Missions. *First Ten Annual Reports of the American Board of Commissioners for Foreign Missions*. Boston: Crocker and Brewster, 1834.

American Board of Commissioners for Foreign Missions. *The Divine Instrumental-ity for the World's Conversion*. Boston: Missionary House, 1856.

Anderson, Betty. "Defining Liberal Education at the American University of Beirut: Education, Protestantism, and Service to Nation." Paper presented at University of Erlangen-Nürnberg, Erlangen, 2005.

Anderson, Rufus. *Missionary Schools (From the Biblical Repository)*. New York, n.d.

———. "A Sermon on the Present Crisis in the Missionary Organizations of the American Board of Commissioners for Foreign Missions." *Christian Examiner and General Review* 29 (September 1840): 57–59.

———. *Report to the Prudential Committee of a Visit to the Missions in the Levant*. Boston: T. R. Marvin, 1844.

———. *History of the Missions of the American Board of Commissioners for Foreign Missions to the Oriental Churches*. Boston: Congregational Publishing Society, 1872, 2 volumes.

Antonius, George. *The Arab Awakening: The Story of the Arab National Movement*. London: H. Hamilton, 1945.

Asad, Talal. "Comments on Conversion." In van der Veer, *Conversion to Moderni-ties*, 263–273.

Ayalon, Ami. *The Press in the Arab Middle East: A History*. New York: Oxford Uni-versity Press, 1995.

Beidelman, T. O. *Colonial Evangelism: A Socio-Historical Study of an East African Mission at the Grassroots*. Bloomington: Indiana University Press, 1982.

Bliss, Daniel. *al-Durus al-awliyya fi-al-falsafa al-'aqliyya* [Primary Lessons in Ratio-nal Philosophy]. Beirut: American Mission Press, 1873.

Bozeman, Theodore Dwight. *Protestants in the Age of Science: The Baconian Ideal and Ante-Bellum American Religious Thought*. Chapel Hill: University of North Carolina Press, 1977.

Brophy, James M. "The Common Reader in the Rhineland: The Calendar as Polit-ical Primer in the Early Nineteenth Century." *Past and Present*, no. 185 (2004): 119–157.

al-Bustani, Butrus. *A'mal al-jam'iya al-Suriya* [Proceedings of the Syrian Society]. Beirut: s.n., 1852.

———. *Qissat As'ad al-Shidyaq* [The Story of As'ad al-Shidyaq]. Beirut: Dar al-Hamra, 1860.

Carter, Paul. *The Spiritual Crisis of the Gilded Age*. DeKalb: Northern Illinois University Press, 1971.

Catalogue of the Syrian Protestant College. Beirut: American Mission Press, 1902–1903.

Cioeta, Donald. "Ottoman Censorship in Lebanon and Syria, 1876–1908." *International Journal of Middle East Studies* 10 (1979): 182.

Comaroff, John L., and Jean Comaroff. *Of Revelation and Revolution, Vol. 2, The Dialectics of Modernity on a South African Frontier*. Chicago: University of Chicago Press, 1997.

———. *Of Revelation and Revolution: Christianity, Colonialism and Consciousness in South Africa*. Chicago: University of Chicago Press, 1991.

Cooper, Frederick. *Colonialism in Question: Theory, Knowledge, History*. Berkeley: University of California Press, 2005.

Davis, John. *The Landscape of Belief: Encountering the Holy Land in Nineteenth-Century American Art and Culture*. Princeton: Princeton University Press, 1996.

Dennis, James S. *A Sketch of the Syria Mission*. New York: Mission House, 1872.

Dennis, James. "al-Madhab al-Darwini" [The Darwinian School of Thought]. *al-Muqtataf* 7 (1882): 233–236.

———. *Christian Missions and Social Progress: A Sociological Study of Foreign Missions*. New York: Fleming H. Revell, 3 volumes, 1897–1906.

Diab, Henry, and Lars Wahlin. "The Geography of Education in Syria in 1882: With a Translation of 'Education in Syria' by Shahin Makarius." *Geografiska Annaler* 65 (1983): 105–128.

Draper, John William. *A History of the Conflict between Religion and Science*. New York: D. Appleton, 1875.

Elshakry, Marwa. "Darwin's Legacies in the Arab East: Science, Religion and Politics, 1870–1914." PhD diss., Princeton University, 2003.

Elsbree, Oliver Wendell. "The Rise of the Missionary Spirit in New England, 1790–1815." *New England Quarterly* 3 (1928): 295–322.

Farag, Nadia. "Al-Muqtataf, 1876–1900: A Study of the Influence of Victorian Thought on Modern Arabic Thought." PhD diss., University of Oxford, 1969.

———. "The Lewis Affair and the Fortunes of *al-Muqtataf*." *Middle Eastern Studies* 8 (1972): 73–83.

Field, James A., Jr. *America and the Mediterranean World, 1776–1882*. Princeton: Princeton University Press, 1969.

Fisk, Pliny. *The Holy Land an Interesting Field of Missionary Enterprise: A Sermon*. Boston, 1819.

Fitzgerald, Rosemary. "'Clinical Christianity': The Emergence of Medical Work as a

Missionary Strategy in Colonial India, 1800–1914." In *Health, Medicine and Empire: Perspectives on Colonial India*, edited by Biswamoy Pati and Mark Harrison. Hyderabad: Orient Longman, 2001.

Fyfe, Aileen. *Science and Salvation: Evangelical Popular Science Publishing in Victorian Britain*. Chicago: University of Chicago Press, 2004.

Gilliam, Robert Truett. "A Muslim Response to Protestant Missionaries: The Case of al-Manar." American University of Beirut, MA dissertation, 2000.

Grabill, Joseph L. *Protestant Diplomacy and the Near East: Missionary Influence on American Policy, 1810–1927*. Minneapolis: University of Minnesota Press, 1971.

Gunson, Neil. "British Missionaries and Their Contribution to Science in the Pacific Islands." In *Darwin's Laboratory: Evolutionary Theory and Natural History in the Pacific*, edited by Roy MacLeod and Philip F. Rehbock, 283–316. Honolulu: University of Hawaii Press, 1994.

Haddad, Mahmoud. "Syrian Muslim Attitudes Toward Foreign Missionaries in the Late Nineteenth and Twentieth Centuries." In *Altruism and Imperialism: Western Cultural and Religious Missions in the Middle East*, edited by Eleanor H. Tejirian and Reeva Spector Simon. New York: Middle East Institute, Columbia University, 2002.

Handy, Robert T., ed. *The Social Gospel in America, 1870–1920: Gladden, Ely, Rauschenbusch*. New York: Oxford University Press, 1966.

Hankins, Barry. *The Second Great Awakening and the Transcendentalists*. Westport: Greenwood Press, 2004.

Hanssen, Jens. *Fin de Siècle Beirut: The Making of an Ottoman Provincial Capital*. Oxford: Oxford University Press, 2005.

Harris, Paul William. *Nothing but Christ: Rufus Anderson and the Ideology of Protestant Foreign Missions*. Oxford: Oxford University Press, 1999.

Hitti, Philip K. *Lebanon in History from the Earliest Times to the Present*. London: St. Martin's Press, 1957.

Hopkins, Charles Howard. *The Rise of the Social Gospel in American Protestantism, 1865–1915*. New Haven: Yale University Press, 1940.

Hopkins, Samuel. *A Treatise on the Millennium*. New York: Arno Press, 1972.

Hourani, Albert. "Bustani's Encyclopaedia." *Journal of Islamic Studies* 1 (1990): 111–119.

————. *Arabic Thought in the Liberal Age, 1798–1939*. Oxford: Oxford University Press, 1962.

Hurani, Ibrahim. *Manahij al-hukm fi nafy al-nushu' wa'l-irtiqa'* [The Procedure for a Judgement Refuting Evolution]. Beirut: American Mission Press, 1884.

Jessup, Henry H. *Fifty Three Years in Syria*, 2 volumes. New York: Fleming H. Revell, 1910.

al-Jisr, Husayn. *al-Risala al-Hamidaya fi haqiqat al-diyana al-Islamiya wa haqiqat al-shari'a al-Muhammidiya* [A Hamidian Treatise on the Truthfulness of Islam and Muhammadan Law]. Cairo, 1905.

Juha, Shafiq. *Darwin wa azmat 1882* [Darwin and the Crisis of 1882]. Beirut: American University of Beirut Press, 1991.

Karmen, Michael. "The Science of the Bible in Nineteenth Century America: From 'Common Sense' to Controversy, 1820–1900." PhD diss., Notre Dame University, 2004.

Kedourie, Elie. "The American University of Beirut." In *Arab Political Memoirs and Other Studies*, edited by Elie Kedourie. London: Cass, 1974.

——. *The Chatham House Version and Other Middle Eastern Studies*. New York: Praeger, 1970.

Khalidi, Mustafa, and 'Umar Farrukh. *al-Tabshir wa'l-isti'mar fi al-bilad al-'Arabiya* [Missions and Imperialism in the Arab World]. Beirut: al-Maktaba al-'Asriya, 1957.

al-Khuri, Khalil. *al-Muqtataf* 9 (1884): 47.

al-Khuri, Nasir. "'Amal falakiyya" [On Astronomy]. *al-Jinan* 20 (1876): 701–705.

King, Jonas. *The Oriental Church, and the Latin*. New York: John A. Gray & Green, 1865.

Kurd 'Ali, Muhammad. "al-'Alama al-Duktur Ya'qub Sarruf" [Professor Ya'qub Sarruf]. *Majallat al-majma al-'ilmi al-'Arabi* 1 (1928): 57–60.

Lambert, Frank. *Inventing the "Great Awakening."* Princeton: Princeton University Press, 2001.

Landau, Paul S. "Explaining Surgical Evangelism in Colonial Southern Africa: Teeth, Pain and Faith." *Journal of African History* 37 (1996): 261–281.

Leavitt, Donald. "Darwinism in the Arab World and the Lewis Affair at the Syrian Protestant College." *Muslim World* 71 (1981): 85–98.

Les Missions Catholiques 9 (1873): 570–571.

Lewis, Edwin. "al-Ma'rifa al-'ilm wa'l-hikma" [Knowledge, Science and Wisdom]. *al-Muqtataf* 7 (1882): 158–167.

——. "al-Madhab al-Darwini" [The Darwinian School of Thought]. *al-Muqtataf* 7 (1882): 287–290.

Lindsay, Rao. "Nineteenth-Century American Schools in the Levant: A Study of Purposes." PhD diss., University of Michigan, 1964.

Makdisi, Ussama. "Reclaiming the Land of the Bible: Missionaries, Secularism and Evangelical Modernity." *American Historical Review* 102 (1997): 680–713.

——. "The Two Deaths of As'ad al-Shidyaq." Paper presented at Birkbeck College, London, 2002.

——. *Artillery of Heaven: American Missionaries and the Failed Conversion of the Middle East*. Ithaca: Cornell University Press, 2008.

al-Marrash, Fransis Fath Allah. *Shihadat al-tabi'a fi wujud Allah wa-al-shari'a* [Nature's Testimony to God and Divine Law]. Beirut: American Mission Press, 1891.

Meyer, D. H. "American Intellectuals and the Victorian Crisis of Faith." *American Quarterly* 27 (1975): 583–603.

al-Midani, 'Abdul Rahman Hasan. *Ajnihat al-makr al-thalatha wa khawafiha:*

al-tabshir, al-istishraq, al-isti'mar [The Three Wings of Duplicity: Missions, Orientalism and Imperialism]. Damascus: Dar al-Qalam, 1975.

Mitchell, Timothy. *Colonising Egypt*. Berkeley: University of California Press, 1988.

Noll, Mark A. *The Rise of Evangelicalism: The Age of Edwards, Whitefield and the Wesleys*. Leicester: Apollos, 2004.

Pels, Peter. "The Anthropology of Colonialism: Culture, History, and the Emergence of Western Governmentality." *Annual Review of Anthropology* 26 (1997): 163–183.

Penrose, Stephen B. L. *That They May Have Life: The Story of the American University of Beirut 1866–1941*. New York: Trustees of the American University of Beirut, 1941.

Phillips, Clifton Jackson. *Protestant America and the Pagan World: The First Half Century of the American Board of Commissioners for Foreign Missions, 1810–1860*. Cambridge: East Asian Research Center, Harvard University, 1969.

Porter, Andrew. "'Commerce and Christianity': The Rise and Fall of a Nineteenth-Century Missionary Slogan." *Historical Journal* 28 (1985): 597–621.

———. *Religion versus Empire? British Protestant Missionaries and Overseas Expansion, 1700–1914*. Manchester: Manchester University Press, 2004.

Post, George. *Mabadi 'ilm al-nabat* [Principles of Botany]. Beirut: American Mission Press, 1871.

———. *Nizam al-halaqat fi silsilat dhawat al-fiqarat* [Vertebrates and the Great Chain of Being]. Beirut: American Mission Press, 1869.

Prucha, Francis Paul, ed. *Americanizing the American Indian: Writings by the "Friends of the Indian," 1880–1900*. Lincoln: University of Nebraska Press, 1978.

Quandt, J. B. "Religion and Social Thought: The Secularization of Postmillennialism" *American Quarterly* 25 (1973): 390–409.

Rauschenbusch, Walter. *A Theology for the Social Gospel*. New York: Abingdon Press, 1917.

Reed, James Eldin. "American Foreign Policy, the Politics of Missions and Josiah Strong, 1890–1900." *Church History* 41 (1972): 230–245.

Sa'di, Lutfi. "The Life and Works of George Edward Post (1839–1910)." In *The Founding Fathers of the American University of Beirut,* edited by Ghada Yusuf Khoury, 151–177. Beirut: American University of Beirut Press, 1992.

———. "Al-Hakim Cornelius Van Allen Van Dyck." *Isis* 27 (1937): 20–45.

Salibi, Kamal S. *The Modern History of Lebanon*. London: Weidenfeld and Nicolson, 1965.

Salisbury, Edward. "Syrian Society of Arts and Sciences." *Journal of the American Oriental Society* 3 (1853): 477–486.

Samrah, Mahmud. "Christian Missions and Western Ideas in Syrian Muslim Writers, 1860–1918." PhD diss., University of London, 1958.

Sarruf, Fuad. *Ya'qub Sarruf*. Beirut: American University of Beirut Press, 1960.

Sarruf, Ya'qub. "al-'Ilm wa'l-madaris al-jami'i" [Science and Higher Education]. *al-Muqtataf* 9 (1884): 468.

———. *al-Hikma al-Ilahiyya* [Divine Wisdom]. Beirut: American Mission Press, 1877.

Schaffer, Simon. "Self Evidence." *Critical Inquiry* 28 (1992): 327–362.

Schölch, Alexander. "Britain in Palestine, 1838–1882: The Roots of the Balfour Policy." *Journal of Palestine Studies* 22 (1992): 39–56.

Sedra, Paul. "Modernity's Mission: Evangelical Efforts to Discipline the Nineteenth Century Coptic Community." In *Altruism and Imperialism: Western Cultural and Religious Missions in the Middle East*, edited by Eleanor H. Tejirian and Reeva Spector Simon. New York: Middle East Institute, Columbia University, 2002.

al-Shadudi, As'ad Ibrahim. *Kitab al-'arus al-badi'a fi 'ilm al-tabi'a* [The Magnificent Bride of Natural Science]. Beirut: American Mission Press, 1873.

Shapin, Steven. "The House of Experiment in Seventeenth Century England." *Isis* 79 (1988): 373–404.

Sharaf, 'Imad. *Haqa'iq 'an al-tabshir* [The Truth about Missions]. Cairo: al-Mukhtar al-Islami, 1975.

Sharkey, Heather J. "Arabic Antimissionary Treatises: Muslim Responses." *International Bulletin of Missionary Research* 28:3 (July 2004): 112–118.

Shumayyil, Shibli. *Sharh Bukhnar 'ala madhab Darwin* [Büchner's Exposition of Darwinism]. Alexandria: Matba'at Jaridat al-Mahrusa, 1884.

Sivasundaram, Sujit. *Nature and the Godly Empire: Science and Evangelical Mission in the Pacific, 1795–1850*. Cambridge: Cambridge University Press, 2005.

Stephanson, Anders. *Manifest Destiny: American Expansion and the Empire of Right*. New York: Hill and Wang, 1995.

Syrian Mission. *Minutes of the Special Meeting of the Syrian Mission Held in September and October, 1855, On Occasion of the Visit of One of the Secretaries of the American Board of Commissioners for Foreign Missions*. Boston: T. R. Marvin, 1856.

Syrian Protestant College. "Declaration of Principles," *Certificate of Incorporation and Constitution*. New York: passed 1864, amended 1882.

Syrian Protestant College. *Annual Reports*. Beirut: s.n., 1963.

Tamim, Suha. *A Bibliography of A.U.B. Faculty Publications, 1866–1966*. Beirut: American University of Beirut Press, 1967.

Tarrazi, Filib. *Tarikh al-sihafa al-'Arabiya* [A History of the Arabic Press]. Beirut: al-Matba'a al-Adabiya, 1913–1933, 4 volumes.

Tejirian, Eleanor H. "Faith of Our Fathers: Near East Relief and the Near East Foundation—From Mission to NGO." In *Altruism and Imperialism: Western Cultural and Religious Missions in the Middle East*, edited by Eleanor H. Tejirian and Reeva Spector Simon. New York: Middle East Institute, Columbia University, 2002.

Thistlethwayte, Lynette. "The Role of Science in the Hindu-Christian Encounter." *Indo-British Review* 19 (1991): 73–83.

Tibawi, Abdul Latif. "Some Misconceptions about the *Nahda*." *Middle East Forum* 47 (1971): 15–22.

———. "The American Missionaries in Beirut and Butrus al-Bustani." *Middle Eastern Affairs* 3 (1963): 137–182.

———. "The Genesis and Early History of the Syrian Protestant College." *Middle East Journal* 21 (1967): 199–212.

———. *American Interests in Syria, 1800–1901: A Study of Educational, Literary and Religious Work*. Oxford: Clarendon Press, 1966.

Topham, Jonathan R. "Science, Natural Theology and Evangelicalism in Early Nineteenth Century Scotland." In *Evangelicals and Science in Historical Perspective*, edited by David N. Livingstone, D. G. Hart, and Mark A. Noll. Oxford: Oxford University Press, 1999.

Van der Veer, Peter, ed. *Conversion to Modernities: The Globalization of Christianity*. New York: Routledge, 1996.

Van Dyck, Cornelius. *Usul al-kimiya* [Principles of Chemistry]. Beirut: American Mission Press, 1869.

Vaughan, Megan. *Curing Their Ills: Colonial Power and African Illness*. Cambridge: Cambridge University Press, 1991.

Viswanathan, Gauri. *Outside the Fold: Conversion, Modernity and Belief*. Princeton: Princeton University Press, 1998.

White, Andrew Dickson. *A History of the Warfare of Science with Theology in Christendom*. New York: D. Appleton, 1896.

Williams, Peter C. "Healing and Evangelism: The Place of Medicine in Late Victorian Protestant Missionary Thinking." In *The Church and Healing*, edited by W. J. Sheils. Oxford: Studies in Church History, 1982.

Winter, Alison. "The Construction of Orthodoxies and Heterodoxies in the Early Victorian Life Sciences." In *Victorian Science in Context*, edited by Bernard Lightman, 24–50. Chicago: Chicago University Press, 1997.

Wolf, Carl J. C., ed. *Jonathan Edwards on Evangelism*. Westport: Greenwood Press, 1958.

Wortabet, Gregory M. *Syria and the Syrians: or, Turkey in the Dependencies*. London: J. Madden, 1856, 2 volumes.

Yared, Nazik Saba. *Secularism and the Arab World*. London: Saqi, 2002.

Zachs, Fruma. *The Making of a Syrian Identity: Intellectuals and Merchants in Nineteenth Century Beirut*. Leiden: Brill, 2005.

Zaydan, Jurji. *Mudhakkirat Jurji Zaydan*, trans. by Thomas Philipp, *The Autobiography of Jurji Zaydan*. Washington D.C.: Three Continents Press, 1990.

———. *Tarajim mashahir al-Sharq* [Biographies of Famous Men of the East]. Cairo: Matba'at al-Hilal, 1922.

Chapter 7

Aksit, Elif Ekin. "Girls' Education and the Paradoxes of Modernity and Nationalism in the Late Ottoman Empire and the Early Turkish Republic." PhD diss., State University of New York at Binghamton, 2004.

Baeva, Sonya. "Dnevnik Makedoniya" ("The Makedoniya Journal"). In *Literaturen Arkiv P.R. Slaveykov*, edited by Petur Dinekov, Georgi Dimov, and Sonya Baeva, 80–146. Sofia: Bulgarian Academy of Sciences, 1959.

———. *Petko Slaveykov: Zhivot i tvorchestvo, 1827–1870 (Petko Slaveykov: Life and Literature, 1827–1870)*. Sofia: Bulgarian Academy of Sciences, 1968.

Baeva, Sonya, et al., eds. *Petko R. Slaveykov: Suchineniya (Petko R. Slaveykov: Writings)*. Vol. 8. Sofia: Bulgarski pisatel, 1982.

Bloch, Ruth H. "American Feminine Ideals in Transition: The Rise of the Moral Mother, 1785–1815." *Feminist Studies* 4, no. 2 (1978): 101–126.

Borin, Julietta Velitchkova. "Les projets d'education bulgares au XIXe Siecle: Affirmation nationale et transferts culturels." PhD diss., Ecole des Hautes Etudes en Sciences Sociales, 1998.

Braude, Benjamin, and Bernard Lewis, eds. *Christians and Jews in the Ottoman Empire: The Functioning of a Plural Society*. New York: Holmes & Meier, 1982.

Brown, Candy Gunther. *The Word in the World: Evangelical Writing, Publishing, and Reading in America, 1789–1880*. Chapel Hill: University of North Carolina Press, 2004.

Butler, Thomas. *Monumenta Bulgarica: A Bilingual Anthology of Bulgarian Texts from the 9th to the 19th Centuries*. Ann Arbor: Michigan Slavic Publications, 1996.

Cholakova, Margarita. *Bulgarsko zhensko dvizhenie prez Vuzrazhdaneto, 1857–1878 (The Bulgarian Women's Movement during the National Revival, 1857–1878)*. Sofia: Albo, 1994.

Clarke, James F. "Konstantin Fotinov, Liuboslovie and the Smyrna Bulgarian Press." In *The Pen and the Sword: Studies in Bulgarian History by James F. Clarke*, edited by Dennis P. Hupchick, 321–327. Boulder, CO: East European Monographs, 1988.

———. *Bible Societies, American Missionaries and the National Revival of Bulgaria*. New York: Arno Press, 1971.

Danova, Nadya. "Bulgarski studenti na ostrov Andros" ("Bulgarian Students on Andros Island"). *Istoricheski pregled*, no. 1 (1996): 32–69.

———. *Konstantin Georgiev Fotinov v kulturnoto i ideyno-politicheskoto razvitie na Balkanite prez XIX vek (Konstantin Georgiev Fotinov in the Cultural, Ideological, and Political Development of the Balkans in the Nineteenth Century)*. Sofia: Bulgarian Academy of Sciences, 1994.

———. "Les Etudiants Bulgares a l'Universite d'Athenes." Paper presented at the Colloque International: Universite, Ideologie et Culture, Athens, Greece, 1989.

Daskalov, Roumen. *Kak se misli Bulgarskoto vuzrazhdane* (*Interpreting the Bulgarian National Revival*). Sofia: Lik, 2002.

Daskalova, Krassimira. *Gramotnost, Knizhnina, Chitateli, Chetene* (*Literacy, Literature, Readers, Reading*). Sofia: Lik, 1999.

———. "Obrazovanie na zhenite i zhenite v obrazovanieto na vuzrozhdenska Bulgaria (Education of Women and Women in the Education of Bulgaria during the National Revival)." *Godishnik na Sofiyskiya universitet "Sv. Kliment Okhridski* 85 (1992): 5–18.

———. *Ot syankata na istoriyata: Zhenite v bulgarskoto obshtestvo i kultura* (*From the Shadows of History: Women in Bulgarian Society and Culture*). Sofia: Bulgarian Group for the Historical Study of Women and Gender, 1998.

Davison, Roderic H. *Essays in Ottoman and Turkish History, 1774–1923: The Impact of the West*. Austin: University of Texas Press, 1990.

———. *Reform in the Ottoman Empire, 1856–1876*. New York: Gordian Press, 1973.

Fortna, Benjamin C. *Imperial Classroom: Islam, the State, and Education in the Late Ottoman Empire*. Oxford: Oxford University Press, 2002.

Frierson, Elizabeth Brown. "Unimagined Communities: State, Press, and Gender in the Hamidian Era." PhD diss., Princeton University, 1996.

Gavrilova, Raina. *Bulgarian Urban Culture in the Eighteenth and Nineteenth Centuries*. Selinsgrove: Susquehanna University Press, 1999.

Genchev, Nikolay. *Bulgarskoto vuzrazhdane* (*The Bulgarian National Revival*). Fourth ed. Sofia: Ivan Vazov press, 1995.

Genchev, Nikolay, and Krassimira Daskalova, eds. *Bulgarskata vuzrozhdenska inteligentsiya* (*The Intelligentsia of the Bulgarian National Revival*). Sofia: State Press Dr. Petur Beron, 1988.

Göçek, Fatma Müge. *Rise of the Bourgeoisie, Demise of Empire: Ottoman Westernization and Social Change*. New York: Oxford University Press, 1996.

Grimshaw, Patricia. *Paths of Duty: American Missionary Wives in Nineteenth-Century Hawaii*. Honolulu: University of Hawaii Press, 1989.

Gulubov, Konstantin. *Petko Slaveykov: Life, Work, Literature*. Sofia: Nauka i izkustvo, 1970.

Hamlin, Cyrus. *Among the Turks*. New York: Robert Carter and Brothers, 1881.

———. *My Life and Times*. 4th ed. Boston: Congregational Sunday-School and Publishing Society, 1893.

Hunter, Jane. *The Gospel of Gentility: American Women Missionaries in Turn-of-the-Century China*. New Haven: Yale University Press, 1984.

Hupchick, Dennis, ed. *The Pen and the Sword: Studies in Bulgarian History by James F. Clarke*. Boulder, CO: East European Monographs, 1988.

Ilchev, Ivan. "Robert Kolezh i formiraneto na bulgarska inteligentsiya, 1863–1878g" ("Robert College and the Formation of a Bulgarian Intelligentsia, 1863–1878"). *Istoricheski pregled* 1, no. 1 (1981): 50–62.

Kaplan, Amy. "Manifest Domesticity." *American Literature* 70, no. 3 (1998): 581–606.

Karabinova, Diana. "A Late Attempt to Find an Integrative Approach through Common Secular Education: Midhat Pasa as Governor of the Danube Province (1864–1868)." In *International Congress on Learning and Education in the Ottoman World*, edited by Ali Caksu, 237–246. Istanbul: Research Centre for Islamic History, Art and Culture, 1999.

Kazamias, Andreas M. *Education and the Quest for Modernity in Turkey.* Chicago: University of Chicago Press, 1966.

Khristov, K., et al. *Russiya i bulgarskoto natsionalno-osvoboditelno dvizhenie, 1856–1876 (Russia and the Bulgarian National Liberation Movement, 1856–1876).* Vol. 1, Part 2. Sofia: Bulgarian Academy of Sciences, 1987.

Kiskira, Constantia. "'Evangelising' the Orient: New England Womanhood in the Ottoman Empire, 1830–1930." *Archivum Ottomanicum* 16 (1998): 279–294.

Kitromilides, Paschalis M. "'Imagined Communities' and the Origins of the National Question in the Balkans." *European History Quarterly* 19, no. 2 (1989): 149–192.

Koycheva, Velichka. "Protestantskoto misionerstvo v Stara Zagora i Bulgarskata obshtestvenost prez 50-te–70-te godini na XIX vek" ("Protestant Missionaries in Stara Zagora and Bulgarian Society from the 1850s to the 1870s"). *Izvestiya na myzeite ot yugoiztochna Bulgaria* 5 (1982): 145–154.

Kuhn, Anne L. *The Mother's Role in Childhood Education: New England Concepts, 1830–1860.* New Haven: Yale University Press, 1947.

Mardin, Şerif. *The Genesis of Young Ottoman Thought: A Study in the Modernization of Turkish Political Thought.* Princeton: Princeton University Press, 1962.

Markova, Z., et al. *Russia and the Bulgarian National Liberation Movement, 1856–1876: Documents and Materials.* Vol. 2. Sofia: Bulgarian Academy of Sciences, 1987.

Meininger, Thomas A. *The Formation of a Nationalist Bulgarian Intelligentsia, 1835–1878.* New York: Garland, 1987.

Merguerian, Barbara. "Mt. Holyoke Seminary in Bitlis: Providing an American Education for Armenian Women." *Armenian Review* 43 (1990): 31–65.

Nachov, Nikolay. *Tsarigrad kato kulturen tsenur na bulgarite do 1877g (Constantinople as a Bulgarian Cultural Center before 1877).* Sofia, 1925.

Nestorova, Tatyana. *American Missionaries among the Bulgarians (1858–1912).* Boulder, CO: East European Monographs, 1987.

Nikov, Peter. *Vuzrazhdane na bulkarskiya narod: Tsurkovno-natsionalni borbi i postizheniya (The National Revival of the Bulgarian People: The Struggle for Recognition of a National Church).* Sofia: Nauka i izkustvo, 1971.

Pailaret, Michael. *The Balkan Economies c 1800–1914: Evolution without Development.* Cambridge: Cambridge University Press, 1997.

Paskaleva, Virdzhiniya. *Bulgarkata prez vuzrazhdaneto* (*The Bulgarian Woman during the National Revival*). Sofia: Otechestven Front, 1984.

Patrick, Mary Mills. *The American College for Girls, Scutari, Constantinople*. Gloucester: John Bellowes, 1898.

———. *A Bosporus Adventure: Istanbul (Constantinople) Woman's College, 1871–1924*. Stanford: Stanford University Press, 1934.

———. *Under Five Sultans*. New York: Century, 1929.

Petkov, Petko. "Amerikanski misioneri v bulgarskite zemi, XIX do nachaloto na XX v" ("American Missionaries in Bulgarian Lands from the Nineteenth to the Beginning of the Twentieth Century"). *Istoricheski pregled* 46, no. 5 (1990): 18–32.

Petrov, Milen V. "Tanzimat for the Countryside: Midhat Paşa and the Vilayet of Danube, 1864–1868." PhD dissertation, Princeton University, 2004.

Porterfield, Amanda. *Mary Lyon and the Mount Holyoke Missionaries*. New York: Oxford University Press, 1997.

Pundeva-Voynikova, Aleksandra. *Bulgarkata prez epokhata na Vuzrazhdaneto* (*The Bulgarian Woman during the National Revival Era*). Sofia: Bulgarian Women's Union, 1940.

Quataert, Donald. "The Age of Reforms, 1812–1914." In *An Economic and Social History of the Ottoman Empire, 1300–1914*, edited by Halil İnalcık and Donald Quataert, 759–944. Cambridge: Cambridge University Press, 1994.

Reeves-Ellington, Barbara. "Gender, Conversion, and Social Transformation: The American Discourse of Domesticity and the Origins of the Bulgarian Women's Movement, 1864–1876." In *Converting Cultures: Religion, Ideology and Transformations of Modernity*, edited by Dennis Washburn and A. Kevin Reinhart, 115–140. Leiden: E. J. Brill, 2007.

———. "A Vision of Mount Holyoke in the Ottoman Balkans: American Cultural Transfer, Bulgarian Nation-Building and Women's Educational Reform, 1858–1870." *Gender & History* 16, no. 1 (2004): 146–171.

Riggs, Martha Jane. *Pisma za mayki ili Rukovodstvo za mayki v dobroto otkhranvanie na detsata im* (*Letters to Mothers, or A Manual for Mothers on the Good Nurturing of Their Children*). Tsarigrad: A. Minasian, 1870.

Robert, Dana L. *American Women in Mission: A Social History of Their Thought and Practice*. Macon: Mercer University Press, 1996.

Ryan, Mary P. *The Empire of the Mother: American Writing about Domesticity 1830–1860*. New York: Haworth Press, 1982.

Sklar, Kathryn Kish. *Catharine Beecher: A Study in American Domesticity*. New York: W. W. Norton, 1971.

Skowronski, Monika. "Die distribution Bulgarischer Volksbucher im 19. und 20. Jahrhundert (bis 1944)." In *Sudosteuropaische Popularliteratur im 19. und 20. Jahrhundert*, 137–158. Munchen: Munchner Vereinigung fur Volkskunde, 1993.

Slaveykov, Racho. *Petko Rachov Slaveykov, 1827–1895–1927: A Sketch of His Life and Memories of Him*. Sofia: Hemus, 1927.

Somel, Selçuk Akşin. *The Modernization of Public Education in the Ottoman Empire, 1839–1908: Islamization, Autocracy and Discipline.* Leiden: Brill, 2001.

Stone, Frank Andrews. "Mt. Holyoke's Impact on the Land of Mt. Ararat." *Muslim World* 66, no. 1 (1976): 44–57.

Stoyanov, Manyo. *Bulgarska vuzrozhdenska knizhnina* (*Literature of the Bulgarian National Revival*). Sofia: Nauka i Izkustvo, 1957.

———. "Nachalo na protestantskata propaganda v Bulgaria." ("The Beginning of Protestant Propaganda in Bulgaria"). *Izvestiya na instituta za istoriya* 14–15 (1964): 45–67.

———. "Petko R. Slaveykov i protestantskata propaganda v Bulgaria" ("Petko R. Slaveykov and Protestant Propaganda in Bulgaria"). *Rodina* 3, no. 3 (1941): 90–98.

Strauss, Johann. "Who Read What in the Ottoman Empire (19th–20th Centuries)?" *Arabic Middle Eastern Literatures* 6, no. 1 (2003): 39–76.

Todorova, Maria. "Language as Cultural Unifier in a Multilingual Setting: The Bulgarian Case during the Nineteenth Century." *East European Politics and Societies* 4, no. 3 (1990): 439–450.

Washburn, George. *Fifty Years in Constantinople and Recollections of Robert College.* Boston: Houghton Mifflin, 1911.

Zhechev, Toncho. *Bulgarskiyat Velikden ili strasti bulgarski* (*Bulgarian Easter, or Passions Bulgarian*). 6th ed. Sofia: Prof. Marin Drinov, 1995.

Zwiep, Mary. *Pilgrim Path: The First Company of Women Missionaries to Hawaii.* Madison: University of Wisconsin Press, 1991.

CHAPTER 8

ARCHIVES
Cambridge University Library, Bible Society Archives (of the British and Foreign Bible Society)

Presbyterian Historical Society (PHS), Philadelphia, Pennsylvania

INTERVIEWS
Nabil Abadir, Director of the Coptic Evangelical Organization of Social Services, Cairo, May 26, 2005.

Menes Abdel Noor, Qasr al-Dubara Evangelical Church, Cairo, May 23, 2005.

John G. Lorimer, Pasadena, California, August 29, 2004.

PRINTED SOURCES
Abdul-Fady (Arthur T. Upson). *High Lights* [sic] *in the Near East: Reminiscences of Nearly 40 Years' Service.* London: Marshall, Morgan & Scott, Ltd. 1936.

Alexander, J. R. "A Great Adventure in the Valley of the Nile." *The Biblical Review* 10:3 (July 1925): 354–382.

———. *A Sketch of the Story of the Evangelical Church of Egypt*. Alexandria: Whitehead Morris Limited, 1930.

Anderson, Benedict. *Imagined Communities: Reflections on the Origin and Spread of Nationalism*, revised edition. London: Verso, 1991.

Atiya, Aziz S. *A History of Eastern Christianity*. London: Methuen & Co., 1968.

Ayalon, Ami. *Reading Palestine: Printing and Literacy, 1900–1948*. Austin: University of Texas Press, 2004.

Batalden, Stephen, Kathleen Cann, and John Dean, eds. *Sowing the Word: The Cultural Impact of the British and Foreign Bible Society, 1804–2004*. Sheffield, UK: Sheffield Phoenix Press, 2004.

Batalden, Stephen K. "The BFBS Petersburg Agency and Russian Biblical Translation, 1856–1875." In *Sowing the Word*, edited by Stephen Batalden, Kathleen Cann, and John Dean, 169–196. Sheffield, UK: Sheffield Phoenix Press, 2004.

Bebbington, David. *Evangelicalism in Modern Britain: A History from the 1730s to the 1980s*. London: Routledge, 1989.

Bowen, Marcellus. *The Bible in Bible Lands: History of the Levant Agency*. New York: American Bible Society, 1917.

Dowling, (Archdeacon) T. E. *The Egyptian Church*. London: Cope & Fenwick, 1909.

Dye, Marjorie, Davida Finney, Adib Galdas, and Samuel Habib. *Literacy—The Essential Skill: A Handbook for Literacy Workers*. New York: The Committee on World Literature Christian Literature, 1964.

Dye, Marjorie. *The CEOSS Story*. Cairo: Dar al-Thaqafa, 1979.

Elder, Earl E. *Vindicating a Vision: The Story of the American Mission in Egypt, 1854–1954*. Philadelphia: The United Presbyterian Board of Foreign Missions, 1958.

Elliott, E. B., ed. *Memoir of Lord Haddo, in His Latter Years, Fifth Earl of Aberdeen*. Fifth revised edition. London: Seeley, Jackson and Halliday, 1869.

Fattah, El Sayed A. "Beirut Conference on Perso-Arabic Braille." In *Proceedings of the World Assembly of the World Council for the Welfare of the Blind* (1954), 75–78.

Finney, Davida. *Tomorrow's Egypt*. Pittsburgh: Women's General Missionary Society, 1939.

Gairdner, W. H. T. *D. M. Thornton: A Study in Missionary Ideals and Methods*. New York: Fleming H. Revell Company, 1909.

Galdas, Adib. *A Village Reborn: The Transformation of the People of a Village in Central Egypt after They Had Learned to Read in an All-Village Literacy Campaign: Told by Adib Galdas of Deir Abu Hinnis to Davida Finney*. New York: The Committee on World Literacy and Christian Literature, 1958.

Hamilton, Alastair. *The Copts and the West, 1439–1822: The European Discovery of an Egyptian Church*. Oxford: Oxford University Press, 2006.

Hasan, S. S. *Christians versus Muslims in Modern Egypt: The Century-Long Struggle for Coptic Equality*. Oxford: Oxford University Press, 2003.

Hill, Richard. "The Government and Christian Missions in the Anglo-Egyptian Sudan, 1899–1914." *Middle Eastern Studies* 1:2 (1964): 113–134.

Hogg, Rena L. *A Master-Builder on the Nile, being a record of the life and aims of John Hogg, D.D., Christian Missionary*. Pittsburgh: United Presbyterian Board of Publication, 1914.

Howsam, Leslie. *Cheap Bibles: Nineteenth-Century Publishing and the British and Foreign Bible Society*. Cambridge: Cambridge University Press, 1991.

Kinnear, Elizabeth Kelsey. *She Sat Where They Sat: A Memoir of Anna Young Thompson of Egypt*. Grand Rapids, MI: William B. Eerdmans Publishing Company, 1971.

Lane, Sarah. "Forgotten Labours: Women's Bible Work and the BFBS." In *Sowing the Word: The Cultural Impact of the British and Foreign Bible Society, 1804–2004*, edited by Stephen Batalden, Kathleen Cann, and John Dean, 53–62. Sheffield, UK: Sheffield Phoenix Press, 2004.

Lansing, Gulian. *Egypt's Princes: A Narrative of Missionary Labor in the Valley of the Nile*. Second edition. Philadelphia: William S. Rentoul, 1864.

Laubach, Frank C. *Teaching the World to Read: A Handbook for Literacy Campaigns*. New York: Friendship Press for the Committee on World Literacy and Christian Literature of the Foreign Missions Conference of North America, 1947.

Laubach, Frank C., and Laubach, Robert S. *Toward World Literacy: The Each One Teach One Way*. Syracuse: Syracuse University Press, 1960.

Martin, Roger H. "Women and the Bible Society." In *Sowing the Word: The Cultural Impact of the British and Foreign Bible Society, 1804–2004*, edited by Stephen Batalden, Kathleen Cann, and John Dean, 38–52. Sheffield, UK: Sheffield Phoenix Press, 2004.

El Masri, Iris Habib. *The Story of the Copts*. N.p.: The Middle East Council of Churches, 1978.

———. *Qissat al-kanisa al-qibtiyya*. Vols. 1–4, Cairo: Maktabat Kanisat Mar Jirjis, 1960; Vols 5–9, Cairo: Maktabat al-Mahabba, n.d.

Noll, Mark A. *American Evangelical Christianity: An Introduction*. Oxford: Blackwell Publishers, 2001.

Philips, H. E. *The Question Box: A Catechism on Missions in Egypt*. [Pittsburgh?]: The Publicity Committee of The Egyptian Mission of the United Presbyterian Church of North America, 1939.

Reid, William J. *United Presbyterianism*. Eighth edition. Pittsburgh: United Presbyterian Board of Publication, 1900.

Roe, James Moulton. *A History of the British and Foreign Bible Society, 1905–1954*. London: The British and Foreign Bible Society, 1965.

Rogerson, J. W. *An Introduction to the Bible*. London: Penguin Books, 1999.

Scouller, James Brown. *A Manual of the United Presbyterian Church of North America, 1751–1881*. Harrisburg, PA: Patriot Publishing Company, 1881.

———. *A History of the United Presbyterian Church*, vol. 11, The American Church

History Series, gen. ed. Philip Schaff et al (New York: Christian Literature Company, 1894).

Sedra, Paul. "Class Cleavages and Ethnic Conflict: Coptic Christian Communities in Modern Egyptian Politics." *Islam and Christian-Muslim Relations* 10:2 (1999): 219–235.

———. "John Lieder and His Mission in Egypt: The Evangelical Ethos at Work among Nineteenth-Century Copts." *The Journal of Religious History* 28:3 (2004): 219–239.

———. "Textbook Maneuvers: Evangelicals and Educational Reform in Nineteenth-Century Egypt." PhD diss., New York University, 2006.

Sharkey, Heather J. *American Evangelicals in Egypt: Missionary Encounters in an Age of Empire*. Princeton: Princeton University Press, 2008.

———. "Christians among Muslims: The Church Missionary Society in the Northern Sudan." *Journal of African History* 43 (2002): 51–75.

Somekh, Sasson. "Biblical Echoes in Modern Arabic Literature." *Journal of Arabic Literature* 26 (1995): 186–200.

Sproul, Christine. "The American College for Girls, Cairo, Egypt: Its History and Influence on Egyptian Women—A Study of Selected Graduates." PhD diss., The University of Utah, 1982.

Strickland, W. P. *History of the American Bible Society*. New York: Harper and Brothers, 1849.

Swan, George. *"Lacked Ye Anything?": A Brief Story of the Egypt General Mission*, Revised edition. London: Egypt General Mission, 1932.

Thompson, John Alexander. *The Major Arabic Bibles*. New York: American Bible Society, 1956.

Trimingham, J. Spencer. *The Christian Approach to Islam in the Sudan*. London: Oxford University Press, 1948.

Virtue, David W. *A Vision of Hope: The Story of Samuel Habib*. Oxford: Regnum, 1996.

Watson, Andrew. *The American Mission in Egypt, 1854 to 1896*. Second edition. Pittsburgh: United Presbyterian Board of Publication, 1904.

Watson, Charles R. "Fifty Years of Foreign Missions in Egypt." In *Foreign Missionary Jubilee Convention of the United Presbyterian Church of N.A., celebrating the Fiftieth Anniversary of the Founding of Missions in Egypt and India*, ed. United Presbyterian Church of North America, Board of Foreign Missions, 76–99. Philadelphia: The Board of Foreign Missions of the UPCNA, 1905.

———. *The Sorrow and Hope of the Egyptian Sudan: A Survey of Missionary Conditions and Methods of Work of the Egyptian Sudan*. Philadelphia: Board of Foreign Missions of the United Presbyterian Church of North America, 1913.

Werner, Roland, William Anderson, and Andrew Wheeler. *Day of Devastation, Day of Contentment: The History of the Sudanese Church across 2000 Years*. Nairobi: Paulines Publications Africa, 2000.

Wolffe, John. "Evangelicals and Pentecostals: Indigenizing a Global Gospel." In *Global Religious Movements in Regional Context*, edited by John Wolffe, 13–108. Aldershot, UK: Ashgate, 2002.

World Council of Churches. *Official Report of the First Assembly of the World Council of Churches*. New York: Harper & Brothers, 1949.

Wosh, Peter J. *Spreading the Word: The Bible Business in Nineteenth-Century America*. Ithaca: Cornell University Press, 1994.

CHAPTER 9

Bargach, Jamila. *Orphans of Islam: Family, Abandonment, and Secret Adoption in Morocco*. New York: Rowman and Littlefield, 2002.

———. "B-A-S-T-A-R-D Biographies: Inside an Invisible Space." Paper presented to Conference on "Family History in Islamic and Middle East Studies," Berkeley, April 2000.

Baron, Beth. "Orphans and Abandoned Children in Modern Egypt." In *Interpreting Welfare and Relief in the Middle East*, edited by Nefissa Naguib and Inger Marie Okkenhaug, 13–34. Leiden: Brill, 2008.

Benge, Janet, and Geoff Benge. *Lillian Trasher: The Greatest Wonder in Egypt*. Seattle: YWAM Publishing, 2004.

Christie, Florence. *Called to Egypt*. Seal Beach, CA: Florence V. Christie Church School Services, 1997.

Danielson, Virginia. "Artists and Entrepreneurs: Female Singers in Cairo during the 1920s." In *Women in Middle Eastern History: Shifting Boundaries in Sex and Gender*, edited by Nikki R. Keddie and Beth Baron, 292–309. New Haven: Yale University Press, 1991.

Elder, Earl E. *Vindicating a Vision: The Story of the American Mission in Egypt, 1854–1954*. Philadelphia: The United Presbyterian Board of Foreign Missions, 1958.

History of the W.G.M.S. 1883–1933. Pittsburgh: WGMS pamphlet, 1933.

Howell, Beth Prim. *Lady on a Donkey*. New York: E. P. Dutton and Company, 1960.

Kinnear, Elizabeth Kelsey. *She Sat Where They Sat: A Memoir of Anna Young Thompson of Egypt*. Grand Rapids, MI: William B. Eerdmans Publishing Company, 1971.

Mishriqi, Samu'il. *Tarikh al-Madhhab al-Khamsini fi Misr*. Cairo: al-Majma' al-'Amm li-Kana'is Allah al-Khamsiniyya, 1985.

Muhafazat Asyut. *Asyut fi 10 Sanawat*. Cairo: Matba'at Nahdat Misr, 1962.

One Hundred Twenty Years of Service in Egypt: Anna Y. Thompson and Margaret A. Smith. Pittsburgh: WGMS pamphlet, n.d.

Program and Needs of the Work of the American Mission in Egypt: Papers Presented to the Mission Association at Its Meeting in Assiut, January 1938. Cairo: Nile Mission Press, 1938.

Seton-Williams, Veronica, and Peter Stocks. *Blue Guide: Egypt*. New York:
    W. W. Norton, 1984.

Sharkey, Heather J. *American Evangelicals in Egypt: Missionary Encounters in an Age
    of Empire*. Princeton: Princeton University Press, 2008.

———. "Missionary Legacies: Muslim-Christian Encounters in Egypt and Sudan
    during the Colonial and Postcolonial Periods." In *Muslim-Christian Encounters
    in Africa*, edited by Benjamin Soares, 57–88. Leiden: Brill, 2006.

Sumrall, Lester. *Lillian Trasher: The Nile Mother*. Springfield, MO: Gospel Publish-
    ing House, 1951.

Trasher, Lillian. *Extracts from My Diary: A Review of God's Gracious Provisions for
    the Needs of the Assiout Orphanage*. Springfield, MO: Foreign Missions Dept.,
    1931–1933?.

———. *Letters from Lillian*. Springfield, MO: Assemblies of God Division of For-
    eign Missions, 1983.

Wissa, Hanna F. *Assiout—The Saga of an Egyptian Family*. Sussex, UK: Book Guild,
    1994.

CONTRIBUTORS

BETH BARON is professor of history at City University of New York (CUNY) Graduate Center and City College. She is the author of *The Women's Awakening in Egypt: Culture, Society, and the Press* (Yale University Press, 1994) and *Egypt as a Woman: Nationalism, Gender, and Politics* (University of California Press, 2005). She is also the current editor of the *International Journal of Middle East Studies* (IJMES).

MEHMET ALI DOĞAN is an alumnus of Bilkent University in Ankara and received his Ph.D. from the University of Utah. In his dissertation he examined the activities of Elias Riggs, one of the most important missionaries to work in the nineteenth century. Ottomon Empire. Doğan is a member of the Department of Humanities and Social Sciences at Istanbul Technical University.

MARWA ELSHAKRY is an Associate Professor of History at Columbia University, and was previously an Associate Professor of the History of Science at Harvard University. Her book entitled *Theologies of Nature: Reading Darwin in the Middle East, 1870–1950* will be published by the University of Chicago Press.

CAROLYN GOFFMAN, a member of the English Department faculty at DePaul University in Chicago, researches and writes on early twentieth-century American women educators in the Ottoman Empire. She lived in Turkey for several years and taught at Boğaziçi University in Istanbul.

KAREN M. KERN is an Associate Professor in History at Hunter College in New York City. She received her PhD from Columbia University in 1999. Her book, *Imperial Citizenship: Marriage and Citizenship in the Ottoman Frontier Province of Iraq*, will appear from Syracuse University Press in 2011.

CHRISTINE LINDNER is an Assistant Professor in the Civilizations Programme at the University of Balamand (Lebanon). She completed her PhD at the University of Edinburgh. Her thesis, "Negotiating the Field: American Protestant Missions in Ottoman Syria, 1823 to 1860," reexamined the early period of Protestant missions in Ottoman Syria through considering the influence of gender on this encounter.

BARBARA REEVES-ELLINGTON is Associate Professor in the Department of History at Siena College, Loudonville, New York. She is coeditor, with Kathryn Kish Sklar and Connie A. Shemo, of *Competing Kingdoms: Women, Mission, Nation, and the American Protestant Empire, 1812–1960* (Duke University Press, 2010).

HEATHER J. SHARKEY is an Associate Professor in the Department of Near Eastern Languages and Civilizations at the University of Pennsylvania. She is the author of *Living with Colonialism: Nationalism and Culture in the Anglo-Egyptian Sudan* (University of California Press, 2003) and *American Evangelicals in Egypt: Missionary Encounters in an Age of Empire* (Princeton University Press, 2008).

CEMAL YETKINER received his PhD in history from the City University of New York (CUNY) Graduate Center in 2010. His dissertation is entitled "American Missionaries, Armenian Community, and the Making of Protestantism in the Ottoman Empire 1820–1860." He is currently an Adjunct Professor in the Department of History at Queens College, CUNY.

INDEX

'Abbasiyya Girls' School (Egypt), 265
Abbot, Eliza, 33, 44, 46
Abbot, Julia, 46
Abbot, Maria, 46
'Abduh, Muhammad, xxvi, 194, 195
Abdülhamid II, Sultan, xxv, 122, 124,
    126, 131, 133, 146, 149, 151, 158n57,
    172, 194; and Hamidian period,
    154n18; and Hamidian spies, 117n2
Abdülmecid, Sultan, 125, 144, 172,
    204n64
Aberdeen, Lord (Lord Haddo), 239–42,
    247, 248
Abu-Ghazaleh, Adnan, 18
Act of Publication (Ottoman Empire,
    1864), 131–32
adoptions, and missionary families in
    Syria, 48–49
Ágoston, Gábor, xxxviin44
Aiken, Edward, 46, 59n83
Aksit, Elif Ekin, 234n34
Albaugh, Gaylord P., 23n21
Alexander, J. R., xxxivn25, 239, 241,
    253n5
Algeria, xiv, xvii, xxii, xln70, 168
Ali Pasha, Mehmet, 144
almanac, and mission press in Beirut,
    171, 184
American Bible Society, xv, xvi, xxix,
    xxxvin34, 5, 138, 245, 246, 247, 250,
    255–56n42, 256n51

American Board of Commissioners
    for Foreign Missions (ABCFM):
    American cultural initiatives in
    Middle East, xiii; American cultural
    mission, xxiv; Bebek Seminary
    and educational policy, 63–79;
    construction years of American
    missionary establishment, 15–16;
    and cultural modernity, 39–40; and
    cultural proselytism, 101–2, 106, 109;
    definitions of home and family by
    missionaries in Syria, 33–52; early
    missions of Levi Parsons and Pliny
    Fisk, 12–15; establishment and first
    foreign missions, 7–10; experimental
    nature of early activities in Ottoman
    Empire, 20–21; first school in
    Beirut, 16–17; hegemonic place of
    in historical literature on Middle
    Eastern missions, xxix; history of
    missions to Ottoman Empire, 124;
    obstacles to American missionaries
    in Middle East of early 1800s, 17–20;
    and Syrian Protestant College, 180
American Christian Literature Society
    for Moslems (ACLSM), xv, 248
American Civil War, 87, 129, 239
American College for Girls (Cairo),
    xxxii, 242
American College for Girls (Istanbul),
    xxiv, xxix, 84–117, 218